**Isaiah W. Lees**
1830 — 1902
*Courtesy of the Bancroft Library*

*"The greatest criminal catcher
the West ever knew."*
William Pinkerton

# Dark and
# Tangled Threads
# of Crime

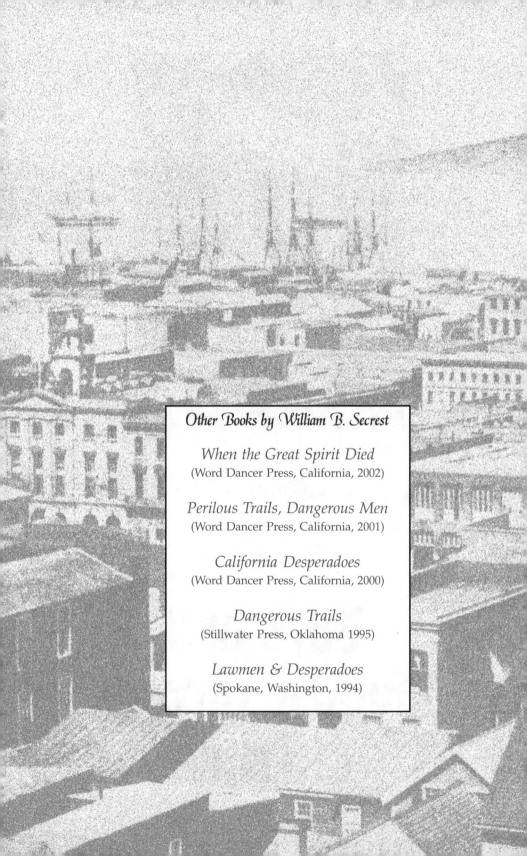

# Dark and Tangled Threads of Crime

San Francisco's
Famous Police Detective,

## ISAIAH W. LEES

WILLIAM B. SECREST

Word
Dancer
Press

Sanger, California

*Printed in the United States of America.*

Published by
Quill Driver Books/Word Dancer Press, Inc.,
1831 Industrial Way • Sanger, California 93657
559-876-2170 / 800-497-4909
*QuillDriverBooks.com*

Word Dancer Press books may be purchased in quantity for educational, fund-raising, business, or promotional use. Please contact Special Markets, Quill Driver Books/Word Dancer Press, Inc. at the above address or phone numbers.

ISBN 1-884995-41-1

**To order a copy of this book, please call
1-800-497-4909.**

*First Printing*

Quill Driver Books/Word Dancer Press Project Cadre:
Doris Hall, Susan Klassen, John David Marion, Stephen Blake Mettee,
Joshua Blake Mettee, Brigitte Phillips
Cover and interior design by William B. Secrest

**Library of Congress Cataloging-in-Publication Data**

Secrest, William B., 1930-
Dark and tangled threads of crime : San Francisco's famous police detective Isaiah W. Lees / William B. Secrest.
    p. cm.
    Includes bibliographical references and index.
    ISBN 1-884995-41-1
1. Lees, Isaiah W., 1830–1902. 2. Detectives—California—San Francisco—
    Biography.
3. Police—California—San Francisco—Biography.
I. Title.
    HV7911.L356S43 2003
    363.2'092--dc22

2003017525

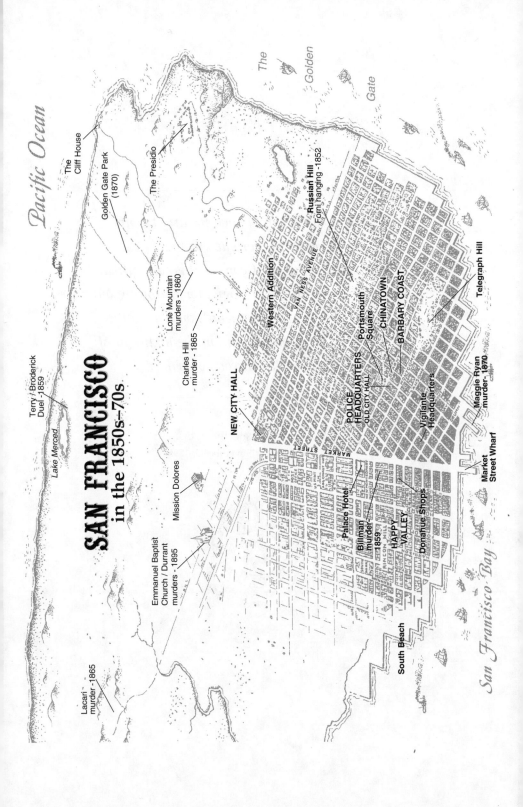

# SAN FRANCISCO
## in the 1850s–70s

Pacific Ocean

San Francisco Bay

The Golden Gate

The Cliff House

Golden Gate Park (1870)

The Presidio

Lacari murder - 1865

Terry / Broderick Duel - 1859

Lake Merced

Emmanuel Baptist Church / Durrant murders - 1895

Mission Dolores

Lone Mountain murders - 1860

Charles Hill murder - 1865

Russian Hill Forni hanging - 1852

Western Addition

VAN NESS AVENUE

NEW CITY HALL

Portsmouth Square

CHINATOWN

BARBARY COAST

Telegraph Hill

POLICE HEADQUARTERS
OLD CITY HALL

Vigilante Headquarters

Maggie Ryan murder - 1870

Market Street Wharf

MARKET STREET

Palace Hotel

Billman murder - 1859

HAPPY VALLEY

Donahue Shops

South Beach

*"A man needs not only such natural talents
as are essential for success in all
professions, but he must come to his task gifted
with a natural aptitude for logic, for reasoning out
from cause to effect—in a word, with a genius
for shedding the noonday sun on the midnight of
dark and tangled threads of crime."*

Isaiah Lees on detective work
*San Francisco Call*, November 5, 1895

# Table of Contents

# Introduction

IT is a commentary on the impermanence of fame that few modern San Franciscans would be able to identify Isaiah Lees, the first Captain of Detectives in the San Francisco Police department. Similarly, it would have been just as difficult to find anyone in San Francisco in the second half of the nineteenth century who was unfamiliar with Captain Lees and his accomplishments.

In "Dark and Tangled Threads of Crime," Bill Secrest begins to set things aright by rescuing Lees from an undeserved obscurity. Isaiah Lees, whose almost 50-year career as a San Francisco police detective gained him an international reputation as one of the world's leading detectives, is reflected in Secrest's biography as one of those rare individuals whose talents and temperament are uniquely suited to their time, place, and situation.

When municipal police departments were first established in nineteenth century cities, the initial concept was that uniformed "preventive" police officers would, by their presence on patrol, inhibit those inclined to commit crime. Some of the proponents of the new system believed that predatory crime could actually be eliminated by these methods.

As a practical matter, no municipality has ever had a tax base sufficient to provide enough preventive patrols to eliminate crime and it soon became evident that something more was needed. Beginning in Boston in 1846, American cities began forming detective police units. Patrol officers would attempt to prevent crime or make an arrest if possible. Detectives were expected to follow up on those cases in which no arrest was made in order to identify offenders, or, when arrests were made, to do the post-arrest collection of evidence necessary to secure a conviction.

The police force established in San Francisco in 1849—the year Lees arrived—was a preventive or protective department; there was no detective element. By early 1851, however, as offenders slipped through the justice system, the *Daily Alta California*, after one particularly egregious lapse, commented that "it should be the duty of some one, when notorious thieves are thus arrested, to hunt up evidence and convict the suspected persons, if guilty."

Like many others, Lees was unsuccessful in his efforts to find gold and he returned to San Francisco where he went to work for the Union Iron Works, south of Market Street. It was there, in 1852, that he received his first taste of the work that was to consume his life.

In September, adjacent to where Lees worked, a Spaniard named Jose Forni was observed by several witnesses to chase down a Mexican named Rodriquez in broad daylight and stab him to death. There was no question that Forni had done the stabbing, but his story was that he had killed the man in self-defense after the

man had tried to kill and rob him of $300 he was carrying. Though not yet a member of the department, Lees became involved in the crime through friendships with police officers and he aided materially in prosecuting the case. Forni was found guilty in District Court and later that year was hanged on Russian Hill before a crowd of thousands, earning the dubious honor of being the first man legally executed in American San Francisco.

In response to a spate of unsolved robberies, several months later the editor of the *Alta* again brought up the subject of establishing a detective police force. "[We] would suggest the organization of a small 'detective police' of about six men here, " he wrote, "who would be selected with the greatest care as to their integrity and capabilities." Nothing was to come of the suggestion at that time, either.

On October 26, 1853, the 23-year-old Isaiah Lees was appointed to the police force, unknowingly putting himself on the ground floor of a new era of police work in the Far West. A year later a basic detective unit was indeed finally initiated.

The new officer's abilities were quickly recognized and he was put in charge of the detective unit with the title of assistant captain. In those early days, Lees and his men had to depend on natural abilities, rather than a criminal science that was yet to evolve. They became incredibly adept at gathering evidence, isolating and prosecuting suspects, and recognizing criminals from meager descriptions originating hundreds of miles away.

Although appointed captain of detectives in 1856, in the turbulent political climate of the early department Lees was soon bounced back to patrolman. Reappointed captain in late 1859, he was to hold that post continuously until appointed Chief of Police in 1897.

Lees led a life of high excitement and drama, ranging from corraling burglars and con men to chasing stage robbers and forgers around the country. His physical prowess, as well as his innovative, psychological approach to fighting crime, made him truly a legend in his own time.

In his detailed study of Lees' career during the second half of the nineteenth century, Secrest takes us from the turbulent days of the Vigilance Committees of the early 1850s to the "Crime of the Century" belfry murders near the century's end. Along the way he records the criminal justice history of the city and the important part Lees played in the story. In accomplishing his task, Secrest shows us the exciting evolution of a fascinating city, the development of the detective police, and the life of Isaiah Lees.

Isaiah Lees has long deserved to be the subject of a full biography, and Bill Secrest is a worthy chronicler of that life.

Kevin J. Mullen, Deputy Chief, (ret.)
San Francisco Police Department

# Acknowledgments

RESEARCHING the story of Isaiah Lees has been a long (over 30 years), difficult, but immensely rewarding task. I must first thank William Roberts, Susan Snyder, and the many other most able custodians at the Bancroft Library, in Berkeley, California, for their help over many years in making the Lees family papers available to me. The early letters, documents, photographs, and other memorabilia were invaluable to my work and shed much light on the personal side of Isaiah Lees' life and career. Research at the Bancroft was always a delightful and enlightening experience.

The staff of the California Historical Society in San Francisco has been very helpful also, always responding to my visits and mail requests with great courtesy and thoroughness. The California State Library at Sacramento has been similarly cooperative, Mrs. Sibylle Zemitus (retired) and others of the California Room staff helpfully catering to my seemingly endless requests for information, old newspapers, special collections, and photographs. The California State University at Fresno, with its microfilm collection of complete runs of the San Francisco *Daily Alta California* and the *Chronicle* has also been invaluable to my research efforts.

Other people and institutions deserve my grateful thanks: Gladys Hansen, archivist of the San Francisco Main Library; the always helpful staff at the Society of California Pioneers; Stephen A. Haller of the National Maritime Museum at Fort Mason in San Francisco; the San Francisco Police Department Credit Union; Donald W. Dickinson of the San Francisco County Clerk's office; the Huntington Library, San Marino; the Metropolitan Museum, New York; Patricia Paladines of the New York Historical Society; Dorothy A. Stratford of the Genealogical Society of New Jersey; James G. Ward of the Passaic County Historical Society of Paterson, New Jersey; the Art Institute of Chicago; the California State Archives, Sacramento; and the National Archives, Washington, DC.

Many individuals have contributed to this project—strangers, friends, and acquaintances, without whose help the story of Isaiah Lees would have been much more difficult to research and assemble. John Boessenecker has not only accompanied me on many research trips, but has provided much material discovered while researching his own projects. His unending talent, friendship, help, and encouragement has been tremendously important. Kevin Mullen, retired deputy chief of the San Francisco Police Department, has also contributed much to this work. A highly skilled historian and writer, Kevin has not only read and criticised the manuscript, but has written an introduction to the work and given me much thoughtful advice on police thinking and attitudes of today and yesterday. The late James Abajian aided me by providing access to his early indexes on Lees. Officer Robert Fitzer of the San Francisco Police Department kindly allowed me to copy several

old police mug books in the department's historical collections. Ron Mahoney, retired curator of special collections, Henry Madden Library, California State University, Fresno, has been extremely helpful over the years in allowing me free access to his collection of San Francisco Police Department mug books and other materials. It was Ron who saved the old San Francisco mug books from being torn apart and sold page by page by an antique dealer. Dr. Robert Chandler, of the Wells Fargo Bank History Room, San Francisco, has likewise provided many items for the Lees story and related bits of early California history. Several important materials were generously provided by the late Dr. Albert Shumate, for whose friendship I am very grateful. My thanks also to Professor Roger Lotchin, Ed Perkins, Greg Martin, Tom Emmens, Bonnie Trask, Christian De Guigne, Mathew A. Bailey, and John Swingle.

My son, Bill Secrest, Jr., made the first survey of the Lees papers for me at the Bancroft. A better historian than I will ever be, Bill has aided me greatly over the years and has my heartfelt thanks. Shirley, my wonderful wife, not only accompanied me on many research trips, but critically read the ms and caught many items that needed further explanation. And, it is always a pleasure to work with Steve Mettee and his great staff at Word Dancer Press. They have done their usual first-class job of preparation and publishing for which I am most grateful.

Perhaps the single, most important discovery of this project was the journals of San Francisco police detective Edward Byram who served under Lees for twenty years. John Ryska, a retired Fresno teacher, acquired the journals from his brother-in-law, a grandson of Byram. The journals proved to be a treasure trove and Mr. Ryska allowed the author complete access to these priceless old ledgers so richly filled with famous cases and details of nineteenth century detective life. Mr. Ryska's friendship and generosity are very much appreciated.

To all the foregoing individuals and institutions, and anyone I may have overlooked, my grateful appreciation for helping to bring together the story of a remarkable man who left his mark on detective method, police tradition and San Francisco history.

William B. Secrest

# Preface

ISAIAH Wrigley Lees was a remarkable man. As a San Francisco police detective for nearly fifty years, few could equal his investigative skills or length of service in fighting crime in the early West. "Above all men," stated a superior court judge at Lees' death, "who have ever been connected with the administration of justice in California, Isaiah W. Lees has done more to vindicate the law and discourage crime." It was a fitting tribute to one of the most colorful, and little-known, of California's pioneer lawmen.

When Isaiah Lees joined the San Francisco Police Department in late 1853, a new era had dawned. The old nightwatchman and constable system of law enforcement was evolving into organized departments better equipped to combat the riots and crime of a growing nation. New ideas and methods were being explored and introduced. There was debate over police uniforms, as well as the new concept of detective officers specializing in criminal investigation and solving crimes.

Lees' police career was all the more significant in light of the setting for his adventures. His story encompasses the beginnings of the rambunctious, gold rush village of San Francisco as it evolved into the financial metropolis of the Pacific Coast. Lees watched as his friends Peter Donahue, Michael de Young, John Nightingale and others acquired fortunes while creating a mighty city. But in the background, in sinister alleys and dead of night, detective Lees worked ceaselessly to maintain order and make his city safe from the spoilers and desperadoes.

Although one of the first west coast police detectives, Lees' methods and the law he sought to uphold were curiously similar to those of today. Then, as now, there were enough legal loopholes to enable a good criminal lawyer to win release of clients on a frightfully frequent basis. Although convictions on circumstantial evidence were much easier to obtain then, the law was still quite liberal in Lees' time. Even at that early period a police officer worked under rules and regulations. And, strict enforcement of the law was usually monitored quite closely by the press.

It is remarkable that Lees appeared on the San Francisco scene when he did and he became the embodiment of the old adage—the right man in the right place at the right time. After trying his hand at various occupations, he found exactly what he was suited for. From the beginning he was the quintessential detective, the tireless investigator who carefully assembled his clues until they made sense. No miracle worker or Sherlock Holmes, Lees always worked very hard to resolve a crime. But he did more. In retrospect, it's clear that he practiced a rudimentary form of criminal psychology, even though he wouldn't have known the meaning of the term.

There are numerous references to Lees' psychological approach to crime fighting—methods which often went beyond police thinking of the day. While testifying

before a legislative commission investigating the San Francisco riots of 1877, the detective captain was asked if he thought Denis Kearney's followers were serious. "I think they are in dead earnest," replied Lees. "When people stand for three hours out in a pouring rain to listen to these speeches, it is an insult to their intelligence to think they are not in dead earnest." Although this is simple, basic logic today, in the 1870s it was difficult for a police officer to look objectively at mobs that had tried to burn and sack the city.

Even more illustrative of his scientific approach to crime was Lees' collection of criminal literature. Sandwiched among volumes of actual crime on his bookshelf were treatises on crop harvests and how they correlated to crime and prostitution. Lees, instincts took him beyond mere recordkeeping and the collection of books on crime. He understood that crime affected everything and everything affected crime.

Probably the most obvious aspect of Lees' psychological approach to crime fighting was his interrogation of prisoners. In an age of tough and often cruel third degree methods, the detective captain realized that kindness would engender more information than brutality. Even in that faraway age, Lees would first inform a prisoner that everything he said would be taken down and perhaps used against him later. In other words, he advised a prisoner of his rights long before any court had mandated such actions.

Friendliness and personal small talk was the key to Lees' interrogation of a suspect. "Man or woman, young or old," recalled Otto "Billy" Heyneman, Lees' personal secretary, "...he always addressed the person by the given name, giving at once a feeling of perfect friendliness." As early as the 1860s, newspaper reports quote Lees as addressing suspects by their first name.

This basic and practical application of the fledgling science of psychology is all the more remarkable in light of Lees' own sparse education. He was truly a self-made man for whom common sense and experience dictated the methods used in his work.

During his long career as a police officer Lees had numerous brutal, personal encounters with desperadoes, yet he never killed a man and seldom fired his pistol at a criminal. As a student of history and his fellow man, he obviously put a high value on human life.

Yet, the man's career was astounding. Anyone reading the San Francisco newspapers of the time, the police record books, and other documents will be overwhelmed at Lees' activities. His steady, day by day apprehension of criminals of all descriptions is impressive enough, but when sandwiched between such classic cases as the Chapman affair, the Bonney case, his life-or-death struggle with Bill Gregg, the epic hunt for Duncan, and so many other incidents, Lees' stature assumes truly epic proportions.

America was just emerging from the period when constables and detectives were primarily concerned with recovering stolen goods, rather than capturing the

thief. Detectives were still often middle-men, negotiating between thieves and the property owners for a percentage of the take. All through the later nineteenth century, detectives were regarded with suspicion because of this traditional alliance with the enemies of society.

"Lees was a splendid friend," Otto "Billy" Heyneman once remarked, "but a bitter, unforgiving, relentless enemy." And, as the powerful detective captain for so many years, Lees had many enemies. Various charges made against him during his career were seldom valid, however.

The most serious allegations against Lees appeared in several books written by Helen Holdredge. In her Mammy Pleasant biography and a book entitled *The House of the Strange Woman*, Mrs. Holdredge asserts that Captain Lees was a notorious blackmailer. She offers no proof, however. Although published as history, the Holdredge books contain so many errors in fact that it is difficult to regard them as anything more than some kind of historical novel.

Far from being regarded as a blackmailer, Lees' honor was seldom questioned during his lifetime. While sometimes deprecating his methods, the local press praised him consistently over the years. "Captain Lees," noted the *San Francisco Bulletin* in 1873 during the celebrated Pereda case, "has an untarnished character for integrity."

There seems little reason to doubt, however, that there was considerable corruption in police ranks during the early days. In the 1850s the city was continually in debt and behind in paying public salaries. When they were paid, the police were issued city scrip which had to be redeemed at a discount. An officer without another source of income would have been hard pressed to survive. To augment his salary meant asking complainants for fees or rewards, running errands for prisoners and lawyers, private police work, and, too often, shakedown rackets among the Chinese and prostitutes.

All through the 1850s and beyond, the police force was practically replaced after each election when a new political party took over the municipal government. "Reorganization," the politicians invariably called it, but it often meant insecurity and emasculation of the department as an effective law enforcement body.

"Full well do I know," wrote New York City Police Chief George W. Walling in the 1880s, "the power of that mighty combination—Politics and Police. ...So long as this combination is allowed to exist, just so long will decay and corruption have a grasp upon that which should uphold the honor, integrity and well-being of our citizens."

Even today Lees is often credited with founding the Rogues Gallery system of photographing felons for identification purposes. Actually, mug shots of criminals had originated almost as soon as photography was invented. A Philadelphia newspaper reported the French police daguerreotyping criminals in 1841 and by the mid-1850s the New York police were utilizing the same system. The San Francisco vigi-

lantes photographed their prisoners in 1851, and Lees apparently initiated the system in the department a few years later.

Prior to 1860 daguerreotype mug shots were kept in cabinets for display, but later paper photographs were pasted in leather books for easier viewing. When Lees retired in 1900, he kept some of the earlier daguerreotypes made prior to 1860, which he had paid for himself. This is the best evidence we have of his being instrumental in the founding of the system in San Francisco.

These old mug books, so important to the early criminal history of California, were tied up in sacks and suspended from the underside of manhole covers during the earthquake and fires of 1906. In the 1960s, the San Francisco Police disposed of many tons of historic records, including these books. Fortunately, they were rescued by someone with an eye for a buck and sold to an antique dealer. Ron Mahoney, an alert university librarian, found them in a shop being torn apart and sold, page by page. They were purchased and a broken run from 1875 to 1915 is now among the holdings of the California State Library at Sacramento. Other volumes have subsequently been located. The earliest two books, beginning with 1860, are in a private collection, but three other early volumes are still held by the San Francisco police department. The writer was allowed access to all these original mug books for this biography. Researching the story of Isaiah Lees was a continually intriguing journey through the back-alley history of a fabulous city. Some of this history has surely eluded me, but I hope a reasonably accurate portrait of the real man is revealed here for the first time.

The great detective once summed up the qualifications of his profession to a curious newspaper reporter:

"A man needs not only such natural talents as are essential for success in all professions, but he must come to his task gifted with a natural aptitude for logic, for reasoning out from cause to effect—in a word, with a genius for shedding the noonday sun on the midnight of dark and tangled threads of crime."

When Lees first joined the department, many of the police officers were inept political appointees or hard characters often as bad or worse than the criminals they must try to control. In an editorial in February of 1854, the San Francisco *California Chronicle* stated: "Whatever may be said of some members of the police, there are men on it who are ever anxious and willing to perform their duty." Yet, a mere dozen years later the department had evolved into what a recent study concludes was "the most efficient, most 'professional' police department in the United States." His sleuthing fame aside, this conclusion is a remarkable tribute to Lees as one who worked for over forty years as detective captain, deputy chief and chief of the department. The much more heralded part-time lawmen of the Old West—Wyatt Earp, Bat Masterson, and the like—were never in the same league with such a man.

Although scarcely known today, in the nineteenth century Isaiah Lees was widely respected in police circles both at home and abroad. By the 1890s he had become the legendary figure whom William Pinkerton once characterized as "the greatest criminal catcher the West ever knew." He was all of that, and I hope in telling his story I have done justice to the man and the early days of his profession.

William B. Secrest
Fresno, California

# A New Life in a New World

AS THE BARQUE *MARY FRANCIS* skirted past Point Lobos and entered the narrow passage called the Golden Gate, her deck was lined with fresh-faced Easterners eager to make their fortune in this rich and unknown land. The ship cruised through the choppy waters past other schooners, frigates, and brigs coming and going, but there were few additional signs of civilization.

Rounding another point of land, the barque was suddenly confronted by a cove choked with hundreds of vessels at anchor. Beyond was a bustling and sprawling village, looking for all the world like a series of anthills with tiny figures moving between a scattered collection of buildings and multicolored tents. Here at last was the fabled doorway to Eldorado—*San Francisco.*

While sailors shouted and the ship maneuvered for anchorage, the passengers gathered along the rail talking and pointing to the scene before them. One, a handsome, clean-shaven boy of eighteen years, smiled broadly. The salt air was strong in his nostrils as he noticed that most of the fleet of anchored ships seemed to be abandoned. Isaiah Lees was here to mine for gold like all his companions. In a year he hoped to return home with a fortune and live happily ever after—the dream of every gold-rusher. This third day of May, 1849, the world was young and anything was possible.

A stiff wind whipped his clothes and tousled hair as young Lees felt an exuberance and excitement he had never known before. He could not foresee that his destiny was not to be a rich miner, but one of the most skilled and famous detectives of his day. Preparing to go ashore with his friends, Lees must have thought of all his brief life's experiences that had brought him to this faraway land, a continent away from home and family.

Young Lees was astounded to see San Francisco Bay clogged with ships whose crews had deserted and rushed off to the gold fields. *California State Library*

19

Originally founded by Alexander Hamilton in 1791, Paterson, New Jersey was the first industrial city in the United States. Hamilton had foreseen that the nation would not truly be independent until it manufactured its own necessities. The great falls on the Passaic River made an ideal power source and the Society for Establishing Useful Manufactures was chartered and put into operation.

Located in the eastern part of the state in the Passaic Valley, Paterson was set amid rolling, wooded hills and scattered farm lands. The village was only twenty miles from the Hudson River and New York, with easy access to overland and water transportation servicing the markets of the country.

Although the new manufacturing township boomed during the War of 1812, the end of hostilities brought inactivity and ruin. By 1825, business had picked up to the extent that some eighteen cotton factories were in operation. Godwin, Rogers and Company was engaged in the production of cotton, wool, and flax machinery, while smaller companies served in jobbing and repair work for the mills. At this time there were eleven blacksmiths, two millwright shops, and one foundry in Paterson, altogether employing over seventy people. By 1835 various iron industries were being established in town and two years later the first locomotive was completed at the shop of Rogers, Ketchum, and Grosvenor. The early census reports show immigrants from Germany, England, France, Ireland, and Canada working in the Paterson shops.

In Oldham, Lancashire, England, John and Elisabeth Lees determined to immigrate to America. The couple already had two boys and a young daughter and despite Elisabeth's pregnancy they prepared for the voyage to the New World in the fall of 1830. Little is known of the family, but they were apparently middle class working people who lived and toiled in the busy village of mills and shops. John Lees was a veteran of the Battle of Waterloo who had left the army at the age of nineteen. He was probably an armourer or blacksmith and in time became a skilled ironworker. Elisabeth Lees' maiden name was Wrigley and the two boys were named Joseph Wrigley and Job Wrigley Lees. Their sister was Mary.

Whether John Lees was recruited to work in America or was merely seeking a new life isn't known, but the family boarded ship in early December. The vessel had barely lost sight of land when it collided with a French brig and had to return to Liverpool for repairs. The ship was still in

Emigrants aboard ship departing from Liverpool to New York in March 1847. *The New York Herald*, April 21, 1847

port on December 25, 1830, when Elisabeth Lees had her baby. The new arrival was christened Isaiah Wrigley Lees and his dramatic entrance on Christmas day presaged a life of excitement and high adventure.

In the states, the Lees family lived in Brooklyn, moving to the Red Hook area of New York sometime later. Eventually, they settled in the manufacturing village on the banks of the Passaic River. John Lees, a master mechanic by this time, obtained work at Rogers and Ketchum's Paterson locomotive works. At the age of six Isaiah began school at the home of a Reverend Father Kyle. His life seems to have been that of a typical boy of the period.

In later years Isaiah delighted in recounting a particular story of his youth. His mother made a dozen blackberry tarts early one day and set them out to cool. Guests were invited for supper and the tarts were for dessert. Mrs. Lees left the house on an errand and when Isaiah came downstairs he discovered his favorite delicacy cooling on the kitchen table.

The boy had missed breakfast and was hungry. Seeing no one about, he ate one of the tarts, which tasted so good he gulped down another. He soon had eaten them all and was feeling decidedly uncomfortable. When Mrs. Lees returned she found her youngest boy in bed groaning with a stomach ache. She called her husband home from work and summoned a doctor who could find nothing wrong with the boy. Isaiah spent the rest of the day in bed.

That evening after supper, Elisabeth Lees suddenly missed the tarts. When she mentioned the disappearance to her husband, a look of understanding flitted across his face. He went upstairs and gave Isaiah "the worst licking of his life." As he told the story in later years, Isaiah had never been able to look a blackberry tart in the face since.

When John Lees died in 1836, Elisabeth did what she could to keep her family together. The older boys went to work in the local mills and when Isaiah was eight years old, he too was employed in the cotton mill of John Nightingale, the father of a young friend. The hours were long and the work boring. When offered the opportunity of going on the road selling notions and cutlery, Isaiah jumped at the chance. Although not yet ten years of age, the boy traveled widely in Pennsylvania and neighboring states. When his mother remarried a man named George Fish, Isaiah joined them at their home in Bulls Ferry, on the Hudson River.

But he missed his boyhood pals. On a visit to see John Nightingale, Bob Hutchison, and other young friends, Isaiah decided to remain in Paterson. Foundry work had stirred an interest and Isaiah became an apprentice at the Rogers Locomotive works. Later he was employed by Samuel Colt, who had set up his Patent Arms Manufacturing Company in an unused room of a silk factory in Paterson. Although Colt was having a great deal of trouble launching his firearms firm, he pioneered assembly line techniques and interchangeable parts for his revolutionary revolving weapons.

When Colt's Paterson factory closed down in 1842, Isaiah was offered a job with Todd and Mackey's hemp jenny manufacturing company. An experienced craftsman by now, the boy traveled to New York and Cuba installing machinery. He later was

The falls on the Passaic River provided energy for Paterson industries and spurred development.
*Author's Collection*

employed by a New York foundry in early 1847, working on the gunboat *Rimac* which was being constructed for the Peruvian government. Peter Donahue, an older boy Isaiah had known at the Rogers shop, was working on the same craft. When the *Rimac* was completed, Donahue signed on as assistant engineer and made the trip to Peru on the first American-built steamer to ever pass through the Straits of Magellan.

Returning to Paterson, young Lees was again employed by Todd and Mackey and later by the Jersey Railroad Company. Paterson was by now a sprawling, smoky factory town filled with shops and teeming tenements. The locomotives, iron goods, machinery, silk, and cotton materials being produced were shipped out to all parts of the country as the frontiers of the young land moved steadily westward.

In these late 1840s Isaiah was a handsome teenager whom years of iron-working had made strong and tough. There had been little time for formal schooling, but the rough mathematics and plans of the machine shops had contributed much to his education. Sensitive by nature, he enjoyed literature of all kinds. He was skilled with his hands and enjoyed his work, but there was a restlessness in him.

Just when the young ironworker met Jane Fisher isn't known, but both families were of English origin. Jane lived at home with her parents, two sisters, and a sailor brother. Her father was a teamster and the family was close-knit and religious by nature. Isaiah and Jane were friends who soon fell in love. They attended church picnics and social events, and relatives and neighbors took it for granted the young couple would eventually marry.

Paterson was an industrial center of the East, choked with smoky iron works, silk factories, locomotive plants, and all the attendant support and trade shops. Isaiah worked for Colt in the building at the far right. *Connecticut State Library*

During 1848 the California gold discovery had startled the country. A trickle of immigrants to the distant Pacific coast quickly developed into a torrent as a gold frenzy spread throughout the nation and across the world.

By the fall of 1848 Isaiah and some of his friends had given in to the tug of California fever. Although in love with Jane, he longed for the adventure of joining the great Gold Rush. His older brother Job was talking of getting married and seemed reasonably satisfied with his life as a machinist. Brother Joseph was working at the shop with Isaiah and also ached with the notion of going West. He had reservations, however, and determined to wait for his younger brother's assessment of the new land.

The Rogers Locomotive and Machine Works in Paterson, 1832. Young Isaiah Lees served his apprentice time as an ironworker here. *Author's Collection*

Isaiah and John Nightingale joined a company forming to go to California. Several members belonged to Isaiah's fire engine company and a series of meetings were held at the firehouse to plan the trip and discuss supplies.

Isaiah's mother was operating a boarding house in Paterson at this time and was concerned about her youngest child. He satisfied her that he was well prepared for the journey and any contingencies. If he didn't find gold, there would always be a need for craftsmen in a raw, new territory.

Leaving Jane would be more difficult. Suddenly California seemed a lifetime away, at the end of the world. She knew he was restless here in Paterson—leading a dreary existence in the shops and listening to the endless clanging on metal all day, every day. In California there would be gold and if not gold, opportunity. They would be married, but first he must go west.

The quiet evenings together were suddenly very precious. The embraces were sweeter. The hand-holding and kisses would have to last a long time. Passage had been booked on the brigantine *Nenumphar*, scheduled to leave New York harbor December 29, 1848.

J. C. Todd, one of Isaiah's early employers in Paterson. *Author's Collection*

5

Isaiah was on the committee that managed the Third Annual Ball of Passaic Fire Engine Company No. 1. Held on the evening of December 1, at the local Odd Fellows Hall, it was a memory for young Lees and his California-bound friends that would sustain them on their long ocean journey.

On Christmas day, Isaiah would be eighteen years old. Jane was a few months older, but both undoubtedly matured these last few weeks before he left. Suddenly, it was time to go.

When Isaiah boarded the *Nenumphar* in New York harbor, Bob Hutchison, Job and Joe Lees, and other friends probably escorted Jane to the wharf. Isaiah carried his trunk and blanket roll up the gangplank, then lined up at the rail alongside his Paterson pals. As sailors scampered about in the rigging and cast lines ashore, the brig suddenly began to move. Isaiah and his friends waved as they watched the gulf of water widen between them and home. Excitement burned in their veins. They were off to California and a great adventure.

Isaiah as he looked in his youth when he was trying to find his niche in life. Probably sketched from a daguerreotype for publication in a newspaper. *Author's Collection*

The *Nenumphar* put in at Vera Cruz, Mexico, on January 12, 1849. The passengers headed overland to Mexico City, then on to San Blas on the west coast. Here the party booked passage on the Hawaiian barque *Mary Francis* for San Francisco. This last stretch of the journey might even be enjoyable, since there were now a number of young women aboard.

San Francisco was found to be a collection of tents, shacks, lean-tos, and frame buildings clustered about what appeared to be an old adobe house on a public square. A tall flagpole designated the place as a headquarters of some kind and later it was discovered to be the post office. Grabbing trunks and bedrolls, the passengers clambored down rope ladders to small boats which took them to a beach called Montgomery Street. Lees and his friends looked around at the exciting scenes that confronted them. They were in the land of gold at last.

In town, Isaiah and Nightingale were thrilled by the sights that surrounded them. Some 3,500 men crowded the streets and structures of the growing town. Just the sounds were exciting; auctioneers called out their wares on the road and in vacant lots, while hammers and saws added to the din. Laborers of every nationality hauled freight up from the beaches, while pack trains tended by colorfully garbed Mexicans were loaded for the long trek back to the mines.

Isaiah and his friends brushed shoulders with Chileans, Hawaiians, British and French sailors, Fiji Islanders, and recently discharged American soldiers. It was a land of new beginnings where doctors and lawyers could be found waiting on tables in a restaurant, while laborers put up a shanty hotel and reaped a fortune.

The Paterson boys pitched their tent in the sand hills and took turns guarding their possessions. They quickly noticed the fleas jumping about, but there was little they could do about it. That night they again strolled through town and determined to leave for the mines as soon as possible, while they had any money left.

Gold had originally been discovered at Sutter's new sawmill on the American River and the flood of incoming miners was spreading out from this locality. Isaiah, John Nightingale, and the two Law brothers were able to book passage on the schooner *Malacadel* which was leaving for Sacramento on May 9, 1849.

Jane Fisher stayed behind while Isaiah looked for a better life in the frontier wilds of Gold Rush California.
*Courtesy of the Bancroft Library*

Gold strikes had been reported on the Middle Fork of the American River and the Lees party headed in that direction. After following the American River to Sutter's mill at Culloma (Coloma), they continued over to the Middle Fork. Many miners were working the river, their tents blossoming like mushrooms along the rocky banks.

Isaiah was surprised to see agriculture had already arrived in the area. "When I went up to mine on the Middle Fork of the American River immediately after my arrival in the state," he later recalled, "I found farms under cultivation in Greenwood Valley...."

The Lees party stopped at a place called Big Bar on the Middle Fork of the American River where they promptly discovered that mining was hard work. They dug prospect holes and hauled the dirt to the river where it was panned or run through a rocker. It was summer in the Sierra foothills and very hot, the thermometer sometimes ranging up to 118 degrees. John Nightingale quickly lost interest in mining and opened a store. Isaiah's company also found mining to be difficult work with little return and headed back to the settlements in late summer of 1849. The disappointed group returned to San Francisco in early August and found an amazing transformation in the city. Another returning miner could hardly believe it was the same town:

A veritable city of 15,000 inhabitants had sprung up with towering blocks and buildings, many of which would vie with those of that time in... New York; where there was water were now docks covered with buildings and still being pushed out further into the bay; a teeming busy throng filled the streets bordering on the water....

Isaiah's brother Joseph met him in San Francisco at this time. We can imagine their elation at meeting so far from home and they must have celebrated that night with their friends. The next day the brothers looked around to see what work they could find. Surprisingly, they discovered two former Paterson neighbors busily setting up a blacksmith shop on the waterfront.

Peter Donahue had been in Peru when news of the Gold Rush arrived. He booked passage for San Francisco and after hearing of a shortage of vegetables in the new territory, invested in a cargo of onions at San Blas. After reaping a nice profit in San Francisco, Peter headed inland for the mines but, like so many others, he was quickly disillusioned.

Returning to the Bay City, Donahue had a joyful reunion with his brother James whom he had not seen in many years. James was a boilermaker and Peter a machinist, and they knew ironwork was certain to be a necessary ingredient in the new territory. Setting up a primitive blacksmith shop, they were soon turning out the iron needs of the town. They were surprised and pleased to see their old Paterson acquaintances and the Lees brothers were promptly put to work.

The shop had been set up at the northwest corner of Montgomery and Jackson streets in an old adobe on the waterfront. It must have been early fall when the brothers installed their hand-operated bellows and charcoal forge and commenced business.

This early view of San Francisco shows the plaza as vacant property while substantial buildings are going up everywhere. *California State Library.*

The shop was busy from the start. The Donahue crews repaired engines, constructed mining tools, fashioned wagon parts, and built most of the cookstoves for the restaurants of the city. Isaiah would later recall that "my brother and I helped to set up the steamer *Mint*, the first one ever turned out from the Union Iron Works," the name later adopted by the Donahue establishment.

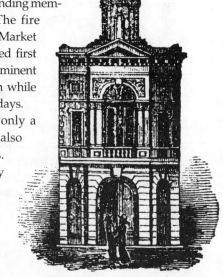

James Donahue. *Author's Collection*

By the spring of 1850 the Donahues had outgrown their quarters. They bought a lot on the waterfront, in an area of sandhills known as Happy Valley, on the southern fringe of the city. The Lees brothers helped erect the new shops on the northeast corner of First and Mission streets. Various commercial establishments were springing up and boarding houses and cottages lined newly established roads.

Michael Donahue joined his brothers at this time. An iron moulder by profession, Michael was a valuable addition to the crew.

Besides steamship repair and maintenance, the shop was supplying a swelling demand for plowshares, castings, fittings, and iron implements of all kinds. Scrap iron from the huge fleet of abandoned ships in the bay was salvaged where the rotting hulks were being burned to clear the harbor.

Working ten to fifteen hours a day, Isaiah was dog-tired at night and apparently wrote few letters home. All day, every day, he worked in the clanging metal shop yards or in the yawning hull of a disabled steamship. It was depressing to realize he had traveled across a continent to find himself again in an iron shop. More and more he thought about returning home.

In early September Isaiah was one of the founding members of California Engine Company No. 4. The fire company's quarters were on the north side of Market Street, near Battery. George Garwood was elected first foreman and many of the members became prominent in city life. Later Isaiah would serve as foreman while helping quell the many terrible fires of the early days.

The volunteer fire companies were not only a safeguard against the menace of fires, but were also prestigious social and political organizations. The companies held grand balls and led every

The California Engine Company No. 4 firehouse cost the city $12,200 for the lot and building, while the volunteer firemen only had to contribute $700.
*Author's Collection*

parade. They competed to see what company arrived first at fires, had the most colorful uniforms, and hosted the most prominent events. Isaiah lived in Happy Valley and was an experienced fireman from his Paterson days. He knew full well how rapidly a fire could destroy a community of predominately frame structures.

For some time Californians had been awaiting news of the admission of the new territory to the Union as a state. On October 18, 1850, the mail steamer *Oregon* rounded Clark's Point and entered the bay, firing her signal guns. The ship's masts were emblazoned with flags and pennants as San Franciscans rushed down to the wharves. An early resident described the stirring scene:

> Immediately the whole of the inhabitants were afoot, and grew half wild with excitement until they heard definitely that the tidings were as they expected. Business of every description was suspended, the courts adjourned in the midst of their work, and men rushed from every house into the streets and towards the wharves, to hail the harbinger of welcome news...Every public place was soon crowded...flags of every nation were run up a thousand masts and peaks and staffs, and a couple large guns placed on the plaza were constantly discharged. At night every public thoroughfare was crowded with the rejoicing populace.... Numerous balls and parties were hastily got up—bonfires blazed upon the hills, and rockets were incessantly thrown into the air until dawn of the following day.

Late in 1850 Isaiah decided to return home. He obtained a leave of absence from the shop to settle some business with Todd and Mackey in Paterson. He wasn't sure just what the future held for him, but he was disappointed with life in the new land. He was also lonely and longed to see Jane.

Acquainted with many of the steamer captains and engineers through his work, Isaiah easily secured a position as assistant chief mate aboard the *Oregon* on its return trip. For the moment, at least, he was jubilant. Whatever his future, whatever his disappointments, Isaiah was going home.

## CHAPTER ONE / NOTES

For the early history of Paterson and New Jersey's Passaic Valley, see L.R. Trumbull's *History of Industrial Paterson*, Paterson: Carleton M. Herrick, 1882 and James B. Kenyon's *Industrial Localization and Metropolitan Growth: The Paterson-Passaic District*, Chicago: University of Chicago Press, 1960.

Brief biographies of Lees appear in Frank B. Millard's *History of the San Francisco Bay Region*, Chicago, American Historical Society, 1924, the *San Jose Pioneer* of September, 1898 and the *San Francisco Argus* of December 31, 1898. The many newspaper obituaries written at his death also contain much information. The story of his birth after the collision at sea was related by Lees to detective Edward Byram, who recorded the incident in one of his diaries.

Lees' family history must be culled from a variety of sources, starting with William P. Filby's (with Mary K. Meyer), *Passenger and Immigration Lists Index, Guide to Published Arrival Records of 500,000 Passengers who came to the United States and Canada in the Seventeenth, Eighteenth and Nineteenth Centuries*, 3 Vols., Detroit: Gale Research, 1981; data from the U.S. Population Schedules, 1840 and 1850 Census, Paterson Township, New Jersey was provided by James G. Ward of the Passaic County Historical Society, Lambert Castle, Paterson; Ella Lees Leigh's three page sketch of her father's life is in the collections of the California Historical Society, San Francisco. The tart story was gleaned from Otto Heyneman's series of articles on his old boss in the San Francisco *Daily Morning Call*, November 27, 1910 through January 29, 1911. Various other newspaper articles contributed biographical material on Lees, particularly the recollections of John Nightingale in the San Francisco *Daily Alta California*, December 4, 1883, the Paterson *Morning Call*, October 17, 1891, the San Francisco *Call*, November 5, 1895 and the San Francisco *Chronicle* of January 2, 1898. The Genealogical Society of New Jersey was helpful, as were various items in the Lees Collection at the Bancroft Library, University of California, Berkeley.

For information concerning Samuel Colt's Paterson operations, see R.L. Wilson's *The Colt Heritage*, New York: Simon and Schuster, 1979.

The sailing of the brig *Nenumphar* was reported in the *New York Herald* of December 29, 1848. A letter from Robert A. Pinkerton to Isaiah Lees dated January 26, 1892, in the Lees Collection at Bancroft, detailed the passenger list of the *Nenumphar* on its 1849 trip to Mexico. For accounts of the gold rush by sea to California consult Oscar Lewis' *Sea Routes to the Gold Fields*, New York: Alfred A. Knopf, Inc., 1949. See also the diaries edited by Robert W. Wienpahl, *A Gold Rush Voyage on the Bark Orion*, Glendale: The Arthur H. Clark Company, 1978.

William Perkins' description of 1849 San Francisco is from the classic *William Perkins' Journal*, Berkeley and Los Angeles: University of California Press, 1964. For a group who made the trek to the same area as the Lees mining party, see Dr. Gaius Leonard Halsey's journal as published in Francisco Whiting Halsey's, *The Pioneers of Unadilla Village, 1784 - 1840*, Unadilla, New York: the Vestry of St. Mathew's Church, 1902, copy in the Bancroft Library.

Biographical material on Peter Donahue is from the James Donahue file in the Bancroft Library and Annie Donahue's *A Sketch of the Life of Peter Donahue of San Francisco*, San

Francisco: Crocker and Company, 1888. See also Ruth Teiser's article, "The Charleston: An Industrial Milestone," *California Historical Society Quarterly,* March, 1946. For a more recent and comprehensive study consult Richard Dillon's *Iron Men: California's Industrial Pioneers, Peter, James and Michael Donahue,* Richmond, Candela Press, 1984.

Articles on the steamer *Mint* appeared in the *Alta* on September 13, 27, and October 1, 1849.

An early description of the Happy Valley area appeared in the San Francisco *Daily Evening Bulletin,* May 17, 1859. Several contemporary references are in *San Francisco As It Is; Gleanings from the Picayune,* edited by Kenneth M. Johnson, Georgetown: The Talisman Press, 1964, and the late Dr. Albert Shumate's *Rincon Hill andSouth Park,* Sausalito, CA: Windgate Press, 1988.

Information on the early fire-fighting companies and California Engine Company No. 4 is contained in the 1850s San Francisco city directories and in Frederick J. Bowlen's "Firefighters of the Past," a typescript in the library of the Society of California Pioneers and "The Exempt Firemen of San Francisco," (no author given), San Francisco, the Exempt Fire Company, 1900, in the same collection. See also Pauline Jacobson's series on San Francisco's early days of fire-fighting in the *Bulletin* of April 29, May 6, 13, 27, June 3, 10, 1916.

The description of the arrival of the *Oregon* is taken from Soule, Gihon, and Nisbet's *The Annals of San Francisco,* New York: D. Appleton & Company, 1855. Lees' first trip back home on the *Oregon* was described in the *Call* of November 5, 1895.

# Love Across the Continent

ON FEBRUARY 22, 1851, Isaiah and Jane Amelia Fisher were married at the Cross Street Methodist Church in Paterson. The ceremony was performed by the Reverend John S. Porter, with many friends and family in attendance.

The couple honeymooned in Jersey City. Isaiah had worked hard the past year and now gave little thought to the future as the happy pair strolled idyllically along the sandy knolls and picnicked on the beach. He knew there must be more to life than the clanging metal, hissing steam, and heated forge that was his world up to now. Still, he didn't want to think about it today or tomorrow.

Returning to Paterson the couple stayed at Isaiah's mother's boarding house. It was late May by now and Isaiah was becoming concerned about his prospects for the future. Joseph had remained in San Francisco and Isaiah finally determined to rejoin him there. At least in the West there was hope that something better would turn up. In any case his money was nearly gone. And, Jane was pregnant.

Isaiah settled Jane in his mother's boarding house knowing she would be well cared for. After borrowing money from friends, he signed on as assistant engineer on a steamer leaving New York in June of 1851.

Once again Jane watched solemnly as Isaiah shouldered his belongings and hurried up the gangplank. Job shouted for him to write about California. Later Isaiah climbed up in the rigging and waved his handkerchief while the big ship moved slowly up the channel. As the vessel became smaller in the distance, Jane must have wondered just when she would see her new husband again.

When his ship dropped anchor in San Francisco Bay on July 21, Isaiah was shocked to find much of the city destroyed by fire. He could see from the ship that the Donahue shops were not in the burnt out area and that the city was quickly rebuilding.

A fire had occurred on May 4, exactly one year after the fourth big fire in the

The May 4, 1851, fire was moderately estimated to have resulted in ten to twelve million dollars worth of damage.
*The Annals of San Francisco.*

city's history. Everywhere in the burnt-out districts, larger and finer structures were being erected, some with brick walls two and three feet thick for future fire protection. Others were of stone. All the old city landmarks had been destroyed.

Isaiah became aware of other changes. The politicians who controlled the city had been replaced at the April election by a slate of more honorable men. The change was long overdue. "At a time," noted the *Picayune*, "when the city required... the best talent and most scrupulous honesty in the administration of her affairs, her public offices were filled by men who possessed neither the ability to comprehend nor the honesty to consult her interests. The consequence...was "the most stupendous system of corruption, fraud and villainy that has ever disgraced...any body of men."

Isaiah was told of the many public meetings held the previous June. The populace had been outraged when municipal officers had voted themselves large salaries at a time when the city was hard pressed to merely meet the basic needs of local government.

Crime had become an increasing problem. The police were poorly paid and many were of inferior character. A hoard of Australian convicts called Sydney Ducks, along with disappointed or out-of-work miners, loafers, con men, and criminals of every description could be found loitering in the Bay City that winter of '51. The situation reached a point where, on June 11, just a few days before Isaiah had left New York, a man named John Jenkins had been hanged by the city's first vigilance committee for the theft of a safe. The committee was organized and conducted by men who felt they had to make a firm stand against those who were preying on the community.

On July 11 a noted outlaw named James Stuart was executed by the vigilan-

tes, with two others being hanged the following month.

There were seventy-five men on the police force at this time, headed by City Marshal Robert Crozier. A good and efficient police force of that number would have been hard pressed to control the thugs in the city, however. One day in June of 1851 the *Alta* reported that "The criminal record of Sunday night is a sad commentary upon the state of affairs in our city, a sad commentary on the inefficiency of our police organization and a fearful exhibition of the dangers to life and property among us."

The instability of the police department was forcefully noted by officer Phineas Blunt in various diary entries. Blunt had been appointed to the force in late 1850 and made the following note in his diary on November 27:

Police officer Phineas Blunt. *Author's Collection*

This morning took my first lesson from Captain Lambert of the station house, he told me that by good management I could make my expenses independent of my regular pay as

policeman. I look upon Mr. Lambert's suggestion as not justified by honest men. I am surprised at his suggestions, but perhaps I ought not be surprised at anything in California.

When a police sub-station was established in Happy Valley, Lees became acquainted with the officers on duty. Other enterprises were being established around the Donahue shops now; a flour mill, sawmills, marine and land engine works, and various boat yards. But Isaiah reported little of life on the Coast in his letters home. He sometimes sent local newspapers to Job and so felt no obligation to comment further. In August he wrote his first letter to Jane from San Francisco:

> Dear Wife:                               S.F. Aug., 1851
>
>     I am in good (health) at present and hope this will find you the same. I send to you by the steamer... a draft on Adams & Co. for fifty dollars. Dear Jane, receive this small amount from yours trully [sic]- I need not ask you dear to excuse the state I left you in as regards money matters for did I not think you would I should be the most miserable of man kind.
>
>     Dear, I shall stay here if I haf (sic) my health and strength until I am able to return to the Karses with a pocket full of rocks, but if my health should fail me I could return immediately. Dear Jane, I want you to wright (sic) and inform me whether or not my absences makes you unhappy for I haf (sic) nothing else in this world but your happiness to study and should it be that you are not happy, command and I obey, cheerfully. Dear Jane take the fifty which I send to you and get whatever you may need and as soon as I can raise two hundred more I will send it and I want you to pay Mr. Tompson one hundred dollars and Mr. Hutchinson fifty dollars. The other fifty will be for yourself. I am not miserable nor yet am I happy without mi (sic) one dear Janey....

Jane quickly responded. Her crudely worded message of September 26, 1851, reflects the yearnings of thousands of women left behind in the Gold Rush at such a tender age—waiting for word to join their loved ones:

> Dear Husband
>
>     I received both your letters and I am glad to hear that you are well and doing well. I feel as well as can be expected. I got my check cashed at the People's Bank and Monday I gave your mother 18 dollars for board. I am going home next week and your mother does not like it. I told her that you promised mother that I could go home... but she did not believe it.... The People's Bank broke on 24 and I have 15 dollars and it ain't worth two cents I paid two dollars five shilling to the lodge. Your mother found her purse and gave me ten dollars and that is all I have had. I suppose that was all she could spare. She has been very good to me since you have been away....Write again as soon as you can for I feel so lonesome.... I don't feel very well but young Notty ain't around yet. I don't want you to come back if you can do better than you can here, but I should like to be where you are. You must write as often as you can and let me know how you are getting along.... Yours til death, Jane Lees

At the shop Isaiah was in charge of the outdoor gangs, working harder than ever repairing crippled riverboats and steamships. His brother Joe was now shop foreman. Soon, the Donahues were again adding to their facilities. At last Isaiah received the letter he had been waiting for:

(Established in 1849.)
North-East Corner of First and Mission Streets,
SAN FRANCISCO.

The above Establishment has been in successful operation for the last seven years, during which time new and extensive Buildings have been erected, and the latest improvements added to the works, which enable the undersigned to supply all demands for

MACHINERY AND CASTINGS
of every description, on the shortest notice, and finished in a style of work-manship that cannot be surpassed.

STEAM ENGINES BUILT & REPAIRED.
QUARTZ MILLS, SAW MILLS, GRIST MILLS, THRESHING MACHINES, HORSE POWERS, GEARING, MALT ROLL-ERS, AND ALL KINDS OF MILL WORK, STEAM-BOAT REPAIRING, BLACKSMITHING, ETC.
Besides the extensive assortment of MACHINERY PATTERNS, attention is called to the new and beautiful designs for
Building Castings, Iron Fronts and Columns for Stores,
Railings for Balconies and Stairs, Door and Window Sills, Study Cores, etc. etc.
ALL ORDERS PROMPTLY FILLED.
PETER DONAHUE, Proprietor.

The Union Iron Works did a big business in ship repair and ironwork as this city directory ad indicates.
*California State Library*

Dear Husband                    Paterson, Nov. 3, 1851

I write to inform you that your little daughter, Mary Jane Lees came to town this afternoon at half past two o'clock after a tedious and hard journey of 15 hours and a half. I am as well as can be expected at present.... Father and mother send their best respects to you and they are as proud as pie with their Grandaughter....Your mother has been up here all day. She is so tickled with the baby. David and Mary Ann send their love to you. Also Job and Sarah and Fred and Peggy. Goodbye dear husband, write soon to your affectionate wife, Jane Lees

Isaiah was exhilarated at the news. Like any new father he was undoubtedly frightened at his new responsibility, but the thought of his family gave him a faith and resolve he hadn't known before. He wrote Jane and for the first time told her she would soon be coming to California. Her reply was enthusiastic, but tempered with concern:

Dear Husband                    Paterson, Jan 4, 1852

Tis with pleasure that I sit down to answer your letter. I received your letter dated Oct 26 and I was glad to hear that you was well and doing well... I am well at present but I have been very sick. I never thought I should get better. My breasts have been very sore. The baby is well but she does not nurse. She has not nursed any since she was five days old and how I am going to come to California I don't know.... Mother wants me to leave the baby. She says I can never get it there alive, but I can't do that. I want you to tell me what you think about it. I would rather stay alone all the days of my life than leave it home or lose it.... I wish a hundred times a day that you could see it.... In your next letter I wish you would send me all the particklers (sic) what things I nede (sic) most out there, when you want to come and all about it.... If you was heare (sic) I could tell you how I love, but I can't write it....I remain yours till death, Jane Lees

The references to the baby proved to be sad and prophetic.

In his next letter Isaiah complained about being depressed and uncertain about the future. He was still stalling on a move, and depressed because he didn't think Jane wrote often enough. He sent her a nice watch, but when she acknowledged the gift in April of 1852, she also complained of his indecision. "If you would only tell me what your plans are I should be more contented." Lees had been seriously ill and this undoubtedly contributed to his melancholy mood.

Finally, his problem was decided for him. Peter Donahue was going east to visit his family and he volunteered to escort Jane and the baby back to San Francisco. Donahue was rapidly becoming a civic leader. At this time he was deeply involved in establishing San Francisco's first gas lighting company and he intended raising some capital and purchasing pipe while on the east coast. "Give me the

16

privilege of supplying this city with gas," he told his brothers, "and I care not for any other fortune."

Donahue apparently headed east in May of 1852. While on the East Coast he visited with his family, then raised funds to buy the necessary gas pipe from a Philadelphia firm. While in New York he married Miss Mary Jane Maguire and the couple honeymooned during his business travels. Isaiah wrote his boss, reporting on the business at the shop. In response, while visiting in Paterson on the last leg of his journey, Donahue wrote to Isaiah in the formal manner of the times, on July 6, 1852:

> Dear Sir:
>
> I received your letter with information of how you were getting along in the shop....When I went to see your wife and child and they was well at that time, but the child took sick about that evening and died about 8 days after I got there. The child was buried in Sandy Hill. I felt sorry, for it was a fine child, but you may thank God that it died before we got to sea. I have not made up my mind when to come as yet and it is better for your wife as she is unwell ever since the child died. You will please give my respects to Mr. Joseph Wrigley....
>
> Your friend, Peter Donahue

Mary Jane had died on June 27, but it was August before the father even knew. Although greatly saddened, Lees looked forward to his wife joining him at last. He found suitable quarters in Happy Valley and obtained the necessary housekeeping supplies.

Peter Donahue was one of the industrial giants of old San Francisco. *California State Library*

In September of 1852, army captain Edward D. Townsend was stationed in San Francisco and rooming in a Happy Valley boarding house. The many sand dunes in the area had by now largely given way to dwellings and businesses of all kinds. Only a few of the hills remained in the eastern portion. Captain Townsend was startled on a Monday afternoon, as noted in his diary entry of the 13th:

> At about half past three in the afternoon, I was awakened from a nap by the screams of a woman and immediately jumped up and looked out the window. I saw a man lying on his back, and another running up the hill pursued by a third with a large stick in his hand. The murderer, for so he proved, was brought to bay at the top of the hill, and the man with the stick demanded of him to "put dowh his knife," which he brandished in a threatening manner until two other men came up to him. When finding his brains would be dashed out with the stick he gave up his knife and was taken into custody. He was a Spaniard named Jose Forni. As soon as I saw the murderer stopped, I ran out to the victim, he was just breathing his last, and expired in two minutes. A purse of gold containing about $300 was found on Forni, who said that the

other had tried to rob him and had stabbed him in the leg, when he wrenched the knife from him and killed him in self defense. I consented to sit on the coroner's jury.

Townsend was one of many who had heard the screams. John Burke had chased Forni up the hill with a club, with John Pensam joining in the pursuit. The two men forced the killer to surrender his bloody knife. Several others ran up and helped guard the prisoner.

Since the murder had occurred almost across the street from the Donahue shops, many of the employees ran out to see what all the shouting was about.

Isaiah took a serious interest in the case. In talking with witnesses and the police he learned that Forni insisted the dead man had tried to rob him and was stabbed in self-defense. Since eleven stab wounds were found in the body, no one really believed him. When he learned the dead man had not been identified, Isaiah volunteered to see what he could find out.

Reading local press accounts, Lees learned all he could of the case. The prisoner was about thirty years old and poorly dressed when captured. He claimed to be a native of Valencia, Spain. The dead man had been well dressed, but carried no identification. In the Recorder's Court on the 15th, however, a witness identified the deceased as one Jose Rodriguez, but there was still no indication where the man lived or worked.

Noticing the victim's fingernails were outlined with a black substance, Lees reasoned he may have worked in a coal yard. Working with several others in the shop, Isaiah began a systematic checking of local coal vendors. At the charcoal yard of one Don Ventura Miro, the amateur sleuths struck paydirt. Rodriguez had indeed worked there and had not shown up for work since payday. Checking local Mexican saloons and gambling halls, Lees found a dealer who remembered both men. Rodriguez had been carrying his money in a sash and when he had tucked away some gambling winnings, the dealer had watched Forni follow him out the door.

Lees gave his information to Officer Hampton North, telling him that in talking with various Mexicans and Spaniards he had learned that no native of Spain would have been wearing a cheap, Mexican sash such as Forni claimed.

Jose Forni as depicted on a San Francisco lettersheet. A lithograph published under the direction of the keepers of the county jail. *Author's Collection*

It seemed clear that the victim had been the owner of both the sash and the money.

On October 13, 1852, a jury was empanelled in the District Court of Judge Delos Lake. By five o'clock the following day the case had been heard and the jury

retired. Two hours later a verdict of "guilty" was reported and Forni was sentenced to hang on December 10.

Lees would never forget this initial excursion into crime. Many years later he would recall to a reporter how "some of the boys at the Union Iron Works and myself dug up most of the evidence that convicted him." It was an exhilarating experience.

The Forni case was soon forgotten in the excitement of Jane's pending arrival. A letter from Panama noted the Donahue party would be sailing on the U.S. mail steamship *Golden Gate* on October 6.

It was 3 A.M. when the *Golden Gate* dropped anchor in San Francisco Bay on October 20. Peter Donahue secured a carriage and was soon escorting his wife, sister, and Jane Lees toward Happy Valley. Isaiah met them at the door of his quarters and in a moment he and Jane were happily embracing. Donahue waved and drove off. There would be time to talk later. Right now, Jane and Isaiah had a lot of catching up to do.

Jane was surprised the next day to see just how sprawling the city was. Happy Valley looked much like Paterson with its boarding houses, factories and shops. Isaiah gave her the grand tour starting with

Judge Delos Lake, who tried the Forni case. *California State Library*

his fire engine house on Market Street where he was now 2nd Assistant Foreman. It seemed as though every nationality in the world was here, from the Chinese who did an endless variety of menial work, to the sightseeing European sailors.

Glittering gambling halls and saloons lined the plaza of Portsmouth Square. John Parrott's new four-story building was under construction on the corner of Montgomery and California streets. Fronted with granite quarried and hewn in China, many Chinese were working on what was to become known as the "Montgomery Block." Down by the wharves, Jane was shown how the bay was being filled in to

Isaiah and Jane lived in Happy Valley for many years. In 1852 they may well have occupied one of the prefabricated cottages shown here among the brush-choked sandhills. *Courtesy the late Albert Shumate*

Jose Forni's hanging as depicted in a contemporary lithograph. *Author's Collection*

gain valuable property for more construction. Much of the fill being used was from the sandhills being levelled in Happy Valley.

Isaiah probably attended Jose Forni's hanging on December 10, 1852. This was the first legal execution in the city's history, and by late morning crowds were assembling around the Russian Hill gallows. By noon three thousand people were milling about, including a disturbing number of women and children.

After a brief statement, the prisoner's arms and legs were tied and a hood placed over his head. At one-thirty the trap was sprung and he dropped to a quick death.

Perhaps Jane's arrival crystallized Lees' determination to make a change. When offered an opportunity to buy into a tugboat partnership with Augustus Van Horn Ellis, he did so. A fellow member of California Engine Company No. 4, Ellis piloted the *Firefly*, while Isaiah served as engineer. They were soon guiding schooners and barges around the bay and easing vessels alongside city wharves. They also towed the old schooner *Waban* to Angel Island where it was utilized as the first state prison.

The tug paid good money, but after nearly a year Isaiah had had enough. Too, Jane complained and worried constantly about a boiler explosion. When she began having strange dreams about the tug, Isaiah used this as an excuse to sell out his share of the business. He had been able to put aside a sizeable nest egg from his profits, however. When one of his old bosses mentioned that he needed some money, Isaiah was able to lend James Donahue $6,000, probably at a nice rate of interest.

Isaiah, however, had decided on another line of work. In talking to a friend at the engine house one day, they discussed the possiblity of his joining the police force. "I had been working pretty hard," Isaiah later recalled, "and John Nightingale, who had been elected assistant alderman, suggested that I go

Isaiah's fireman friend and tugboat partner, Augustus Van Horn Ellis.
*Courtesy of the New York Historical Society*

on the force and take a rest. At that time the policemen were appointed by the aldermen and assistant aldermen."

Isaiah mentioned the idea to Jane that night. Aside from his appointment, he must be recommended by ten other citizens and approved by the boards of aldermen and the mayor. He already knew several police officers and felt confident of his position.

He had rules, regulations, and duties to learn. There were currently fifty-six officers on the force, including City Marshal Brandt Seguine, Captain Hampton North, Assistant Captain Richard Monks, and two sergeants. The balance were patrolmen who also did duty as clerks, jailers, and bailiffs. Sometimes officers were detailed as investigators—to detect clues that would identify the perpetrators of crimes.

Isaiah learned the arresting procedure and filed the details away in his head. Felony arrests could be made at any time, while a misdemeanor arrest could not be made at night unless the warrant was endorsed by a magistrate. A defendant must be notified of the intention to arrest and not be subjected to any more restraint than necessary. Arrests could be made without a warrant under certain circumstances and entrances to a dwelling could be broken down if an officer gave notice but was refused entrance.

Other regulations had to be digested: the duties and responsibilities of police sergeants, captains, and assistant captains. Officers must remain on their beats during fires to prevent looting. They must also be familiar with pertinent city ordinances.

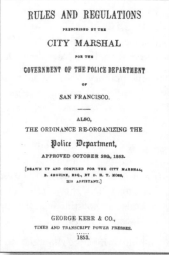

Title page of the 1853 San Francisco police regulation book. *California Historical Society.*

He would have to obtain a pair of handcuffs and buy a pistol. Wells Fargo model Colts were popular, as were pepperboxes that fit easily into a back pocket.

Fifty Special Police had been appointed the previous December. These "Specials" were not paid by the city, but were under control of the marshal. They patrolled specific areas and were paid by merchants and property owners.

At a meeting of the Common Council on October 28, 1853, Isaiah and the other recruits were officially appointed San Francisco police officers and sworn in. Jane Lees must have had serious reservations about her husband's newly chosen line of work, but she could not interfere again.

## CHAPTER TWO / NOTES

A notice of the marriage of Isaiah Lees and Jane Fisher appeared in the *Paterson Intelligencer* of February 26, 1851. The couple's honeymoon in Jersey City is noted in a letter of Isaiah to Jane on June 4, 1852. Various other letters make it clear Jane was living at the boarding house of Isaiah's mother while the newlyweds were separated. All letters are in the Lees Family Papers in the Bancroft Library.

In a letter to Isaiah dated August 24, 1851, Job Lees comments on his family and his interest in California. See also Job and his family, listed in the 1850 U.S. Census Schedule for Paterson and Passaic County, New Jersey. Job apparently had planned to travel to California with Jane, but got cold feet at the last moment. See his letter to Isaiah dated November 23, 1851. Isaiah's debts to friends are also mentioned in Job's letter to his brother on April 25, 1852. Isaiah discusses his trip back to California in the San Francisco *Call* of November 5, 1895. His friend Bob Hutchison wrote that he saw him in the shrouds waving a handkerchief. He also mentioned seeing Job and Jane on the wharf. See Hutchison's letter to Isaiah dated at Yonkers, New York, December 3, 1851.

Contemporary accounts of the 1851 San Francisco fires can be found in the various city newspapers of the time. See also Kevin Mullen, "Torching Old-Time San Francisco," in *The Californians*, January / February, 1991, and the previously cited *Annals of San Francisco*.

The newspaper quote on crooked local politicians appeared in the *Picayune* of July 8, 1851. The San Francisco Vigilance Committee of 1851 is dealt with at great length in Hubert Howe Bancroft's two volume, *Popular Tribunals*, San Francisco, The History Company, Publishers, 1887. See also Mary Floyd Williams' *History of the San Francisco Committee of Vigilance of 1851*, Berkeley, University of California Press, 1921. For an excellent current appraisal of conditions at that time, see Kevin Mullen's *Let Justice Be Done*, Reno, University of Nevada Press, 1989.

In June of 1851 the *Alta* referred to the police as "ignorant, incompetent, negligent, and their general inefficiency... is freely spoken of by the public." Phineas Blunt's diary is in the Bancroft Library.

Isaiah's letter to Jane in August, 1851, and Jane's response are in the Lees Family Papers in the Bancroft Library. The Lees brothers work at the Donahue shop is referred to in the 1895 *Call* interview. Isaiah's concerns about his future are alluded to in letters in the above referenced Lees Papers.

Information on Peter Donahue's pioneering gas lighting company and his trip to the East was gleaned from previously cited sources in the Bancroft Library.

The Townsend quotes are taken from *The California Diary of General E.D. Townsend*, edited by Malcolm Edwards, Los Angeles, The Ward Ritchie Press, 1970. The Forni case was given extensive converage in the San Francisco *Daily Whig* of September 14, 15, and 16, 1852. The *Alta* covered the trial on October 15 and 19. The press makes no reference to Lees' involvement in the case, but there seems no reason to doubt his statement to the *Call* reporter in 1895. The proximity of the murder to the Donahue shop makes the story all the more plausible.

A complete passenger list of the *Golden Gate* was published in an *Alta* "Extra" on October 20. On the roster were "P. Donahue, Jr., Mrs. Donahue, Mrs. Leese (sic), Miss Donahue." A good picture of San Francisco at this time can be had from the previously cited *San Francisco as It Is, Gleanings from the Picayune, 1850-1852*. The Forni execution was covered in the *Herald* and *Alta* of December 11, 1852.

Invented in New York in 1828, the original tugboats were small, steam riverboats converted to tow or push larger craft in and out of harbors. The first steam-turned, propeller tugboat in New York was the *Sampson*, built in 1850 at a cost of $4,500.

Lees' daughter, Ella Lees Leigh, recalled her father's brief stint as a tug operator on the bay. "My mother had such strange dreams about the boat that she persuaded him to sell it," she wrote some years later. Ella stated that several days after the boat was sold it blew up and the crew was drowned. Lees himself, in the *Call* interview, recalled, correctly, that the tug was sold to "some parties in Oregon" and "was lost at the mouth of the Columbia River." The *Alta* of March 8, 1854, confirms this. Ella Lees Leigh's brief biographical statement concerning her father is in collections of the California Historical Society. John Nightingale also refers to Isaiah's tugboat days in the *Alta* of December 4, 1883. Apparently the tugboat business paid quite well and Isaiah had a comfortable bank account when he sold out. He was able to invest in some property, according to John Nightingale who stated Lees loaned James Donahue some $6,000 at about that time. See the Nightingale article in the *Alta* referred to above.

Isaiah's discussion with John Nightingale is quoted from the previously cited 1895 *Call* article. A copy of the 1853 Rules and Regulations prescribed by the City Marshal for the Government of the Police Department of San Francisco is in the collections of the California Historical Society.

When Isaiah Lees joined the San Francisco Police Department he wore no uniform and although a badge was issued, they were seldom worn openly. Handcuffs cost about $12 for a Derby or Hiatt Company pair from England, or a set manufactured by the Towers Manufacturing Company of Brooklyn, New York. Early handcuffs had been completely handmade, but by the 1850s they were being molded in parts, then finished by hand and assembled. Handguns were cap and ball and most officers carried a knife in case their pistol misfired. Lees was still carrying his knife in the 1890s. Handcuff data is from Patterson Smith and Officer Dominick Palermo, Assistant Curator of the New York Police Museum. See also the *Daily California Chronicle* of February 8, 1854 and the San Francisco *Examiner* of September 20, 1891.

A handwritten manuscript giving a notebook history of the San Francisco Police Department up to 1853 is in the collection of the author. It was compiled by Luke Fay (1861–1933) from old newspapers and documents.

# Riots and Renegades

A BRIEF ARTICLE IN THE *ALTA* reported the beginning of one of the most colorful careers in American police history. Eager to commence his new calling, young Lees was lumped together with the group of new officers:

> THE NEW POLICE - The policemen elected by the Common Council on Friday night will be sworn into office by the Mayor today. Most of the persons appointed are raw and green hands, and with their qualifications as policemen we are not acquainted. The appointments of North and Monks as Captain and Assistant Captain are excellent. They are both old policemen and obliging, efficient and gentlemanly...

Isaiah had no illusions about his new job. This was the greatest training ground for fledgling lawmen in the world. There were confidence men, horse thieves, burglars, political thugs, and ex-convicts from all over the world. The city numbered some 50,000 people now with just over one hundred police to protect them. Police headquarters was at City Hall, the old Jenny Lind Theater building which had been bought and refurbished for municipal offices. The cell blocks were in the basement while the marshal and captain's rooms were located upstairs and referred to as the "upper offices."

Lees quickly found he was in rough company. Just a few days after swearn in, officers Nugent and Shaw had an early morning pistol duel in a Dupont Street bordello. During the fracas Police Captain James McDonald was injured. Although a good officer, McDonald had himself stabbed a man the previous year in another whorehouse, after nearly wrecking the place during a drunken spree.

"I was a patrolman just three weeks," Lees was to recall years later. "I was on Stockton Street the first week. That was the boulevard, the Van Ness Avenue of the city then. The second week I was put on the Kearny Street beat, from Sutter to Washington streets. My side partner, who had Kearny Street north of Washington, was Henry J. Kerrison.... At the end of my fortnight on Kearny Street, I was transferred to the detective department as one of the four assistant captains. In other words I had charge of the detective department, ranking as an assistant captain...."

Lees' memory was apparently faulty here since an existing pay voucher for November 1853 lists him as a patrolman drawing a salary of $150 per month. He was probably given a temporary appointment and it wasn't until late the following year that he was officially promoted to assistant captain. There is no doubt, however, that he quickly assumed his sleuthing duties, probably some time in December of 1853, when a $300 per month appropriation was added to the budget for a detective department.

Detectives were a new concept in crime control. The idea had been given significance by a French ex-convict named Francois Eugene Vidocq, who had tired of a

life of crime and volunteered as a Paris police informant about 1809. Vidocq enlisted other criminals as informants and spies and he quickly rose in police ranks. He founded the Brigade de la Suerte, the first detective bureau, and pioneered the use of disguises, stool pigeons, detailed criminal records, and other innovative investigative methods. The Suerte was so effective that British Scotland Yard was established in 1842. The term "detective police" was coined by an English journal shortly after this and the idea spread to the New World. By 1846 the Boston, Massachusetts, police had their own three-man detective unit.

Lees found his detective work was only an adjunct to his other duties. The police were spread very thin with everyone from the marshal to patrolmen constantly on call to maintain order in the fledgling city.

The city was hopelessly in debt and Isaiah's $150 salary was paid in municipal scrip which had to be sold at a discount. To make ends meet, many officers had to work on their time off, run errands for prisoners and lawyers, ask for fees from complainants, or shake down gamblers and prostitutes. Lees had made a nice profit when he sold the tug and he invested in property from which he received rentals. Still, it was frustrating.

In late 1849 the Town Council had ordered forty-nine badges for the new police force. The badges consisted of a gold button the size of a ten dollar gold piece for the marshal, and silver buttons for officers. The emblem, attached to the officer's coat collar, was the only identification to be seen. Now, in December of 1853 there was talk that the New York and Philadelphia police had adopted uniforms. Al-

When Lees first joined the police force the old Jenny Lind Theater had been refurbished into a police headquarters and courts building. To the left is the El Dorado, scene of Horace Bell's excitement.
*California State Library*

James Casey was a political thug with a New York prison record. *Author's Collection*

though not a new idea, the concept was cussed and discussed locally as noted in the *Daily Placer Times and Transcript*:

> THE POLICE - We have been rather amused at the arguments used by some of our contemporaries in advocating the wearing of a uniform by our police. One of them... that without a uniform they might be disposed to skulk when they were wanted to stop a row. Now we happen to know these gentlemen well and... many of them would require very little "hurrying up," to induce them to "go in," when a muss is on the carpet....

Lees had watched with interest as government developed in the Bay City. The municipal machinery had been created in the image of New York, shaped as it was by David Broderick and other ex-residents of that eastern metropolis. It had all the benefits and vices of the ward and Tammany systems and when the warning of the 1851 vigilantes had worn off, citizens again became aware of political thievery, increased crime, and fixed elections. The situation became particularly obvious late on a Friday afternoon, February 17, 1854.

A group of Democratic party faithful had adjourned a meeting at the Mercantile Hotel on Pacific Wharf and crowded into the establishment's barroom. Many prominent politicians were on hand as well as a generous sprinkling of thugs and toughs who made themselves useful during elections by guaranteeing results. When a barroom fight turned into a riot, the proprietor called the police and Sergeant James Towle and two officers responded. As the lawmen shouldered their way through the crowd to the proprietor, they recognized the troublemakers as thugs with records of many prior arrests.

When Towle held up his hands and shouted for the rioters to go home, he was greeted by curses and laughter. Martin Gallagher, a waterfront boatman, grabbed Towle and in a moment the three officers were being pummeled by a dozen drunken thugs. James P. Casey, another of the trouble-makers, showed a constable's star and announced he was an officer and would arrest Towle. The sergeant agreed to leave with Casey so as to get him out of the building. As they reached the door,

Edward J. K. Kewen was attorney for the rioters at their hearing. *Author's Collection*

Marshal Seguine, Captain North, and other officers helped hustle Casey and one James Turner into a hack.

The drunken Casey and Turner were finally subdued and jailed, while Sergeant Towle and three other officers returned with warrants for the balance of the rioters. Some of the toughs had retreated to a ship in the bay where a contingent of their pals were joining a filibustering expedition. They were still drinking and were now surrounded by some fifty henchmen. Although Towle and his men managed to clamber aboard and arrest Gallagher and two others, they were badly beaten in the process. By the time Towle's detail had limped back to the station house, a dozen more of the rioters had been arrested. Seventeen cursing, drunken thugs and politicians had been in their cells but a short time when city bosses began showing up. The *Alta* chronicled the unfolding drama in its issue of February 19:

> ...All these men are well known as the men who control our primary elections and during the evening the marshal's office was beseiged by politicians and office holders of every grade endeavoring to obtain the discharge of the prisoners. The scene in the station house is beyond description. The officers were hustled and bruised, and Captain North was himself thrown down and beaten. Every epithet that could be found in the slang dictionary was applied to the Marshal, Captain North and the officers....

When the prisoners were refused release, the politicians obtained a writ of habeus corpus from State Supreme Court Justice Alexander Wells. Another of the New York Tammany Democrats, Wells stomped into the station house at one-thirty in the morning and served the writ. Sergeant Towle was on duty at the time and in no mood for such a travesty. The writ called for the release of the prisoners the following morning, but Towle refused to honor it and asked about its legality. Although Recorder Baker also thought it improper to release the men, it was decided not to ignore a supreme court judge's order. Sneering and cursing, Casey and his cohorts were released as the glowering police officers stood by and nursed their bruises.

"After the parties were discharged," commented the *Alta*, "some of them proceeded immediately to the Mercantile Hotel where they threatened the life of the proprietor and used toward him the most insulting and abusive language. These are the facts in the case and we leave the public to form their own opinions of the dignity and

A small steamship and a sailing vessel are docked alongside Brown's Mercantile Hotel on the Pacific Street wharf, where the riot was initiated. From a woodcut in an early San Francisco directory. *Kevin Mullen Collection*

justice of our courts." Wells was later reported celebrating with his clients at the Union Hotel bar.

Appalled at this turn of events, the police threatened to resign as a body, and the following Monday morning a letter signed by forty-five officers was presented to Mayor C. K. Garrison:

Mayor Cornelius K. Garrison.
*Annals of San Francisco*

The Police Officers of this city deem this a fitting opportunity to express, in plain terms, their feelings in regard to the late disgraceful riot. Ever since the organization of a police force in this city, most of the actors in the late disturbance, and men of their calibre, have been a greater source of annoyance to that corps, and the public, than all the other lawbreaking populace put together.... The public and their officers have been set at defiance. Is it to be wondered at then if the Police, after having been beaten, abused and struggling with drunken ruffians, should feel incensed at the conduct of Judge Wells in unlocking their prison doors at midnight to turn them out upon an unguarded community? Whilst Policemen must stand by with folded arms and meekly receive the scoffs, the jeers and threats of deadly vengeance of midnight brawlers? If they afterwards see that midnight habeus corpus judge imbibing in a dram-shop, festooned by the released rioters and grogshop politicians, and listen to his honor assert with an oath, "That he would not allow four or five rascally, thieving policemen to arrest men and keep them confined all night; that he had the power and by G - d he meant to use it!"... The police appeal to your Honor, the Public and the Press. They are and ever have been willing to do their duty. They ask your Honor and the People to stand by them. They have sworn to support and try and execute the laws, and if sustained they will yet triumph despite the jackals of party, the self-styled "election makers."

Assuring the police the rioters would be punished, the Mayor managed to stall the mass resignation.

Lees had signed the petition along with most of the department and was apparently the first officer singled out for punishment by the recent rioters. If this was the case, they had selected the wrong man!

The following Sunday Isaiah had accompanied his engine company to an early morning fire. Afterward, as he sat in a small restaurant having a cup of coffee, a group of firemen led by their chief, Charley Duane, walked in and also called for coffee. Lees knew Duane and William "Wooley" Kearny, a leading spirit at the recent riot and a prominent local thug. And it was apparent Wooley was drunk and had mischief in his eye.

An ex-New Yorker, Kearny was a prize fighter whose scarred and battered face made him an effective precinct worker during local elections. In February of 1850 he had won a grueling twenty-five round prize fight on an island in the bay, even though thirty pounds lighter than his Australian opponent.

As Lees watched, one of the firemen walked behind the counter and began breaking crockery and bottles. Jumping to his feet, the officer ordered the man to stop just as Kearny seized him by the throat and the fight was on. Duane grabbed Wooley and tried to drag him from the shop as Lees was attacked by another thug named Nick Perezo. Isaiah was trading punches with his new assailant, when suddenly the thugs broke and ran. He grabbed Kearny and held his pistol on him until he promised to behave.

In a brief account of the fight captioned "An Effect of the Habeus Corpus," the *Alta* reported "Officer Lees succeeded in getting Carney (sic) to the station house. Carney appeared very ready to go and...assured the officers that he didn't care about being arrested, as he would send to Judge Wells and get his discharge.' Carney was kept in custody, however, although strong efforts for his release were made by some of his political friends."

Isaiah had received a severe blow in the brawl and one eye was completely closed. "The officer..." reported the *Herald*, "presented rather a damaged countenance in court yesterday."

The following day Kearny published a letter in the *Alta* denying he had made comments about Judge Wells. He had been at the same fire as Lees and afterwards drank too much brandy and was "led into the commission of an act which I most deeply regret.... I presume that I can pay the penalty without incurring the odium of being a law-breaker, or assailant of the law officer...." One wonders just what Kearny thought he was guilty of? In any case the judge fined Wooley $75 and Perezo $100.

As he walked about the city, Isaiah watched the steady improvements being made. The rutted, muddy streets filled with garbage and debris in 1849 were now graded and many covered with planking. However, women hated the wooden streets with the splinters that snagged and tugged at their long skirts. The cost of the planking had run as high as $3,000,000 according to one estimate, much of the expense as yet unpaid. Cobblestones were being tried out now on Washington Street, between Dupont and Stockton. At nearly 47¢ per square foot, however, this too was quite expensive.

Civic progress was never more in evidence than on the evening of February 11, 1854. As crowds of people lined the sidewalks, gaslight lit up the city streets for the first time. Walking down the crowded thoroughfares, Isaiah well-remembered how Peter Donahue had gone east for the gas pipes and returned with Jane.

Next to City Hall stood the elegant El Dorado gambling hall, an establishment fully as legendary as its name. Here the doors never closed, as sports from all over the world tried their luck at the roulette, faro, and rouge-et-noir tables—tables often groaning under the weight of gold. Working men drank and played at the Arcade, Polka, and other middle-class saloons, but at the El Dorado only the finest was served. Some thirty cosmopolitan drinks were obtainable at the bar, while splendid velvet curtains, mirrors, and large, gilt-framed paintings made every patron feel like a millionaire.

Horace Bell, a Los Angeles resident, visited the El Dorado while patrolman Lees was still walking his Kearny Street beat. Sauntering among the crowded tables, Bell met an old friend named Clayton Sinclair. Telling Bell he had won some $20,000 and was determined to break the bank, Sinclair gave him a bill of exchange for $5,000, together with his boat ticket for safe keeping. He intended going home in style the following day. Bell placed the ticket and money in the safe at his hotel, then returned to watch his friend slowly lose his winnings. In a short time Sinclair demanded that Bell return his funds. When he refused, Sinclair took a diamond pin from his shirtfront and asked a gambler to loan him $500 on it. "I gave a thousand dollars for this pin today," he remarked. A female voice behind him asked to see it and as Sinclair turned to hold it up to the light, a Chinese man snatched the pin and sprinted for the back door.

Horace Bell, a colorful soldier, lawyer and newspaper editor who chronicled an early Lees adventure.
*Author's Collection*

Bell plunged after the thief. He followed him outside, through a card room and restaurant, then down a flight of stairs to a basement. He found himself in a kitchen filled with other Chinese who blocked his way. They insisted the thief had doubled back in the confusion and gone back up the stairs. Bell knew better, having caught a glimpse of him going through a far door.

By this time two policemen and a gathering crowd were filing into the basement. As the Chinese were searched, Bell looked into the storeroom where he had seen the thief disappear. Except for a pile of bags full of rice, the chamber was empty. The room seemed to have swallowed the fugitive.

Interior of the El Dorado gambling hall and saloon.
*The Annals of San Francisco*

Remaining on guard, Bell asked one of the officers to return to headquarters and request Captain McDonald to join him. In a short time McDonald and Lees arrived and Bell told them the story.

"Lees at once took the matter in hand," recalled Bell, "and ordered all the Chinamen present, except the steward, to the lock-up—cleared the kitchen of the crowd, and then proceeded to investigate. It was then two o'clock in the morning."

Querying the steward concerning all the Chinese in the kitchen, Lees was told they were all cousins. Stepping into the storeroom, he asked why there were only sacks of rice in there and nothing else. "Chinaman eat much rice," grinned the steward who was holding a candle in the dark room. Lees bent over and began cutting the fastening on one of the rice bags when suddenly the steward threw the candle to the floor and dashed for the door. McDonald was too quick for him, however, and he was quickly handcuffed and in custody.

Opening the rice bag it was found to contain only dirt. Isaiah opened several more bags and found the same thing.

"By Jove, Mac," exclaimed Lees, "we've got the biggest thing out. I see through the whole thing. You take this fellow to the lock-up and return immediately with every man you can bring. See that they are well armed...."

As they waited for the reinforcements, Bell asked the officer just what was going on.

"About a week ago," reported Lees, " at four o'clock in the morning, I stopped on the crossing between Palmer, Cook and Company's corner and the corner opposite, and was listening to a noise I heard in the direction of Pacific Street. Everything was still, and I distinctly heard picking, as though miners were at work directly under my feet. I remained and listened until daylight, and have watched the thing ever since. They have worked to the sidewalk on the Kearny Street side of the bank. They are burglars tunneling to the bank vault, and we are now guarding the mouth of their tunnel. We have bagged the batch, young man...."

When McDonald returned with a half dozen armed policemen, Lees removed several of the bags and revealed the mouth of the tunnel. It was about two feet wide and only tall enough to admit someone on hands and knees. Pushing a lantern ahead, Lees entered the tunnel and soon a pistol shot was heard in the distance. Bell and the officers gathered anxiously around the tunnel entrance and in a few minutes the detective backed out, dragging a wounded Chinese burglar. Lees was painfully injured by a blow from a crowbar in the hands of the thief who had taken Sinclair's pin.

Chinese immigrants.
*Annals of San Francisco*

When the whole gang had been carted off to the station house, Lees continued to investigate. Under the stairway was a closet containing burglar tools and counterfeiting equipment. Years later an old-timer, reminiscing about the El Dorado, recalled the episode:

I remember well when an attempt was made by a number of Chinese burglars to tunnel their way into Palmer, Cook and Co's bank. The Chinese were very successful at passing off counterfeit coin. I believe they got off with upward of $20,000 in "twenties" at the Alhambra and El Dorado alone.

Restaurants of every nationality could be found throughout the city. To everyone's delight, all were serving real butter at last. Lees remembered the "butter" shipped up from Chile wrapped in cornhusks in 1849 and '50. It smelled thickly of hog's lard and most suspected this was the principal ingredient. Now local tables featured real butter produced by newly established dairies in Sonoma, Petaluma, and Santa Clara. "Hot rolls sing out with a brilliancy in connection with it," rejoiced a Bay City resident.

In early July of 1854 the *Alta* chronicled the establishment of two special police stations. This gave the police four different locations for depositing criminals and hopefully would make them more efficient in checking a burgeoning crime rate.

After a squabble with Mayor Garrison in mid-July, Marshal Seguine was suspended from duty and replaced by Hampton North. The replacement was generally well regarded since "Captain North," stated the *Alta*, "has won the respect and the confidence of the community by his manly actions...." His men were probably not quite so enthusiastic. They knew him to be a sometime martinet who was overly concerned with personal authority.

Isaiah was thrilled when his second child was born on October 23, 1854. Jane was just fine and they named the tiny girl Josephine.

Lees' appointment as assistant captain of police was received on December 5, 1854. The added authority would make his job as detective that much easier.

After this first year on the force, Isaiah must have wondered if he had made the right career move. Salary was no incentive. The city was still several months behind in paying the police via its discounted scrip. It was a thankless job that put him in constant contact with the worst elements of society. He had been beaten in riots, scorched at fires, and threatened by politicians.

But he loved his work! It was exhilarating and provided challenges and rewards undreamed of in other occupations. Here he would sink his roots and grow up with the city. There was no more lingering doubt and confusion about returning to Paterson. San Francisco was his home.

## CHAPTER THREE / NOTES

The article on the new policemen appeared in the *Alta* of October 31, 1853. The population of San Francisco was 34,776 in 1852 and 56,802 in 1860, so 50,000 would be a rough figure for 1853. See Gladys Hansen, *San Francisco Almanac*, San Francisco: Chronicle Books, 1975.

The San Francisco *Daily Placer Times & Transcript* of October 31, 1853 reported the Nugent-Shaw gun fight. Police Captain James McDonald was injured also. McDonald was a very tough character. Although regarded as a good lawman, the *Alta* of February 24, 1852, reports one of his drunken sprees when he terrorized and wrecked another Dupont Street bordello. During the melee he fatally stabbed a man named Carrol who tried to intervene. Hiding out on the local prison ship *Euphemia*, McDonald was captured by Billy Mulligan and Jim Hughes, two local toughs. After a prolonged trial, McDonald was freed by a hung jury. The police were roundly scored by the local press for trying to shield one of their own. See the *Alta* of February 25, 26, 27, 29, March 8, and May 13, 1852.

Lees' quotes are taken from an interview published in the San Francisco *Morning Call* of November 5, 1895. For the pay voucher referred to, see "Ancient Payroll of Police Department", *2-0 Police Journal*, San Francisco, September, 1928, copy in the San Francisco Public Library. San Francisco Ordinance, 1853, 183-5, 199, 171 as reported in Hubert Howe Bancroft's *History of California, Vol. VI*, San Francisco: The History Company, Publishers, 1888, documents the "Detective Police" appropriation.

Information on Vidocq is found in the notes section of Chapter 6. For a derivation of the term "detective," see Sir James Augustus Henry Murray, *The Oxford New English Dictionary on Historical Principles, etc.*, Oxford: Vol. III, The Philological Society, 1897. The first police detectives in this country were constables who would seek out criminals and recover stolen property for a fee from the victim. To be effective, detectives would use stool pigeons and otherwise consort with criminals. This, and the fee, or reward, system, combined to give detectives a bad name throughout the nineteenth century. Many detectives did indeed succumb to the criminal environment and opportunities. See David R. Johnson's *Policing the Urban Underworld*, Philadelphia, Temple University Press, 1979; Roger Lane, *Policing the City, Boston 1822–1885*, Cambridge: Harvard University Press, 1967. An excellent contemporary account is George W. Walling's *Recollections of a New York City Chief of Police*, New York: Caxton Book Concern, Limited, 1887. See also the article "A Detective Police," *The Pioneer*, San Francisco, Vol.II, No. 6, December, 1854.

An account of the police beats and their various other duties appeared in the *Alta* of February 24, 1854. Even the marshal, or chief, did street duty in those days and everyone worked seven days a week. For an article on police pay see the *Alta* of January 6, 1854. The 49 badges ordered in December of 1849 cost $600 as noted in the previously cited Luke Fay document. The reference to the New York and Philadelphia police adopting uniforms appeared in the *Daily Placer Times & Transcript* of December 24, 1853. The local comment about uniforms was quoted from the same paper of January 7, 1854.

The Mercantile Hotel riot was well covered in the local press and was a frightening example of the manipulative powers of the local body politic. Both the *Alta* and the

*California Courier* carried long articles and editorials on February 18 and 20, 1854. Those arrested were all strong-arm thugs of the Democratic Party, the so-called "election-riggers" who controlled the voting precincts. The attorney for the rioters, E. J. C. Kewen, published a long article in the *Courier* defending Judge Wells' right to give bail for the prisoners. The *Courier* summed up the feelings of most when it stated "we have but little respect for the personal liberty of those whose chief use of it seems to be to violate the personal liberty of others." The police officer's statement to the mayor appeared in the *Courier* of February 21, 1854. In a prophetic comment, the *Courier* asked, "Do the courts want a revival of the Vigilance Committee?"

The fire Lees attended on the morning of the Kearney fight had started at two in the morning in a Kearney Street building, as reported in the *Alta* of February 19, 1854. Personal data on Wooley Kearney is from the *Alta* of February 17, 1850 and James O'Meara's *The Vigilance Committee Of 1856*, San Franciso: James H. Barry, Publisher, 1887. Lees' fight is reported in the *Alta* of February 20, and the *Herald* of the 21st, 1854. Kearney's letter appeared in the *Alta* the following day.

The grading and construction of the streets is often mentioned in the contemporary press, but a good overview can be found in Roger W. Lotchin's *San Francisco, 1846–1856, from Hamlet to City*, New York: Oxford University Press, 1974.

# A King in a Stew Over Mulligan

BY 1855 CITY GROWTH had become phenomenal. Structures sprinkled over the hills, spreading out from the vicinity of the plaza, and the plank roads covering the four miles out to the old mission were becoming lined with commercial establishments.

Although real estate had been depressed the previous year, the bay was now being filled in by leveling the many sand hills in the city. The resulting "water lots" brought much needed revenue into the city coffers. Corner water lots sold for around $15,000 each, with regular lots costing about half as much. The Montgomery Block was constructed on a water lot and, with the new Custom House, could rival large structures anywhere in the country.

But for all the impressive construction, the city's crime rate was very much keeping pace with civic growth and it was at this time Isaiah had one of the closest calls of his life. He enjoyed telling the story in later years:

> It happened on Jackson Street, near Dupont...when that was a lively part of town. I saw a fellow pick up a cobble and heave it through the window of Maggie McCormick's saloon. Then he walked along quietly toward Kearny Street just as if nothing had happened. I slipped after him and said in a quiet way as I drew to his side:
>
> "What made you throw that cobble through that window?"
>
> "Did you see me throw a cobble through that window?"
>
> He was a cool chap and tall and athletic, but I couldn't see his face as the night was dark.
>
> "Yes," I said, "I saw you do it, and I'm an officer and I arrest you for it."
>
> "Oh that's alright," he said cheerfully, and began to whistle as we went along together.
>
> Just as we got opposite a little cul de sac he let drive at me. I ducked and got the blow on the top of the head. If I'd got it on the jaw, as was intended, it would have knocked me out.
>
> Well, the little alley was as dark as a tunnel, but I piled in after my man and ran full against him. I grabbed him but this fellow's pistol was a short one and he let me have the whole five shots. I felt every one of them sting me and thought he'd made a sieve of my body. But that was no reason why I shouldn't attend to business, and I did that as soon as possible by getting the empty gun away from him. The hammering I gave that fellow was awful, but he deserved it. I beat his head with the gun and stabbed him with its muzzle til I bent the barrel...when I'd worn myself out on him I took him down, and he was a sight to behold with the blood on him....

At the station Lees booked his prisoner then rushed off to see a doctor. Expecting to be shot through and through, he was surprised to learn his silk under-

shirt had deflected the bullets, leaving five, red welts around his body. "They reached so far around my back," Isaiah later recalled, "that the doctor had to hold a looking glass for me so that I could see them."

Putting on his shirt, Lees rushed back to the station with blood in his eye, but his prisoner was gone. He had been released on $25 bail. In his rush to get his wounds cared for, Isaiah hadn't explained the circumstances to the desk sergeant. "I've never seen him from that day to this," commented the lawman.

Isaiah and Jane were living in a three-room apartment in Happy Valley at the time. She must have been horrified when she saw the welts around his body, but he pacified her as best he could.

When Brandt Seguine was fired by the mayor, John McKenzie served as city marshal for a brief period. The new marshal was in court with Lees and several other officers in April of 1855 assisting in the prosecution of a burglar gang. As he testified against the four defendants, Isaiah was reminded he was still learning his profession. When asked to explain the various tools found in the thieves' possession, he began describing the function of "slung shots, chloroform" and lock

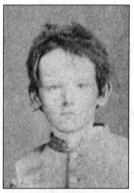

The son of a San Francisco police officer, Bobby Durkin was a lifelong criminal beginning in the 1850s.
*Author's Collection*

"gimmys," but was interrupted by McKenzie. The marshal pointed out that various professional and potential burglars were in the audience and it wasn't a good idea to be explaining these tools in open court. All but one of the gang were convicted without further testimony.

Although tough and merciless when necessary, Isaiah felt a genuine compassion for some offenders. In time it became apparent that many criminals had come from desperately poor backgrounds, with a resulting lack of opportunity. Most were from the big city slums with all their crowding, filth, and degradation. They became outlaws to survive. Lees watched young thieves like Bobby Durkin, scarcely more than babies, and knew they were headed down this grim, dark path.

As he interrogated criminals, the young detective gradually became aware of how their minds worked. By questioning them about their families and showing an interest in their lives, he could subtly shift the conversation to areas of his investigation. Gradually he discovered the twisted corridors of the criminal mind and how to use it in his work.

While fighting a fire with his company on May 18, Isaiah had his hand badly smashed in a collision with another engine company. Jane must have wondered just what to expect next.

Hampton North was elected marshal in July. Lees and North had been quite friendly in the past, but now he found his new chief increasingly moody and distant.

Lees purchased a chain and whistle in August of 1855, the instrument having met with general satisfaction as a means of calling for aid during the past few years.

The following month there was a proposal to reorganize the police. Besides specifying that officers should be citizens of the country and of good moral and physical character, it was proposed the force be increased to eighty men. There was to be one captain, three assistant captains, and seventy-six officers. The proposed ordinance further specified that uniforms were to be adopted by the police. "It consists," noted the *Alta*, "of a single-breasted, blue frock coat with silver-plated buttons and standing collar; upon the collar the number of the policeman is affixed; he wears a glazed cap with the word police inscribed, and pantaloons with a stripe. The uniform is neat and well-chosen."

James King of William brought a fiery brand of journalism to 1850s San Francisco. *Author's Collection*

Lees must have been relieved when the re-organization ordinance failed. It had suddenly occurred to him that he had never applied for citizenship in his adopted country.

Although houses of prostitution had been abolished by ordinance the previous year, by the fall of 1855 it was increasingly apparent that such houses were becoming as blatant as ever. Some one hundred bordellos were reported in an eight-block area bounded by Clay, Broadway, Kearny, and Stockton streets. Mary Blane, Belle Cora, and other richly attired madams paraded the streets as brazenly as though they were public officials.

In early October a newly established newspaper began rocking the local political boat. The editor of the *Daily Evening Bulletin* was a man with the medieval-sounding cognomen of James King of William, to differentiate himself from oth-

New planked streets and solidly constructed brick and stone buildings characterized the city in the later 1850s. *Author's Collection*

ers of the same name. A former banker and merchant, King was an eloquent and frustrated reformer. In early November he complained of a lack of enforcement of the prostitution laws, for which Marshal North took an editorial beating:

Gambler Charles Cora.
*Author's Collection*

> If the city council find that they have not power or lack the will to remove Mr. North and make him do his duty, we will have the records searched and learn who owns the houses rented to these people; and we will publish their names, that the respectable portion of the community will know who to admit and who to reject from their firesides. It's no use trying to dodge the *Bulletin*, gentlemen!

The *Bulletin* was the talk of the town and the subscription list grew by leaps and bounds. King quickly zeroed in on the banking house of Page, Bacon and Company, linking them to shady doings and the corrupt state of local government. When a bank emmisary dropped by to discuss economics, the *Bulletin* printed a full report of the meeting. Nothing more was heard from that quarter.

Lees well knew the shabby pasts of some of the characters being exposed in the *Bulletin*. Despite his rash and overwrought style of journalism, King seems to have been a respectable and honest man. He had been an early, and wealthy, city banker, but through the calumny of an employee had lost everything. He found employment with Adams and Company, but in February of 1855 that concern also became insolvent. Although he had his detractors, King seems to have conducted himself through all these hard times with the utmost honesty and dignity. And, as grand jury foreman in 1853 he had stood up to threats of violence from Hamilton Bowie and other politicians whose activities were being investigated.

Tough and vituperative in his attacks, King was quick to print a retraction when necessary. Often he printed both sides of controversies, no matter what reflection this cast upon him. Threats became a way of life with the gritty editor and many thought it just a matter of time before someone shot him.

On the evening of November 17, 1855, gambler Charles Cora shot and killed United States Marshal William Richardson in a Clay Street doorway. The two had quarreled the previous night at the theater, Richardson objecting to Cora and his mistress sitting behind him. A Mexican War veteran, Richardson was reportedly a mean and frequent drunk, but the shooting of a federal lawman by a gambler left street crowds buzzing for the next few nights.

Cora and his mistress, Belle, had arrived in San Francisco from New Orleans in late 1849. While his woman oper-

Gunman, gambler, and prize-fig[ht] promoter, Billy Mulligan was al[so] a notorious ballot box stuffer.
*Author's Collection*

ated bordellos in various gold camps, Cora gambled and both became quite wealthy. They were settled in San Francisco now and Belle began talking to the best attorneys in the city to defend her lover.

Despite much talk in the streets of vigilance committees and hanging, by morning most of the excitement had melted away. Aside from an editorial noting that prostitutes should not be allowed in theaters where they must mingle with respectable people, editor King was reasonably restrained concerning the shooting. When Cora became the recipient of a hung jury and King discovered he was being guarded in the county jail by the notorious Billy Mulligan, moderation was thrown to the winds:

Yankee Sullivan, an escaped Australian convict, became a champion prizefighter in America, then a thug and ballot box stuffer in California.
*Author's Collection*

> ...If Mr. Sheriff Scannell does not remove Billy Mulligan from his present post as keeper of the county jail, and Mulligan lets Cora escape, hang Billy Mulligan, and if necessary to get rid of the sheriff, hang him—hang the sheriff! ...What a mortification to every lover of decency and order, in and out of San Francisco, to think that the sheriff of this county is an ex-keeper of a gambling hell; his deputy, who acts as keeper of the county jail, is the notorious Billy Mulligan....Merchants of San Francisco, mechanics, bankers and honest men of every calling, hang your heads in very shame for the disgrace now resting on the city you have built.

Mulligan was indeed one of the worst of the local thugs. As a boy growing up in the tough tenements of New York City he had been apprenticed to a barrel-maker, but soon degenerated into a gambling and boxing promoter. He early learned to rig elections and intimidate voters for Tammany Hall, but when he was hauled in on a burglary rap, Billy skipped out for New Orleans. He was said to have served in the Mexican War, then came to California during the Gold Rush.

In San Francisco Mulligan teamed up with Yankee Sullivan and Chris Lilly, two other notorious prize fighters, gamblers, and political thugs. In 1842 Lilly had distinguished himself in New York state by pummeling to death the first man to die in the American ring. Sullivan, whose real name was Francis Murray, was an escaped convict from Australia. He was once boxing champion of the country and had many notable fights, whipping the tough John Morrissey in New York in late 1853. It was Sullivan who had stuffed James Casey into a supervisor's office when Casey hadn't even been on the ballot. "Yankee" was an elections judge at the time, yet couldn't read or write. These men and their cronies had much to do with controlling the elections in San Francisco.

In late December Isaiah was pleased to see his name on the police re-appointment list. A new officer named Henry H. Ellis had been listed, also. He was just a year older than Lees, and the two men got along well from the start. Ellis had been a foundry worker and sailor who had come to California from Maine just a few months after Lees. He too had briefly labored in the mines, returned east for a bride, then again turned to the sea.

"It was in 1855 that I was appointed a member of the police force," Ellis recalled in later years. "Since childhood I had been a student of men....I could glance at a man and instantly note his characteristics of countenance, manner, dress, and carriage, and could recognize a person from his back as readily as from his face. This was a valuable asset in the game I was to follow."

Lees' good friend and fellow police detective, Henry H. Ellis. *John Boessenecker Collection*

In early February of 1856 the *Bulletin* again assailed City Hall for being in arrears in police salaries. Editor King pointed out that officers were paid in city scrip which was seldom worth its full value. At $150 a month, King computed, the six-month pay loss of a policeman was as shown here:

Of course any dissatisfied officer could always resign. The officials knew full well that in December there had been over 400 applicants to fill 30 police appointments.

In late January of 1856 a group of Monumental firemen finished their watch at two o'clock in the morning. Walking to their homes, they ran into Billy Mulligan and a drunken crowd of bullies at the corner of Clay and Kearny streets. Mulligan snarled a crude insult at the firemen and was told by Tom Riley that he better not repeat it. Billy peeled off his coat, but took a decided beating from the tough Riley, until the two were separated by their friends.

**July - scrip pay worth - $ 97.50**

| | |
|---|---|
| August | $ 100.00 |
| September | 100.00 |
| October | 80.00 |
| November | 80.00 |
| December | 75.00 |

**Loss of $367.00**
**$532.50 instead of $900.00**

Editor King was furious over the incident. "What now is to be done with Billy Mulligan for his brutal assault the other night on Thomas Riley? ...Will anybody arrest Mulligan, or will he go free? Will Sheriff Scannell keep him in office? A fine Deputy sheriff, truly!" Isaiah arrested the thug without incident, but he was released when no one pressed charges.

Hampton North was constantly quarreling with his men. Undoubtedly some of the trouble originated in the pay problems and accusations of the press, but many were surprised when on February 18 North suspended four of his best officers; Captain McDonald, Assistant Captain Lees, and officers R. B. Monks and Sam Stevenson. McDonald was the first to be tried before the three police commissioners, consisting of the president of the board of supervisors, Mayor James Van Ness,

42

who was also the police court judge, and North.

The marshal had charged McDonald with unofficerlike conduct after he had removed a prisoner without permission. North had been unavailable at the time and McDonald had needed the prisoner to locate some stolen property. The marshal regaled the commissioners with a litany of complaints and accounts of misconduct.

Throughout the hearing North and McDonald hurled charges at each other—at one point Mayor Van Ness having to jump between them. When both the mayor and Officer John Nugent supported McDonald's position, North was furious. The board finally found the officer not guilty and restored him to duty.

Two days later the charges against Lees and Monks were also dismissed. Realizing there was a serious problem in the police ranks, however, the board noted that "we at the same time recognize the authority of the marshal, and the necessity of obedience to his orders on the part of subordinates in the police department...." All four officers were returned to duty with no loss in pay.

Lees wasn't disappointed when North gave him one of the worst beats in the city. Old-timers on the police force were still telling the story forty years later. North had assigned Lees to a district out near the army Presidio. There was a particularly rowdy saloon in the area where soldiers were always causing trouble. Police officers dreaded the assignment. Fearless as usual, Isaiah headed straight for the soldiers' hangout. Unknown to him, Marshal North intended to keep an eye on his troublesome subordinate and followed him. The rest of the story was recalled in an old newspaper account:

> Both officers reached there about the same time, and, as usual, there was a fight in progress, with sixteen men in the battle, and Lees and North realized their inability to prevent the melee. All they had was their revolvers, and they did not feel like shooting the soldiers down, so they retired for a consultation. North didn't know what to do, but Lees did. He jumped out and tore two pickets off the fence. One he gave to North and the other he took and started into the saloon. "Stop that fighting!" he shouted, "or we'll take every mother's son of you to jail." The situation appeared so preposterous that the soldiers closed in on the two officers and the fun began. Lees and North laid out nine soldiers and the others fled for

The army Presidio near San Francisco. *California State Library*

their lives. The picture of those two policemen marching in nine badly battered government soldiers and locking them up in the old calaboose was a sight to behold. When it was over North turned to Lees, put out his hand, and said "Shake, I'll never mistrust you again,"

Although no names are mentioned, the incident was probably reported in the *Bulletin* of March 6:

The U.S. Troops.- Some of these boys who have been allowed the "freedom of the city" for the time being, have been cutting up such pranks as to cause their arrest. Their first valiant attack was on the Presidio Hotel, where failing to obtain as much liquor as they wanted, they broke a number of windows in revenge. They afterwards attacked other buildings performing the same exploit, and yesterday they made a rush on the city Hall and demolished windows in the Tax Collector's office, for which the police conveyed them to the station house. Last evening several of them attacked a police officer, who with the assistance of other officers, took them also into custody....

In late February a prototype of a new police badge had been displayed. "It is silver, small, but exceedingly neat in appearance," noted the *Bulletin*, "with the name and number of the officer, and a handsome device engraved on it. When worn on the left breast of the coat we think it would be a mark sufficiently distinct to make the officer known."

A uniform had finally been adopted by the department, also. It was a simple frock coat, single-breasted, of blue beaver cloth with a velvet collar. The new coats and badges were to be officially worn by all officers beginning on Sunday, March 9, 1856.

Edward McGowan had arrived in California in October of 1849. He was one of the thousands of political hacks who were to muddy the state's political waters during Gold Rush days. While serving in the Pennsylvania State Assembly McGowan had gained renown by stabbing a local newspaper editor in a bloody brawl. Deserting his family in Philadelphia, he had skipped out just one step ahead of a bank robbery investigation. A Democrat and lawyer who jumped onto the patronage bandwagon at every opportunity, he became a power in California where he served as a justice of the peace, county judge, treasurer of the State Marine Hospital and State Commissioner of Immigration. Popular in his party, "Ned" McGowan was elected to chair the state Democratic convention of 1854.

The new uniforms as depicted in a contemporary engraving, although this coat is double-breasted.
*Author's Collection*

Despite his official positions, McGowan was no better than the thugs, whores, and sleazy politicians with whom he consorted. Judge Alexander Wells, of Mercantile Hotel riot fame, was a particular crony, the pair being all too typical of those

involved in California politics.

Only the previous December the *Bulletin* had chronicled Ned's attempt to blow up the residence of prostitute Fanny Perrier, with whom he had formerly played house. The venal judge's natty appearance sheltered a tough character.

On the afternoon of March 21, 1856 Captain McDonald found McGowan chatting with a friend on Montgomery Street and served him a summons to testify in the case of a local bordello madam. "Sharp words passed between them," commented the *Bulletin,* "and McGowan grossly insulting McDonald, the latter struck him twice with his cane. McGowan drew a revolver, when the bystanders interfered and separated them."

In talking to officer Jim Green one day, Isaiah casually suggested that North and others might have set McDonald up by having him serve the summons on McGowan in an effort to get him killed. When North was informed of what was said, he was furious.

Isaiah was making out a report at city hall when North stormed up and confronted him. "I hear you have been trying to create a difficulty between Captain McDonald and myself," he barked. "If you repeat it, I will take care of you!"

Lees denied the charge, but North kept up the verbal attack.

"If you say anything more about me, or predjudicial to my character, I'll pull your nose."

The infuriated Lees pulled his pistol. As North rushed forward with an upraised cane, McDonald jumped between them and snatched Lees' weapon. Officers Ellis, Green, Sergeant Blood, and several bystanders all witnessed the shouting match that now transpired as Lees was shoved from the room and into the hall.

"I'll remember you for this, old fellow," warned North as he followed McDonald and Lees into the hallway.

"You may if you please," shot back Isaiah.

"If you give me any more impudence, I'll lock you up."

"You might if you please," again shouted Lees, but as the marshal ordered Green and the other officers to arrest him, Isaiah jumped back and drew his knife. "Nobody can arrest me," he yelled. Several officers had seized Lees by this time and North helped haul him off to a cell downstairs. He was probably only held until he cooled off, but when later relating the incident to Jane he must have thought his police career was at an end.

Perhaps worry about the future was the reason he paid his landlord, R. L. Ripley, eleven months rent on April 1. If worse came to worst they would at least have a roof over their heads. He and Jane could always get by, but they had the baby to think of now. He had little hope for a police future when he appeared before the police commissioners on April 3.

At the hearing, witnesses all told the same story. North admitted he "had known Lees for a long time; he had always been a good officer." After Ellis, Saulsbury,

and several others testified, it was ruled the commissioners would meet the following day when McDonald could be present. All of those present agreed that Lees was an excellent officer and of good character. As he left the room, Isaiah must have had mixed emotions. Perhaps his career wasn't over after all.

When the commissioners met the following day, Captain McDonald corroborated the other witnesses. The board adjourned to reach a decision, then returned in ten minutes with the following resolution:

Mayor
James Van Ness.
*Author's Collection*

> Resolved, that the suspension of officer I. W. Lees be and is continued until the 22nd day of April, and that he be deprived of his pay from the date of his suspension by the Marshal during the continuance of same.

Lees must have had a relieved look on his face as he stood up now for a final word from Mayor Van Ness.

"The board," remarked the mayor, "gives you all credit for being a good officer, one of the best in the department; but it is necessary that insubordination should be discountenanced. The Board must sustain the Marshal in suspending you...."

Under other circumstances, Isaiah might have relished some time off. He had been working long, hard hours and Jane was undoubtedly pleased he could spend some time with her and the baby. Perhaps there was time for a drive out to Russ' Gardens one weekend and an evening at Apollo Hall on Pacific Street, where the very popular balls and social events were held. Just a stroll through the bustling city together was pleasant, watching it grow up around them.

Isaiah couldn't have been eager to face North again, but his friends were glad to see him when he returned. Everyone cautioned him, however, that North was still edgy and quarrelsome.

## CHAPTER FOUR / NOTES

Information on the growth of the city can be found in the contemporary press, in Hubert Howe Bancroft's works, and in Roger W. Lotchin's excellent, *San Francisco, 1846–1856, from Hamlet to City*, New York: Oxford University Press, 1974.

Lees told the story of his being shot at various times. The account quoted here is a long and detailed version published in the *Examiner* on February 16, 1890. A briefer account appeared in the same paper on March 1, 1896. The story was recounted again in the *Examiner* at the time of Lees' death in 1902. In this version he is quoted as saying that he saw his assailant again some years later. Lees wouldn't give a name, but said the fellow was "worth his millions and was a United States Senator." Helen Holdredge, in her unreliable *House of the Strange Woman*, San Carlos: Nourse Publishing Company, 1961, identifies the would-be killer as John B. Weller, senator and later governor of California.

The Lees' living quarters and details of personal expenditures made during this period are taken from the Lees Collection in the Bancroft Library. There is a great mass of receipts, notes, clippings, letters, and other ephemera that can only be utilized when some knowledge of his life is acquired.

The incident of Lees testifying in court against the burglars appeared in the *Alta* of April 19, 1855.

Although sometimes exaggerated, Lees' secretary, Otto Heyneman, has left some fascinating reminiscences of the great detective's methods. His series appeared in the old San Francisco *Call* between November 1910 and January 1911. Particularly informative was the article titled "How the Old Master Applied the Third Degree."

The story of the fire and Isaiah's injury was reported in the *Alta* of May 19 and the *Herald* of May 20, 1855.

Lees' purchase of a chain and whistle is indicated by a receipt in the Lees Collection in the Bancroft Library. The *Placer Times & Transcript* reports Marshal Crozier sending a silver whistle to Sacramento marshal William M. White in August of 1853. The *California Chronicle* on June 24, 1855, reports Jake Chappell blowing his whistle to summon aid one night. The police uniform ordinance was announced in the *Alta* of September 22 and 24, 1855.

The data on the number of bordellos in the city was incorporated in a report of the Judiciary Committee of the Board of Assistant Aldermen as noted in the "Continuation of the Annals of San Francisco" in the *California Historical Society Quarterly*, June 1938. King's editorial threatening to expose the bordello landlords appeared in the *Bulletin* of November 7, 1855.

Editorial complaints about lack of enforcement of the ordinance against houses of prostitution began in the *Bulletin* on November 6, 1855. They continued through the month, Marshal North's visit to the editor being reported on the 13th. For background on James King of William, see the biography by Stanton A. Coblentz, *Villains and Vigilantes*, New York: Thomas Yoseloff, 1957 and Hubert Howe Bancroft's *Popular Tribunals*, Vol. Two, San Francisco: The History Company, Publishers, 1887.

Notice of California Engine Company No. 4's new uniforms arriving from the East appeared in the *Alta* of October 27, 1855.

Charles Cora's story is given in all of the great mass of 1856 Vigilance Committee publications, including the above cited *Villains and Vigilantes* and *Popular Tribunals*. See Pauline Jacobson's series in the San Francisco *Bulletin* beginning on October 7, 1916 for much little-known data. Curt Gentry's *The Madams of San Francisco*, Garden City: Doubleday & Company, 1964, gives other detail. The killing of Marshal Richardson is given much coverage in the *Alta* of November 18 and 19, 1856, and many subsequent issues. The *Bulletin*, of course, has much information on Cora during this period. See also Thomas L. Raynor's "Corrections and Addenda to the Article on the San Franciso Vigilance Committee of 1856," *California Historical Society Quarterly*, December, 1929.

Billy Mulligan's early life must be gleaned from a variety of sources. His "own story" was related to a New York newspaper and republished in the *Bulletin* of November 15, 1856. A New York attorney related more of Mulligan's life in a *Bulletin* article of January 16, 1863, while the *San Francisco Police Gazette* of September 2, 1865, gave a long account of his career as a sporting figure. Additional details appeared in the Stockton *San Joaquin Republican* of December 20, 1860. Mulligan's rowdy career is related in William B. Secrest's "There Once was a Badman Named Mulligan," *Real West*, August, 1984.

For information on Christopher Lilly, Yankee Sullivan, and other early prize fighters and their political connections see Elliot J. Gorn, *The Manly Art, Bare-Knuckle Prize Fighting in America*, Ithaca and London: Cornell University Press, 1986 and George W. Walling, *Recollections of a New York Chief of Police*, New York: Caxton Book Concern, Ltd., 1887.

The Ellis quote is in Henry Hiram Ellis' *From the Kennebec to California*, Los Angeles: Warren F. Lewis, Publisher, 1959. As a detective Ellis was honored many times for his services and later served as chief.

The graph showing the loss in scrip pay is from the *Bulletin* of February 11, 1856. Mulligan's scrap with Tom Riley and the resulting events were reported in the *Alta* and *Bulletin* of January 28; Lees' arrest of the thug was reported in the *Alta* of January 29 and Mulligan's release was noted in the *Bulletin* of January 4, 1856.

Marshal North's suspension of Lees and three other officers appeared in the *Bulletin* of February 19, 1856. Notice of McDonald's and Lees' hearings appeared in the same paper on the 25th and 27th. The *Examiner* of March 1, 1896, recorded Lees' and North's fight with the soldiers.

The new police badge notice appeared in the *Bulletin* of February 21, 1856.

Edward McGowan's history is aptly recounted in Carl I. Wheat's, "Ned, the Ubiquitous," *California Historical Society Quarterly*, March, 1927. Other biographies are John Myers Myers, *San Francisco's Reign of Terror*, Garden City, New York: Doubleday & Company 1966, and McGowan's own work, *The Narrative of Edward McGowan, Including a Full Accont of the Author's Adventures, etc.*, San Francisco: 1857. Bancroft's *Popular Tribunals*, Vol. two, devotes a good deal of space to the rascal also and there is much information in the contemporary press. McGowan's scrap with Captain McDonald is reported in the *Bulletin* of March 21, 1856.

Lees' scuffle with Marshal North and the resulting hearings were fully reported in the *Bulletin* of March 25 and April 4 and 5, 1856.

# Vigilante Days

LEES AND HIS FELLOW OFFICERS WATCHED IN DISMAY as North continued bickering with his men. In late April John Nugent was called on the carpet.
An officer since November of 1852, Nugent was a tough, efficient, and hard-
working lawman. He had aroused the marshal's ire by searching a pawnbroker's
shop for stolen goods without first notifying North. Both men were bitter over
the incident.

As Nugent was standing in the marshal's office on May 2, he looked up to see
his superior glaring at him.

"North," he growled, "what are you looking at me for? You must have something particular against me."

North stepped over to his subordinate and grabbed him by the arm. It was the
Lees scuffle all over again.

"Nugent, I don't want any trouble with you
and I don't want you about city hall. If you want to
go out in the sand hills with me, you son of a bitch,
well come on!"

Nugent tore himself away from the marshal's
grasp and pulled his pistol.

"I'm no son of a bitch, but I'm going to make
your wife a widow!" Before he could cock the
weapon, policemen Blood and Durkee seized him
and assisted North in dragging him downstairs
where he was thrown into a cell.

On May 9 Nugent had a hearing before the
police commissioners. He testified to circumvent-
ing the marshal only because to do otherwise would
have meant losing some stolen goods. The commis-

Officer John Durkee.
*Author's Collection*

sioners ruled that Nugent had taken emergency action
and the charge was dismissed. North left the room muttering after the commissioners stated they would rule later on the personal clash between the two men.

The constant skirmishing between North and his men had the town talking. A
"citizen's" letter in the *Bulletin* echoed what many were thinking about the quarrels
of the marshal and his men:

> Editor *Bulletin*: It is evident there is something rotten in the Police Department. The
> evil, whatever it may be, seems to be on the increase for scarcely a week passes by without

finding the City Marshal in some difficulty with his subordinates. I think I know the cause of the difficulties, but such is the official condition of our city it is dangerous to tell the truth at all times....We are told that as much as $200 per month is paid by Whipple's gambling house for an immunity from police surveillance. We are also told that all the Chinese hells on Dupont street are taxed the same way. It is said that certain controlling influences are exercised over police officers, so as to restrain them in the performance of their duties....

After the letter appeared Marshal North burst into the *Bulletin* office and demanded the letter writer name names. He was not accommodated, however. Whatever the problem, something did indeed seem to be stimulating trouble in the department.

On the evening of May 7, 1856, Lees located two noted thieves eating dinner in the Railroad Saloon. Billy Foster had recently escaped jail at Sacramento, while his partner, Charlie Wilson, was wanted for a large jewel robbery in Oakland. There was no resistance during the arrest, but while on the way to the station house Foster asked if he could say goodbye to a friend on Sansome Street. The lawman foolishly agreed and as the trio cut across a dark street Foster suddenly turned and grabbed Lees by the throat, calling out for help from Wilson. Isaiah whirled and slammed Foster into a wall, then knocked Wilson down before he could get into action. Drawing his pistol, Lees marched the two suspects to the station house with no more detours.

Banker William T. Sherman was later a prominent general during the Civil War.
*California State Library*

In his constant feuding and exposure of unsavory institutions and politicians, editor King of the *Bulletin* was making many enemies. James P. Casey was a particular target. He had recently "stuffed" himself into a supervisor's office and his record of rigged elections, brawls, and shooting scrapes made him a notorious figure.

After founding his own weekly newspaper, the *Sunday Times*, Casey apparently added blackmail to his list of avocations. Banker William T. Sherman recalled the new supervisor had rented space for his paper in Sherman's bank building, but had moved out just before both he and his press could be heaved through the window. Casey was emulating the *Bulletin* by attacking various institutions in the city, but unlike the *Bulletin*, Casey wanted his palm greased before he would ease up. Also, unlike the *Bulletin*, no one paid any attention to Casey's modest sheet. "So far as we are concerned," wrote Sherman, "the paper might be published in Ireland."

When editor King exposed Casey's New York prison record, the tough little politician was furious. He stormed into King's office on May 14 and demanded to know why his personal life was being exposed. King ran him out. "If necessary," screamed the departing Casey, "I will defend myself."

As he left to walk home that evening King passed alongside the Montgomery Block, then started across the planked street. He seemed deep in thought and was startled to hear a shout. Looking up he saw Casey about fifteen paces away aiming a pistol at him from the middle of the street. He had shouted a warning and fired at about the same time. The editor staggered as blood began staining his shirtfront. Several by-standers helped King to a nearby express office where he was made comfortable and physicians summoned.

Supported by friends, Casey fled to a nearby police sub-station seeking protection. Marshal North, Lees, and several other officers arrived shortly afterwards and shoved their way through growing crowds of excited people. In the distance a fire bell was sounding.

It was decided the county jail was the safest place for the prisoner and a hack was summoned. With Charley Duane, Billy Mulligan, and other thugs aiding as escorts, Lees and North hustled the prisoner into the hack. Duane later claimed to have threatened the crowd with his pistol to keep them from over-turning the vehicle.

As the hack clattered off down the street, the mob fol-lowed yelling threats and curses. Suddenly an open sewer trench was seen bisecting the road ahead and the hack driver reined up his animal. Looking back at the gaining mob Lees shouted, "Go on, man, you've got to go!" Using

Casey shot King in the street, in front of the express office with the awning, next to the four story Montgomery Block building, shown here in 1856. *Author's Collection*

his whip, the driver plunged his hack toward the ditch and successfully crossed it, galloping on down the street. News of the shooting had by now spread throughout the city and cries of "Lynch him!" followed the carriage up to the jail doors.

Charles Cora, still in jail and waiting for a retrial, looked on grimly as the terrified Casey was ushered into a cell. "Casey," he growled, "you've done us both in!"

North, Lees, and a collection of other officers now formed a knot in front of the jail and warned back the swelling crowds of excited men. They were a minnow cautioning a whale to behave. Everywhere men were joining the crowds in the streets, while figures were beginning to appear on the roofs of surrounding buildings.

When Tom King, brother of the wounded editor, began to harangue the hordes of people, policeman John Nugent tried to arrest him, but was blocked by the crowd. The mayor then attempted to address the mob, but was quickly shouted down with cries of "How about Richardson? Where is the law for Cora?" and "Down with such law!"

Attempts by officers to arrest speakers and agitators were resisted, and John Nugent's skull was fractured by a brick-bat. By eight o'clock that evening a reported ten thousand people had collected on Montgomery Street, between Clay and Washington.

As volunteers formed to reinforce the police, groups of businessmen were assembling with the idea of re-establishing the old vigilance committee of 1851. That night William T. Coleman was again persuaded to lead a new committee and newspaper announcements proclaimed a meeting for the next day. Despite opposition from the governor, city officials, attorneys, and most politicians, huge crowds lined up to join the new organization. Establishing headquarters at a building on Sacramento Street, the vigilantes quickly enlisted thousands of volunteers, who were formed into militia companies. The police and local government were helpless against such odds. The city was in a state of near anarchy.

The surrender of Casey and Cora at the San Francisco county jail. An engraving made from a dagerreotype and published in the *Illustrated London News*, July 12, 1856. *Author's Collection*

Those opposed to the vigilance committee on legal grounds now found themselves in a frustrating position. When banker Sherman was asked to make an assessment of how best to defend the jail in case of an attack, he only grudgingly accepted. "The duty," he confided in a letter, "was a most disagreeable one, to defend...two such scoundrels as Casey and Cora." Although unalterably opposed to the vigilantes, Sherman grudgingly wrote that the "Committee has such an organization that they can do what they please and if they stop short when they have executed Casey and Cora, which they must, and have warned off the shoulder strikers; which they are doing it will be the most wonderful movement of this kind in history...."

William T. Coleman was the vigilante chieftan in 1851 and '56. *Author's Collection*

Editor King had meanwhile been moved to a room in the Montgomery Block where he died on May 20, 1856. Bells tolled throughout the city and most business buildings were draped in black.

Two days previous to King's death, Lees and North were present and watched thousands of armed vigilantes marching in formation up Broadway and taking up positions facing the jail. A cannon was aimed at the door and Coleman demanded Sheriff David Scannell surrender Casey. The sheriff, his deputies, and others doing guard duty, now watched helplessly as Coleman was admitted and led a wide-eyed Casey from the jail and into a waiting carriage. Marshal North accompanied the group. As the vigilante troops moved off towards their headquarters, huge crowds watched the history-making event.

An hour later Cora was also brought to the committee rooms and when King died both prisoners found themselves in the hands of the popular tribunal. After a prompt trial, Casey and Cora were hanged from the windows of "Fort Gunnybags," the vigilante headquarters, on May 22, the day of King's funeral. Thousands watched the terrible scene.

The police force was to all appearances suspended from duty during this period, as vigilantes patrolled the streets. Lees and his fellow officers watched as Casey's long funeral procession filed from the Crescent Engine House and headed towards the cemetery next to the Mission Dolores. The grim-visaged Wooley Kearney brought up the rear of the sad parade.

King's funeral wound its way toward Lone Mountain Cemetery with some five or six thousand people in the procession. Thousands more lined the streets.

With Casey and Cora out of the way, the vigilantes extended their war to other areas. Judge McGowan, implicated in the King shooting by several witnesses, now fled town, heading south. Yankee Sullivan, Billy Mulligan, and other political "shoulder-strikers," found themselves in vigilante cells at Fort Gunnybags. David Broderick himself, the Democratic political boss, was at one point questioned, but was not detained.

The police at times worked with the vigilantes who had their own police force and chief. Years later Lees reminisced about those stirring times:

Wooley Kearney's crooked patent ballot box with secret compartments for thousands of "Stuffed" ballots. *Popular Tribunals*

> Well, I dug up the patent ballot box.... That ballot box was an object lesson in itself. I surrendered it to the Vigilance Committee. Of course it wasn't quite regular to do that, but if I hadn't given it up gracefully, they would have taken it...

The detective was probably remembering a raid on Wooley Kearney's shack on Mission Street. Caught unawares, Wooley was quickly hustled off to the committee's rooms along with a trick ballot box which was later displayed at Fort Gunnybags. A false bottom and side allowed votes to be added and many ballots from a Democratic primary contest in July of 1854 were found in various compartments.

With vigilante police patrolling the city, there was little for North and his men to do. "The City Hall is nearly deserted—courts all adjourned," noted the *Bulletin*. Several more political bullies were meanwhile taken into custody as the vigilantes continued their heralded "cleansing" of the city. Most of those arrested were Democrats, although Charley Duane was a Whig.

Early in June, Marshal North resigned and disappeared. Indications are that he had been warned by the vigilantes to leave town. To further complicate matters, Captain McDonald, next in line for the marshal's job, suffered a heart attack and was confined to bed. Jim McElroy, acting captain since McDonald's illness, was now promoted to acting marshal. When McDonald died in early July, McElroy was elected city marshal by the board of supervisors. On July 27, Lees and others on the force paid their last respects to the veteran McDonald at his funeral.

For all their secrecy and strutting about, the vigilantes were very businesslike and official about their operations, as reported in the *Bulletin* on June 21, 1856:

DAGUERREOTYPES of the NOTORIETIES - A daguerreotype artist was engaged yesterday at the Vigilante Committee rooms in taking miniatures of the notorieties who were to be sent

Gambler Dan Aldrich was one of the undesirables daguerreotyped by the Johnson brothers. With various others, he was shipped out of town by the vigilantes on July 5. This contemporary engraving was published locally.
*Author's Collection*

off by the Sierra Nevada....We will doubtless soon have lithoraphs or woodcuts of them all. It is said that Cunningham and Purple twisted and turned considerably and that it was only after several trials that correct likenesses could be procured.

The article referred to the forced exile of toughs and ballot box stuffers from the city by the vigilantes. On June 5, Charley Duane, Martin Gallagher, Billy Mulligan, Edward Bulgar, Billy Carr, and Wooley Kearney were given one-way tickets on a steamer leaving the city. Exactly one month later six more undesirables were shipped out of town on the steamer *John L. Stevens*.

As a lawman Lees must have had reservations about the vigilantes. Still, he realized that the poorly paid and outnumbered police had been mismatched against the criminals and politicians of old San Francisco. Too, many of the police were political appointees and tools of these same politicians. After the Mercantile Hotel imbroglio, the police must have appreciated something being done, even by a determined band of vigilantes acting outside the law.

"There is no doubt," penned banker Sherman, "we have had a bad administration of law here, and more than a share of rowdies; but I think the committee itself no better, and if we are to be governed by the mere opinion of the committee, and not by officers of our own choice, I would prefer at once to have a dictator...." Most San Franciscans, however, supported the vigilantes.

Jane must have liked the beard Isaiah had grown. It made him look the part of the noted detective whom the newspapers constantly sought out for stories. From an old newspaper print. *Author's Collection*

When State Supreme Court Justice David S. Terry stabbed a vigilante in a dispute over a prisoner, he was hauled into Fort Gunnybags and jailed. Fortunately the victim recovered and the vigilantes grudgingly released their political "hot potato."

In late July Joseph Hetherington shot and killed Dr. Andrew Randall in a dispute over money. Isaiah arrested the killer, but was forced to give him up to the vigilantes. On July 29, 1856, Hetherington and a criminal named Philander Brace were hanged by the vigilantes before a huge crowd of people.

After various parades and festivities, the vigilantes retired from their work in late August. The police were once again in control and the courts resumed operation.

On July 22, the *Alta* listed four newly appointed captains of police. Lees was nominated by President Whelan of the police commissioners, while Jim Towle, John O'Brien, and Richard Monks made up the other new officers. Lees was the first Captain of Detectives and it was a proud Isaiah who grabbed his wife that evening and gave her the good news. He was only twenty-five years old that troubled summer of 1856.

On the evening after the vigilante grand review, a particularly vicious crime

was committed at a house in Washington Place. Maria Lafourge, a French prostitute, stepped outside her cottage to investigate some suspicious sounds. Not seeing anything, she turned to go back inside when suddenly a vial of acid was thrown at her. As the deadly fluid bit into her face and neck, she ran screaming across the street to a saloon and gasped out what had happened.

It was eleven o'clock that night when Lees arrived and found the woman out of her head from pain and unable to answer questions. Earlier she had accused Thomas Chieto, her lover, of the crime, saying they had been having trouble for some time. Looking about her room, Lees noticed vitriol burns on some curtains and a chair. A careful search outside turned up a small, wide-necked bottle that had formerly contained ox-marrow hair dressing. A man's handkerchief was folded and wrapped about the bottle.

Chieto operated a two-room saloon in the basement of a brick building on Dupont Street. After discovering the bottle at the Lafourge place, Lees went straight to Chieto's saloon and arrested him. Quickly searching the rooms, the detective found a trunk full of clothes, all of which bore the same laundrymark as the handkerchief at the Lafourge home. Leaving an officer in charge of the saloon, Lees took his prisoner and the trunk to the station house where he questioned the prisoner before locking him up.

Although unable to obtain any significant information from the suspect, Isaiah had noticed what appeared to be burns on his trousers. When a drop of vitriol was applied to the trousers, the resulting burn matched the existing damage.

After tending business in another part of town, Lees returned to find Chieto had been released on bail and taken his trunk and burned trousers with him. The detective was furious. Cursing the officer on duty, he rushed to Chieto's saloon and again searched the place over the proprietor's objections. He located the burned trousers which had been rolled up and hidden under the bar. They were noticeably damp, as if an effort had been made to remove the stains and burns.

Searching the place more carefully this time, the detective found a cork that didn't fit any other bottle in the saloon. It did fit perfectly into the bottle found at the Lafourge house. While going through a pile of rubbish in a dark corner, Lees found a container of vitriol. A little footwork to tie up some loose ends and he was ready for an indictment.

Although an eye was destroyed and she was badly scarred, Madame Lafourge managed to testify at Chieto's trial in late October. Lees had by now located various witnesses, including the druggist who had sold the vitriol. His detailed testimony on the evidence sealed Chieto's fate, as reported in the *Bulletin*:

> ...The judges and attorneys all remarked that it was by far the most remarkable case they had ever witnessed. On an examination of the investigations and discoveries of Capt. Lees, of the police, the reader will be reminded of the famous "Officer Bucket of the Detec-

tives," characterized by Dickens in "Bleak House." Captain Lees has certainly displayed a great deal of ingenuity and has approved himself very good in the detective line and deserves credit....

It was a classic instance of Lees' detective work—the collection of many bits of evidence, luck and just plain hard work that had to be any good detective's trademark. The comparison to a Dickens character, however, marked the beginning of the Lees' legend.

Although sentenced to ten years at the state prison, Chieto managed to escape the following year.

James F. Curtis, the vigilante police chief, was to be Isaiah's new boss. Curtis had also been a member of the 1851 vigilantes. *Author's Collection*

In early October Isaiah was elected to represent California No. 4 on the Board of Delegates. He couldn't spend much time with his fire-fighting pals anymore, but wanted to do what he could.

The new vigilante-spawned Peoples Party won big at the November elections with ex-vigilante police chief James F. Curtis elected city marshal. It was commonly whispered around town that Curtis, who had been born in Boston in 1825, lived with an ex-prostitute named Lou Moore. At this time the city marshal title was changed to chief of police, as was customary in most larger cities.

But for all his good work and press notices, in early December Isaiah and the other three police captains found themselves dismissed from the force by the police commissioners during one of the periodic reorganization efforts. The officers were furious and maintained they could only be removed for dereliction of duty. When they were offered free legal services by several lawyers, the commissioners saw the handwriting on the wall. Lees and the others were reinstated, but they were reduced in rank to patrolmen.

Although still in command of the detective force, as the new year of 1857 arrived, Isaiah found himself again just a private in the ranks.

## CHAPTER FIVE / NOTES

The North-Nugent squabble is well covered in the *Bulletin* of May 3, 7, and 12, 1856. The "Citizen" letters appeared in the same paper on May 7 and 9th.

Lees' arrest and fracas with Foster and Wilson is given in detail in the *Alta* and *Bulletin* of May 8, 1856, while accounts appeared in at least two other San Francisco papers, also. The Sacramento *Daily Union* mentioned the capture on May 10.

Various letters of banker William T. Sherman written during the 1856 vigilante takeover of San Francisco are extremely illuminating of the period. These letters have been printed in various publications over the years, but are all reproduced in *The San Francisco Vigilance Committee Of 1856, Three Views*, Los Angeles: The Los Angeles Westerners, 1971. Excellently edited by Doyce B. Nunis, Jr., this book reprints various works of William T. Sherman, William T. Coleman, and James O'Meara and gives an excellent overview of the vigilante period from three divergent points of view. See also Frank Meriweather Smith (ed.), *San Francisco Vigilance Committee of 1856*, San Francisco: Barry, Baird & Co., 1883. Hubert Howe Bancroft's *Popular Tribunals*, San Francisco: The History Company, Publishers, 1887, although flawed by a biased approach, is still a worthwhile account of those troubled times. For a flavor of the period a study of contemporary newspapers is particularly rewarding.

Thomas King assumed his dead brother's duties as editor at the crusading *Bulletin*.

A more recent interpretation of vigilante morals and methods is Robert M. Senkewicz's *Vigilantes In Gold Rush San Francisco*, Stanford: Stanford University Press, 1985. Sherman's San Francisco career is covered in Dwight L. Clarke's, *William Tecumseh Sherman: Gold Rush Banker*, San Francisco: California Historical Society, 1969.

Lees' involvement in the rescue of Casey in the hack is given in the *Examiner* of May 19, 1895, while Charley Duane's reminiscences of the event were published in the same paper on February 27, 1881.

Lees' recollection of the ballot box incident is taken from an article in the *Call* of November 5, 1895. The account of the raid on Wooley Kearny's shack appeared in the *Alta* of May 30, 1856.

Marshal North's resignation was published in the *Bulletin* of June 11, 1856. The vitriol case was reported in the *Bulletin* of August 19 and 20, 1856. Details of the investigation and trial were published in the *Bulletin* of October 25 and 26 of the same year.

Notice of Lees' election to the Board of Delegates of his engine company was reported in the *Alta* of October 8, 1856. For an informative monograph on James Freeman Curtis, see Dr. Albert Shumate's *James F. Curtis, Vigilante*, San Francisco: San Francisco Corral of the Westerners, 1988.

Lees' dismissal from the force and reinstatement is reported in the *Bulletin* of December 4 and 13, 1856.

# Prostitutes and Plaza Thieves

WATER WAS IN LIMITED SUPPLY when Lees first landed in San Francisco. Baths in hotels cost twenty-five cents and water sold on the street at five to twelve cents a pail, or three dollars a barrel. Some of the city's water was from local springs or wells, but much of it was brought across the bay from Sausalito in specially constructed boats. Water carts plied the streets replenishing the supplies of residences, businesses, and restaurants. Jane, Isaiah, and little Josephine probably shared water with neighbors so it wouldn't become stale.

Although discouraged by his demotion, Lees determined to stay with his new profession. Some fine officers had been lost, while others were rapidly becoming disillusioned by the attrition caused by political cronyism and patronage. Still, Isaiah kept hoping that one day the politicians could be made to stay out of police business.

There was little Jane could do but listen to her husband's complaints. She was terrified of the life he led, but he had sold the tugboat at her insistence and she could not ask him to abandon this new career. She knew he had found what he had been looking for now. His new work was the breath of life to him.

On March 24 the police raided a French gambling house. The place was cleverly shielded from discovery, but Detective Jake Chappell and Officer E. J. Saulsbury managed to break in on the heels of a customer who was being admitted. They were confronted by one Madame Botan who carried a large Bowie knife and several derringers. A huge woman, Madame Botan and several gamblers held the two officers at bay until police reinforcements arrived. Alexander Peyre, the owner, was taken into custody along with his woman and an assortment of gamblers and patrons.

Arriving from France, South America, Hawaii, and the French Marquises, the early French immigrants to California made many contributions to the new country. It was the bad element, however, who were most conspicuous. The French immigrants settled along Jackson Street, then along Commercial when it was opened to Kearny, and the area soon became known as Frenchtown. Maria Lafourge had been a French prostitute in an area where hundreds of others plied their ancient trade. Despite their vocations, early San Francisco editor Frank Soule noted that it was these French women who were most responsible for giving the town "ease, taste and sprightly elegance" in those early years.

When the steamer *Brother Jonathan* arrived at San Francisco on April 23, a middle-aged Oregon merchant stepped ashore and looked around. Taking a room at the Rassette House, Isaac Hutchings prepared to take in the sights of the colorful Bay City. It was to be an experience he would never forget—an adventure all too familiar to many visitors in early San Francisco.

Hutchings' first stop was a barber shop where he was trimmed and perfumed for the evening entertainments. He asked the barber for the nearest daughter of joy and was directed to Alice Atkins' room on Jackson Street. Here he spent the next two nights, with Friday afternoon being spent in a carriage ride around the city with Alice. After several stops to purchase various articles for Miss Atkins, the couple had an early Saturday breakfast and Hutchings paid Alice ten dollars. At the bordello of Rose Church, he struck up a conversation with Eliza Cooney, whose paramour, John Cooney, had been shipped out of town by the vigilantes the previous summer.

Rose Church, as she appeared in the 1860 San Francisco police mug book. *Author's Collection*

When Hutchings didn't return to his hotel, several of his steamer acquaintances became concerned. He was known to be carrying a large amount of money and friends informed Chief Curtis of the disappearance.

Detectives Isaiah Lees and Henry Johnson were assigned the case. Johnson was new on the force, but he had a long background in police work. Born in Scotland about 1818, he had served on the Glasgow police force and later was a detective in Melbourne and Sydney, Australia. After arriving in San Francisco in 1855, he had been appointed a Special Policeman and Isaiah quickly recognized him as a clever detective. They began their investigation Sunday afternoon.

During a search of all the cribs and brothels of the area, no trace of the missing man could be found. The detectives finally located a witness who had seen an older man in a carriage with Lizzie Cooney. After locating the prostitute at Rose Church's place, the lawmen felt sure the victim was there. Chief Curtis had joined his men by now and the three officers entered and began a search. In a dingy, second story room they found their man. As Lees and the other officers burst through the door, Hutchings was barely able to cry out,

Rose Church's description in the 1860 police record book. *Author's Collection*

"Thank god, I am saved! I am saved!"

The victim was nearly naked, lying on a bed unable to move from the effects of drugs and liquor. Cooney had plied him with champagne and taken him for

60

another carriage ride during which he had bought her numerous gifts and articles of clothing. After their return to Rose Church's place, they consumed more wine and Hutchings was taken up to a bedroom. Before long the victim knew something was wrong, as reported in the *Alta*:

> By this time the poison of the drugs was affecting him strangely; every limb seemed paralyzed and powerless; he had no control over them, but remained stretched out upon the bed utterly helpless, and at the mercy of the two she-devils; and yet, strange to say, his head remained clear and he retained full possession of his mental faculties....In this deplorable condition he remained for several hours. Liz did not return, but about 11 o'clock Saturday night Rose Church came into the room, sat upon the bed and commenced fondling him, and helped him to some more poisoned liquid which he was afraid to refuse. She then blew out the light and while sitting by his bedside, took from his body a...money jacket containing about $750; he knew what she was doing, but had not the strength to resist her. In this state of stupor and helplessness he remained a close prisoner in the room for twenty-six hours, until the officers came to his rescue.

The case was scheduled in police court for May 7 with Lees as the principal witness. He must have privately resented these up-country tourists who got themselves into life-threatening situations by their own reckless behavior.

Rose Church received a light sentence and was soon back in business. Only about twenty-two years old at the time, she had already been convicted several times for midemeanors. A native of New Zealand, Rose always gave her livelihood as a barmaid. She spoke with an Irish accent and was described in police records as "Height five feet, two inches, Weight 120, Hair black, Eyes blue, High cheek bones, thin face, teeth much decayed—nose and forehead deeply scarred by a burn..." Her police record notes that she died in San Quentin.

Following the Church-Cooney hearing on May 8, the police court enjoyed a good laugh. Mike Taylor had visited a Chinese brothel and after leaving couldn't find a five-dollar gold coin he kept in his wallet. Dashing off to police headquarters, he secured a warrant for the girl's arrest and had her hauled back to the station. When asked for a deposit to assure he was going to press charges, Mike reached for his money and was surprised to find the missing gold piece hidden in a fold of his wallet. The girl was then released and Mike thrown into jail for drunkeness. Judge Henry Coon later had the wit to fine Mike exactly five dollars.

In late April Lees and Henry Johnson located a suspect in the saloon of James Mulloy. Arresting John Cook, they were ushering him out when Mulloy rushed up and asked what was going on. He offered to give bail and demanded a warrant, which the officers didn't have.

Police judge, and later mayor, Henry Coon. *Author's Collection*

"That's the way a thief would act in coming into a man's house," blurted out the saloonkeeper and Isaiah promptly knocked him down. Scrambling to his feet, Mulloy rushed to the bar for help. His bartender snatched a pistol and was threatening to start throwing some heavy glass tumblers when Mulloy's wife ran into the room.

"For God's sake," she wailed, "don't commit murder!"

One of the saloon patrons told Cook he should go with the officers and, with Mulloy yelling after them, the trio proceeded to the nearest station house.

On May 1 Lees was called before the police commissioners, charged by Mulloy with misconduct. After a hearing in which both sides testified, the commissioners rendered a verdict that Mulloy had unlawfully interfered with an arresting officer. Lees was then mildly reprimanded and returned to duty.

With the coming of spring and summer the city's population began thinning out as miners, gamblers, and drifters headed inland for the mining country. Lees is constantly mentioned in the press arresting minor thieves and recovering stolen property, mostly in conjunction with Henry Johnson.

Charles Coffee, the toughest of the "Plaza Thieves," who were exhibited. From the 1860 San Francisco police mug book.
*Author's Collection*

On July 16 the store of Hipolite Stampf, on Third Street, was robbed. He had foolishly left the premises for a few moments and returned to find the cash drawer emptied of over $500 and a valuable gold watch. The city was being plagued by a group of young thieves at this time and Detective Jake Chappell learned that several prominent members had just left for Sacramento. The suspects, Charles Coffee, John Farell, and Bobby Durkin, were nabbed by the Sacramento police, whom Chappell had alerted by telegraph. They were found to have a large sum of money in their possession and were returned on the next steamer. Lees and Johnson were meanwhile investigating yet another robbery at the Eureka Lodging House.

After picking up a local burglar and thief named "Mugg" Peterson, the two detective officers quickly learned of an accomplice named "Briney" John O'Brien and soon had him in custody. Next, a witness was found who had seen O'Brien and four others gathered in an alley behind the Catholic church on Market Street. They appeared to be dividing money and since this occurred immediately after the Stampf robbery, a tie-in seemed certain.

Lees and Johnson visited the alley and carefully went over the area described by the witness. Nearby they found a buckskin bag identified by Stampf as that taken

in the robbery. Further investigation established Charles Coffee, his brother Cornelius, John King, and "Red-Head" Burns as the four engaged in dividing the loot with "Briney" O'Brien in the alley.

"Much credit is due Officers Lees and Johnson," reported the *Alta*, "for their promptness and shrewdness in ferreting out and arresting the above parties."

Mickey Grant. A woodcut made from his daguerreotype that appeared in *Spirit of the Times. Author's Collection*

While leafing through the July 11, 1857, issue of the *Bulletin* Isaiah noticed a brief story on the death of the famous French detective, Francois Eugene Vidocq. He had read Vidocq's autobiography and been impressed with the account of the beginnings of the French Surete, the detective force of Napoleon's time. The great detective's recordkeeping, his stress on careful investigations, and the plodding detail work upon which success depended, all made so much more sense now.

Isaiah knew well the importance of recordkeeping. In 1852 former police Captain George Casserly had provided a device to measure the height of prisoners. He had also kept a book containing descriptions of noted criminals and recommended the department take daguerreotypes of the more notorious offenders.

Lees had to buy his own notebooks and other supplies, as did many public officials. Henry Johnson and European thieves had told him how criminal portraits had been taken by the French and Belgian police almost since the beginning of photography in 1839. He was aware that the 1851 vigilantes had made daguerreotypes of several prisoners and, of course, the vigilantes of the previous summer had taken portraits of their captives, also. It was a good idea and daguerreotypes were made of the more important prisoners whenever possible. Lees found a newly arrived photographer from Hong Kong who would make criminal portraits for five dollars each. Most of the cost was paid by Lees and Curtis, however.

Chief Curtis was becoming increasingly irritated by the gangs of young petty thieves roaming the city. The Coffee brothers, "Red-Head" Burns, Bobby Durkin, Mickey Grant, and many others were constantly being arrested, yet were seldom convicted or were quickly out on bail. Lees knew them all. It was frustrating for the police to bring in these young thugs, then watch them get off with a light sentence. Twenty-

"Red-Head" Burns, another of the "Plaza Thieves." *Author's Collection*

year-old William Keefe was a good example.

Lees and Johnson had arrested Keefe the previous May on a charge of larceny. He had set a fire in the O'Meara Building and during the resulting excitement had robbed several rooms. In trying to locate the stolen property, the officers had backtracked and found he had recently been released from the Sacramento chain gang. He had lived in various local hotels under different names, but although the detectives could prove he was the thief, little of the stolen property was recovered. At this time Keefe was back doing business as usual.

William Winters, alias "Brockey." From the 1860 San Francisco police mug book. *Author's Collection*

On August 2 Lees, Saulsbury, and Johnson arrested Mickey Grant on a charge of grand larceny. He had taken rooms at the Clinton Temperance House after midnight, robbed one of the lodgers of over $600, then skipped out before five that morning. Grant had a criminal history dating back to 1851 and had served several terms in state prison, aside from various tours of duty on the local chain gang. Although the suspect seemed obviously guilty, it could not be proven and he was released after a police court hearing. For Chief Curtis, however, this was the straw that broke the proverbial camel's back.

Under Curtis' direction, Isaiah took officers Johnson, Chappell, Saulsbury, and Welch and rounded up fourteen of these local thieves and deposited them at City

The young thieves were exhibited on the San Francisco Plaza as shown here in the mid-1850s. Police headquarters is at the far right, with the arched doors. *Author's Collection*

Hall police headquarters. Some had charges against them, but most were picked up merely as known thugs and thieves. Curtis had them daguerreotyped, then announced he was going to display the prisoners on Portsmouth Plaza. The plan was for local shopkeepers and hotel people to see them there and be on the lookout in the future.

On the day of the exhibition a large crowd lined the plaza fence along Kearny Street to view the novel proceedings. At ten o'clock Chief Curtis stepped out of City Hall leading his string of prisoners. Since the plaza was directly opposite City Hall, Curtis walked across the planked street and pushed back the crowds. There was a neat, iron picket fence surrounding the square now. Inside were newly planted trees and a lawn, crisscrossed with walkways. "As soon as they made their appearance on the street," chronicled the *Spirit of the Times*, "the crowd rushed helter-skelter pell mell to obtain the most favorable positions from which to view the disgraceful exhibition."

The prisoners were handcuffed on either side of a heavy rope and guarded by a detachment of officers. In tow were "Brockey" Winters, Mickey Grant, William Keefe, "Browney," William Harrison, Sam Miller, William Burns, Henry McDermott, Ah Bing, George Shultz, Davis, John Fisher, Frank Steele, "Mose" Emory, Henry Bates, Ah You, Bill Clark, and Charles Coffee. One of the worst of the crew, Coffee, was the most outraged over this humiliating treatment, as reported in the *Spirit of the Times* of August 15, 1857:

The procession was followed by an immense crowd to the Plaza where the display took place. It was with some difficulty they reached the place, however, in consequence of the obstinancy of Charles Coffee, one of the gang, who threw himself upon the ground refusing to walk, and had his clothes torn from him in being dragged there. As soon as he reached the spot he commenced swearing and abusing the officers in the most violent and vindictive manner. Some one in the crowd handed him a large bowie-knife, with which he cut himself loose from the rope, and slipping the shackles from off his hands, threw himself into a defiant attitude and dared anyone to approach him under pain of death. He did not maintain this position long, however, for Capt. Anderson, of the police, seized his arms and wrenched the knife from his grasp. Coffee then broke clear of the crowd, and made his way back again to the city prison. The rest were more quiet and subdued in manners and were ranged in line with one end of the rope

Portion of an article in the *Alta* of August 11, 1857, describing the exhibition of thieves on the plaza.

*Author's Collection*

### CITY ITEMS.

PUBLIC EXHIBITION OF THIEVES. — Several days ago a number of persons, the majority of whom were young men, under the age of twenty, who were known to the police as common thieves, or rather who were known to have no business and no visible means of support, but lived vagabond lives, and were suspected of being the perpetrators of all the petty thefts and daring burglaries lately committed, because they had all or nearly all been tried and convicted of some offence before the Police Court, were arrested by order of Mr. Curtis, Chief of Police, and locked in the station house, where they remained until yesterday morning. On Saturday Mr. Curtis expressed his determination to take the whole band out on Monday morning, and parade them with placards upon their backs, through the Plaza, to allow the public an opportunity of knowing and guarding against them. The intention of the chief was reported in several of the morning papers, and before the hour of ten yesterday the City Hall was thronged with hundreds of persons eager to witness the sorry sight. After considerable difficulty, the officers got all things ready for the start. Several of the prisoners objected to going and swore they would die first. Some of them stripped off their shirts, under the impression that they would not be taken ; but they

William Keefe, another of the Plaza group. *Author's Collection*

tied to the flagstaff....

The prisoners were exhibited for some two hours, although Curtis' zeal went completely unappreciated. "The spectacle," grumbled the *Alta*, "was disgusting and revolting in the extreme. There seemed to be but one expression in regard to it... disappointment...."

The board of supervisors called a hurried meeting when they heard of the affair. Severely castigating Chief Curtis for this "violation of the law," resolutions were passed condemning the exhibition and absolving the board of any involvement.

Curtis must have been furious when he released the prisoners. Exactly one week later Mickey Grant and Billy Harrison were picked up for several room robberies in the What Cheer House, while two nights later Lees and Johnson picked up "Red-Head" Burns for the same dodge in the Bay City Hotel. Curtis could smile and snarl, "I told you so!" but critics could ask what good his parade had done when all the "Plaza Thieves," as they were being dubbed, were doing business as usual a few days after being released.

Isaiah's home life was sporadic, but he adored three-year-old Josephine and spent what time he could with her. With seven-day work weeks and investigations making his hours even longer, time with his family was indeed precious. Jane was proud of her husband's fame and smiled at the excited chattering of neighbors at his adventures. She learned to cope with his life, but it was impossible not to worry. Somehow she managed to keep her mind occupied with home and other projects.

Chief Curtis, shown here in his Civil War uniform, was bitterly censured in the local press for his Plaza exhibition. *Author's Collection*

## CHAPTER SIX / NOTES

The contemporary press gives much interesting information on transportation and water sources as they developed, but Lotchin's brief references are also informative.

The constant turnover of officers on the police force during the 1850s is apparent in city directory lists, as well as the fairly frequent rosters of new appointments appearing in the local press.

The French gambling house raid was reported in the *Alta* of March 25, with a more detailed account in the *Marysville Herald* of March 29, 1857 as reprinted from the San Francisco *Globe*.

The comments concerning French immigrants is taken from the previously cited *The Annals of San Francisco*, together with the "Continuation, through 1855" compiled by Dorothy H. Huggins in the edition published by Lewis Osborne, Palo Alto: 1966.

Information on Henry Johnson is from the 1860 San Francisco Federal Census and the *Alta* of August 1, 1875.

Mr. Hutchings' misadventure with the two local cyprians is recounted in the *Alta* of April 28, 1857. Data on Rose Church is from a San Francisco police identification book of the early 1860s in the collection of John Boessenecker. The police court hearing of the affair, as well as the Taylor incident, was reported in the *Alta* of May 8, 9, 1857.

Lees' trouble with saloonkeeper Mulloy is described in the *Alta* of May 2, 1857.

The Hypolite Stampf robbery and aftermath is reported in the *Alta* of July 19, 1857.

Vidocq died in Paris on May 11, 1857, and is generally accepted as a pioneer in police detective methodology. Originally a criminal himself who served galley and prison terms, Vidocq recognized the folly of his life and became an undercover policeman in Napoleonic Paris. Hiring ex-convicts as aids, he became phenomenally successful in capturing criminals by infiltrating their gangs and in the use of stool pigeons. He founded the Brigade de la Suerte in October of 1812 and pioneered the use of scientific and innovative techniques for solving crimes. Elaborate recordkeeping, descriptions of criminals and their methods of operation, and the collection of clues and evidence made him eminently successful and he was a literal legend in his own time. Later he operated the world's first private detective agency. As friend and associate of Victor Hugo, Balzac, and Dumas he was the hero of many of their novels and stories. Poe is said to have freely used him as the protagonist of his several detective stories, also. There were many editions of his autobiography over the years. The author has a copy of *Memoirs Of Vidocq*, published in Philadelphia by Peterson & Brothers in 1859, a treasured gift from his son, William B. Secrest, Jr. A modern biography is Samuel Edwards' *The Vidocq Dossier*, Boston: Houghton Mifflin Company, 1977.

Captain George Casserly's contributions to the police department were reported in the *Alta* of April 20, 1852. Lees' own personal recordkeeping was frequently mentioned in the press of the time and re-stated at the time of his retirement in 1900. Sergeant Tim Bainbridge, in charge of the department's records, reported in the *Chronicle* of January 5, 1900 that he still had several of the early record books compiled by Lees "at his own expense, paying $2,500 out of his own pocket for the work." Bainbridge also mentions Lees' early collection of

daguerreotype mug shots, "taken prior to 1860." For more data on Lees' recordkeeping, see the *Chronicle* for January 3, 1900.

When camera exposure time was cut from minutes to seconds in the early 1840s, criminal mug shot portraiture became practical and was promptly put into use. The German newspaper *Munchener Morgenblatt* noted in November of 1841 that the Paris police were taking daguerreotypes of all criminals passing through their hands and attaching them to their respective reports. The Philadelphia *Public Ledger* on November 30, 1841, reported the same thing. For an extensive investigation into origins of police mug shot photography, see the papers of Harris B. Tuttle, former consultant to the Law Enforcement Photography Department at the Eastman Kodak Company, in the Photographic Archives Collections, University of Louisville Library, Louisville, Kentucky.

Little is known of the beginnings of mug shot photography in this country. Allan Pinkerton is sometimes credited with establishing the first Rogues Gallery in this country about 1857, but this is undoubtedly wrong. In the papers of the 1851 San Francisco Vigilance Committee is a receipt for four daguerreotypes at six dollars each. See *Papers of The San Francisco Committee of Vigilance of 1851*, edited by Mary Floyd Williams, Berkeley: University of California, 1919. Both Bancroft, in his *Popular Tribunals*, and the San Francisco *Bulletin* mention the 1856 Vigilance Committee daguerreotyping prisoners. For some information on early San Francisco police photography of criminals, see "The First Rogues Gallery in the World," by Theodore Kytka, in *Camera Craft*, March, 1901, a photographic monthly published in San Francisco. The title is not correct, however. Kytka was a noted handwriting expert and worked with Lees on many cases.

A portrait and some biographical data on William Keefe appeared in the California *Spirit of the Times* of August 15, 1857. The *Bulletin* of May 5, 1857 gives the details of Lees and Johnson arrest of Keefe for the O'Meara Building fire.

The round-up of the "Plaza Thieves" is briefly noted in the *Alta* of August 8, 1857. There is good coverage of the exhibition in the *Spirit of the Times* and also in the *Alta* of August 11 and 18. The *Bulletin*'s reporting of the incident appears from August 10–13. One letter-writer in the *Bulletin* notes that New Orleans police put placards on the backs of criminals with their crime printed in large letters and parade them through the streets.

The re-arrests of Coffee, Grant, Harrison, and others for various crimes is reported in the *Bulletin* of August 15 and 17, 1857.

Men worked seven days a week during most of the nineteenth century and unpaid time off was usually acquired by being replaced by a substitute. Police officers worked these same, long hours. It wasn't until the 1920s that the eight-hour day and a six-day work week took root in the U.S. and abroad due to the rise of labor unions and more advanced machinery. See Commons, J.R., and others, *History Of Labor In The United States*, New York: 1918.

# Archy and the Cornelia Affair

AS THE YEAR 1858 DAWNED ON THE BAY CITY, Lees must have wondered just when some stability could be established in the department. Four years earlier there had been forty-eight regular patrolmen and seven officers, including the chief. Despite the phenomenal growth of the city, the current manpower report listed thirty patrolmen, four captains, and the chief. And, even when not on the increase, crime was constantly becoming more complex and expensive.

In late January Chief Curtis listed some $800 in expenses incurred in recapturing the notorious burglar Alexander Orlanski, who had recently escaped from the city prison. This included a fifty-dollar reward offered by the police. Between 1856 and 1858, over $1,900 in contingency expenses had been incurred by the department, most of it coming from the chief's own pocket or being on credit.

The press constantly mentioned the work of Lees and Henry Johnson. They arrested shoplifters, burglars, fugitives, and con men of every kind and description. The hours were long and hard.

Alexander Orlinski, the notorious burglar. Despite the chains, he managed to escape and was not recaptured. From the 1860 police mug book. *Author's Collection*

"It means work all the time," Isaiah would later comment on his detective work, "the hardest kind of work, both mental and physical. It means the sacrifice of home comforts and entertainments and delights. You must be always ready for work. Criminals refuse to consult your convenience in the perpetration of their crimes." Often he wouldn't be home for days at a time and Jane gradually came to accept their erratic lifestyle.

In an intriguing prelude to the troubles soon to engulf the country, Charles Stovall brought a slave to California. Born in Mississippi, Archy Lee was only nineteen years old, but was wise enough to know that in California he was no longer a slave. He escaped in Sacramento, but was captured and brought before a judge who ruled there was no California law that would force him to return to Stovall's charge. Free again, Archy traveled to San Francisco where Stovall again had him arrested—but once more he was declared free by a local judge. As he was leaving the courtroom, however, Archy was arrested by a U.S. marshal under the Fugitive Slave Law.

When the case eventually reached the state supreme court, Archy once more was freed, but Stovall managed to again seize him and made plans to quickly leave

the state. The black population of San Francisco, concerned about Archy's fate, had supplied funds and moral support for his courtroom appearances. Now many of them gathered at the Vallejo and Market street wharves after hearing rumors that Stovall and his vassal would be sailing on either the *Orizaba* or the *Golden Age*.

Lees and Chief Curtis had also heard the rumors. On March 6, 1858 Isaiah and Henry Johnson began watching the two ships with orders to prevent Archy from being taken aboard either boat at all costs. Staking out the wharves, the detectives spent all night watching the two steamers. When dawn lightened the sky, neither had seen a sign of Archy Lee.

A red-eyed Lees and Johnson compared notes in the morning, then again split up—Isaiah watching the *Orizaba* and Johnson the *Golden Age*. Hordes of black citizens and others were crowding the wharves as rumors traveled like wildfire. Every carriage and small boat in the area was scrutinized, but Archy was nowhere to be seen.

By eleven o'clock it was whispered along the wharves that Archy was to board the *Orizaba* by a small boat put out from North Beach. Several Whitehall boats manned by stalwart blacks immediately pushed off to thwart any such move.

When the suspected steamer cast off and moved out into the bay, Henry Ellis and Deputy Sheriff D. W. Thompson were aboard with the appropriate warrants. Two Whitehall boats had been tied to the stern of the ship for use if needed. The officers walked about the decks hoping for a clue or loose talk of some sort, but by now Lees was worried that they had missed their chance.

The coastal steamer *Orizaba* as it appeared during the Archy Lee excitement.
*California State Library*

While in the bow of the ship, Isaiah glimpsed a man waving a handkerchief towards shore. Edging closer, he overheard remarks that assured him a showdown was imminent.

"There they are!" The words called Lees' attention to a small boat approaching from the east. Directing Ellis to stand by the starboard gangway, Lees and Deputy

A plea for financial aid to help secure
freedom for Archy Lee appeared in the
*California Chronicle. Author's Collection*

Thompson covered the port side and waited
quietly for the boat to come alongside. As it
drew nearer, Isaiah recognized Stovall, who
was accompanied by three other men. Archy
was seen crouching in the bottom of the boat.
In a few more minutes the small craft was
alongside.

"Keep off! Keep off! There are officers
on board!"

Someone was shouting at Lees' elbow
as Stovall frantically tried to push his craft
away from the larger boat. The *Alta* gave a rousing account of the exciting scene:

> A rush was made by some of Stovall's friends to keep the officers back, but Lees sprang
> down into the boat, at the risk of jumping through her, and seized Archy by the collar. The
> steamer was then in the utmost confusion, yells and cries arose above the roar of the escape
> pipe, some applauding the intrepidity of the officers, and others hooting at the interference
> with the man and his property. In the midst of all this, Lees picked up the trembling negro
> and passed him up like a sack of potatoes to Thompson, who bent down from the guards to
> receive him, and in a twinkling Archy was in the custody of the authorities. During the time,
> Stovall and his friends, both in the boat and on the steamer, swore that the boy should not be
> taken, threatening to blow the top of the officer's head off, see his damned heart, etc., but
> Lees being used to such scenes, considered them only as incidents in the course of events,
> and continued his duties quite composedly.

After herding Stovall aboard the steamer, Lees
served him with his kidnapping warrant. By this time
all the passengers were on deck, the yelling crowd creating a noisy and confusing scene. Detective Ellis
ploughed a course through the mass of humanity, with
Archy following and Lees and Thompson bringing up
the rear with Stovall. Clambering down the gangway
to one of the waiting Whitehall boats, the officers and
their prisoner headed for shore.

A Whitehall boat on the bay.
*California State Library*

Large crowds lined the Market Street Wharf hoping for a glimpse of the celebrated prisoner. The many
black people in the crowd sent up rousing cheers as Lees and his men put up their
oars and climbed onto the wharf. The officers were the heroes of the day. After being
escorted downtown by the mobs of spectators, they safely lodged Archy in police
headquarters.

A long series of hearings and trials resulted in a federal decision that Lee was
free, and he eventually returned to live out his life in Mississippi.

Judge Henry Coon's police court saw a steady stream of customers. The court itself was in City Hall, the old Jenny Lind Theater building that had been remodeled at such great expense several years before. An *Alta* reporter, bored with the day after day listing of the drunks and brawlers, took an imaginative look at the court one day in early 1858:

> THE JENNY LIND THEATER - The private rehearsal at Judge Coon's theater yesterday was not so well attended as usual. But few persons were present in dock, owing, perhaps, to the fact that the "stars" were not out on the night before....Judge Coon sat in judgement over them, and passed upon them as they deserved. The first called were those who had undertaken the part of "Edward Middleton," in the play of the "The Drunkard." Judge Coon fined them $5 each for overdoing the thing....Next came three comic actors - two males and one female - who had attempted a private rehearsal of the old comedy, "Family Jars." They had not done it well, and His Honor discharged them. Lewis Miller offered himself as a feeble imitator of Jack Sheppard. He went to the International Hotel, entered a gentleman's room, opened a bureau drawer and was in the act of removing sundry shirts therefrom when a waiting maid came in unannounced and spotted the play. Judge Coon will take toll from Miller this morning.... John C. Cushing rehearsed the tragedy of the "Bloody Hand" and threw a knife at a man. Judge Coon will teach him the epilog of the play this morning. Carmel Ramirez took the difficult character of "Borachio, or as Drunk as Bacchus" and played it to perfection....

Lees must have chuckled at such articles. He was an avid newspaper reader and watched with interest the blooming of the Bay City presses. There were a dozen newspapers in the early 1850s and now in 1858 the fourth estate was as robust as ever.

In keeping tabs on crime in other parts of the country, Lees frequently read the Eastern papers, also. These were as popular in San Francisco as the local journals, particularly to the incoming steamers. Newsboys would buy bundles of the *New York Herald*, the *Boston Journal* and the *New Orleans True Delta* from Jerry Sullivan, the popular news dealer. Meeting every arriving steamer, the newsboys would sell their imported papers at anywhere from twenty-five to fifty cents each. Lees couldn't help comparing these enterprising young scamps with their criminal counterparts. Many were orphans or cripples with the same cruel background, yet one turned to crime while the other made a living by hard work.

By the late 1850s the importance of criminal photography for identification purposes was being recognized in the United States. Only the larger cities could afford this innovation, but a few progressive departments photographed prisoners whenever possible. The Saint Louis police were photographing criminals at this time, while the New York police had their own photographer and a collection of some 450 portraits in what they referred to as their "Rogues Gallery." The portraits were displayed in glass-doored cabinets where the public was invited to view them.

Criminal portraits had often proved useful to the San Francisco officers. Lees and Curtis had a growing collection of likenesses accumulated over the past few years, as reported in a March issue of the *Alta*:

CHIEF CURTIS' GALLERY OF ART- Chief Curtis has been gradually introducing a new feature into his police arrangements. For the last few months he has taken to collecting the photographic portraits of the most noted thieves, burglars and state prison birds who have come under his supervision. As fast as one of these gentry passes through his hands, he walks him up to a daguerrian gallery, gets an infallible likeness, and is thereafter prepared to identify him as occasion may require, and, in the event rewards are being offered, can give a minute description of the fugitive....Some of them - Orlanski, for instance - are taken manacled and chained, these ornaments adding greatly to the Jack Sheppard look of the wearers....

Daguerreotype of Manuel Canto, a criminal from the first, early San Francisco police mug shots made circa 1857. *Author's Collection*

But with pay still irregular and low at best, the police would have to continue paying for such frills themselves. It made rewards all the more important.

In mid-March of 1858 Isaiah's daughter Josephine became ill. Just four years of age, she was idolized by her parents and Isaiah had delighted in the precious moments he could spend with her. Suddenly it was over, as chronicled in the *Alta* on March 15:

DEATH OF A PET CHILD - Officer Lees met with a sad bereavement yesterday in the death of his beautiful little daughter, Josephine, at her father's residence. She was the pet of the family, and it leaves a void in the mother's heart which can never be filled. The funeral takes place today at 2 P.M. when friends are requested to attend.

Isaiah was crushed. It had been very difficult to accept his first child's loss, but now after living with little Josie and watching her grow and mature, her death was nearly more than he could bear. The following day there was a brief church service, followed by a reception at the Lees home on Stevenson Street. It was late afternoon when the last straggling friends left and Jane and Isaiah were suddenly alone in the stillness of their home.

Towards the end of the month big, black clouds came boiling up from the west and torrents of rain pelted the city. The dark, dreary weather only emphasized the memories and loneliness of Jane and Isaiah.

In late February the brig *Cornelia* sunk off the coast of lower California. Captain Henry Bennett and his crew came ashore by boat at Cape San Lucas, then traveled overland to San Diego. From there they all took passage on the steamer *Senator* for San Francisco.

In the Bay City the *Cornelia's* crew went straight to police headquarters, where they told a strange tale of robbery on the high seas. Chief Curtis and Lees listened carefully.

The seamen insisted that, rather than sinking as the result of damage in a storm, the ship was scuttled by the captain and mate. The crew had been herded below decks while a cargo of some $19,000 in Mexican silver coin was taken ashore and hidden. The ship was then abandoned and sunk.

Several passengers aboard the *Senator* had overheard the *Cornelia* seamen discussing the affair and reported to the police, also. One of these men was a Lloyds of London agent named Green. Working with Lees and Johnson, Green interviewed Mr. Thomas Bell, who had been the San Francisco consignee of the Mexican coins. It was learned that interested parties in Mexico had discovered the plot and taken out insurance on a nonexistent cargo. Captain Bennett had signed a false bill of lading for $30,000. The captain swore the ship's log had gone down with the ship, but it was discovered in the mate's trunk. Everything seemed to be coming together for the detectives.

Under careful questioning by Lees and Curtis, Captain Bennett and the mate finally confessed to the plot. They earnestly denied, however, scuttling the ship. With the statements of the ship's steward and two other crew members, the case seemed complete, although the U.S. attorney decided he had no jurisdiction in the matter. Curtis and Lees had their own ideas about how the case should be resolved.

Selim Woodworth, a prominent merchant, vigilante and law and order advocate. *Annals of San Francisco*

On March 30, 1858, the pilot boat *Fanny* pulled away from the Jackson Street wharf and headed out towards the Pacific Ocean through the channel called the Golden Gate. His maritime experience made Lees the perfect choice to lead the expedition and he was accompanied by Jake Chappell, Officer Sayward, and Selim Woodworth,

Early day tugboat leaving the wharf at San Francisco. *Author's Collection*

a prominent businessman. Captain Bennett and Mate Lenart were along as prisoners to help locate the purloined treasure. The weather was ominous and the water choppy as the small craft cleared the entrance to the bay and headed south toward the southernmost point of Baja California. On the open sea the water was considerably rougher.

On April 8 the *Fanny* dropped anchor off Cape San Lucas, at the furthest tip of Baja California, and the expedition prepared to go ashore. There was a crude village of huts clustered about the beach

and the sudden appearance of a group of strangers sparked very natural fears that a filibustering expedition had landed. With many of the local inhabitants following along, Captain Bennett directed Lees and his men to where the treasure was buried. Some nine sacks of coin were hauled down to the beach and within a half hour were safely stowed aboard the *Fanny*. An American named Richie was ill in the village and Lees talked briefly with him to determine if he were mixed up in the affair. After leaving him some late copies of the *Alta*, Isaiah directed Jake Chappell to accompany a wood and food gathering party while he and the others returned to the *Fanny*.

They had no sooner returned to their anchored craft when a canoe came alongside and the local alcalde was helped aboard. Dressed in a ragged old uniform, Don Domingo Vertelete brandished a cane signifying his office.

The alcalde got right to the point. What right did these filibusters have coming ashore in Mexico and digging up treasure from under his very feet? He further demanded that the money be counted and a report made and duty paid.

Selim Woodworth looked at Lees, then began conversing with the miffed magistrate. He chatted on almost any subject he could think of, except the pilfered treasure. Lees meanwhile had secured a bottle of brandy and began pouring drinks. As the alcalde was being stalled on deck, the treasure was carefully packed and concealed in the hold. When the now pleasantly-addled Don Domingo left for shore, Lees and Woodworth knew he would be sending for the nearest troops as soon as he sobered up. They would have to leave the moment supplies had been taken on.

When a sailor didn't return with the supply detail, Lees and his men held a conference. Someone proposed they leave without the missing sailor, but this was voted down. Lees finally led another armed party ashore.

The dinghy had no sooner been hauled up onto the beach when Isaiah saw the lost sailor stagger from an adobe and make his way towards them. He had been held captive by three local senoritas who had kept him full of Aguardiente as a means of stalling the gringos until troops could arrive. Telling the locals they would be coming ashore for provi-

The village at Cape San Lucas was made up of huts such as this as sketched by J. Ross Browne a few years after the Lees expedition.
*Harpers Magazine, 1868*

sions in the morning, Lees and his men rowed back out to the *Fanny* and awaited nightfall.

It was ten o'clock that night when Lees directed the anchor be quietly hauled up and the *Fanny* headed north along the coast. After a rough trip taking three times longer than the initial voyage, the little pilot boat chugged into the Vallejo Street wharf on April 28 and Lees reported to police headquarters.

Thomas Bell. *Author's Collection*

Curtis was delighted at the success of the venture. He took the recovered money, nearly sixteen thousand dollars in Mexican silver dollars, and deposited it in John Parrott's bank. After informing Lloyds' agent Green and Thomas Bell of his intentions, Curtis declared himself and his associates as salvors and owners of the treasure.

Agent Green was appalled. His company was the logical owner of the captured treasure. When Thomas Bell, to whom the treasure had originally been consigned, declared that Curtis and his men were not entitled to any salvage, Curtis promptly withdrew the funds from the bank. Bell had originally refused to invest in Curtis' recovery scheme and when the chief took possession of the money, Bell issued a warrant for his arrest. Having supposed Lloyds would make good on the stolen coin, Bell apparently knew better now. Curtis remanded himself to the custody of the sheriff, but was released on his own recognisance. The *Alta* considered the whole scheme a glorious coup:

> In reviewing this transaction from the first, it is evident that the Chief is entitled not only to the full credit for originating, boldly taking the responsibility and incurring the expense of this plan, but that his exertions and those of his associates in the matter merit an allowance of salvage. The whole affair, from the arrests made in March up to its triumphant consummation, has been conducted with great skill and judgement.

In late May word arrived on the schooner *Flying Dart* that several of the conspirators had been imprisoned in Mexico. It wasn't until July 9 that an arbitration board settled the matter, however. Nearly $2,000 was allowed Chief Curtis on the expenses of the operation, while he, Lees, and others were re-

A waterfront scene in old San Francisco. *Author's Collection*

warded with 40 percent of the recovered treasure. After several incidental expenses were paid, the officers divided a net of just over $5,000.

There was still no police fund for emergencies. When the officers rented horses to chase fugitives, they used credit or their own cash. Curtis was becoming weary of the situation and pleaded with the board of supervisors for compensation:

> Gentlemen: Herewith please find a bill of advances made by me for necessary expenses or police purposes... amounting to $373.30, which I respectfully request may be audited and ordered paid.
>
> The late murder of a German citizen on Jackson Street, and the escape of the murderer, affords a striking proof of the necessity which exists for a fund to be appropriated to meet the expenses attending the detection and arrests of criminals. Upon the day this murder was done, the press was supplied from this office with the name and description of the party, who has since been indicted by the coroner....
>
> Officers have been on the alert throuhout the city, and among the shipping, and have been sent to the remote points of our own county, as well as to San Mateo and Contra Costa. Through the kindness of the Chief of Police of Sacramento, we have been furnished with a photographic likeness of the fugitive, and have forwarded copies to adjoining counties....
>
> In every report which has been made from this office to your Honorable Board for the past two years, the necessity of this fund has been urged without avail. Our police ask no reward for arresting a fugitive or criminal, but simply desire their expenses...be met by the county....
>
> James F. Curtis, Chief of Police

Curtis further complained that even when contingency funds were available, he was paid in scrip worth eighty-five cents to the dollar and he still lost money.

## CHAPTER SEVEN / NOTES

Police Department manpower reports appeared in the local press from time to time during the early years, making it fairly easy to track the growth of the department. In the 1850s city directories also carried a complete listing of the police force. This particular report was given in the *Daily Alta California* for February 5, 1858. Later the *Municipal Reports* published this information annually.

An article giving a detailed listing of the expenses in recapturing Orlanski appeared in the *Alta* of January 23, 1858.

Captain Lees' quote on detective work was reported in the *San Francisco Call* of November 15, 1895.

There is much coverage of the Archy case in the contemporary press, but detailed information on Lees' part in the affair appeared in the *Alta* of March 6, 1858. For an overview of the complete affair, see Rudolph M. Lapp, *Archy Lee: A California Fugitive Slave Case*, San Francisco: The Book Club of California, 1967.

The humorous account of Judge Coon's police court appeared in the *Alta* of January 26, 1858.

Much interesting information on early San Francisco newspapers and newsboys appeared in a feature article in the *Call* on January 29, 1882, entitled "Newsboys of Old." See also Edward C. Kemble, *A History Of California Newspapers, 1846–1858*, Los Gatos: The Talisman Press, 1962.

Probably the most complete study of the origins of criminal photography is Harris B. Tuttle's "Notes on the History of Photography in Law Enforcement," *Finger Print and Identification Magazine*, October, 1961. Harris, a former consultant to the Law Enforcement Photography Department at the Eastman Kodak Company, deposited his valuable research papers at the University of Louisville Library, Louisville, Kentucky. The article referred to appeared in the *Alta* of March 14, 1858.

The death of Josephine Lees is chronicled in the *Alta* of March 15 and 16, 1858.

Captain Lees' adventure recovering the hijacked treasure is recounted in the *Alta* of March 31, April 3 and 29, May 1, 7, 21, and June 6, 1858. The *Call* of April 28 gave additional details.

Chief Curtis' plea to the Board of Supervisors is contained in the *Alta* under the date of June 25, 1858.

# Mrs. Billman and an Express Robbery

CHIEF CURTIS WAS DEFEATED at the fall elections. His successor was Martin J. Burke, a London physician who had emigrated to America and practiced medicine in Milwaukee. Coming to San Francisco in 1850, Dr. Burke operated two drugstores and a foundry. An energetic man, the new chief had been a vigilante with Curtis, but he had his own way of doing things.

The *Fireman's Journal* reported a quantity of fire hydrants had been completed by a local foundry and some thirty-five locations selected. This could aid greatly in fire protection, but water pipes still had not been adequately installed throughout the town. The growing Bay City was some $92,000 in debt to the gas company and other creditors and it seemed at times as if the municipal machinery would grind to a halt. George Hossefross, the street superintendent whom Isaiah knew through the fire companies, was also complaining about the condition of the city thoroughfares.

In later years Chief Burke became quite wealthy dealing in Bay Area real estate. *Robert Chandler*

On January 6, 1859, officers George Rose and John McKenzie ushered a large, struggling black man into the city prison. The prisoner, John Croger, had been "insulting women on Pacific Street." He was an old offender and a year earlier had tried to knife Lees as the officer attempted to arrest him. As Croger continued to struggle, Officer John Durkee gave him a well placed kick that convinced him to settle down.

In jail, Croger was later being removed from his cell when he made a break for the door. Isaiah, Henry Johnson and Jake Chappell were nearby at the time and rushed to aid in restraining the prisoner. As Croger continued to struggle, the three detectives gave him a sound beating to convince him they meant business, then heaved him into a cell.

Officer John McKenzie.
*Kevin Mullen Collection*

When another prisoner filed charges against the officers for the Croger thrashing, the police commissioners ruled that force could indeed be used to subdue an unruly prisoner. Croger was considered such a menace that he was placed aboard a ship bound for some Pacific islands, as had been done during vigilante days. Later, word was received that the ship's captain had hanged the desperado on an island in the Indian Ocean after Croger murdered the ship's second mate.

On the morning of February 8, 1859, Isaiah was detailed to investigate a stabbing on Battery Street. Taking Henry Johnson with him they interviewed several witnesses to the assault on Louis Guzman, a local porter. While playfully throwing mud at some friends the previous night, Guzman had accidentally hit a seaman named Gustave P. Yenner in the face. Yenner and a companion named Miller had a shouting match with Guzman just prior to the stabbing and in the confusion the assailant had escaped.

Guzman had identified Miller as his assailant and by ten o'clock that morning Lees and Johnson had escorted the suspect to where the dying Guzman lived on Lafayette Place.

The detectives brought several other seamen along with Miller and asked Guzman to pick out his assailant. Miller was immediately pointed out, but he vehemently denied the accusation. He insisted that Yenner must have done the deed and was so emphatic that Lees finally concluded he was telling the truth. Yenner was later arrested aboard the Danish ship *Caroline*. When taken to headquarters, he finally confessed to stabbing Guzman, but claimed it was in self-defense. Meanwhile, the victim had died from his wound.

The trial in late April was a confusing affair. Miller had left town and Yenner was still claiming self defense. His counsel, however, insisted Miller was the guilty party and the conflicting testimony resulted in an acquittal. A disgruntled juror's letter was published in the *Bulletin* the following day:

> ...The whole weight of testimony was in favor of the prisoner. All the evidence for the prosecution tended to establish his innocence in the minds of the jury. It was proved to have been almost physically impossible that he could have done the deed; while the statement of Guzman, persisted in up to the hour of his death, showed that the wound was inflicted by a man named Miller. That man was allowed to leave the city with the knowledge and permission of the police! Either, then, the jury were bound to believe the statements of the above named officers that Yenner had confessed...or believe all the other evidence going to prove the contrary. A motive, too, was shown why the officers desired to have Miller liberated, as his evidence was of importance in a case then pending before the U.S. Circuit Court, in which they had some interest....

Lees did not fear in an investigation and sent the following note to his superior officer:

> San Francisco, April 27, 1859
>
> To M. J. Burke, Chief of Police - Sir: Having seen in this evening's *Bulletin* a card signed "A Juror," which censures the conduct of the officers who made the arrest in the Guzman case, and though I have been a member of the Police Force in this city since 1853, yet this is the first time that I have been charged with malfeasance in office; and as I value more than life my good name, therefore I most urgently request that you will at once hold an investigation into my conduct in this affair. Respectfully yours,
>
> I.W. Lees

The following day Lees had his hearing before two of the police commissioners, Chief Burke, and Mayor Ephraim Burr. Both men wanted to dismiss the meeting since no charges had been preferred, but Isaiah insisted on presenting witnesses to show he had acted properly. Still, the commissioners refused to take the time. The officer then demanded that he be allowed to make some remarks on the case. "The main point in what he said," reported the *Bulletin*, "was that he had nothing to do with the release of Miller. He had no authority to release the prisoner once arrested." The hearing was promptly terminated after Lees' remarks.

One evening as Isaiah read his paper, Jane calmly remarked she had been to see the doctor. She smiled as her husband looked up in alarm. She was pregnant. The detective grinned broadly as he gave his wife a gentle hug. He was going to be a father again.

Early on Sunday morning, February 20, 1859, Lees answered a knock at the door of his home to find Officer J. H. Hesse on the porch. There had been a murder the previous night, just around the corner from the Lees home. Quickly pulling on his coat, Isaiah accompanied

Mayor Ephraim W. Burr.
*Author's Collection*

Hesse to a row of frame houses where groups of people stood around talking. Henry Johnson ushered Lees into the house at 27 Jessie Street where they found one Albinus Billman lying on a bed. He was dying and unable to speak. He had been attacked on the back porch, his head and hands had been terribly crushed and he was bleeding. Besides Mrs. Billman and her small child, several other boarders lived in the house. Moses Tate, a negro friend of the Billmans, was also present when the detectives began their investigation. It was to develop into a strange and complex case.

Mrs. Albinus Billman instigated the murder of her husband, while others paid for the crime. A woodcut from the *California Police Gazette*.
*Kevin Mullen Collection*

Mrs. Mary Ann Billman was originally from Arkansas where she was married to a man named Magnus. A short time after her husband died, she had a child. Sometime later she left for California, arriving in San Francisco in January of 1858. The family slave, Moses Tate, travelled with her, but upon his arrival he was apparently regarded as being free. Later, Tate admitted to intimacies with Mrs. Magnus when they lived in Arkansas.

In the Bay City Mrs. Magnus lived as a prostitute, at one time residing at the brothel of the notorious Rose Church. She met her brother-in-law, James Magnus, in the city and apparently posed as his wife for a time. Another

relationship developed with a man named John Kelly, a messenger at the Custom House. Moses Tate meanwhile was hired as a cook on a schooner owned by Magnus and his partner, one Albinus Billman.

Moses Tate's mug shot indicates how police photography had not yet been standardized.
*John Boessenecker Collection*

Magnus had introduced his partner to his sister-in-law and was present when the two were married on Christmas day, 1858. Mrs. Billman made no pretense of loving her husband and seems to have continued a liaison with John Kelly.

On Saturday evening, February 19, the Billmans invited a Mr. M. P. Hayden, James Magnus, and Moses Tate over for a game of cards. They drank some wine and played cards until about ten o'clock, when the guests left and the Billmans retired.

Shortly after midnight there was a knock at the back door. Billman got up and opened the door, then turned to get a candle and was struck repeatedly with a blunt instrument until slumping to the floor mortally injured. Bloody handprints and gore were all over the room.

Lees and Johnson quickly went to work. Tate, who had been brought to the house earlier with other witnesses, acted suspiciously from the start. The detectives both noticed he was jumpy and wanted to get out of the house and he was promptly taken into custody, along with John Kelly and Magnus. Mrs. Billman's four-year-old daughter had told the officers she had seen Moses beating her "papa" while her mother looked on. Tate was immediately elevated to the status of prime suspect.

The detectives interviewed everyone connected with the case. Friends of Mrs. Billman testified to her loose character. A black man who lived next door to the Billmans told the officers he had seen Moses in the alley between the houses around two or three that Sunday morning. This was substantiated by another witness. Camille Belanger, Tate's landlady, not only contradicted his story of retiring before twelve o'clock on the fatal evening, but testified that he had returned around three o'clock, wearing a different hat than the one worn when he left.

Late Monday afternoon Detective Johnson was in city hall when he was summoned to the basement prison. After some stalling, Moses Tate confessed he had gone to the Billman house early that Sunday morning with John Kelly and a man named Mike Kelly. He had met the two men downtown and on the way over to Jessie Street they had talked of killing Billman, presumedly so his wife could obtain several of her husband's properties. According to Tate, Mike Kelly had killed Billman when he had answered their knock. Moses repeated this story to Lees, Chief Burke and other officers, although all the evidence pointed toward Moses, alone, as the killer.

At the inquest, Lees offered lengthy testimony on the investigation. After two days of hearings, the jury found that Billman had come to his death at the hands of Tate, John or Michael Kelly and that James Magnus and Mary Ann Billman were accessories before or after the fact.

On March 3 the grand jury indicted Tate, Magnus, and Mrs. Billman, but exonerated the Kellys, largely because Moses's testimony was that of a co-conspirator who admittedly participated in the murder. The trial commenced on March 21 in the Twelfth District Court where Tate was convicted on a wealth of circumstantial evidence and sentenced to life imprisonment.

Mrs. Billman was tried in early May, but was acquitted after the jury deliberated some twenty-six hours. Magnus was automatically acquitted at the same time. "She absolutely danced with delight to think how she had escaped," grumbled the *Bulletin*.

In August the *California Police Gazette* reported:

> It was supposed at the time of Mrs. Billman's release from custody that she would retire from public life, and either leave the state or quietly subside into obscurity, but the fact of her opening a low house of prostitution...is proof of her entire callousness to all the better feelings of a woman, and she should be driven from her present place....

Many years later Lees was to comment that "It took a lot of hard work to present the case against Moses Tate....Of course Tate was abetted by Mrs. Billman, but it's hard to convict a woman, you know."

The police had recently become aware of the gradual return to San Francisco of various troublemakers exiled by the vigilantes in 1856. These men were not only unrepentant, but Martin Gallagher had sued and collected from the shipowner who had taken him away. In New York, Charley Duane and Wooley Kearney had also sued vigilantes who arrived in town, while Billy Mulligan sought vengeance by physically assaulting members of the committee who arrived in New York.

Late on the night of August 1, a Freeman and Company express wagon pulled up in front of its San Francisco office. Tompkins, the express messenger, helped several clerks carry six leather treasure bags into the office where they were routinely opened and the contents checked. Instead of gold dust, however, one of the sacks contained metal shot and iron bolts wrapped in paper. The shipment had just arrived on the Sacramento steamer under Tompkins' care and he had checked the shipment when it had been first received. The robbery was quickly reported to Chief Burke.

It was one o'clock in the morning when Lees was given the particulars of the case. Taking Jim Bovee, Johnson, and Chappell with him, Isaiah talked to the Freeman people and learned exactly what their treasure-handling procedure was. A man named Joseph Augell had been driving the wagon, while one James Mulhare was the

company porter. They had driven the wagon to the wharf where Mulhare had met Tompkins on the boat. When Tompkins asked Mulhare to pick up some packages for

him, the porter asked if they shouldn't take the treasure ashore, to which Tompkins agreed. Mulhare took two bags to the wagon, then returned and both he and Tompkins put the remaining four bags into the vehicle. Tompkins checked with Augell to make sure there were six bags in the treasure chest, then the three men, and a friend of Mulhare's named "Ashpan Jack," drove over to the express office at California and Montgomery streets.

Lees glanced over at Henry Johnson. It was obvious a bag switch had been made somewhere between the boat and the express office. Mulhare's demeanor had made him a likely suspect and Bovee was sent to arrest him. Later a search of the porter's home turned up an empty express sack. Acting on a hunch, Isaiah checked a grocery store a few doors from Mulhare's house on Stevenson

**James Mulhare, the larcenous express agency clerk.** *Author's Collection*

Street. The detective wasn't surprised to find identical twine and wrapping paper used to wrap the bolts and shot in the dummy express sack. Connor, the store owner, wasn't informed of the investigation. Lees later explained:

> I took a directory and made a list of all the saddlers in the city, and I then set out to find who made the bag. After asking a dozen or more I entered Hanson & Trapp's place and showed them the bag. Mr. Hanson said he made it. I took Hanson to Freeman and Company's office and showed him all the employees of the office. He could not identify any of them as the man who had ordered the bag made. Mr. Higgens brought in the express bags and Mr. Hanson picked out the one that had been brought in as a pattern. I then went with Hanson around town to search for the man who had ordered the bag. I saw Connor and it suddenly occurred to me that he might be the man. I went for Hanson and we went into Connor's grocery to get a drink. As soon as Hanson saw Connor, he gave me a wink and whispered that he was the man who had the bag made. I then arrested Connor. He was greatly excited....

Checking further, Lees discovered Mulhare and Connor to be old friends—a brother, Patrick Mulhare, testifying that they had known Connor for twenty years. The bolts in the dummy express bag were traced to Freeman and Company's blacksmith shop, while other local saddlers identified Connor as having asked about having duplicate express bags made. Lees quickly had the case ready for an examination in the police court.

After three days' testimony before Judge Coon, the prisoners were ordered to appear before the next court of sessions. The *Alta* was again delighted with the work of the officers:

> Too much credit cannot be given to Chief Burke and the untiring and efficient detectives, Lees, Johnson and Chappell, for their exertions in ferreting out the perpetrators of the robbery, whom they have followed up step-by-step until the evidence seems almost incontrovertible.

The Archy Lee case had made Californians increasingly aware of the polarization of society on the issue of states rights and slavery. Many of the duels fought in the state during the past decade originated among Chivalry Democrats and those opposed to Southern views. When United States Senator David Broderick wouldn't politically support Chief Justice David S. Terry of the state supreme court, events were set in motion which would result in one of the great tragedies of early California.

David Terry was a hot-headed Southerner. A capable attorney, Terry had a history of violence in both his private and public life. When Senator Broderick refused to retract statements considered offensive by

David Broderick, the Democratic political boss.
*John Boessenecker Collection*

Terry, the latter resigned his office and a duel was arranged by friends. Although against the law, dueling had long been condoned on the Pacific Coast, even though public opinion was gradually turning against the ancient custom. Few men in public life had the courage of James King of William who had refused to fight a duel and reasoned against engaging in such affairs.

Broderick had tried to avoid the meeting, but after hearing other enemies were waiting to challenge him also, he agreed to the contest hoping to discourage the others.

It was common knowledge that a duel was scheduled, but Chief Burke and his detectives couldn't learn where or when. Finally, Burke, Lees, Chappell, and Ellis dressed in old clothes and watched the Broderick home. It was in a sparsely settled area and the lawmen had to bury themselves in the sand to keep hidden. When Broderick did leave home, he was followed by the rag-tag group of policemen to the dueling grounds near Lake

Texan David Terry was a violent man who would be shot down in another personal encounter many years later. *Author's Collection*

Merced. Burke recalled later that he and his men pinned on their badges, climbed a fence, and headed straight for the duelists. Hundreds of partisans lined the rolling hills. Calhoun Benham, one of Terry's principals, approached Burke's party and flatly stated they would be shot by Terry sympathyzers if they tried to interfere. It was a desperate moment.

Burke refused to be intimidated. He belonged to the same Masonic lodge as Benham and gambled that there would be no shooting. He and his men walked past Benham and read their warrant to Terry, Burke commenting that as a supreme court justice, the judge should set an example.

"Why don't you arrest Broderick?" growled Terry.

"I will," returned the Chief, "just as soon as I arrest you."

Police Judge Henry Coon heard the case and ruled that although dueling was a crime, an attempt to duel was not illegal. The incident was dismissed. Furious Broderick adherents watched helplessly as another meeting was arranged for the

following day. Disgusted with the whole affair, Burke refused to interfere further.

On September 13, 1859, Terry mortally wounded Broderick in a duel held just over the San Mateo County line, near the original location. Three days later the senator was dead.

Although not relishing the job, Isaiah and Henry Ellis were given a warrant for the arrest of Terry. Crossing the bay to Oakland, they headed south for Terry's farm and home in Stockton. Years later Ellis recounted the experience to another officer:

> Lees and I procured a warrant against Terry and had it properly endorsed. We then proceeded to Terry's home. When we arrived within about one hundred feet of the house, a window was thrown open and Calhoun Benham, Tom Hayes, Sheriff O'Neal and Terry leveled shotguns at us and told us to halt. We did so and announced that we were officers with a warrant for Terry. He stated that he was certain that he would not receive a fair trial and feared violence at that time, but agreed to surrender three days afterwards at Oakland. Knowing that he would keep his word in this, as we also knew what he would do when he told us that if we came nearer to his house they would all shoot, we decided to allow him to dictate terms....

The Leonidas Haskell home, at Black Point, where Broderick died. The bay and Angel Island are in the background. *California State Library*

The detectives returned empty-handed, but it was generally agreed they had showed good judgment in handling the matter. Terry's case was not tried, but he was so severely criticised for the killing that he soon after left for the Virginia City mines.

In the fall Isaiah an-

nounced there would be a little more salary for his family. Jane knew instantly what he meant and proudly read the announcement in the *Alta* on October 11:

> CAPTAIN OF POLICE - Mr. Isaiah W. Lees, for many years connected with the detective police of this city, has received the appointment of Captain of Police by the Board of Police Commissioners. Mr. Lees is in every respect qualified for the position and no appointment could have been more judicious.

When Frederick W. Lees was born on October 20, Isaiah was pleased beyond measure. As they showed the baby to friends and neighbors, the new parents were well aware of the delicate balance between life and death in such a tiny life. There were so many ways to lose a child—so many small graves at Lone Mountain Cemetery where Josephine had been laid to rest.

On November 19, Jake Chappell was hauled into the station house after a drunken brawl on Pacific Street. Luckily, Jim Bovee and another officer had taken him in hand. Lees could only grind his teeth at such behavior. Drinking to excess just didn't pay in this business. Jake Chappell was a good detective, but in his personal life he was often a fool.

In December Lees noticed the dog Chuffy gnawing on a bone in a corner of the city hall jail. Glancing at a nearby cell, he shook his head as he saw Francisco Fuentes eating his meal as well. Chuffy was Fuentes' pet dog, a small cur of uncertain antecedents who had lost a foot in some forgotten accident. Everyone at the station knew Chuffy. His master was an incorrigible chicken thief who was currently serving his tenth term on the chain gang. Chuffy followed the gang out each day, watching patiently as his master worked on the city streets, then following him home to jail each evening. At meal time Chuffy wagged his tail until a scrap was thrown his way. He seemed to accept his position in life. And, when Fuentes was released and engaged in yet another chicken-hunting expedition, Chuffy would be cheerfully limping along behind him, inevitably waiting to be caught and returned to the chain gang.

## CHAPTER EIGHT / NOTES

Information on Martin Burke is in his 1887 "Dictation" in the Bancroft Library, in the *Daily Morning Call* of February 4, 1884, and in the Dagget Scrapbooks, California State Library.

The information from the *Fireman's Journal* and the growing indebtedness of the city appeared in the same paper under date of January 17.

An article on the stabbing of Guzman appeared in the *Bulletin* of February 8, 1859. A report of the trial was given in the same paper on April 26, while the letter from "A Juror" appeared the following day. Lees' letter to Burke was published in the *Bulletin* of April 28 and his hearing reported in the same paper the following day.

Isaiah and Jane were living on Stevenson Street, just one block away from the scene of the Jessie Street murder in Happy Valley. The crime was announced in the *Bulletin* of February 21, 1859, with long follow-up articles appearing on February 23, 24, 26, March 22 and 23. Mose Tate's conviction was announced in the *Bulletin* of March 24 and his sentence reported in the same paper on March 26, 1859. Mrs. Billman's trial and acquittal were detailed in the *Bulletin* of May 6 and 7, 1859. The *Alta* also gave the murder good coverage, while the *California Police Gazette* printed a map of the crime scene with its article on February 27, 1859. The quote pertaining to Mrs. Billman is taken from the *Gazette* of August 27, 1859. Lees' remarks on the case appeared in an interview published in the *Daily Morning Call* of November 5, 1895.

The return of the more notorious thugs exiled by the vigilantes is chronicled in the contemporary press and any of the standard histories, such as Bancroft's *Popular Tribunals*. A typical account of Mulligan beating up an unsuspecting vigilante in New York city was reported in the *Bulletin* of September 30, 1856.

Many more of Lees' arrests and investigations are reported in the press during this period, but only a sprinkling are mentioned in this chapter.

The express robbery case is detailed in the *Alta* beginning on August 3, 1859 and in the *California Police Gazette*. Long articles on the case appeared for the next few days. Connor received a 14-year sentence at San Quentin, while Mulhare got off with a 5-year term.

For some political background of the period, see James O'Meara, *Broderick and Gwin*, San Francisco: Bacon and Co. Printers, 1881; David Williams, *David C. Broderick: A Political Portrait*, San Marino: The Huntington Library, 1969, and A. Russell Buchanan, *David S. Terry of California, Dueling Judge*, San Marino: The Huntington Library, 1956. Chief Burke's own story of the arrest of the duelists is contained in his "Dictation" in the Bancroft Library. The ill-fated trip to arrest Terry in Stockton was related by Henry Ellis in Thomas S. Duke's, *Celebrated Criminal Cases of America*, San Francisco: The James H. Barry Company, 1910. Of course, there was much coverage of the duel in the press of the time. The Haskell House still stands, one of the oldest in the city. Fort Mason now occupies much of the site.

The date of Frederick Lees' birth was found among the papers in the Lees Collection at the Bancroft Library. Jake Chappell's brawl was noted in the *Alta* of November 21, 1859. The story of "The Chain Gang Dog" appeared in the *Alta* of December 25, 1859.

# The Horrible Affair at Lone Mountain

JANUARY OF 1860 WAS BITTER COLD. Isaiah spent a good deal of time on the street and was glad to reach his warm home at night.

On January 18 he attended the funeral of John Nugent at the Monumental Engine House opposite the plaza. Nugent had been a police officer since the early 1850s and although he had been tough and a hard drinker, Lees remembered him as being concientious and brave as a lion.

When a notorious eastern "sharper" was spotted coming down the gangplank of a docked steamer, Chief Burke was quickly informed. He called in Captain Lees and the two decided on a novel plan of surveillance to make sure the visitor had no opportunity for mischief. Two detectives were assigned to never let him out of their sight, as reported in the *Alta*:

> Did he get into an omnibus, one of his vigilant pursuers was at his side. Did he enter the theater, vis a vis with him was one or the other of the argus-eyed watchers. Wherever he went he either saw or felt the presence of the detectives, and so closely was he followed up that he was unable to consummate the rascality for which he had visited the city, and in sheer desperation he determined to leave town. The whole of this figuring was conducted with the utmost silence. Neither of the detectives ever spoke a word to him, or he to them, but each knew the other—no introduction was needed.

This fellow told an acquaintance he had tried every trick to throw the detectives off his trail, but to no avail. His "shadows" were standing on the wharf looking everywhere but at him as he boarded the Sacramento steamer to leave town. "We have heard of...drumming out of a regiment," chuckled the *Alta*, "but this is the first instance within our recollection that a man has been watched out of town."

The first Pony Express rider left Saint Joseph, Missouri, on April 3, 1860. When he galloped into Sacramento some eight days later, the telegraph reported the first rider was on his way to the Bay City and a hastily-formed committee made plans for a massive celebration. Isaiah's fire company was notified to take part in a grand parade, while announcements of the festivities were made at all the local theaters. Large bonfires were kindled on the streets, while excited people mingled everywhere. Engine companies, bands, and large crowds of citizens began converging at the Broadway wharf where the steamer *Antelope* would land with pony and rider.

It was around midnight when the brightly decorated horse and rider descended from the *Antelope* and moved into the center of the procession amid deafening cheers. Most of the police were on duty and Isaiah and his men moved among the crowds watching for the inevitable pickpockets and con men who delighted in such occa-

sions. It was nearly dawn before Lees was able to go home, after prowling among the celebrating crowds for most of the night.

During the summer word was received that Hampton North had died in Philadelphia. He had returned to his home town after the vigilantes had suggested he leave town in 1856. Apparently his wife on the West Coast had been abandoned, but when she read of his death in the press, she headed east to claim a $50,000 estate North had left to other relatives.

In July the steam paddy was gnawing away at yet another sand hill on Stockton Street. Preparations were also under way to launch the narrow gauge railway out Market Street to the mission. This was to be the first mechanical transporatation in the city. Elegantly upholstered and decorated cars were being built, each with twenty-six seats and mirrors at each end to make the interiors appear larger. The Albion Foundry was constructing the steam engine, while Peter Donahue's Union Iron Works was to furnish the wheels and undercarriage.

Captain Lees had been watching a gang of Boston pickpockets and burglars for some time. Their headquarters was a Pike Street groggery, and when enough evidence had been gathered, Isaiah had the thieves picked up. The capture resulted in a spirited editorial from the *Alta* editor:

> No city in the United States is so orderly as San Francisco. During the past year, out of $49,000 worth of goods stolen, $40,000 worth were recovered. No crime of any magnitude has gone undetected, and in the year, the six cases of murder were mostly reduced to manslaughter, and in every instance the perpetrator has been brought to justice. Our citizens may well congratulate themselves upon having such a reliable...police force.

In early August Chief Burke prepared to update his jail facilities below City Hall. Five new cells were to be added, each to be nine feet long and six feet wide. The cells would have board floors and be ventilated, top and bottom. A water closet and a sewer would hopefully also be constructed. Gas had already been installed and a water system would be introduced. Burke had lobbied long and hard for the improvements.

In September Isaiah attended the ten-year reunion of California Engine Company No. 4. George Garwood, the popular butcher at the Washington Market, had been first foreman of the fire company. William T. Coleman, the recent vigilante chief, had also been a member, along with Gus Ellis, Lees' partner on the *Firefly*.

William S. O'Brien later made millions in Virginia City, Nevada. *California State Library*

William S. O'Brien, the genial partner of the Auction Lunch Saloon, was also a member. Isaiah would sometimes drop by his saloon for a delicious free lunch of

the famous fish stew, slabs of ham, and corned beef. Jane and Isaiah attended the fire company grand ball held at Tucker's Academy of Music on the 10th.

The evening of October 23, 1860, ushered in one of the most horrifying mysteries of old San Francisco. A man rushed into Chief Burke's office with news that a murder had been committed in the hills west of town. Isaiah had already gone home so Burke took along Captain William Douglass and Officer Conway. The informant, a man named Gladding, knew little of the crime, but a boy who lived near Lone Mountain Cemetery had stopped by his house and told him his mother and sister had been murdered. The boy was on his way into town to get his father who worked as a carpenter when not tending his small farm.

It was dark and cold when Burke and his men arrived at the isolated house located out in the sand hills and scrub oak. A few farms were nearby, but it was a lonely area several miles out from the settled portions of the city. Some people had already gathered at the scene and Burke walked into the yard where lanterns cast a harsh light and threw shadows on a scene of hideous slaughter.

Mrs. Susanna Johnston lay stretched out on the ground before the door of the house. Her head was terribly gashed and mutilated, but she appeared to be still alive. Her daughter, Margaret, lay inside the house near the stove, her head also brutally torn and bleeding. She was dead. Nearby was an ax, clotted with blood and hair. Several physicians had arrived, but there was little they could do for the mortally injured Mrs. Johnston. The husband and father, Theophilus Johnston, and his young son David who had discovered the crime, paced about the yard in numbed shock.

Burke quickly gathered what information he could concerning the bloody occurrence. After discovering the murder, David Johnston had run to the nearby dairy farm of Martin Marran. The two had then returned and extinguished a smoldering fire in the house and did what they could for Mrs. Johnston.

A man named William Cook had been hired recently to look after the Johnston's cattle. As he was missing, he immediately became a prime suspect. It was quite late by now and Burke hurriedly sent officers to cover all roads, steamer offices, and wharves. The missing Mr. Cook seemed to be the best lead, but there were still many unknown factors.

The chief and his detective force were on the scene early the next morning. In the light of day they quickly discovered another body under some bushes. It was the missing Mr. Cook. Suddenly the lawmen were back to square one. There was a dearth of clues, but they kept doggedly on the job. Somewhere, there had to be an answer to the terrible crime.

Cook had been murdered in the same manner as Mrs. Johnston and her daughter—with blows to the head dealt with an ax. His hat and new boots wexe missing, but these seemed to be the only items taken from the premises. Nothing had been broken open, ruling out robbery as a motive. After thoroughly going over the immediate area, the detectives fanned out to interview neighbors.

At Martin Marran's dairy farm Captain Lees talked to a worker named Tom Hineberg. The detective listened carefully as Hineberg told of Cook having previously worked for Marran. The night before the murder he had visited the dairy to collect some back wages, but Marran had stalled and said he couldn't pay him at that time. There were other stories of Marran accusing Cook of stealing a blanket and some money. Marran had also complained of Cook's doing a poor job cleaning his milk cans when he worked there. When Hineberg left the area to go to work on a Stockton ranch, Lees had him shadowed. He learned from the laborers on the ranch that Tom had left San Francisco as a result of the murder and because he was afraid.

In 1860, the corner at California and Sansome streets was on the edge of where San Francisco had built out into the bay. The buildings were impressive here in the very heart of the city, but a few miles to the west it was still wild and undeveloped farmland.
*California State Library*

Lees, Johnson, and Ellis searched Marran's house and yard but could only come up with a hat he supposedly wore on the day of the murder. Other bits of information suggested Marran as a suspect, but there was nothing conclusive. The detectives kept working.

On Sunday morning, October 29, the crowds were just beginning to file out of the Congregational Church and Saint Mary's Cathedral in the area of Dupont and California streets. As the people spilled onto the sidewalk, suddenly there was the explosion of a shotgun. William Crowell, standing on a street corner, had fired both barrels at the Catholic congregation. Luckily his aim was high and he was quickly collared by Officer Spooner. At the station house it quickly became obvious that Crowell was demented. Isaiah stared at the fellow and decided to try a ruse. Crowell had been babbling about cleaning out all the Catholics, or "Romans," as he called them.

"Why did you commence your slaughter on so small a scale out at Lone Mountain the other day?" Lees watched him carefully.

"Oh, I didn't do that," returned Crowell without batting an eye. "My plan is different from that."

It was apparent he knew nothing of the murders, although rumors quickly spread throughout the city that the killer had been captured. Lees kept his men searching for leads and clues, but the investigation seemed to be going nowhere. Meanwhile, he spent what time he could campaigning for Burke, who was running for re-election on the "Peoples Ticket." He won handily in November and City Hall settled back to normal again.

On December 23 a letter appeared in the *Alta* decrying the lack of results in the Lone Mountain murders. Lees and Burke must have winced when they read how "...weeks and even months have passed since the bloody deed was consummated, and yet no definite action has been taken with regard to ferreting out the fiend, or fiends, guilty of the crime." The letter went on to suggest the offering of a reward to spur interest in the case. The public and press were unaware of the ongoing detective work until the first police court examinations were held on the 27th.

Several private rewards had been offered by now and a citizen finally swore out warrants for Marran and Hineberg, charging them with the murders. Lees must have been uncomfortable when he arrested Marran and brought him in to City Hall. There was evidence, but barely enough to sustain a prosecution. And, he didn't like rewards in a case like this. They usually brought out a lot of superfluous leads that had to be checked out to the detriment of the undercover work that might result in hard evidence.

At this time Lees went aboard the Sacramento steamer to look for three Mexican thieves who had stolen some $20,000 worth of ore from a Washoe (Nevada) mine. He found the suspects, but they declined to come along peacefully and Lees was having a lively scrap when the ship's captain entered. Thinking several of his passengers were being assaulted, Captain Chadwick tackled the officer with the result that Isaiah was considerably roughed up. The battered detective arrested Chadwick, along with the three suspects, but later in police court the two captains agreed to dismiss the charges against each other.

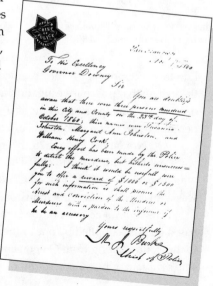

Letter from Chief Martin Burke to Governor John G. Downey asking for a reward in the Lone Mountain murders.
*California State Archives*

Jane, busily preparing for the Christmas holidays, was taken completely by surprise when her bruised husband came home. She recovered quickly and fussed over him until he had to return to headquarters.

First accounts of the Lone Mountain tragedy were misleading, as indicated by the *San Francisco Herald* of December 27, 1860.

They were living on Vallejo Street now, near Stockton. It was a nicer area and nearer the better stores and shops. A few days before Christmas a fierce storm blew in, buffeting the city in wind and rain. By Christmas morning it had abated and the sun peeked out occasionally through intermittent showers. Theaters were well patronized, but still most people preferred to stay home.

On December 27 the police court hearings on the Lone Mountain murders were gavelled to order. A long list of witnesses had been summoned, with Lees testifying on the 29th. The hearings lasted until just after New Year's Day, with a case of circumstantial evidence being made out against Marran. On January 4, Judge Cowles decided there was enough evidence to hold Marran without bail. Tom Hineberg, or Hanberry as he was now being referred to in the press, was released. His testimony turned out to be helpful to Marran. Isaiah was uncomfortable about the whole business.

Marran was eventually released and the terrible Lone Mountain murders were never resolved. It was a haunting incident, a scene the detectives couldn't forget. The sight of those chopped and mutilated bodies at the Johnston farm was seared into their memories, yet they seemed helpless in finding a significant clue. Despite the exhaustive police investigation and various theories developed over the years, officially it was to remain one of the blackest mysteries of old San Francisco. But perhaps there was a resolution, after all.

On November 23 and 25, 1874, two accounts of the Lone Mountain murders were published in the *Bulletin*. The scenario of the 23rd has Marran as the villain who quarrelled with and killed Cook over the money owed him. When the murder was witnessed by Margaret Johnston, she was murdered also, along with her mother.

The *Bulletin* account of the 25th is much more intriguing. Apparently, this was based on data supplied by one of the police detectives, who is not named. According to this source, a brig from Oregon entered port the week preceding the murders. The ship's captain, a man named Pinkham, had become a raving maniac during the trip

and, after attempting to kill his mate with an ax, had been put in irons. His wife took charge of him after his arrival and he seemed to become rational again. On the day of the murders Captain Pinkham reportedly went to his ship and obtained a tallysheet of the cargo, then left to return home. It was the last heard of him for three days.

On the evening of the murders a man answering Pinkham's general description was seen washing himself in a lake near the Johnston farm. Later this same man attacked a family out near the coast, but was driven off. He had been seen carrying a pair of boots, such as those missing from the murdered Cook. Detectives later found a portion of a torn tally-sheet near the lake where the man had been seen washing. When Pinkham later showed up at his home, his wife hustled him aboard his steamer and they immediately departed for the East.

The *Bulletin* article closed by stating that "Five years ago the detective who was best informed regarding these circumstances visited Augusta, Maine, the former home of Captain Pinkham." He learned that Pinkham had been placed in a lunatic asylum by his wife and that insanity of a particularly virulent form was hereditary in his family. Both his father and brother had also committed heinous crimes before being committed to asylums.

This "best informed" detective was undoubtedly Henry Ellis. Both Ellis and Lees had traveled to the East with the Society of California Pioneers in 1869. What would have been more natural than for Ellis to visit his own hometown of Watertown, Maine, while he was on the trip. And, Watertown is only about twenty-five miles from Augusta! Although no one by the name of Pinkham is listed as being admitted to the only asylum in Maine between 1860 and 1862, he may have been received under a pseudonym to avoid family embarrassment. Significantly, there is a David Pinkham listed in the 1850 U.S. Census for Augusta. His age is reported as twenty-five and his occupation listed as steamboat captain.

## CHAPTER NINE / NOTES

Notice of Officer John Nugent's death is in the *Alta* of January 19, 1860. Nugent had served a prison term for shooting a man in a drunken quarrel in 1854. The *Alta's* account of the gambler being "watched" out of town appeared on January 25, 1860.

There was much hubbub in the press concerning the arrival of the first Pony Express rider, a detailed description of the celebration appearing in the *Alta* of April 14, 1860.

Hampton North's death is reported in the *California Police Gazette* of July 7, 1860. The work of the steam paddy is mentioned often in the press, as its "insatiable maw" gobbled up the city's sand hills and filled in the bay. Two particularly interesting articles concerning these activities appeared in the *Alta* of April 16 and June 7, 1860. The Market Street Railroad article is in the *Alta* of July 1, 1860.

The capture of the Boston gang of thieves was recorded in the *Bulletin* of July 23, 1860. The *Alta's* editorial on the police appeared in the August 4 issue. Improvements in the city prison are detailed in the same paper of August 8. The anniversary celebrations of Isaiah's fire company and the Society of California Pioneers are both noted in the *Alta* of September 6, 1860.

Data on California Engine Company No. 4 and its members can be found in the early city directories and other publications cited previously. For information on William S. O'Brien's Auction Lunch saloon, see Amelia Ransome Neville's *The Fantastic City*, Arno Press, and Oscar Lewis' *Silver Kings*, New York: Alfred A. Knopf, 1947.

The *Alta* announced the Lone Mountain murders on October 24, 1860, in a long article. For the following week the local press gave much coverage to the terrible event. William Prescott Crowell's sashay against the "Romans" was reported in the *Alta* of October 29.

Lees' fight with the Mexican suspects and Captain Chadwick is reported in the *Bulletin* and *Alta* of December 23, and mentioned in the Stockton *San Joaquin Republican* of December 25, 1860. The Lees' various home addresses over the years can be checked through the city directories. Information on the Washington Market is from the *Alta* of December 14 and 27, 1860.

Hearings on the Lone Mountain murders began on December 27 and were given good coverage in the *Alta* and the other local newspapers through the rest of the month. There was little testimony of substance, however. In the California State Archives, Governor's Reward Files, there exists a letter written by Chief Burke on November 14, 1860 asking Governor Downey to offer a reward of $1,000 or $1,500 for information leading to the arrest of the murderer. Correspondence with Jeffrey E. Brown, Reference Services Branch, Maine State Archives, Augusta, January 27, 1986, established information regarding the Pinkham family.

# A Most Remarkable Case

ALTHOUGH CHIEF BURKE WAS RE-ELECTED the previous November, a craggy-faced politician named Abraham Lincoln had also won election and the nation wondered if he would be up to the troubled times that seemed to lie ahead. Most political pundits promised trouble and Isaiah Lees heard the talk all around him—talk of a Pacific Republic separate from the Union. California was a Free State, but much of the population was of Southern origins and they resented the high-handed antics of the North. The Democratic Party had been strongly entrenched in California from the outset and felt that state sovereignty must be maintained at all cost. In the streets and saloons there was talk of dividing the state or actual secession, if it came to that!

Isaiah was disgusted in early January when Jake Chappell was again charged with misconduct. Lichenstein, the pawnbroker he had previously tangled with, accused him of not paying a seven dollar debt. He was also charged with using insulting language to the editor of the *California Police Gazette*.

As if this wasn't enough, a drunken Chappell was involved in a Dupont Street bagnio row where he had used his pistol to force one of the women to submit to him. His hearing before the police commissioners began on the 10th and Isaiah anticipated the result. Chief Burke did not want any aspersions cast on his department—least of all on his famous detective officers. A patrolman might be cast to the wolves to show Burke's concern for the quality of the department. He did not, however, intend to have one of his best detectives make him look bad. Isaiah wasn't disappointed when Chappell got off with merely a fine.

Lees, Chappell, and Johnson were working on a burglary case when the body of Auguste Hirsch was discovered. The corpse had been found across the bay, just off the road in the San Antonio district of East Oakland. Hirsch's head had been nearly severed from his body. Captain Douglass was put on the case until Lees could get free.

Isaiah had recently received a communication from the New York police warning of two burglars named William Burns and Robert Tanin. Lees traced them to a series of robberies and by January 15 had them in custody. By the time Isaiah became involved in the San Antonio murder case, a reported business partner of Hirsch, Edward Bonney, was a serious suspect. Friends of the dead man had gotten up a subscription to defray the cost of a police investigation outside San Francisco.

Bonney and Hirsch operated a Clay Street bookstand. On a Sunday morning, January 13, 1861, Hirsch left on a business trip to San Jose. He had some $600 in company money with which to start a new branch of their bookstall operation. Bonney claimed he had accompanied his partner across the bay where they had

rented a buggy. At San Antonio Hirsch met two French friends who had gotten into the buggy with them. Bonney had driven them about for awhile, but had left them in San Antonio while he had returned the buggy to Oakland where he spent the night. Monday morning he caught the ferry to the city and later in the day the body was discovered. An inquest turned up no pertinent information and Hirsch was buried as Lees began his investigation.

On the Friday following the discovery of the body, Chief Burke and detectives Lees and Johnson picked Bonney up at his bookstall and crossed the bay to Oakland. Here they hired a buggy and retraced the route taken by Hirsch and Bonney the previous Sunday. Questioning the suspect extensively as they traveled about, Lees performed the inquiry while Burke kept notes on everything that was said. For the better part of two days the officers and suspect drove around, and every detail of the murder was probed and examined.

Battery Street, constructed entirely on landfill in the bay, was lined with some impressive new buildings. *California State Library*

Bonney was caught in several small deceptions. At first he claimed to be a partner of Hirsch, but later admitted being merely a clerk. When they visited the spot where the body was found, Bonney said he had only been a few hundred yards out on that road. Later he let slip that he and Hirsch had indeed been several miles out.

During the investigation Lees learned the suspect had bought a necktie at an Oakland store. When asked about it, Bonney claimed to have lost his own necktie. Lees then pointed out that two neckties, fastened together, were found secured to the back of the buggy he had used. At that the suspect became excited and admitted that one of the ties was his. They were used to support the back of one of the Frenchmen while all four of them were riding in the buggy.

At the first opportunity the detective questioned the stable operator. The buggy hired that day, he was told, could not have supported four men. It was not constructed to carry such a load and the springs would have broken down unless they had gone but a very short distance on a very smooth road.

Lees and his men next sought out witnesses in the surrounding country. Several farmers had seen a buggy that day with but with only two men in it. All agreed that one of the persons appeared quite still, as if sick. A young boy, James Howard,

saw the two men in the buggy and remembered they had driven by him twice. He too noticed one of the men appeared sick and was leaning back. He got a good look at the man who was driving, and when Lees later accompanied him to the station house, he quickly picked out Bonney as the man he had seen. An arrest could now be justified.

Little by little a picture was being formed. In talking to the stable owner Lees discovered a small support missing from the seat of the buggy Hirsch had used. The support had been intact when the vehicle was hired. At the same time the detective learned that the horse used that day had a peculiar defect in its hoof. Traveling back to where the body was found, Lees made a minute examination of the ground. Suddenly, he saw the missing buggy seat support. More searching revealed a print of the defective hoof. Two more bits of the puzzle had been eased into place.

Chief Burke, Lees, and several other officers accompanied Bonney to the hearing held at San Antonio on January 25. Lees' affadavit charging Bonney with murder was read to the court and a parade of witnesses gave their testimony. Isaiah gave a long account of his investigation and discoveries. The following day Bonney was indicted for murder by the grand jury. The detectives would keep gathering evidence until the trial in mid-July.

The changes taking place in the West were forcefully brought home to Lees in February. The prior December Henry Johnson was approached by Maria Escobal, a resident of his district. She had been living with a cabinet maker named Haley and became suspicious when he hadn't returned home for several days. In checking, she found a tin box hidden under the floor was missing, also. The woman's $2,500 in savings had been in the box and when questioned by Johnson she recalled catching her lover looking on as she was reburying her treasure. Johnson promptly consulted with Captain Lees.

George W. Matsell. *Author's Collection*

The two lawmen next checked with Haley's employer and found he had sold his tools under the pretext of having to visit Petaluma. The tools, worth some $150, were sold for only $15 so as to get rid of them quickly. A check of steamship offices provided several suspects and finally the two officers were sure that Haley, using the name Hamm, had sailed for New York on December 21.

Lees sent a Pony Express letter to ex-Chief of Police George W. Matsell, of New York, asking him to detain Hamm when he disembarked. Matsell held the fugitive until Haley/Hamm agreed to make out a bank draft for the missing money. He was then released. Lees and Johnson next secured an indictment and a requisition from Governor Downey for the surrender of Haley to California authorities. Although he put up a desperate fight to avoid extradition,

Haley was penniless without the stolen money. Finally he surrendered in February of 1861. The *Alta* was delighted with the local lawmen:

> ...The reputation of Officers Johnson and Lees of our police force is well known in New York... and a firm reliance on them has been placed by Mr. Matsell throughout the whole of this transaction. The rapidity of inter-communications overland by Pony, stage and telegraph combined, must act upon the fears of ill-doers in the future, as escape from justice, by steamers to the Atlantic states, or Europe, is now rendered an unsafe procedure, as the intelligence will precede the individual.

Reading of his exploits in the *Alta*, Isaiah couldn't help noticing a long article on a local Saint Patrick's Day gathering. As the meeting was being adjourned someone had shouted "three cheers for the Union" and the crowd responded with a deafening exhibition. There were more and more Union demonstrations in the city as men began to choose sides. The Cotton Confederacy, by its stubborn refusal to compromise and its actual forcing the abandonment of various military posts in the South, was forcing this choice. Isaiah realized such actions might very well lead to the ugliest kind of war—a civil war. And, the two sides seemed to be headed on a collision course!

The recent success of the detectives prompted curious scenes of public confidence at police headquarters, as noted in the *Alta:*

> A lady lately called on the chief and in a business-like manner said, "Doctor, I have had my watch stolen; please set one of your detectives at work and I will call for it in an hour!"

When Jane became pregnant again, Isaiah promised her a larger apartment. He found a nice place on Clay Street and it was here, on April 1, 1861, that Annie Laurie Lees was born. Fred was nearly a year and a half old now and Isaiah delighted in his two babies. He undoubtedly felt guilty at not being able to spend more time with them, but hopefully there would be more time later.

On April 2 Officer Charles McMillan was fined twenty days' pay for being unnecessarily rough with a prisoner. A young man had cursed him on the street and when McMillan attempted to take him into custody, the boy showed fight. The officer knocked him down and had to drag him forcefully off to the station. McMillan found it necessary to thump him again at headquarters. When the boy's friends reported the incident to the *Alta*, there was a hearing before the police commissioners and the officer was docked twenty days' pay.

In its article, the *Alta* editorialized that "the policeman's life is apt to brutalize" and this brought a spirited rebuttal from a group of officers. Lees must have smiled grimly. Of course policemen were apt to be brutalized! Theirs was a thankless task, for the most part unappreciated by fellow citizens. It would be difficult not to be brutalized—or at least become less sensitive in the way that a physician becomes inured to observing pain and suffering. It was a defense mechanism for lawmen who must spend the greater part of their time in contact with thieves, pimps,

killers, con men, whores, and degenerates of every description. Isaiah could only try to be tolerant of men like Captain McDonald, John Nugent, and Jake Chappell who couldn't shake off the aura of violence which seemed to pervade their very souls. For himself, he made every effort to lead a normal existence. "I try to forget that phase of my life when I go home," he once commented.

Later this month there were excited groups of people on every street corner talking about the seige and surrender of Fort Sumter. On April 27 thousands gathered for a huge Union meeting, with patriotic speeches and mass declarations of loyalty. San Franciscans—or Californians for that matter—were putting aside arguments and discussions of the worsening situation. It was a time for decision.

The mass meeting of San Franciscans at Market and Post streets on May 11, 1861, where the city declared its loyalty to the Union. *Author's Collection*

During the big Union rally, Isaiah and Henry Johnson were more concerned with counterfeits than Confederates. Taking samples of bogus coin to the local banks, they had met with some forty merchants, only one of whom had discerned the phony money. The counterfeit was of the highest quality and had arrived recently on the *Golden Age*, from England. Those who brought it, however, had escaped into the city.

On May 11 another giant Union rally was scheduled and Burke wished all his men could participate. This was impossible, of course. "The officers," noted the *Alta*, "are wanted where they can be of service in looking after certain well-known thieves who infest the city when great crowds are gathered." An estimated 20,000 people attended the rally—this with a city population of nearly 70,000.

In late June Isaiah heard that Wooley Kearney had made two unsuccessful attempts to hang himself in his room in the Potrero District south of town. Poor, ugly Wooley. His delerium tremens was so bad now he couldn't even commit suicide.

On July 14 the Bonney case finally came to trial. The affair seemed quite plain to Lees now. The evidence was wholly circumstantial, but so clear that he felt confident of a conviction. All the witnesses and evidence indicated there had never been four men

in the buggy, as Bonney had alleged. On the contrary, many witnesses had seen just two men in the vehicle that day—one of them clearly identified as Bonney and the other described as a "sick," unmoving figure.

Although Hirsch's body was exhumed and traces of a drug found, Lees wasn't able to isolate the poison. Still, it seemed clear what had happened. Bonney had drugged Hirsch with a bottle of wine during the trip. He had then propped up the unconscious victim in the buggy by securing him to the back of the seat with the two neckties. Then he had driven about for some time looking for a location where he could leave the body. Finding a secluded spot, Bonney dragged Hirsch from the buggy, laid him on the ground and slashed his throat with a razor. The murder weapon was probably dropped in the bay as he returned to San Francisco.

The Alameda County courthouse at San Leandro, where the Bonney case was tried. *John Boessenecker Collection*

The trial was held in San Leandro and on the fourth day Lees was given due credit for his work by a correspondent of the *Alta*:

> Captain I. W. Lees, of San Francisco, the detective who principally "worked up" the case, and who finally took Bonney into custody, was on the stand the whole of yesterday and nearly all this forenoon....The importance of his evidence was so obvious that the defending counsel resorted to every method which ingenuity could dictate or law allow to involve him in inconsistencies, but so far as I could see, without success....

On the last day of the trial Isaiah listened carefully to the summing up by the eloquent defense attorneys. The evidence was totally circumstantial, they insisted, and many similar cases were cited where such data was used to wrongfully convict. Chief Burke and Lees were attacked for being suspiciously concientious—they were obviously seeking to add to their reputations by convicting an innocent man. One of the lawyers even read a poem Bonney had written to his mother.

The prosecution, headed by H. S. Love, concisely detailed the wealth of damning testimony and evidence. Everything pointed overwhelm-

The hanging of Edward W. Bonney on May 9, 1862. A woodcut published in the *California Police Gazette*. *Author's Collection*

ingly to the guilt of the accused. The verbal assaults on the police officers and the many allusions to Bonney's family only underscored the failure of the defense to prove their case.

After remarking on the "remarkable" aspects of the trial and circumstantial evidence, the judge retired the jury at 4:30 on the afternoon of July 28, 1861. By seven o'clock that evening, the jury returned with a verdict of "guilty." Isaiah was congratulated on all sides, but he was relieved to get out of the hot and crowded courtroom. Bonney was later sentenced to hang.

In early August Lees heard the shouts on the street when first news was received of the federal disaster at Manassas. The papers were full of it. The *Alta* seemed to think that a large, decisive battle was eminent and everyone hoped so.

The polarization of city residents was effectively illustrated on the morning of September 22. Dr. William Scott, pastor of the large Calvary Presbyterian Church, was a Southerner who refused to involve his congregation in the politics of war. When the minister equated Jefferson Davis to George Washington, he was hanged in effigy. An unruly mob gathered to see what might happen when the minister appeared to preach that Sunday morning and both Burke and Lees were on hand, along with several officers, to ensure order.

The Rev. William A. Scott, a most controversial pastor.
*California State Library*

After the service Scott walked to his carriage as shouting crowds began converging on him. With great difficulty the police closed around the minister and finally got his carriage underway.

Scott had conducted the services for Josephine Lees' funeral and Isaiah spoke with him several times about the dangers of his position. The minister had previously been hanged in effigy for opposing the vigilantes in 1856 and he now saw that he might very well be a catalyst for local bloodshed. A short time later he left for England, beginning an eight-year exile from the city.

Anyone doubting the legendary status of Isaiah Lees had only to peruse *The California Magazine* in November, 1861. In a novel titled "The Mysteries of San Francisco," a police officer called "Captain Rees" makes an appearance during a trial. No one in the city had any doubts that the character was based on San Francisco's famous sleuth.

## CHAPTER TEN / NOTES

The gathering war clouds were as apparent in San Francisco as in any Eastern city. Lincoln's election was reported in a Pony Express dispatch in late October of 1860 and the local press was filled with rumors and speculations. For an interesting personal reminiscence of this period, see Neville's *The Fantastic City*. A broader look at the politics of the time can be found in John P. Langellier's "The Union Forever: Bay Area Military Maneuvering in the Civil War," *The Californians*, January/ February 1985. See also Robert Chandler's excellent article on the military intrigues and misconceptions on the support for a Pacific Republic: "The Mythical Johnston Conspiracy Revisited: An Educated Guess," *The Californians*, November/December 1986. Also helpful for an understanding of the period is Theodore H. Hittell's, *History Of California*, Volume IV, San Francisco, N.J. Stone & Company, 1898.

In late 1859 Lees is mentioned by the *California Police Gazette* as being a member of the Republican County Convention, but this is one of the few notices of his involvement in local politics. He was finally naturalized on June 2, 1866, according to data supplied by the late James T. Abajian.

The *Alta* detailed Jake Chappell's troubles on January 11, 1861. Lees' involvement in the capture of Burns and Tanin is noted in the *Alta* of January 16.

The Hirsch murder case was another of Lees' classic investigations where he compiled such a compelling amount of circumstantial evidence that guilt could not be denied by any rational person. *Duke's Celebrated Criminal Cases Of America* gives a brief account of this case. The *Alta* of January 15 and 16, 1861 carried first news of the discovery of Hirsch's body. More articles on the crime appeared on January 20 and 21, while a long account of Bonney's justice court hearing appeared in the *Alta* of January 25, 1861.

The Haley investigation was detailed in the *Alta* of March 1. The tribute to the detectives appeared in the *Alta* on March 27, 1861.

Lees' Clay street and other addresses can be traced in contemporary city directories and also in the Lees Collection at the Bancroft Library. His daughter's birth is noted in the collection, as it was in the local press.

Officer McMillan's troubles and the resultant squabble can be found in the *Alta* of April 4 and 5, 1861. Commentary on the fall of Fort Sumter appeared in the *Alta* of April 25, 1861. On April 28 the same newspaper carried excellent coverage of the great Union rally and Lees' investigation of the counterfeit coin. Wooley Kearney's attempts at self-demise were reported in the *Alta* of June 26.

Bonney's trial was reported at great length in the *Alta*, beginning on July 17. Long and detailed reports of the proceedings appeared in that newspaper under dates of July 26, 27, and 29, 1861, with many references to Lees' testimony and sleuthing activities. The detective captain always regarded this case as one of his most important accomplishments.

On August 2 Bonney was sentenced to be hanged. An account of the execution appeared in the *California Police Gazette* of May 10, 1862. Some documents and Lees' testimony are in the San Quentin Prison Papers, Edward W. Bonney (File 1342), California State Archives, Sacramento.

Reports of the Battle at Manassas, or Bull Run, appeared in the *Alta* of August 8, 1861.

For Reverend Scott's troubles in war-time San Francisco, see Clifford M. Drury's *William Anderson Scott: No Ordinary Man,* Glendale, Arthur H. Clark Company, 1967. Enlightening also is Annegret Ogden's article, "Reverend Traitor—A Voice for Principle," *The Californians,* January/ February, 1985. The local press gave much attention to Reverend Scott's questionable attitudes both before and after he was hanged in effigy on September 22, 1861. Neville also mentions the incident.

My thanks to John Swingle, of the Alta California Bookstore, for calling my attention to "Captain Rees" in *The California Magazine.*

# Murder Most Foul & the Chapman Affair

IN MARCH OF 1862 a Chinese wash house operator was murdered at his Pacific Street shop. A man named Ah On was suspected and when Officer Rose and Chief Burke arrived, a woman pointed out where she had seen a bloody Chinese man running from the area. Officer Rose disappeared into Chinatown while Chief Burke cordoned off the area, but the elusive oriental could not be found.

As the dragnet spread out over the city, Isaiah Lees, Jake Chappell, and two other officers entered another wash house on Rincon Point. Isaiah noticed a pile of blankets in a corner. Drawing his pistol, he began tossing aside the blankets and in a moment the fugitive was revealed. Ah On readily admitted the killing, but claimed self-defense after being struck with a flat iron during an argument. Lees turned him over to other officers, then informed Burke of his catch.

The Chinese were becoming an increasing concern in the city. The Chinese Quarter was centered between Jackson and Broadway and Kearny and Dupont. Lees was continually amazed that the teeming and squalid tenements could exist in such close proximity to the rich shops and offices of Montgomery Street, a mere block away.

In the course of investigations he had sometimes slipped into a twelve-foot-wide alley off Jackson Street that entranced the Quarter. Once inside, visitors quickly disappeared into another world. Alleyways and narrow thoroughfares splintered off from the brick and shanty-lined walkway into a dilapidated, gloomy, and progressively sordid area peopled by prostitutes, laundries, gambling halls, drug dealers, thugs, and poor Chinese of every social level and description. The *Daily Examiner* described the Quarter well:

> Down in the dark cellars, where from morning to night no ray of sunlight ever enters, hundreds of these wretched creatures have lived. Their only sleeping place a rough mat stretched upon a wooden bunk fastened against the bare bricks, without any means of drainage or ventilation, existing in habitual filth of the most loathsome description upon the wages of the most degraded sensuality. Here, too, we see

A street scene in San Francisco's old Chinatown. *California State Library*

the depots to which the chiffonier (rag and scrap collectors) carries his motely collection of waifs and strays. Yards filled with rags of every kind, pieces of bone, old metal, paper and rubbish without end, swelter and rot in the sun and rain, and contribute their share to the horrible stench which arises from these crowded dens like a silent warning to the city....

Yet for all the shadows of Chinatown, it was a colorful place on the surface. Sailors, sightseers, and tourists were already discovering the crowded streets and alleys filled with import shops, markets, restaurants, theaters, and joss houses. They were charmed by their mysterious hosts, the clanging and twanging music, and the colorful paper lanterns rimming the balconies and doorways. And, for those with more erotic tastes, the Chinese supplied a variety of saloons, gambling dens, and bordellos filled with slave girls.

All this was ruled by the wealthy Chinese merchants who controlled the Quarter—the leaders of the Six Companies that represented the old country districts from which the Chinese had emigrated. The Quarter was a microcosm of their homeland. Although other nationalities were clannish, the Chinese absolutely refused to assimilate into traditional American life.

A police officer holds a recalcitrant Chinese suspect's head still for his mug shot. The prisoner is obviously displeased. *Author's Collection*

Officer Patrick Crowley, later chief, in his new police uniform. *Author's Collection*

The search for Ah On had involved many officers and Lees and Burke were delighted when ten more policemen were appointed in early June.

In November the new police uniform was adopted. The coat was a single-breasted, gray color that extended to the knees. It had a small, turn-down black velvet collar and black buttons. The trousers and vest were of the same material. Matching caps had a leather bill. Later Chief Patrick Crowley recalled: "We wore gray on account of the dust, for Montgomery Street was a sandy place and we chose things for durability....I remember the clothes were of fine French cloth and we thought they were tip-top." Isaiah and his men, of course, seldom wore uniforms.

Dr. Burke and his predecessors were not desk officers. They were frequently in the field and led their men in most important raids. Lees and Burke often disguised themselves as vaqueros, discharged soldiers or sailors and visited the disreputable saloons where thieves and confidence men congregated. Here they would pick up news on recent robberies, on the expected arrival of thieves, and other bits of information. Jane had long ago constructed her life around her husband's long and unpredictable work hours.

In early March of 1863 Captain Lees received word of a rebel privateer being armed and equipped to commence raiding along the coast. The principals in the plot were Asbury Harpending, Alfred Rubery, and Ridgley Greathouse, all local businessmen and vocal secessionists. Harpending, a wealthy miner, had recently returned from Virginia where he had obtained approval from Jefferson Davis for a scheme to seize California for the Confederacy, or so he later claimed. Returning to the Coast he discovered a cooling of enthusiasm among many of his supporters, but Harpending and his partners still determined to push ahead with their plans.

After various attempts to buy a fast schooner, both locally and in British Columbia, Harpending noticed the arrival in port of the *J.M. Chapman* on February 17. The craft had made record time from the East and had beaten the U.S. sloop of war *Cyane* from Panama. This was just the ship the plotters had been looking for. The schooner was purchased and stocked with muni-

Asbury Harpending, a secessionist with big ideas.
*Author's Collection*

tions and a rebel crew was told to be ready to sail at a moments notice. Captain William C. Law was hired to command the *Chapman* just as final arrangements were being made. The plan was to sail down the coast, outfit her in Mexico, then commence raids on the treasure ships plying the coast.

One day a steamship agent asked Isaiah to call on Dr. John T. McLean, surveyor for the Port of San Francisco. McLean had received word that a group of secessionists had been trying for some time to purchase a ship to outfit as a privateer. These men had been watched, but Captain Law had gotten a little too full one night at the Tehama House. He had confided the sailing plans of the *Chapman* to a friend who promptly notified Dr. McLean.

Alfred Rubery, the young Englishman with high connections.
*Author's Collection*

The detective captain quickly made his plans. Disguising several of his men as sailors and longshoremen, a twenty-four hour watch was put on the *Chapman*. The *Cyane* commander was advised of the plot and promised two boatloads of sailors and marines to be ready to move instantly. The tugboat *Anashe* was rented and kept under steam around the clock. Boarding the tug, Isaiah and naval port officer W. B. Farwell began their long, cold vigil.

On the night of March 14, numbers of men began boarding the *Chapman*, a beam of light appearing each time a hatch was opened to admit them below decks. All night long Lees watched the proceedings and he became convinced the *Chapman* would attempt to slip out through the Golden Gate before daybreak. This in itself was strictly against the law, since the cargo had not been declared. At dawn the

moorings were cast off and the *Chapman* began drifting out into the bay. Lees and his men quickly went into action.

As two boatloads of men put out from the *Cyane*, Lees ordered the captain of the *Anashe* to pull alongside the escaping craft. In a few minutes policemen, sailors, and marines were scrambling aboard the privateer. Lees found Rubery and third mate Alonzo Libby and quickly searched them before turning them over to one of his men. After checking the forecastle, the detective cautiously took a lamp down into the hold. A moment later he yelled up to Farwell:

The Confederate pirate schooner *J.M. Chapman*, right, under the guns of the U.S. sloop-of-war *Cyane* in the left foreground. A sketch by San Franciscan G. E. Bigelow, as published in *Frank Leslie's Illustrated Newspaper*, May 9, 1863. *Author's Collection*

"There's fifteen or twenty damned rebels hidden down here, just under the hatch."

Lees cleared all the armed crewmen from the hold and herded them onto deck along with Harpending, Greathouse, and Rubery. Following a pre-arranged plan, the prisoners were then deposited at the federal installation on Alcatraz Island. After the *Chapman* was safely moored to the mail company's wharf, Isaiah went to work.

Scouring the ship minutely for evidence, Lees carefully collected small bits of paper and pulpy matter he found in the hold. Harpending and his cohorts had burned as many documents as they could, then tore, chewed up, and scattered what was left. "Nevertheless," Harpending later recalled, "out of the destruction Captain Lees gathered together the scraps and by piecing them together and guessing at the missing parts, collected some evidence that was produced against us in court later on."

In cases marked "machinery" were found cannon, pistols, muskets, and cutlasses, along with plenty of shot, powder, and caps. The fantastic plot, up to this

point merely rumor and heresay, was suddenly very real. With more careful planning, there was no telling what the Rebs might have accomplished. At a hearing the rebel pirates were scheduled to be arraigned in early September.

On the evening of May 3, 1863, word was received of a murder committed out on the San Bruno Road, in Visitacion Valley. The area was near the county line, and when Lees left for the site, he took the coroner, as well as several officers, with him.

At the scene Lees interviewed Pasquelina Larcari, wife of the dead man. She had been out walking with her husband, Pietro, when suddenly a man jumped out from behind a rock and shot him. It had happened so fast she hadn't seen the assassin. Although the woman claimed to have stayed with the body for some time before reporting the crime, Isaiah noted the body was still warm. He had been shot four times, a bullet through the chest proving mortal. The *Alta* later reported:

Mrs. Pasquelina Larcari. *Author's Collection*

> The woman is very reticent. Her account of the affair as given us is not only unsatisfactory, but improbable. Captain Lees had a long conference with her and may have gleaned facts which will come out in the preliminary examination of the case. The woman is meanwhile detained for safekeeping..

Lees knew he had to act fast. Every moment of investigation was time the killer could be using to escape. He knew the woman was the key to the crime and continued

Francisco Pizano, the other man. *Author's Collection*

questioning her. She insisted no one had quarrelled with her husband and she knew of no motive for the murder. In checking her statements, however, the detective discovered that an acquaintance named Francisco Pizano was missing. After first insisting she knew nothing of the man, Mrs. Larcari then hedged and thought perhaps she had met him once, but that was all. In further questioning Lees learned Pizano was not only a frequent visitor to the Larcari home, but that there had been violent scenes between him and Larcari. When advised of this, the woman finally admitted Pizano had been a good friend, but nothing more.

Isaiah felt sure Pizano was involved and put his men to checking all steamers leaving port. Telegraphed descriptions were sent to the outlying districts also, but without results. He felt sure the fugitive was still in the city and detectives were kept busy following up every clue. The murder had been committed on a Sunday and by the following Saturday Pizano had been located and jailed. By now events were moving swiftly.

A mutual friend of the Larcari family and Pizano had also been seen on the road that Sunday carrying a weapon. Isaiah discovered that this friend, one Giocomo Bruzzo, had disappeared after suddenly coming into some money. A witness remembered Bruzzo had recently bought a bright-red, flowered handkerchief which he wore around his neck. With this clue Lees and Ellis stopped a man on the street who not only wore such a neckerchief, but otherwise answered Bruzzo's description. Incredibly, although not Bruzzo, the man proved to be a friend of the wanted man. Just that morning he had received a letter from Bruzzo asking that he forward some clothes to him at Sacramento. Lees and Ellis were on the next riverboat to the capital city.

Giocomo Bruzzo, the killer. *Author's Collection*

Operating on the slimmest of clues, the lawmen tracked the fugitive from Sacramento to Folsom and then Placerville. By sleeping in out-of-the-way farmhouses and riding the railroad without purchasing a ticket, Bruzzo avoided attention. His distinctive neckerchief, however, had been noticed along the way, and the detectives tracked him toward Virginia City.

Telegraphing ahead for the city marshal to hold the fugitive if he showed up, Lees and Ellis arrived to find their quarry waiting for them in the local jail. It had been quite a chase.

On the return trip Bruzzo steadily maintained his innocence, denying he even knew Larcari or of his death. When Lees told him his friend Pizano had told them Bruzzo had admitting the killing, he adopted a surly, but more subdued attitude.

Lees could now deduce that the woman and Pizano had conspired to murder her husband, Bruzzo being the instrument of the crime. At the coroner's inquest the testimony of the three made the conspiracy all the more apparent. Now it was everyone for himself. "That the murder lies between the three, the woman, Pizano and Bruzzo," commented the *Bulletin*, "like the converging point of a tripod, is very apparent....Subsequently, when all were arrested, each confined his story to those particulars leading to convict the other and clear himself."

On May 25 Bruzzo finally confessed to the actual murder, insisting Pasquelina Larcari and Pizano had talked him into it. The woman steadily maintained her innocence, but Lees shook his head. The story was as old as the Bible. Isaiah testified at great length during the police court hearing, where a fall trial was subsequently set for the trio. Most of the spectators were Italians.

Isaiah's low-key Republican politics paid off early this same month when he was appointed a deputy U.S. marshal for northern California. This didn't conflict with his police work and merely made him available for government investigations.

The bloody war in the East shocked Californians and crowds of San Franciscans gathered around the war dispatches tacked up in front of newspaper offices. When

word of the federal victory at Gettysburg reached the city in early July of 1863, there were cheers and parades in the streets. The rebel sympathizers were quieter than ever in the city saloons.

In early July Lees and Henry Ellis were investigating the vicious murder of William LaMeet out on the old Mission Road. The dead man had been living with the wife of one Andrew Cummings, who had beaten and killed LaMeet with the help of Henry Wallace. The two detectives were returning to town on a warm afternoon, and as the buggy rattled along the rutted road, the king bolt suddenly fell out. They had been traveling at a fast pace and the vehicle lurched violently off the road and flipped over.

Ellis was thrown clear, and as he staggered to his feet, he saw Isaiah painfully crawling from under the buggy. He helped his friend get clear and made him comfortable. Lees' ankle was already swelling and it was clear he was badly injured. The trip back to the city was long and painful for Lees and the physician put the detective to bed before examining his leg. The incident was reported in the *Alta* the following day:

> Severe Accident - We regret to learn that detective officer Lees was thrown out of a buggy yesterday afternoon on his way into town from beyond the Mission Dolores. His left leg, at the ankle, suffered a compound fracture and it is by no means certain that it will not have to be amputated....

Although his leg was saved, the detective was many months in recovering from the accident and had to be completely immobilized to assure proper healing. To keep up with his workload and maintain liaison with headquarters, two officers were detailed to the Lees home. It was an ordeal for someone used to so much activity, but all he could do was make the best of things. A year later he was still crippled and walking with a cane.

On October 5, Isaiah hobbled into court to testify in the *Chapman* case. Many minute bits of paper found in the hold had been restored and proved to be bills of

Mission Dolores was some distance west of town, but the area around it was still sparsely settled.
*Annals of San Francisco*

lading and other documents damaging to the defendants. This and other evidence was quite conclusive and on October 16, Judge Stephen J. Field sentenced Harpending, Rubery, and Greathouse each to a ten-year prison term and a $10,000 fine. All the other crewmen took the oath of allegiance and were released.

The *Chapman* case thrilled the country and was the most noted Civil War incident on the West Coast. Although given much credit for his work, Isaiah would have undoubtedly traded it all for a good left leg. He was getting around on crutches now, however.

On the 19th Judge Sawyer sentenced all three of the Larcari murderers to life imprisonment, while their lawyers scrambled to file appeals. Henry Wallace and Andrew Cummings, the killers of William LaMeet, received ten year terms for their brutal crime.

Henry Wallace, who, with Andrew Cummings, committed the drunken, brutal murder of William LaMeet. *Author's Collection*

On October 29, 1863, Chief Burke received a telegram from Portland, Oregon. It was from a prominent Idaho businessman named Hill Beachey who had been deputized to pursue a party of men suspected of killing and robbing merchant Lloyd Magruder and four companions in the Bitteroot Mountains. Magruder and Beachey had been close friends and when he became convinced there had been a murder, Beachey relentlessly pursued the suspects.

Arriving at Portland from Lewiston he learned the suspects had already taken a steamer for San Francisco. Unwilling to wait for the next boat, Beachey took the first stagecoach south, after telegraphing Chief Burke to apprehend the suspects on the Oregon boat, saying he could be reached at either Yreka or Sacramento on his way down. Burke turned the case over to Captain Lees.

Isaiah selected officers John Evatt, Alfred Clarke, and John Greer to assist him. The Oregon steamer had already arrived and the difficult job of locating the fugitives was begun. It seemed likely they would take their stolen gold dust to the local branch mint for processing, and Isaiah called on D. W. Cheesman, the assistant treasurer. Cheesman verified that a large amount of dust had been deposited on October 29 by parties calling themselves "James M. Romaine, Dan. Howard & G. Clark." This information, coupled with data gleaned from passengers on the Oregon boat, narrowed the search down to two rough-looking men who had taken a room on Dupont Street. A watch was put on the house and when a well-dressed stranger called there, he was in turn followed as he joined a companion at the Lick House, a reputable hotel.

Lees was sure he had his men spotted now, having recognized one as a former San Quentin inmate. David Renton had served time for a Sacramento felony, but had escaped in 1860. He was now using the name "Dan Howard." The detective's suspicions were further confirmed when he surreptitiously entered the fugitives' rooms and found more armaments than respectable men would be carrying. Officers Clarke and Greer were assigned to arrest Romaine and Howard, while Lees and Evatt were to capture one Chris Lowery and one Billy Page at the Dupont Street house.

When Lowery and Page returned from a drive out to the mission, they had no sooner entered their room than Lees and Evatt walked in on them. As Evatt held a shotgun on the pair, Isaiah told them to put up their hands, but Lowery glowered and hesitated. Later it was learned he had been the one who actually killed Magruder. Lees told him again to raise his hands, this time drawing his own pistol. The killer did as he was told and both men were searched and herded off to the city jail where their two companions soon joined them.

On the evening of October 30, Isaiah sent a telegram north:

> To Hill Beachey: I have arrested Renton and have found six thousand (6,000) dollars. You must get down as soon as possible or they will be discharged on habeas corpus.
>
> Lees

Arrest of Four Fugitive Murderers from Idaho Territory—Strategy of our Police.

On Thursday last a telegram was received by Chief Burke from Hill Beachy, Sheriff of Lewiston, Idaho Territory, asking for the arrest of William Page, Chris Lowery, James Romaine and Daniel Howard, for having murdered two traders named Lloyd Magruder and Charley Allen, in the woods some 200 miles from Lewiston. The case was entrusted to Capt. Lees and such other assistants as he should require.

The steamer from the Northern coast had arrived before the despatch was received, and the police were therefore obliged to hunt for their game after the passengers had dispersed. Nothing discouraged, however, by the apparent difficulty of picking out four murderers (two of whom were entirely unknown to any of the police) in a city as large as San Francisco, the detectives went to work. After having drummed up and examined many of the passengers who came by the steamer, and found that they were not entitled to a return ticket to Idaho at the expense of that young Territory, their attention was attracted to two rough-looking strangers who had taken lodgings at an obscure house on Dupont street, near Market, pretending that they came from Oregon to recuperate broken constitutions and desired a quiet and secluded room.

The police at once instituted close and unceasing watch of the premises, and finding that their men were visited by a very genteel looking young man they set

San Francisco *Daily Evening Bulletin*, November 4, 1863. *Author's Collection*

A lawyer had already interested himself in the suspects' case and Lees knew he must act fast. He did all he could to gain their confidence and encouraged them in thinking they would soon be free on a writ of habeas corpus. Howard, or Renton, was terrified of being returned to prison. Later, Page claimed Lees and their attorney were promised all the money but a thousand dollars if they could get free. Closely guarded, the prisoners were kept together in the hope they would make incriminating remarks to each other, but they proved to be quite tight-lipped.

Isaiah now had custody of the mint certificate which he had taken from one of the prisoners. He knew nothing of Magruder at this point, but was certain that either lawyers or the government were likely to get the money now. Hopefully, he might be in for a slice of the pie and he had better acquire some control. He wanted to get the money into a bank until legal disposition of some kind could be made. This was his usual procedure.

Following through on his plan, Isaiah had Romaine endorse the mint certificate, then called on Cheesman to make sure the document was in order. The detective was advised that it was, but that it wouldn't be payable until November 7. In any case Cheesman had ordered a stop payment until it could be determined just who the proper owner was.

Hill Beachey was determined to avenge his friend's murder. And he did. *Author's Collection*

When Beachey arrived in town on November 2, he promptly contacted Burke and Lees. He was told Cheesman planned to stop payment on the mint certificate

and that one Daniel McNeill was going to swear out a writ of habeas corpus for the release of the prisoners. Beachey had obtained extradition papers from Governor Leland Stanford and hoped to be on the next steamer heading north with his prisoners. Now he was becoming bogged down in legal entanglements.

"The success of the officers," noted the *Bulletin*, "in arresting these men reflects great credit upon them, and it were a pity if any legal quibble set the murderers free."

Isaiah brought Beachey up to date and told him of his plan to get the money out of the mint and into a bank where it could be dealt with. Beachey must have agreed with him. He now needed have a lawyer to look out for his interests and Lees recommended his good friend, Reuben H. Lloyd.

All parties agreed that Lees should obtain possession of the money until proper legal dispensation could be made. But Cheesman still refused to honor the certificate. When Beachey finally obtained jurisdiction over the prisoners, he turned the certificate over to one Maurice Dore to continue trying to collect the money for Magruder's wife. Reuben Lloyd was to aid in any legal work.

On the morning of November 18, 1863, Beachey headed north with his prisoners on the steamer *Pacific*. Page broke down and confessed to the murders and, thus, escaped hanging with the others. All but Howard, or Renton, also confessed to the terrible crime.

Lees' instincts about the government were quite sound. It took much legal squabbling and a threatened lawsuit before some seven thousand dollars were finally surrendered to Mrs. Magruder.

Page's accusation that Captain Lees had made arrangements to keep all but $1,000 of the stolen money sounded quite suspect to anyone not knowing the clever lawman. The Oregon *Boise News* seems to have been the only critic of the detective's reported actions, however. After publishing that portion of the confession pertaining to Lees, the *News* snorted:

> And this is the Captain Lees whose praise has been sounded from lip to lip along the Columbia from its source to the ocean, for the active part he took in bringing the murderers to justice, and to whom resolution after resolution of thanks has been introduced in the Idaho Legislature.

There was apparently no criticism in the local press. The Bay Area fourth estate was used to the canny operations of their famous detective who usually followed the same procedure of establishing friendly terms with his prisoners and banking any disputed funds. Actually, a police commission investigation, instigated by an angry Lees, would later praise the detective for his work and clear him of any wrong-doing.

## CHAPTER ELEVEN / NOTES

The *Alta* of March 24, 1862, detailed the story of the Chinese killing and capture of the suspect by Lees. The description of the Chinese Quarter is taken from the *Daily Examiner* of April 4, 1866. A more moderate and later view is Thomas B. Wilson's, "Old Chinatown," *Overland Monthly*, September, 1911. Information on the Chinese Six Companies can be found in Corinne K. Hoexter's *From Canton To California*, New York, Four Winds Press, 1976.

The announcement of the ten-man addition to the police force appeared in the *Alta* of June 3, 1862. Discussion of the new police uniforms appears in the same paper on September 3 and November 15, 1862. Patrick Crowley's reminiscence was in the *Chronicle* of March 1, 1896. Disguises utilized by the police are reported in Martin J. Burke's 1887 "Dictation" in the Bancroft Library.

The story of the Chapman capture and subsequent events is taken from the contemporary press, primarily the *Bulletin* of March 16, 25, 26, May 26, September 7, 10 and October 1, 3, 1863. Lees' trial testimony was reported in the *Alta* and *Bulletin* of October 6 and 7, 1863.

The conclusion of the trial and sentencing of the prisoners was reported in the same papers on October 12, 16, and 17, 1863. Asbury Harpending recalled these events in *The Great Diamond Hoax and Other Stirring Incidents in the Life of Asbury Harpending*, San Francisco, The James H. Barry Company, 1913. Harpending's somewhat flawed account was expertly critiqued by Robert J. Chandler in "The Chapman Case Reexamined," *The Californians*, January / February, 1985. For a national view, see *Frank Leslie's Illustrated Newspaper* (New York) for May 9, 1863.

The *Alta* of May 4, 1863 carried one of the first reports of the murder of Pietro Larcari, although his name is given as "Pedro Carlton." The *Bulletin* carried long stories on the resulting investigation on May 11, 12, 15, 22, 23, 25, 27, and June 3, 1863. Sentencing of the conspirators was reported in the *Bulletin* of October 19, 1863. The conspirator's names were spelled variously in different sources. Newspaper accounts refer to Giocomo Bruzzo, while a police identification book calls him J. Baptiste Bruzzo, alias Briones. The San Quentin Prison Register lists him as "Juan B. Bruzzo." His sentence was commuted in 1876, while Mrs. Larcari was pardoned in 1869 and Pizano in 1871.

Lees' appointment as a deputy U.S. marshal for the northern district of California was noted in the press at the time. The original, large certificate of appointment signed by U.S. Marshal Charles W. Rand is in the Lees Collection in the Bancroft Library.

The *Bulletin* carried a long article on the brutal LaMeet murder on July 8, with follow-up reports on July 10, 11, and August 15, 1863. Lees' buggy accident was reported in the *Alta* of July 10, 1863. Mark Twain once humorously suggested in an article that the recuperating Captain Lees should not have been allowed several policemen as nurses, but instead should have paid for his own medical attendants. As usual, Mark was more interested in a good story than the truth. Lees was second in command of the police department and kept quite busy while laid up. Any officers assigned to his sick room were there for errands and liaison with Chief Burke and the department. Several policemen could hardly have been of much use in nursing a smashed ankle. At the time of the accident, the

great humorist was still in Nevada. See the *Golden Era* of January 21, 1866 for this humorous, but unfair, article.

Lloyd Magruder, a prominent merchant of Lewiston, in the new territory of Idaho, was murdered and robbed on the night of October 11, 1863. News of the suspects' arrival in San Francisco and their capture appeared in the *Alta* and *Bulletin* on November 4, 5, and 6, 1863. Cheesman's reasoning for holding up the stolen funds is given in the *Bulletin* of November 16 and in a letter to Secretary of the Treasury Salmon P. Chase on December 16, 1863 in the National Archives, Washington, DC. The suspect's attorneys argued in the 4th District Court that a territory could not legally extradite prisoners from a state. The matter was taken before the state supreme court and Beachey finally won custody. See the *Sacramento Bee* of November 10 and 11, 1863. For the supreme court decision, see Tuttle 23 California Reports, 585-592. The killer's confessions and trials are covered in the Walla Walla *Washington Statesman* of December 12, and the Portland *Oregonian* of February 4, 1864. The police commissioner's investigation of Lees' conduct in the case was reported in the Idaho *Boise News* of April 30, 1864 and the Marysville *Daily Appeal*, April 2, 1864. It can be assumed that Lees hoped for a share of the stolen money, since he often applied for rewards during his career. His integrity, howerver, was seldom questioned. My grateful thanks to Tom Emmens, of Eugene, Oregon, for providing much material and guidance on the Magruder case. Tom is the pre-eminent authority on this most interesting and complicated bit of Northwest history. For an interesting account of the case, see Julia Conway Welch, *The Magruder Murders*, Eagle Point, Oregon, Falcon Press Publishing Co., Inc., 1991

# Thieves, Thugs, and a Man Named Twain

CHIEF BURKE CALLED A MEETING of all the "Specials" in early January of 1864 to explain that until the legislature restored such authority, the Special Police had no more power than an ordinary citizen. Amended city ordinances no longer permitted the police commissioners to appoint Special Police officers. Actually, this meant the Specials were no more than watchmen and threatened to become a serious blow to the regular police force. Without the services of the Specials, the department would be seriously undermanned.

While a petition to the legislature was awaiting action in the matter, it was decided the "Specials" could be appointed constables and retain their authority to arrest and bear arms. This was objected to, but Lees' old partner, Henry Johnson, volunteered to be a test case. On January 18 Police Judge Shepheard ruled that such "Special Constables" could only be appointed for a specific action. Johnson had been arrested for carrying arms, but the case was dismissed since the judge felt there was no criminal object in the affair. For the time being, it was decided the Special Police would have to be appointed deputy constables, by other constables, even though this too was probably illegal.

On January 31 Billy Mulligan walked down the gangplank of the steamboat *St. Louis* and stood once again on a San Francisco wharf. Quickly appraised of his arrival, Burke and Lees were relieved when the badman immediately left for Sacramento to visit his brother, Barney.

Lees was aware that Mulligan's career had been going downhill lately. After serving a term in Sing Sing for assaulting a policeman, he had helped organize a New York regiment for the war, but had been refused a commission for himself. He had married a prominent New York bagnio madam, but he had been drinking more than ever when he decided to return to the West Coast. The old days were gone, however, as was facetiously noted in the *Call* on February 2, 1864:

> BILLY MULLIGAN - This individual, who years ago, when taking his departure from San Francisco, was accompanied to the steamer by a large number of our most respectable citizens, returned on Sunday and, strange to say, has created no excitement amongst his former admirers.

Isaiah was shaken in early March when his infant daughter, Annie Laurie, died. She would have been three years old the following month. The funeral was held at their Clay Street home and Lees was grateful that he could immerse himself in his work.

On the afternoon of May 21, Isaiah and Henry Ellis were walking down Montgomery Street when Ellis stopped to talk with Robert McDougal, a former policeman. As Lees stood nearby, a stockbroker named D. S. Levy walked up from the

opposite direction and engaged him in conversation. Lees had known Levy since he had served as a witness for one of his cases. When Levy began loudly denouncing the nearby McDougal for calling him some hard names during a saloon argument, Isaiah cautioned him that McDougal was just a few steps away. Levy hadn't noticed the former officer, but now quickly stepped over to where Ellis and McDougal stood talking.

"If you don't stop calling me a thief, Mac," blurted out Levy, "I'll murder you!"

"I'll call you anything I please," responded McDougal, "you damned Jew son of a bitch!" He emphasized his remark by throwing a punch that dropped Levy to the sidewalk.

Although aware of the enmity between the two men, Lees was taken completely by surprise by their actions. Shifting his cane for use as a club if need be, Isaiah jumped between the combatants as Ellis grappled with McDougal. Suddenly, a shot was fired just as McDougal struck Lees a glancing blow. As someone snatched a small calibre pistol from Levy, Lees struck McDougal several times with his cane, knocking him down. A woman standing nearby received a bullet wound in her arm and was hustled off to a doctor as the two officers herded the combatants over to police headquarters. It was a senseless affair, and Isaiah was grateful he hadn't reinjured his ankle.

Judge Shepheard held a hearing in police court several days later where several witnesses were examined. Nearly all the participants were deemed guilty and fined, with the exception of Ellis. Levy paid $100, McDougal $40, and Lees was tagged with a $15 donation, although it was allowed that he may have used his cane "with more force than was necessary" because he was a cripple. All were relieved that nothing more serious had occurred.

A new "locals" reporter began work on the *Daily Morning Call* in early June 1864. Just when Lees met young Sam Clemens isn't known, but it was probably in police court where both men spent considerable time. Police business was an important part of the local scene that Clemens was covering. Arbiter of all the petty misdemeanor cases, as well as more serious preliminary hearings, the police court was once described by Clemens in a not (for him) too-exaggerated a manner as the following:

Samuel L. Clemens had become "Mark Twain" by the time he arrived in San Francisco. *California State Library*

> The room is about 24 x 40 feet in size, I suppose, and is blocked in on all sides by massive brick walls; it has three or four doors, but they are never opened—and if they were they only open into airless courts and closets anyhow: it has but one window, and now that is blocked up... there is not a solitary air-hole as big as your nostril about the whole place. Very well; down two sides of the room drunken filthy loafers, thieves, prostitutes, China chicken-stealers, witnesses and slimy guttersnipes who come to see, and belch and issue deadly smells, are banked and packed, four ranks deep—a solid mass of rotting, steaming corruption...

Clemens had arrived in town from Nevada about ten days after one of the city's earthquakes, but he was able to chronicle the next tremor on the evening of June 23. "There were three distinct shocks," he wrote, "two of which were very heavy, and appeared to have been done on purpose, but the third did not amount to much...."

In late October Lees read in the *Alta* that Wooley Kearney had come off second best in a saloon disagreement:

> Badly Beaten. - Wooley Kearney, famous in the early days of San Francisco, was terribly beaten in a scuffle in a saloon on Kearny street early on Tuesday morning. Some difficulty occurring between him and the bar-tender, the latter brought a champagne bottle to bear on Kearney's countenance in such a manner as to transform it into a tolerably good representation of a fresh made blood pudding. The bar-keeper is under arrest....

Isaiah must have grinned at the description. Poor Wooley was so ugly any change in his face would be an improvement.

While walking down Kearny Street one day with Henry Ellis, Lees caught sight of a familiar face. Patrick Toomey was one of the more noted footpads of the time, a so-called "Barbary Coast Ranger," who had plagued the city since Gold Rush days. In the late fifties Toomey had pulled off a number of succesful crimes, but had skipped off for China before the police could nab him. Toomey spotted the lawmen just as Lees was pointing him out to Ellis. The "Ranger" quickly ducked into a saloon and pretended to be reading some posters as the officers stepped in after him. He was edging back towards the door when Lees spoke to him saying, "How are you, Pat?" Toomey ignored him.

Patrick Toomey, as he appeared in the 1865 police mug book. *John Boessenecker Collection*

"How are you, Toomey?" reiterated the detective. Slowly the thief turned and with a blank look asked if Lees was speaking to him. "Yes, I am," Isaiah responded. "Then I have to tell you that my name is not Toomey at all."

"Yes," countered Lees, "your name is Patrick Toomey and you have that name in India ink on your arm."

Kearney Street in old San Francisco. *Author's Collection*

Still putting on an outraged act, Toomey quickly pushed up his shirt sleeves and presented both arms for the officer's inspection. Although he was tattooed, there was no name. Lees was about to admit his mistake when he noticed something peculiar in the folds of a large and beautifully detailed American flag tattooed on Toomey's arm. Looking closely, Isaiah could see the letters "P. Too" within the flag, and Toomey pulled away and began straightening his sleeves.

"Yes," he growled, "I'm Toomey, and you bastards have no right to bully me like this. Yes, I'm a thief and I'll work for no man and it's your job to try and catch me if you can. Unless you have a warrant, you have no right to lay your damn hands on me."

Flanking the thug, Lees and Ellis grabbed him by both arms and dragged him off to headquarters. There was no charge against him, but Lees had Captain Douglass take him around to the principal hotels and restaurants of the city so the proprietors could watch out for him. One of the hotel keepers immediately recognized the thief. "Ah," he smiled, "an old Ranger, one of the Broom Rangers I presume!" This latter reference was to a name applied locally to McClellan supporters, and Toomey was outraged.

"Sir," he bellowed to Douglass, "I demand protection. I came here to further the ends of justice, not to be insulted!"

Toomey was released with a warning that he would be watched.

On a Saturday night a few weeks later, Toomey was observed standing over a fallen man. When a bystander approached, the thug calmly stated that his friend

On a rare day off, Isaiah (far left) pours drinks for several friends as they relax in a carriage. The locale is inknown, but thought to be a local race track. The police captain in foreground wears a top hat.
*Courtesy of the Bancroft Library*

had imbibed a little too freely and would he mind watching while he went for a hack. Of course, he never came back and the prostrate man was discovered to have a severe cut on the head and empty pockets.

Later that same evening another pedestrian was knocked down on Jackson Street and robbed of a gold watch. Officers Greenwood and Hepworth picked up Toomey a few minutes later. There was little doubt the thug richly deserved the four-year vacation he later received to San Quentin.

Captain Lees took Officer Alfred "Nobby" Clarke along when he arrested Lewis Mahoney on December 19, 1864. Various local burglaries had been particularly nervy affairs and when Isaiah spotted Mahoney in town he was sure he had his man. He had jailed Mahoney many times and twice sent him to San Quentin. "Mahoney is an industrious thief," commented the *Alta*, "and takes anything, with feet or without, on which money can be raised. He believes that Captain Lees is his evil genius, and not without cause, for three-fourths of his imprisonment he has served on arrests made by Captain Lees." When Lees and Clarke picked him up, the thief was wearing a heavy gold watch and pistol stolen from a steamboat steward. Other loot was in his possession and Isaiah advertised for the owners to call on him at his office in City Hall.

Lewis Mahoney spent much of his colorful career in state prison. *Author's Collection*

Some of Mahoney's feats of thievery were so audacious as to border on the hilarious. Lees recalled how once, out near the mission, Mahoney had stolen a saddle at a ranch and then sold it down the road. From that house he had taken several hogs and herded them to the next dwelling where they were sold. At this place he took a calf which was sold further along the road. Mahoney was a thief of the worst sort, but certainly an imaginative one.

Loan shark, police officer and lawyer, Alfred Clarke retired as a very wealthy man. *Author's Collection*

There were those who thought officer Nobby Clarke was as bad as Mahoney. Clarke was a promoter, had many friends in City Hall, and had developed usury into a fine art within the department. As he loaned out money to his fellow officers at exorbitant rates, it was said that on payday Nobby had as long a line at his table as the paymaster.

## CHAPTER TWELVE / NOTES

Chief Burke's meeting of the "Specials" was reported in the *Alta* of January 5, 1864. Other notices appeared in the same paper on January 6 and 19.

Billy Mulligan's return to the city was chronicled in the *Alta* of February 2, 1864, and noted in several other papers. His attacks on former vigilantes in New York were duly reported in the California press; see the *Bulletin* of July 30, 1856, and the *Santa Cruz Sentinel* of October 4 of the same year. He had told a Sacramento reporter just before being shipped out of town that he had "spotted" members of the committee and "would get even." And he frequently did. Californians were kept appraised of Mulligan's New York misadventures in the *Alta* of December 2, 1860, and the *San Joaquin Republican* of December 15, 1860, and January 3 and 5, 1861. The *Bulletin* never missed an opporunity to print a derogatory item concerning the former Bay City badman.

Mulligan left San Francisco to visit his brother Barney in Sacramento, but found that his brother was in Nevada. Billy joined him there and had his celebrated duel with Tom Coleman near Austin as reported in the *Reese River Reveille* of April 21, 1864.

The death of Annie Laurie Lees is recorded in clippings in the Lees Collection in the Bancroft Library.

Lees' involvement in the McDougal-Levy fracas was covered at length in the *Alta* of May 22, 25 and 26, 1864. Mark Twain's San Francisco sojourn, and the articles attributed to him in the local press, is detailed in *Mark Twain's San Francisco*, edited by Bernard Taper, New York, Toronto, London, McGraw-Hill Book Company, Inc., 1963, and *Clemens Of The Call, Mark Twain in San Francisco*, edited by Edgar M. Branch, Berkeley and Los Angeles, University of California Press, 1969.

Wooley Kearney's brawl was noted in the *Alta* of October 20, 1864.

The story of Lees and Ellis picking up Pat Toomey appeared in the *Alta* of October 24, 1864. Listed as "Patrick Grady Toomey, alias William Smith, alias Short Hair" in a contemporary police record book, Toomey's tattoos are minutely described, along with all other identifying marks and features. Toomey was reportedly born in Boston and was 28 years old at this time. He was pardoned out of San Quentin in April of 1866. The mug book with Toomey's portrait and the accompanying description book are in the collection of John Boessenecker.

The Mahoney capture was detailed in a long article in the *Alta* of December 20, 1864. Officer Clarke was on the force in various capacities for many years and later became a wealthy and prominent attorney; see the summary of his career by Dick Brill in his "Looking Back" column in *West Bay*, November 4, 1984.

# Chapter 13

# A Sagebrush Bohemian

ISAIAH HAD FOLLOWED WITH INTEREST the experiences of the many prominent San Franciscans in the war. Edward Baker, the distinguished attorney and orator, had been killed early at the disastrous Union action at Ball's Bluff. Lawyer Henry Halleck, builder of the Montgomery Block, was one of Lincoln's leading generals, as was "Fighting Joe" Hooker. William T. Sherman, the erstwhile San Francisco banker, had also emerged as a prominent Union general who had just recently achieved widespread notoriety for his "march to the sea" through Georgia.

Other local citizens had joined the Confederacy and were heard from occasionally. Although he followed the war news, Isaiah had little respite in his work. Late 1864 found him working with some sleazy characters in trying to resolve a counterfeiting case.

Lees had been gathering evidence against a man named William Farrell, alias Minnie Price, but was thwarted each time he seemed to be making headway. Finally he employed a local character named Indian Ned Wellington who had a variety of unsavory connections. Chief Burke had kept another character on the payroll as his private clerk. Despite his checkered past and several aliases, Burke seems to have genuinely liked T. B. Fargo, who was living with a Pike Street prostitute at the time. It was known that Farrell had brought $10,000 in "queer" currency from the East and it was imperative that both Farrell and his counterfeit be taken at the same time.

William Farrell, alias Minnie Price, was a cagey operator, but no match for Lees and his detectives. *Author's Collection*

Detective Henry Ellis brought Wellington to Lees' office one day in December 1864. Several decoys had already tried to gain Farrell's confidence, but without success. Wellington knew him already. The plan was to have Indian Ned introduce Fargo to Farrell and see what would develop. Fargo was given watches and other pawn shop items which could be represented as stolen goods. At the right time Wellington took the disguised Fargo to a downtown saloon and introduced him to Farrell. The two hit it off, but Lees knew Farrell was keeping tabs on Fargo to verify his identity.

After winning the counterfeiter's confidence, Fargo mentioned having just brought in a cargo of stolen goods from New York. He was on his way to Idaho and was trying to find some "queer" money to take along. Farrell was noncommittal. The following day the men met again and Fargo displayed his "stolen" goods. Thinking he now had information he could use against Fargo if anything went wrong, the

goods were exchanged for $1,500 worth of counterfeit. Farrell then accompanied Fargo to the wharf and the Portland boat.

On January 2, 1865, Lees arrested Farrell as a receiver of stolen goods. The startled counterfeiter shouted his objections, insisting the goods had been obtained in trade. When confronted by Fargo, he accused him of selling the stolen goods, while Fargo shouted the goods had been paid for in "queer." Fargo was then ushered from the room and Isaiah went into his act.

"Now Mr. Farrell, this is an awkward situation, but I hope we can count on you to testify against Mr. Fargo. The money you gave him was counterfeit, however, and you must give it up. You have no choice in the matter. I can guarantee that the coin you give up will not be used against you."

Farrell saw he was trapped. While reluctantly leading Lees to the hidden coins out in the sandhills, he tried to escape, only to find the cold barrel of a pistol pressed to his forehead. The hidden coin was missing, but detectives later found it in the possession of a Farrell confederate.

Confronted with the whole story, Farrell was furious. When Lees told him he would be charged with passing phoney coin to Fargo, Farrell screamed that he had been promised the coin would not be used against him. Smiling sweetly, Lees shook his head.

"I promised not to use the coin you gave up against you, and I won't," rejoined the detective. "What I will use against you is the coin you gave Fargo!"

The *Alta* of January 6, 1865 reported:

> Captain Lees and Officer Ellis are deserving of especial credit for the activity and energy they have displayed in this matter, and the skill they exhibited in laying out the work for their subordinates to do, in order to make the chain of evidence perfect in every link.

Although Farrell was put away for six years at San Quentin, Isaiah must have hated working with characters like Wellington. Such men were always unreliable and Indian Ned had a record of burglaries, shooting scrapes, and mix-ups of all kinds. Still, without him the Farrell case might have taken much longer or never been successfully concluded.

In mid-March Isaiah investigated a corpse recovered from a shallow grave in San Souci Valley, west of the city. Decomposition was such that identification was impossible. The head was terribly battered and when several pawn tickets and a business card failed to lead to identification, Lees looked about desperately for other clues. There seemed to be none.

At the Death House the body lay unrecognized until local physician L. T. Henry remembered an article in a British medical journal. A London doctor had recently restored the facial features of a decomposed body through the use of various chemi-

cals, and Dr. Henry now prepared to perform the same experiment. With the coroner's permission, the body was placed in a watertight shell to which was added a pound of hydrochloric acid and twenty pounds of salt. In three hours the body was re-

moved from the shell and sponged off with clean water. A bucket of water charged with chlorine gas was now splashed over the head of the corpse, after which a stream of pure chlorine gas was passed over it. To the amazement of Lees and the other observers, the bleached face had assumed recognizable features again. In a short time the body was identified as one Charles T. Hill, a young man recently arrived from New York.

Lees and Ellis now went to work. A woman who had traveled with Hill from the East directed the officers to his boarding house on Dupont Street. The landlady identified Hill as a boarder and reported he had disappeared on February 20. She recalled also that a young man had come by the next day and asked for Hill's personal effects. When she had refused, the man left, but she was able to give a good description. He was young, tall, and light-complexioned, with curly hair and a fresh cut running down one side of his face.

Tom Byrnes' mug shot clearly shows the gash on his cheek that helped convict him. *Author's Collection*

Lees remembered a young burglar he and officer Fuller had arrested recently. The description fit, even to the facial cut, and he was sure the fellow was still in jail. Back at the station house the two detectives confronted the prisoner, one Thomas Byrnes. He fit the description exactly. In his belongings, the lawmen found keys and other personal property of the murdered man, including an imitation diamond pin often represented by Hill as being genuine. The lawmen exchanged grim glances.

Blood spots on some clothes further tied Byrnes to the crime. Confronted with all the evidence, he finally admitted going for a buggy ride with Hill that night of the 20th. They had driven over to the Cliff House, but while returning had an accident and lost a horse. Riding the remaining animal back to the stable, Byrnes brought back another horse and dropped Hill off, while returning the rig to the stable. Further grilling of the suspect elicited serious contradictions. Meanwhile, other possessions of Byrnes were identified as having belonged to the dead man.

On the evening of March 15 Chief Burke and Captain Lees escorted the suspect to the Death House. Con-

The 1865 San Francisco police record book with Tom Byrnes' description and other data. *John Boessenecker Collection*

fronted with the corpse, Byrnes gasped and turned white. He pretended to examine the body, but denied it was Hill, insisting he had seen him after the 20th and received a letter from him dated at Sacramento. The letter, of course, had been lost. Lees continued interrogating him, pointing out identified clothing on the corpse. Byrnes still insisted the body was not that of Hill.

Returning to jail in a hack, Isaiah turned to the prisoner. "One thing I may as well tell you, Tom. The hitching strap which you took out on the horse you got that night was found in the grave with Hill and has been recognized!"

Byrnes blanched and blurted out that he didn't believe it. Lees stroked his beard. "It's true, Tom, and it was tied to a piece of the straw rope the stableman gave you to repair the buggy."

Circumstantial evidence in the case was overwhelming and Isaiah was certain of a conviction. Strangely enough, all the evidence suggested Hill had laid the groundwork for his own death by bragging to friends of the value of his diamond. Byrnes had committed murder for an imitation gem worth five dollars.

Unrepentant to the end, the brutal killer was convicted and hanged in September of 1866.

On April 6, 1865, word was received of the fall of Richmond and Petersburg. General Lee's surrender at a place called Appomattox was announced a few days later and the town went wild. Spotty military actions were still being reported, but it was over at last. Before any celebration could be organized, however, the city was shocked by news of the tragic event at Ford's Theater.

When word of Lincoln's death was received on April 15, immediate

A spectacular news photograph of the time shows Burke's officers and some soldiers protecting a Confederate newspaper during the rioting on April 15, 1865, after word of the death of President Lincoln was received. *Lincoln Museum, Fort Wayne, Indiana*

plans were made to insure peace and security in San Francisco. Chief Burke assembled every available member of the force for duty, while Mayor Henry Coon called out all local militia units.

Crowds gathered on street corners and rumors and late news from the East was discussed and repeated. Rebel sympathizers were particularly scarce this day. Mobs of excited men roaming the streets finally decided to vent their fury on several rebel-oriented newspapers. Storming into the offices of the *Democratic Press*, the mob hurled chairs and type into the street and destroyed the presses. When Chief Burke and some fifty officers ran up the street, the crowds quickly moved on to sack other offices. It was several days before the city returned to normal.

In a town overstocked with newspapers, no one paid much attention when Charles and Michael de Young founded a small journal in early 1865. Charles was twenty and Michael just seventeen at the time. With their mother, an older brother, and a gaggle of sisters, the boys had arrived in the city in the late 1850s from Saint Louis, Cincinnati, and points east.

Charles already had some printing experience and, borrowing a twenty-dollar gold piece from their landlord, the brothers launched the *Daily Dramatic Chronicle* on January 17. Primarily an advertising vehicle for city theaters, the

Charles de Young. *California State Library*

new paper was distributed free to hotels, saloons, and restaurants. The boys hoped one day to convert their small sheet into a real newspaper.

It was a lucky coincidence that Michael de Young happened to be at the telegraph office when news of Lincoln's assassination arrived. Rushing back to his office, Mike and his brother got out the only extra on the tragedy and scooped all the big dailies.

The de Youngs allowed Mark Twain to use one of their desks to write dispatches for the Carson City, Nevada *Daily Appeal*. Mark had been in the doldrums lately. Laid off at the *Call*, he was trying to pay bills with freelance work. He paid for the desk by occasionally writing items for the *Chronicle*.

In early July Isaiah was acting chief while Dr. Burke was ill. On the morning of the 8th, a Chinese laundryman ran into headquarters and reported being shot at while in his shop. Lees sent officer Charles McMillan to look into the matter and promptly forgot it. McMillan found the bullet and from its position concluded it had come from the Saint Francis Hotel, across the street. Further investigations suggested the shot had been fired from Billy Mulligan's second floor room. Mulligan had returned to the city from Nevada and was making a particular pest of himself. He had been on a protracted drunk and

Mark Twain, on the brink of his literary career in San Francisco. *California State Library*

129

was babbling about someone who was going to "get" him. The previous night he had voluntarily placed himself in the city jail because of delerium tremens.

McMillan went up to Mulligan's room and knocked, but the drunken badman shouted for him to go away. He had pushed his bed against the door and piled several trunks on it. The officer talked to him for some time, but Mulligan insisted someone was trying to get him and he would shoot the first man who entered the room.

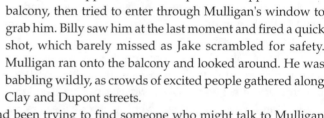

Finally, the officer left to seek the counsel of Captain Lees.

McMillan found Isaiah in court and briefed him on their way over to the Saint Francis. Lees tried to converse with Mulligan, but he was still irrational. Leaving McMillan, Chappell, and officer McCormack with instructions to try and grab him, Lees returned to testify in court. McCormack, meanwhile, went out onto Dupont Street to try to attract Mulligan's attention and allow McMillan to enter his room.

Jake Chappell had another plan. He slipped onto the balcony, then tried to enter through Mulligan's window to grab him. Billy saw him at the last moment and fired a quick shot, which barely missed as Jake scrambled for safety. Mulligan ran onto the balcony and looked around. He was babbling wildly, as crowds of excited people gathered along Clay and Dupont streets.

Billy Mulligan as he appeared as a second at the Heenan-Sayers fight in England, April 17, 1860. *Author's Collection*

Other lawmen had been trying to find someone who might talk to Mulligan and finally located Jack McNabb, a gunman and desperado of the same stripe. McNabb was ushered over to the hotel where Mulligan was bellowing and pointing his pistol at the crowd from the head of an outside stairway. Yelling that he wanted to come up and talk, McNabb took several steps up the stairs, despite Mulligan's warning that he would shoot.

"Come on, Billy, let's have a drink together. It's all right."

McNabb coaxed his way up the stairs, all the while covered by Mulligan's pistol. Suddenly there was a shot and McNabb staggered. With a widening red stain on his chest, the wounded man made his way back downstairs and lurched off to find a doctor. A half hour later the crowd received word he was dead.

After several other attempts to capture him, Mulligan fired at some retreating lawmen and killed a young man on the street. Lees had meanwhile consulted with the district attorney. It was finally determined that every effort should be made to take him alive, but the police could shoot him if necessary. Lees stationed Officer Hopkins in a window across the street. A last attempt would be made to take him alive.

Isaiah again entered the hotel and went upstairs. Mulligan's room was at the top of the stairs and the detective captain kept up a steady parlay with him. A drugged

glass of brandy was left at his door, but Billy drank it with no apparent ill effect. Every time Lees thought he had him in a rational frame of mine, Mulligan would begin raving again.

"All right, Lees, I know your game," he railed. "They're trying to sneak up on me. Get out of here, quick. I don't want to kill you, but I will! Get out!"

Rushing to another window, Mulligan pushed it open and was stepping onto the balcony again when officer Hopkins fired from across Clay Street. The crowd gasped as the badman was flung backwards into a hallway, his brains splashing over the walls. He was stretched out full length on the floor when Isaiah and other officers finally forced their way into the room. Mulligan had always been a fashionable dresser, wearing kid gloves and the finest tailored coats and brocaded vests. Looking down at the whiskey-stained, bloody corpse, Isaiah could hardly believe it was the same man. The *Alta* summed up the emotions of the city in its description of the funeral cortege and shipment of the body to Sacramento:

> ...There was an evident feeling of relief in the mind of the community that it was at last rid of the presence of a thoroughly bad man who had been a terror and a disgrace to it from the day he entered it until the day of his violent death. No church bell tolled....

Eighteen new policemen were appointed after the mid-October elections. The *Examiner* charged that some nine hundred seekers of police appointments were induced to work for the re-election of Police Judge Philip Shepheard, who was supported by the mayor and police chief. This was a common trick that had been used many times in the past. At least Shepheard was a competent and experienced jurist about whom Mark Twain had written: "It is indeed a fortunate thing for the community that we have such a man as Judge Philip Shepheard on the bench...."

There was a huge Fourth of July parade just a few days prior to Billy Mulligan's killing. The celebration hailed the end of the war, also. *California State Library*

Mark had been busy making a name for himself. His witty, acerbic dispaches to the Nevada *Territorial Enterprise* were picked up and reprinted by other papers and cussed and discussed throughout California. An astute student of human nature, Twain knew the best subjects for ridicule and sarcasm were those the pub-

lic could identify with. And he knew controversy got people talking. As a police reporter he had seen the seamy side of courts and the law. He knew some police officers accepted bribes or weren't too interested in recovering stolen property when a reward wasn't offered. He watched too as lawmen ignored the abuse of Chinese on the street.

Chief Burke was regarded by some as a pompous dictator who made his men work for his election and weeded out ambitious officers who threatened his own position. For whatever reasons, Twain began a series of articles belittling the police in general and Burke in particular. An early sample of his campaign appeared in the *Territorial Enterprise* in December 1865:

> One may easily find room to abuse as many as several members of Chief Burke's civilian army for laziness and uselessness, but the detective department is supplied with men who are sharp, shrewd, always on the alert and always industrious An ordinary policeman is chose with special reference to stature and powerful muscle, and he only gets $125 a month, but the detective pays better than a faro bank. A shoemaker can tell by a single glance at a boot whose shop it comes from, by some peculiarity of workmanship; but to a bar-keeper all boots are alike...
>
> Detective Rose can pick up a chicken's tailfeather in Montgomery street and tell in a moment what roost it came from at the mission...
>
> Deteclive Blitz can hunt down a transgressing hack-driver by some peculiarity in the style of his blasphemy.
>
> The forte of Lees and Ellis is the unearthing of embezzlers and forgers. Each of these men are best in one particular line, but at the same time they are good in all....The detectives are smart, but I remarked to a friend that some of the other policemen were not. He said the remark was unjust—that those other policemen were as smart as they could afford to be for $125 a month. It was not a bad idea....

The blossoming humorist had barely launched his campaign when tragedy struck in early January of 1866. "When Mark worked for us," recalled Michael de Young, "he had the bad habit of lifting his elbow too high on numerous occasions. He used to go on late night sprees. He was noted for that and, like a good Bohemian, he ran up bills and owed money right and left."

On one of these sprees, Twain was arrested while roaring drunk. He was hauled unceremoniously off to the city jail where he spent the night ruminating on his misfortune. In the morning a disheveled, hungover Twain woke to find his arch rival grinning at him through the bars. Albert Evans, of the *Alta*, had been feuding with Twain for some time and now saw a chance to really crucify him. He did so in a dispatch to the Nevada *Gold Hill News* late in January.

Referring to Twain as a "sage-brush Bohemian," Evans suggested he could avoid further trouble with the San Francisco police if he sought the company of gentlemen when on a binge, rather than "Pacific street Jayhawkers. When being

escorted to the station house," warned Evans, "...do not lay down on the ground and compel them to drag you... Dragging your legs on the sidewalk always aggravates a policeman, and you are apt to get kicks for your pains....When you have been searched, and your tobacco and toothpick [knife] safely locked up, go quietly into the cell and lay down on your blankets, instead of standing at the grating and cursing...."

Mark wisely ignored the assault, attacking Evans from other directions. We don't know whether he increased the venom in his police articles because of his night in the pokey, but he kept up the momentum without a backward glance. On January 21, the *Golden Era* reprinted the following article from the *Enterprise*:

> Ain't they virtuous? Don't they take good care of the city? ...Isn't it shown in the fact that although many offenders of importance go unpunished, they infallibly snaffle every Chinese chicken thief that attempts to drive his trade, and are duly glorified by name in the papers for it? And ain't they spry?...ain't they friskey? Don't they parade up and down the sidewalk at a rate of a block an hour and make everybody nervous and dizzy with their frightful velocity?

Twain was making a name for himself. He cared little for absolute accuracy so long as there was a kernel of truth to his stories. His articles were being picked up by inland papers and being discussed over dinner tables and saloon bars and that was what was important to him. "Chief Burke and his pets," noted a Mariposa newspaper, "are getting warmed up by 'Mark Twain,' as you may notice in the columns of the *Territorial Enterprise*."

In early February Twain published a particularly obnoxious, albeit hilarious, article on Chief Burke. The humorist, however, was showing signs of whipping a dead horse. It was known he was looking for another job and the police no doubt would have liked nothing better than to find him one in New York...or China! No in-depth, investigative reporter, Twain's often superficial knowledge of his subject was admitted in one of his last articles, published in the *Examiner* on February 10. Speaking of the police, he noted:

> I have abused the department at large, because I could not find out who were the guilty parties and who were the innocent. I knew there were many honest, upright, reliable and exellent men on the force, but then, on account of the questionable surroundings it would have been a hard thing to prove it! Therefore I refrained from asserting the presence of this virtue—I had a delicacy about making a statement which would be difficult to substantiate, and perhaps impossible. It was safe enough to say that in general they were rather a hard lot, because that didn't require any proof! Some of the policemen are very tender about their character...then why do they sit still and see their brethren bring them into disrepute?—Why don't they root out the bad element from the force? If they choose to keep their mouths shut and not expose the shortcomings of their brethren, they must just accept the natural consequence, and consent to be suspected themselves. Lord! So far from trying to purge their ranks of men who disgrace them, they are ready at a moments notice to shield such men and hush up their malpractices....

Lees must have smiled. There was some truth to what Twain wrote, of course, yet so much he didn't know. Certainly there was an inept element on the force, and there always would be so long as politics were involved in police affairs and appointments. And wouldn't the soon-to-be-great humourist have been delighted to learn that Chief Burke was a paid agent of the French government, charged with preventing recruiting efforts in San Francisco against Maximillian's Mexican government?

Still, Twain's allegations had drawn blood. In early February an investigating committee, acting in conjunction with the police commissioners, was looking into charges of police corruption. Lees' old friend, John Durkee, who was now the city fire marshal, had accused policemen of refusing to protect property during fires unless they were paid. This and other misconduct was being investigated, all adding fuel to—and possibly the result of—Twain's articles. When Mark left for the Sandwich Islands as a correspondent for the *Sacramento Union*, there were those in San Francisco who were not sorry to see him go.

Isaiah's fame as an officer and his years of association with the fire department had made him a prominent member of the community. In early February he and Jane attended the exclusive reception and banquet held for General W. H. L. Barnes at the Baldwin Hotel. The reception committee consisted of such names as William Coleman, J. C. Flood, Lloyd Tevis, and Governor Frederick Low.

On June 1, 1866, Isaiah was sworn in as a naturalized citizen of the United States. It was something he had put off for years, but it was a situation that had become increasingly important to him. He would be chief one day and nothing must stand in the way.

Chief Burke faced an election in the fall and worried about securing his party's nomination again. When he lost the nomination to Constable Patrick Crowley, the doctor busied himself in other occupations. Lees had got along well with Dr. Burke and always admired his energy and abilities. A flood of memories rushed over Isaiah as Burke made the rounds of the stations, shaking hands for the last time as chief.

When he left office in early December, the ex-chief entered the real estate business with his customary drive and intensity.

Lees' friendship for Chief Burke is indicated by a photograph of the good doctor in the Bancroft Library, inscribed to the detective captain. *Author's Collection*

## CHAPTER THIRTEEN / NOTES

There are many excellent sources detailing San Francisco's involvement in the Civil War, including the contemporary press. Bancroft's *History Of California, Volume VII* covers the period, as does Neville's *The Fantastic City*. See also William Martin Camp's *San Francisco, Port Of Gold*, Garden City, Doubleday & Company, 1948, and Oscar Lewis' excellent *The War In The Far West, 1861–1865,* Garden City, Doubleday & Company, 1961.

Details of the Farrell counterfeiting case are given in the *Alta* of January 6, 1865, and January 12, 1866. Mark Twain's comments on the case were published in *Mark Twain: San Francisco Correspondent, Selections From His Letters To The Territorial Enterprise; 1865–1866,* edited by Henry Nash Smith and Frederick Anderson, San Francisco, The Book Club of California, 1957. For a participant's account, see also Henry Ellis' *From The Kennebec To California.*

In a companion volume to the police Rogues Gallery book containing Farrell's mug shot, he is described as follows: "Farrell, alias Minnie Price, William, Occupation - harness maker, age 28, Height 5 ft, 9 1/2 inches, Weight - 165, Complexion - light, Eyes - blue, Hair - auburn, Scar of a cut on right ear...." Several tattoos were also described. He was released from San Quentin in March of 1870. Both of the above books are in the collection of John Boessenecker.

Details of the Hill murder case are contained in a long *Alta* article on March 16, 1865. See also the brief account in Duke 's *Celebrated Criminal Cases of America*. The *Alta* of September 4, 1866, carried an extensive account of Byrnes' execution. Although he never confessed to the crime, in his final comments on the scaffold Byrnes readily admitted he would not be standing where he was that day if he had heeded the teachings of his parents.

Telegraphic dispatches kept San Franciscans quite current on war news. By March of 1865 it seemed obvious the end was in sight and large celebrations were held in the city to herald Union victories. The April 16, 1865, issue of the *Alta* announced the death of President Lincoln and gave a good idea of the despair and disorder that prevailed in San Francisco. The police were criticised in some quarters for being slow to act against the rioters and in their fury the mob destroyed several small newspaper offices that were neutral or not of pro-Union sentiment. See John Bruce's lively account in *Gaudy Century*, New York, Random House, 1948.

Information on the De Young family was obtained from the *San Francisco Chronicle* of February 16, 1925, and from Ira Rosenwaike's "The Parentage and Early Years of M.H. De Young: Legend and Fact," *Western States Jewish Historical Quarterly*, April, 1975. Bruce's *Gaudy Century* was also helpful. In one of his notebooks, Edward Byram, later one of Lees' detectives, referred to the early *Chronicle* as "a notorious, libelous sheet."

The death of Billy Mulligan was well chronicled in the *Alta* and *Examiner* of July 8 and 9, 1865. A San Francisco correspondent of the *Grass Valley Union* furnished a particularly good account to that up-country newspaper. The local *California Police Gazette* published a sympathetic story of Billy's life and death, picked up from a "New York exchange." The article concluded, "There were worse men than Billy Mulligan." Well, maybe, but from

most accounts there seemed to be good reasons that the *New York Times* titled its brief article on Mulligan's demise "The Death of a Dog."

Reports of the appointment of new policemen and the methods used to elect officials in municipal elections appeared in the *Examiner* of October 7 and 23, 1865.

Mark Twain's lively articles found humor in nearly any subject and covered much more ground than just his spirited campaign against the police. Particularly useful for information on Twain's West Coast career was *Mark Twain: San Francisco Correspondent*; Franklin Walker (editor), *The Washoe Giant In San Francisco*, San Francisco, George Fields, 1938; and the previously cited *Mark Twain's San Francisco* and *Clemens Of The Call*. Personal information on Twain has been gleaned from Albert Bigelow Paine's *Mark Twain: A Biography*, Vol.I, New York, Harper & Brothers, 1942, and the more recent *Mark Twain's Notebooks And Journals, Vol. I, 1855–1873*, edited by Frederick Anderson, Michael B. Frank, and Kenneth M. Sanderson, Berkeley, University of California Press, 1975.

The early sample of Twain's abuse of the police appeared in the Virginia City *Territorial Enterprise* of December 19, 1865. The Michael de Young quote is from *Gawdy Century*. Twain's feud with Albert Evans of the *Alta* is nicely covered in the previously cited *Mark Twain: San Francisco Correspondent*. His article castigating the police for their laziness and "frightul velocity" originally appeared in the *Enterprise,* also.

# Highwaymen and Patronage

ISAIAH HAD KNOWN THE NEW CHIEF, Patrick Crowley, for many years. Born in New York in 1831, Crowley had come to California in early 1850 and worked in the mines. Like so many others, he became discouraged and returned to San Francisco where he engaged in boating on the bay. In 1854 he was elected a justice court constable and served in that lucrative position for many years.

Early on the morning of February 12, 1867, Chief Crowley rushed into Isaiah's office. There was a riot in South Beach and all off-duty officers were to report to headquarters.

For some time there had been grumbling about Chinese being employed instead of white men to do excavation work on some private property. Now the trouble had taken a violent turn. Dividing his forces, Crowley himself led the officers who confronted the rioters as they moved toward Market Street and the central portion of the city. The chief was armed with his revolver, a knife, a riot club, and a sawed-off shotgun filled with birdshot.

Pat Crowley was a tough and experienced Irishman who made an excellent chief of police. *Author's Collection*

Isaiah and several of his detectives were with Crowley and recognized John Stork, Bill O'Hearn, Gat Jones, and other thugs with police records. Crowley made a brief speech, announcing he was going to keep the peace and for them to go home and abstain from further acts of violence. The chief was cheered by the mob, even as they denied causing any trouble. Slowly, the crowds drifted off in groups.

Later, the police learned of extensive property damage and injury that had occurred. A white foreman had been savagely beaten, as well as a number of Chinese. Buildings had been torn down or burned and the crowd was heading for the mission to attack a Chinese labor force there when dispersed by the police. Twelve men were arrested out of the mob of four hundred, but little could be proved against them. The Chinese had been maligned for years, but this latest trouble singled out a serious spreading tumor of racial unrest.

A scene during the anti-Chinese riots as pictured in the contemporary *California Police Gazette*. *Author's Collection*

Occasionally Isaiah participated in another of those strange little dramas that broke the monotony of the constant war on crime. Chief Crowley called him into his office in late April of 1867 and handed him a telegram from New York. The message reported one Aaron Meyer having skipped town with some stolen property...and a thirteen year-old girl. When the steamer *Arizona* docked at San Francisco, the chief of detectives was there to greet the couple.

Meyer was jailed, but his companion refused to leave him. There were no charges against her and she turned out to be a bright and pretty blonde named Deckla Miller. She and Meyer both denied any property had been stolen and told a harrowing tale of parental objections to their marriage, which had driven them across a continent. The girl had no friends in town and Crowley and Lees talked to the prisoner at some length trying to resolve the problem. Meyer insisted he had stolen nothing and finally offered to give up all his property as a condition for bail. If the goods were not claimed, they would revert to him. When he was released he was penniless, but Crowley insisted he keep $120 to tide him over until the situation was resolved.

There was one more problem to settle, however. Young Miss Miller had been living with Meyer up to this time and the lawmen were determined to make an honest woman of her. She turned out to be sixteen, rather than thirteen, and when the couple eagerly agreed to be married, Chief Crowley, Captain Lees, and several others escorted the happy pair to a nearby minister.

A waterfront scene in old San Francisco.
*California State Library*

In August Isaiah and Henry Ellis were summoned to the local United States customs office. Collector John F. Miller wanted them to investigate what looked like a fraud case pertaining to a cargo of liquor on the schooner *Sarah*. The ship had sailed from San Francisco on June 18, 1867, with 175 barrels and 100 cases of double-distilled spirits. There was a $16,000 insurance policy and bonds on the cargo in the amount of $90,000. On June 25 the *Sarah* had returned to port for repairs, then sailed again on July 9. Word was received on July 25 that the ship had capsized in storm waters off Santa Cruz and Captain John W. Swan and two of the crew had managed to reach shore in a small boat. Two other seamen were reportedly drowned.

Collector Miller was concerned. A wrecker had reported no cargo had been found, yet there was not enough damage to allow barrels and cases to have been washed away as the captain had reported. Too, the *Santa Cruz Times* reported sev-

eral recovered barrels marked "alcohol" had in fact been filled with fresh water! If Lees and Ellis would undertake an investigation, Miller assured them they would be eligible for any rewards or shares of forfeitures. Isaiah must have smiled at Ellis. Here was a nice opportunity to unravel a crime and be well paid for it.

The two lawmen interviewed Captain Swan and one of his men and found enough discrepancies in their stories to arouse even more suspicions. Second Mate Charles Hoy was located aboard a small schooner he had just purchased. He had paid $500 for the craft, yet had been reportedly penniless when last in port. There had by now been reports of the *Sarah* having been seen to the north, at Drake's Bay, after initially leaving port.

Reporting their findings to Collector Miller, Isaiah and Ellis asked for a ship to take them to Drake's Bay. The U.S. revenue cutter *Wayanda* was put at their disposal and the two lawmen were soon at sea and headed north. A careful search of Drake's Bay disclosed a barely discernible cave which, because of the rough sea and breakers, was quite difficult to enter by small boat. Once inside, the officers quickly spotted a large quantity of barrels and cases covered by canvas sail. About one fourth of the *Sarah's* cargo had been discovered. With great difficulty the goods were taken aboard the *Wayanda* for the return trip.

Back in town, Isaiah and Ellis pulled together the details of the case for Collector Miller. The scheme was apparently hatched by Captain Swan and his crew. The crewmen reported drowned were probably ficticious names utilized to make the wreck seem more dramatic. Although he maintained from the first that he was an innocent victim of the crime, Captain Swan made his escape from a federal marshal in early September. Neither Lees or Ellis believed owner Charles Lord was involved in the fraud.

The two detectives watched helplessly now as the case ran its course. The *Sarah* was forfeited to the United States and sold for $2,350. The insurance company was paid $1,200 for salvage, while the recovered liquor was also forfeited to the United States and sold for $2,847.50. In addition, $32,400 was paid to the government for forfeited bonds. Lees and Ellis angrily discovered that only $211.26 remained as their share of the negotiations. They petitioned the government for $8,000 as their share of the forfeited bond funds, but their request was refused. Even though all parties agreed that the two lawmen had successfully resolved the case, U.S. Secretary of the Treasury George Boutwell ruled that the bond money was not legally considered part of the spoils. The detectives could only salve their wounded pocketbooks by the complimentary remarks in the local press.

The Democrats had swept the previous month's city elections, bringing more bad news; a new police commission was going to reinstate political patronage in police appointments. Isaiah and his fellow officers gritted their teeth for the hard times to come.

Lees encountered Bill Gregg some days later. Gregg was a notorious thug and highwayman who calmly informed the lawman that he would never again submit

to arrest and whoever tried to take him, did so at his own peril. Isaiah just smiled and walked off.

On December 28, Mayor Spaulding of Oakland was robbed on the street. When the two highwaymen were described to Captain Lees and Officer Fred Fuller, both concluded that Gregg and Tom Jackson were the thieves. Although the lawmen kept on the lookout for the next few days, the suspects weren't expected to stay in the area.

Bill Gregg gave Lees one of his toughest battles.
*Author's Collection*

On the first day of 1868 Isaiah had been invited to supper by a local operatic singer named Madame Gillotti. Jane and the children were in the East and he was looking forward to a home-cooked meal. Asked to bring a friend, Isaiah brought Fred Fuller along and on the way they stopped at the San Jose railroad depot across the street from the singer's home. Fuller followed his chief into the building knowing such visits seldom had a specific reason. They were instinctive. As Isaiah looked around the building, he was startled to see Bill Gregg and his partner over in a corner. In a moment the officers were eye to eye with the two thieves, Lees facing Gregg and Fuller keeping pace with the retreating Jackson.

"You're under arrest, Bill," announced Lees. "We know you did that Oakland job the other night."

Suddenly Jackson dodged around Fuller and ran. He plunged out the door with the officer close behind him, but Isaiah was careful not to take his eyes off Gregg. Edging closer, Lees could see his quarry meant to fight, but when the detective tried to draw his pistol, it caught in his coat pocket. As Gregg pulled his own four-barrelled Remington, Lees was on him. He caught the desperado in a vise-like grip, pinning his arms to his body so tightly he couldn't maneuver the pistol. Gregg thrashed about furiously trying to break the lawman's grip. Suddenly he twisted loose and savagely bit

Tom Jackson was a notorious stage robber and highwayn
*Author's Collection*

Isaiah's hand, which held the desperado's pistol. grimacing in pain, Lees kept his arms locked around the struggling thief. Unable to free his arms, Gregg tried desperately to bite Lees in the face, but the detective butted him in the nose with his forehead.

Summoning all his strength, Lees heaved the thrashing Gregg into a window, showering glass in every direction. A bystander now came to the lawman's assisance and the two managed to grab Gregg's pistol, although he still fought frantically.

"Stop it, Bill, or I'll blow your head off!" snarled Lees.

Gasping for breath, Gregg glowered at his captors, but he ceased struggling. Isaiah made him empty his pockets and a complete set of burglar's tools and keys were dumped on the floor. In a few minutes Fuller returned, prodding Jackson before him. He had fired several shots at the fleeing robber and finally captured him as he fled from an abandoned house on Market Street. Jackson had tried to throw away Spaulding's watch, but it had been recovered. The captives were deposited at the station house, while Isaiah sought first aid for his bleeding hand. Needless to say, the two disheveled lawmen were a little late for Madame Gillotti's dinner.

"In conversation with Chief Crowley last night," reported the *Bulletin*, "he [Gregg] said that this is no place for him to operate; that Montana is his field; that the police here are too shrewd for him and he talked very cooly about the constant interference which they make in his 'business.'"

Gregg had a long criminal history. He had served two prison terms and had escaped twice. His last conviction had been for robbing the home of Sheriff Bob Paul of Calaveras County.

Officer Frederick L. Alming was a San Francisco Special Policeman in 1868.
*Kevin Mullen Collection*

Lately there had been a change around city hall—a tension felt by nearly everyone on the force since the last election. Provines, the new police court judge, let it be known that he would put up with no nonsense from police officers. When patrolman Ben Lynes tried to arrest a foul-mouthed drunk on the street, his friends had rallied around and defied the lawman. In the melee Lynes had clubbed one of the crowd, but had lost his prisoner. The drunk had charged the officer with assault and Provines had fined him $300 or thirty days in jail. The *Alta* wailed:

> The policy under the former administrations since the days of the Vigilance Committee was to fine rioters for resisting the officers, but it now appears to be to fine the officers for resisting the rioters.

When the new police commissioners met on January 12, the lawmen's worst fears were confirmed. Some eighteen officers were removed and an equal number of rookies appointed. Captain Welch and Sergeant Jim Evrard were among the dismissed—both good lawmen with excellent records. Later Chief Crowley told Isaiah he had voted "no" on all the dismissals, but had been overruled by Provines and

Mayor McCoppin. The department looked forward to the next commissioner's meeting with a very real feeling of dread.

It had been an ugly winter in other ways. Smallpox and various virulent diseases had caused many to flee the city. Isaiah had packed Jane and the two children off to visit his mother in Paterson until the city was again safe. Little Fred was nine years old now and daughter Ella, who had been born on October 31, 1859, was eight. Both parents were terrified at the thought of losing another child and a visit to the East seemed the safest course. Isaiah missed his family and wrote often.

The dismembering of the police force continued, as reported in the *Alta* of May 18:

> GONE OVER THE BAY—D. H. Rand, who has been connected with the San Francisco Police force either as a regular or special, almost ever since our city had a police force at all, and was one of the most determined and efficient men ever in the city service, having been arbitrarily removed from his position...to make room for a political favorite, has taken service at Oakland...making the third San Franciscan now in that position, Officer Conway having been induced to go over there a year since....

Mayor Frank McCoppin was disliked by the veteran officers after installing the patronage system in the police force. *Author's Collection*

By the end of the month three more special officers were removed, one of them being the noted George Rose. He had been a good officer and received much press notice for his work, but when he complained of the dismissal, it was pointed out that for some time he had been paying another officer to tend to his beat. Rose reportedly only visited the area to collect his pay from his Chinese employers.

Isaiah only occasionally saw his old friend Henry Johnson any more. Besides his Special Policeman duties, Johnson was being retained as detective for the Pacific Mail Steamship Company and was a member of Tom Ansbro's private detective agency. Johnson also frequently aided Wells Fargo in tracking down stage robbers.

Isaiah wrote to Jane on June 29. It was a rambling letter in which he mused about buying or building their own home. He was lonely and wrote a note to the children and told Jane she could telegraph for money any time they were ready to come home. His mother could return with them, he wrote; "Give her my love and kisses." On July 11, 1868, Lees telegraphed Jane $500 to procure their passage home.

The police force, because of the increasing number of raw recruits, was under constant criticism in the press. Frequently, officers of one political persuasion would ignore trouble at meetings of the other party. Too, there were increased, needless shootings by officers as well as numerous minor infractions of duty. Although the political dismissals continued, some of the lawmen began to fight back. When the

commissioners tried to remove Special Officer Henry Johnson from the force, they were promptly taken to task by his employers...and probably by Lees and Crowley. Johnson was reinstated the following day.

The combination of demoralization and inexperience in the police ranks peaked during the October political campaign. The troubles became so obvious that Mayor McCoppin asked to address the whole department. On the evening of October 29, the mayor lectured the lawmen on their duties. They must not behave as partisans at political rallies and must enforce the law without respect to political affiliations. When he had finished with politics, the mayor admonished the lawmen for smoking while in uniform, for sitting on boxes when they should be patroling their beat, and for other derelictions of duty. Chief Crowley also lectured the men on their obligations. Old timers on the force looked on glumly. They knew, as did Crowley, that the mayor was largely responsible for many of the problems, even though others maintained the dismissals could have been avoided if the police had only cleaned up their own house.

Despite all the grumbling, the Democrats were able to maintain a slim majority at the November elections. The sole Republican victory was Chief Crowley. "If we had lost that office," wailed the *Alta*, "matters would look very blue indeed."

Smallpox still raged in the city, and Isaiah wondered if he had brought his family home too soon. There were thirty-three deaths during the week of December 13, but by the end of the month the number of new cases was down considerably. Too, the new cases seemed to be of a less malignant character. The city had suffered primarily because vaccination seemed ineffective against this particular strain of the disease. In any case, the worst seemed to be over and San Franciscans were returning to resume life in the Bay City.

## CHAPTER FOURTEEN / NOTES

Details of Patrick Crowley's life appeared in the San Francisco *Examiner* of March 1, 1896, and in an early San Francisco scrapbook containing many clippings relating to police matters and nineteenth-century crime held by the Fresno City and County Historical Society.

The South Beach riot received much press coverage, my account being taken from the *Call* of February 24, 26 and 27 and the *Alta* of February 13 and 24, 1867. The *California Police Gazette* also reported incidents of the rioting. Chief Crowley's armament on that day is referred to in Kate Hays Crowley's "Chief of Police Crowley," *San Francisco Police and Peace Officer's Journal*, Vol. VII, December, 1929. Kate Crowley also recalled her mother was so concerned that her husband would be injured, she prepared his bed and laid out all the necessary materials a physician might find useful in an emergency.

The affair of the schooner *Sarah* is given extended coverage in the *Alta* of August 11 and 12, 1867. Captain Swan's unexpected departure is noted in the *Alta* of September 7. Forty-first Congress, 1st Session, House of Representatives, Ex. Document No. 4 contains lengthy reports on the case by Special Treasury Agent Samuel Purdy, Collector John F. Miller, Captain Lees, and Henry Ellis. Lees' and Ellis' printed Petition for Relief and accompanying Statement of Facts concerning the case are in the Bancroft Library.

Details of the Bill Gregg encounter are reported in the *Bulletin* of January 2 and the *Alta* of January 3, 1868. Captain Lees' scrap with this desperado was frequently referred to in later years when feats of bravery by the police were being enumerated. See the *Examiner* of February 16, 1890, the *Chronicle* of September 2, 1894, and Detective Byram's comments on Gregg and Jackson in Volume 3 of his notebooks. Jackson's later stage robbing career is detailed in *Report Of Jas. B. Hume and Jno. N. Thacker, Special Officers*, Wells Fargo & Co's Express, etc., San Francisco, H.S. Crocker & Co., 1885, and this author's *Perilous Trails, Dangerous Men*, Clovis, CA., Word Dancer Press, 2002. Sentenced to ten years in San Quentin, Gregg was pardoned conditionally in September of 1875.

The case of Officer Lynes is reported in the *Alta* of January 9, 1868. The first meeting of the new police commissioners and the dismissals and new appointments to the police force are covered in the *Alta* of January 13 and 15, 1868.

Jane Lees' and the children's visit to Paterson at this time coincided with a terrible epidemic in San Francisco and the writer has assumed this was a primary reason for the lengthy visit. It also came as an opportunity to show off the kids to friends and relatives. George Rose's removal from the force is noted in the *Alta* of May 29, the reasons being listed in the same paper on June 4, 1868.

Two letters Isaiah wrote to his family in Paterson at this time are in the Lees Collection in the Lees Collection, the Bancroft Library.

Mayor McCoppin's address to the police force was printed in the *Alta* of October 30 and reports of the local election which was so disastrous to the Republicans is reported in the same paper on November 4, 1868. The smallpox and vaccination problems are reported in the *Alta* of December 13 and December 27, 1868.

# Little Maggie Ryan

SYDNEY-TOWN, THE COLLECTION of shacks, cheap shops, saloons, and brothels frequented by Australian thugs in the Gold Rush days, had evolved by the mid-1860s into an area referred to as the "Barbary Coast." No one knew the name's origins, but it seemed fairly obvious that some drunken sailor had seen similarities between that African hellhole and the embarcadero at San Francisco.

Pacific Street was the core of the "Coast," originating near Montgomery and running west to Stockton Street. The ugly collection of dance halls and dives spilled over into such arterial thoroughfares as Kearny and Dupont, which in turn helped feed other hellholes along Jackson and Broadway. Various narrow sidestreets with the colorful names of Bull Run, Deadman's Alley, Murder Point, and Moketown slashed into adjoining blocks and offered cheap rooming houses for denizens of the Coast. The whole area was almost completely made up of cheap hotels, music halls, saloons, and brothels where waiter girls would prostitute themselves for a quarter on up.

Some of the more prominent dives were the Bella Union, the Dew Drop Inn, Brooks' Melodeon, the Occidental, the Bull Run, and the Thunderbolt. Most had music of some sort and waiter girls with whom you could dance or dally, but you had better check your pockets when you left. Many of these deadfalls were in cellars, the cheapest being beer saloons with wooden benches lining the walls, filthy sawdust on the floor, and an

A Dupont Street dive on the old Barbary Coast. *Author's Collection*

aromatic atmosphere that only a drunk could stomach. All such places housed a floating population of thugs, thieves and con men ready to pounce on unwary tourists and travelers. The local press ran almost daily accounts of these robbers, as typified by the following *Alta* notice:

> On Wednesday night an elderly gentleman from the country, named Joseph W. Wilson, went around the city to "see the sights," and in his travels wandered into the region of the Barbary Coast...where he entered a saloon and, after partaking of some refreshment...he was set upon by two individuals who pulled him to the floor, and succeeded in taking from him his gold watch and chain....

The thieves were identified and arrested by the police, but this was seldom the case and the general feeling was that persons gullible enough to go into the Barbary Coast pretty much deserved what happened to them.

Early on the morning of October 26, 1869, Isaiah was informed that a body had been found at the rear of the Thunderbolt Saloon. Murders were frequent enough in the area, but most victims were found floating in the bay or otherwise disposed of. The dead man was a Frenchman named Hypolyte Frinquenelle. The officer who had reported the body brought in Samuel Carr, one of the owners of the place, for questioning. Frinquenelle had been drunk when he came into the place, stated Carr, and had several more drinks with two girls during the evening. When the girls left, the victim seemed to be asleep and Carr and his partner left him in front of the place and went home.

With Ben Bohen and two other detectives, Isaiah hurried over to the Kearny Street location of the Thunderbolt. Instructing the other officers to check for witnesses, Lees and Bohen looked for clues in the immediate vicinity of the body. While there were no traces of a crime being committed, the two lawmen agreed that there were positive indications that the body had been deliberately placed in front of the saloon.

Girls hustling drinks in a Barbary Coast deadfall. A crude woodcut from an 1869 *San Francisco Police Gazette*. Author's Collection

Confronting Carr and his partner Charley Kyle with their suspicions, the officers were now told the drunken man had originally been taken out back of the saloon, and not the front. Isaiah and Bohen then searched Kyle's room and were rewarded by finding Frinquenelle's watch and purse. Isaiah noticed the watch was still running and was able to establish that no one but Kyle had been in the room during the last few hours.

After presenting the saloon man with their evidence, the lawmen were not surprised when he frantically denied ever seeing the watch and purse. Under more questioning, Kyle finally admitted that he and Carr had robbed their patron when the other customers had left. Everything was falling into place now. When Captain Lees asked Carr what he thought of Kyle's statement, he replied:

"It is good as far as it goes."

Isaiah felt sure he knew what had happened. The Frenchman had been given a drug in his liquor and either it was too strong or it caused some kind of reaction that killed him. Lees was no doubt relieved that the case had been resolved so easily. When an autopsy confirmed the body had been poisoned, the saloon keepers were easily convicted and sentenced to long prison terms.

The new year of 1870 was ushered in with the usual assortment of Barbary Coast brawls and a city prison full of moaning and battered drunks. The newly elected police judge, W. D. Sawyer, seemed promising and walked into police head-

Captain Lees was becoming a legend in his own time due to his clever detective work.
*Author's Collection*

quarters on January 1 and asked to see Friday night's collection of inebriates. Below in the cells, Judge Sawyer proceeded to give a stern lecture to the bleary-eyed prisoners, then had them all released. The judge remarked to the policemen and reporters present that if the custom proved to be legal, from now on he would pass sentence on drunks in the city prison instead of the courtroom. All agreed that it was an excellent idea.

Trying to get a group of sick and wobbly-legged carousers into the courtroom had always been difficult and embarrassing. After they got there, it was even worse. "The precipitate admission," noted the *Bulletin*, "of a score of besoted men into the close Police Courtroom produces in the place a stench of stews that would make a Caesar swoon...."

The end of the month brought

Officer Appleton Stone.
*John Boessenecker Collection*

a particularly ugly case before the department. On January 24 a man burst into the Harbor Police headquarters with news that he had found the body of a small girl under the wharf at Drumm and Pacific streets. Officer Langan accompanied him back to the spot where seven-year-old Maggie Ryan was lying dead on the cold rocks surrounding the pilings. Bruises on her face and neck, coupled with torn and discarded clothes, told the terrible story all too well. She was the daughter of a poor waterfront family who had reported her disappearance to all the police stations the previous night.

Isaiah took Henry Ellis, Ben Bohen, Appleton Stone, and Officer Sellinger with him to the scene of the crime. They could find no clue whatever. The area of the murder was on a filled-in portion of the bay, a section of rock and sand where the city had built out over the water. Besides the bare wharves, there were warehouses, boating shacks, and other waterfront structures built on pilings which sheltered a subterranean area of mud, rocks, sewage, and refuse of all kinds. Rag pickers collected junk under these wharves and streets, while others lived directly in the reeking tract.

Some thirty or forty feet from where the body was found, Lees discovered a small pair of shoes which had apparently belonged to poor Maggie. Nothing else could be turned up and the lawmen began the laborious task of locating witnesses who had seen anything suspicious. A boy named Connors remembered seeing a

man the previous day. He thought he could recognize him and was told to report back if he saw him again. A short time later young Connors returned with news that he had just seen the fellow under the wharves.

The dark and dangerous areas under the San Francisco wharves were filled with rubbish and refuse and were a breeding ground for crime of every sort. *Author's Collection*

Bohen and Officer Finnigan were detailed to proceed under the wharves behind the man, while Lees and Ellis ran to cut him off from another direction. Chief Crowley and Jim Gannon took a different route, while officers Colter and John Coffey dropped down beneath the streets from the other side. A frantic chase resulted in only a brief sight of the fugitive, and Crowley hurried back to headquarters to round up more officers. Captain Lees quickly divided the new men into squads to search particular sections and arrest anyone emerging from beneath the wharves.

By now crowds were gathering along the streets. A shot rang out when an officer fired at the fugitive, but it was a miss. Shortly after two o'clock in the afternoon the suspect emerged from under India Dock. A cry went up from the crowd and as the man ducked back under the wharf, four officers were on him. Colter was closest and grabbed him with both arms. In another moment officers Dugan, Bonner, and Coffey had seized him also and he was dragged up onto the pier.

As they moved across the wharf with the prisoner, the lawmen quickly found themselves in the midst of a surging crowd of several hundred people. There was pushing and shouting now, but in a few minutes Crowley and Captain Lees stepped in on either side of the captive. Getting uglier by the minute, the mob closely followed the phalanx of officers as they made their way along the six blocks of Pacific Street leading to police headquarters.

When a large stevedore grabbed the shirt of the terrified prisoner, Crowley lashed out and knocked him down. The other officers were cracking heads with their clubs now, and Isaiah pushed and punched several others. Within a block of City Hall another group of officers rushed up and reinforced their comrades, joined by crowds of lawyers and judges who had heard the noise.

**By Western Union Telegraph.**

SAN FRANCISCO, January 26.

This city was in a state of dreadful excitement yesterday. Strong men would talk of the horrible manner in which the late Maggie Ryan had been ravished and murdered, and shed tears while they vented their curses upon the fiend who committed the crime. The entire detective force, aided by officers specially delegated for the purpose, were searching for some clue to the guilty person. At half past eleven o'clock yesterday a boy came to the Police Office and stated that a man was on Clark street who had been in the habit of tampering with children, and, from his actions, was thought to be the person wanted. The officers hastened to the spot. The man saw them coming and fled under the wharf, and was pursued, but escaped for the time

Stockton *Daily Evening Herald*, January 26, 1870. *Author's*

As the lawmen rushed along the last few steps toward headquarters, a strange thing happened. Suddenly the surging crowds fell back and began cheering while shouting the names of Chief Crowley, Captain Lees, and the other dauntless men who had defied them to save the captive. In another moment the prisoner was safe.

While Isaiah changed his filthy shoes and trousers, he observed the excited prisoner. He was a stout man in his early twenties, of medium height, and with dark hair and mustache. When asked, he stammered that his name was Charles Quinn. He was too upset to question fully at this time, so Isaiah left him in custody of Crowley and several detectives, then headed back to the wharves.

During the search Lees had picked up bits of information on another prime suspect in the case. Before nightfall the new suspect was in custody and Isaiah had the testimony of several children to whom he had made indecent proposals. "Probably," commented the *Bulletin*, "the career of this man and others of the same stripe would not have been for a long time interrupted, but for the awful sacrifice of little Maggie Ryan."

When Quinn confessed to raping the child, it became obvious the right man was in custody. Although he steadily maintained Maggie had been alive when he left her, his criminal history and mental problems seemed to clearly implicate him. Quinn was convicted of his hideous crime and later died in San Quentin.

The Ryan family was miserably poor and hard-pressed to eat on a regular basis, much less pay for a funeral. Over six thousand people attended the last rites, with many donating something for the family. The *Bulletin, Alta,* and *Chronicle* also took contributions. The police managed to put together a small offering as well. The city's sympathy went out to the family which already had little of this world's goods and had then lost something as precious as a child.

One of Isaiah's forgery cases proved more interesting than most. Early in the year George Howard and Lewis Brotherton arrived in the city and took rooms at a local hotel. They seemed to have enough money to live well and in a short time left town, taking the train east. They joined an older brother of Lewis, George C. Brotherton, on the way and all three returned to San Francisco and registered under assumed names at separate hotels.

Forger Lewis (or Louis) Brotherton.
*Courtesy the Bancroft Library*

On May 13, 1870, Howard made a small purchase in the general store of Treadwell & Company. The clerk was given $50 to pay a $14.25 charge and Howard asked for change in the form of a check. The money

was to be sent to a friend who was a drinker, he explained, and he would rather not give him cash. The clerk obligingly gave Howard a check for the balance.

The following day Lees stopped on the street to talk to George Hickox, a local banker. There had been a number of innovative bank forgeries in the East recently, and the detective was keeping close tabs on the local money emporiums. He had just told banker Hickox of a suspicious occurrence with a broker named Davis when Hickox remembered a large transaction at his bank that day. A man was due in this very morning to buy some $16,000 in greenbacks. It was a large sum and Lees accompanied him back to his place of business. They arrived a few minutes too late. John Spear, Hickox's partner, had just delivered the greenbacks for a check drawn on Treadwell & Company.

Isaiah looked carefully at the check, then suggested they immediately visit Treadwell's and make sure it was genuine. At the store the cashier pronounced the check legitimate, but the amount was wrong. A quick check of dates and stubs established the bank had been very cleverly duped.

Captain Lees gathered what information he could, then rushed back to headquarters. It was a new trick—the same Eastern dodge about which he had been voicing concern. Forgers used chemicals to erase the amount from a check, then substituted new figures in a larger amount. At the station Isaiah sent men off to cover all the boat wharves and train stations. Lees himself covered the most obvious escape route, the Sacramento steamer dock. He had a good description of Howard and promptly recognized him as he boarded the boat.

Back at headquarters the well-oiled machinery of the detective force was put into full gear. Howard was quickly linked to the Brothertons who were picked up in Stockton by Isaiah and Ben Bohen. Both men had large amounts of cash and the detectives returned to the city with the prisoners and their baggage. Brushes and a vial of white powder were particular evidence. Much work was still to be done in gathering witnesses and breaking down the details of the crime.

After a preliminary hearing, the trial was scheduled for August 19 in the municipal court. Howard plead guilty and Isaiah could concentrate on the Brothertons. Witnesses

Ben Bohen was quickly developing into a shrewd member of Isaiah's detective team. *Author's Collection*

clearly established that the trio had been seen together all over the city. Other circumstantial evidence clearly linked them to the crime and Lees concentrated on proving that the powder found in possession of both Howard and the Brothertons had been

used to erase the figure on the check. When the defense intimated that the powder (chlorate of potash and carbonate of soda) might be used as a poultice for eye trouble, a physician testified this was not likely. A chemist named James Howden was next put on the stand. He testified that the powder in question, when put into a solution, could be used to erase ink from a check. Both he and Isaiah demonstrated the procedure and it seemed likely the compound had been used for just that purpose.

Isaiah left nothing to the jury's imagination as he produced the bits and pieces of circumstantial evidence that would insure a conviction. He was a master at such work, and many lawyers and spectators in court watched his demonstrations in awe. He produced testimony that the powder, while not damaging the check, did remove the sizing from the paper. Lees showed that some rice in possession of the accused could be boiled and applied to the check paper to restore the sizing. Between tracking down witnesses and the constant court appearances, Isaiah was relieved when the jury pronounced the brothers guilty late that month. All three men were sentenced to fourteen years in prison on September 24.

Lees was sure the convicted men had prior records in the East. They were thought to be from New York and Philadelphia, but no records could be found in those cities. He kept trying, especially when the brothers managed to obtain a new trial from the supreme court. A disappointed Isaiah saw a $5,000 reward going right out the window.

On November 12 Isaiah read in the *Bulletin* that a Sacramento police officer had supervised the comparison between a bullet taken from an accused man's pistol and one that had been taken from a wound in a man's hand. Identical markings on the two bullets indicated both bullets had come from the same pistol. The detective smiled. If true, this could be an important weapon in the war on crime.

A few days later a man and his wife entered the station house and described how they had just been robbed on Market Street. They left their luggage for a brief moment, only to return and find it gone. While a report was being filled out, Ben Bohen happened to overhear the details, a situation which was reported in the *Bulletin* on November 17:

> While the description was being given, Detective Bohen hastened out of the office, and before the record had been written, came back bringing the property and the two thieves who had stolen it. He knew there is but one place, a "fence," where such articles could be sold, and calculated that he could reach there before the thieves....He calculated rightly, met the "young men" and captured them with the stolen articles in their possession.

## CHAPTER FIFTEEN / NOTES

A good informal history of San Francisco's early tenderloin district is Herbert Asbury's *The Barbary Coast,* New York, Garden City Publishing Company, Inc., 1933. For a contemporary report see the *Chronicle* of November 28, 1869. The Barbary Coast reference quoted is from the *Alta* of April 16, 1869. The Frinquenelle murder is covered in the *Chronicle* of November 4, 1869. Carr was sentenced to life in prison, but was pardoned in 1877. Kyle's life sentence was commuted in 1878.

Judge Sawyer's unconventional police court proceedings were reported in the *Bulletin* of January 1, 1870.

Maggie Ryan's murder and subsequent events were reported in the *Alta*, the *Bulletin* and the *Chronicle*, of January 26 and 27, 1870. In later years Pat Crowley recalled that the Maggie Ryan case was the most exciting of his career. See the *Examiner* of March 1, 1896.

The Howard and Brotherton case is given extensive treatment in the *Bulletin* of August 20, 22, 23, and 24, 1870.

The ballistics item appeared in the *Bulletin* of November 12, 1870. Ben Bohen's tour de force is noted briefly in the *Bulletin* of November 17, 1870.

# Hoodlums and the Pereda Case

ISAIAH AND CHIEF CROWLEY both recommended Henry Ellis to replace Captain James McElroy, who had died in January of 1871. Ellis had a splendid record as officer and detective, and Lees was delighted when the commissioners made the appointment on January 12.

The city's slum areas had long been a breeding ground for crime, but the police were becoming increasingly aware of a different breed of young criminal. Banding together in vicious gangs, these thugs pilfered stores, robbed old people on the street, and often senselessly attacked Chinese, homeless vagrants, and others. "Hoodlums," these boys were called, and they ranged from twelve to twenty-five years in age. The Bobby Durkins of the city were bad enough, but even they didn't club victims into insensibility for no reason at all. Like wolves, these packs of thugs gathered in alleys and vacant warehouses to plan their depredations, then at night returned to their lower-class homes.

Newspaper sketch of a hoodlum.
*Author's Collection*

In early June Officer Cook broke up a fight among a crowd of these boys, but was set upon by others and severely beaten. Two brothers named Farley were picked up and fined ninety-five dollars for the incident. "A few more such heavy fines," naively commented the *Bulletin*, "will check the career of the young roughs who infest the city and who perpetrate some outrage every day."

Chief Crowley's annual report noted the police force entailed a mere one hundred officers and four captains, besides himself. According to the latest city census, this meant one officer for every 1,445 inhabitants. New York had one officer for every 461 people, Dublin one officer for every 303 residents, and London one for every 410 citizens. Actually, the chief didn't include all the Special Police, bringing his total local figure down somewhat. The *Bulletin* insisted, however, that San Francisco had neither the slums nor the political upheavals to justify increasing the department at this time.

When Isaiah occasionally enjoyed a respite in criminal activity, he enjoyed a leisurely lunch at home with Jane, a discussion of books with publisher Anton Roman, or an afternoon chatting with John Nightingale at his office. He sometimes attended social gatherings, but Jane was a homebody who cared little for such things. She was involved in various charities, but beyond a small circle of close friends, didn't go out much unless Isaiah insisted.

The previous January there had been a robbery a continent away on the Spanish island of Cuba. Isaiah received word of the incident in a telegram from Harry N.

Davies of the Pinkerton National Detective Agency. Alerting Lees to the robbery of the army barracks at Santiago de Cuba, Davies reported four men had stolen some $300,000 in army payroll and other funds. The gang had split up, but one Buenaventura Pereda had gone to New York with his share and indulged in some lavish living. The Spanish minister had engaged the Pinkertons to retrieve the money, but by the time Pereda had been located he had disappeared. Lees was advised the fugitive was expected to flee to San Francisco.

There was no extradition treaty with Spain at this time, and Pereda could not simply be arrested and turned over to the Spanish government. Lees was warned to pick up the fugitive and get him to give up the money voluntarily. It was a ticklish business. The detective would be laying himself open to a charge of false arrest if he wasn't careful and Pereda had the money to purchase the best legal talent in the city. Isaiah showed the telegram to the local Spanish consul, who had not yet been advised of the crime.

Since there would be a nice percentage of the loot to split with the Pinkertons if he could pull it off, Isaiah went to work. There seemed to be no doubt as to the fugitive's guilt.

Arriving in San Francisco on June 5, Pereda registered under an assumed name at

the Occidental Hotel. By the time he had been located, however, he had already left on a steamer for Lima, Peru.

By September 11, Pereda had returned to the Bay City and Lees quickly had him spotted at the Gailhard Hotel. Detailing Ben Bohen to watch him, Lees accompanied Chief Crowley and an interpreter back to the hotel. Pereda was interrupted at dinner and escorted to his room, where Lees and Crowley confronted him with what they knew. He was assured he was not under arrest and that any action he took would have to be voluntary. As the interpreter explained the situation to Pereda, the fugitive became increasingly alarmed.

When asked how much money he had, the Spaniard produced a sack

What better place for thieves and con men from the East to hide out than San Francisco, on the other side of the continent. *Author's Collection*

containing some $8,000. A search of Pereda's trunk disclosed a collection of bills and drafts such as had been mentioned in the first Pinkerton dispatch. After Isaiah reported being authorized to settle the affair, Pereda became indignant and insisted $4,000 be returned to him. When Lees refused, he asked for $2,000 and the detective told him they would see the Spanish consul about it.

"No, no," Pereda frantically exclaimed. "If you do that neither of us will get anything! Here, take whatever you want from the bag and I will take the rest."

"No," said the detective. "We don't do business like that."

All the funds that could be found were placed in a carpet bag and given to Pereda, then the four men went downstairs and hailed a hack. Lees directed the driver to the Spanish consul's house, where he informed Consul Camillo Martin of Pereda's custody. The official was asked to meet them at the chief's office that evening, where the money would be counted and voluntarily turned over to the officers. Hopefully the matter could be settled that night.

Everything seemed to be falling into place. Pereda's aliases and his illogical story of a boy giving him the money in Havana didn't make sense. His claim to being a deserter from the Spanish army also put him in a bad light. That evening, when Consul Martin arrived at police headquarters, Pereda anxiously asked if he were going to be returned to Cuba.

Just how tough the lawmen had been up to this point is anyone's guess. As has been seen, civil rights for criminals was carefully monitored by elements of the local press and the police had been reasonably careful since the days of the Plaza incident. Another mitigating circumstance was the officers' responsibility to obtain the money voluntarily from Pereda. They could pressure him in many ways—let him know there was a good case against him—but he must surrender the stolen funds voluntarily. We can be sure, however, that the lawmen put on a tough show for the fugitive.

In the presence of the consul, all of Pereda's funds were counted and stacked on a table. The total was $28,000. Lees then asked Crowley to draw up a paper stating in effect that Pereda was turning over all his funds to Captain Lees. "The document was read over to him," Lees recalled later, "and he objected to a clause. Another paper was drawn and after it had been read several times, he signed it."

The following day, Isaiah took Pereda to the Bank of California, where he deposited all tangible funds. Various other bank drafts were endorsed over to Lees, following the detective's instructions. All the money was now in the bank, with all negotiable notes endorsed over to Lees. Since he couldn't be arrested, Pereda was given $1,000 and told to leave town. It was now simply a matter of turning the money over to Pinkerton and collecting the reward.

Then it happened. Lees explained the evolving situation to Pinkerton Superintendent Harry Davies in a telegram dated September 26, 1871:

> I recovered $28,000, including drafts. Since then he (Pereda) retained a lawyer to commence suit for recovery under circumstance. I was compelled to get aid from the Spanish Consul of this place, which will necessitate me to make settlement with the Spanish government through him. Will advise you more fully when I get out of the hands of lawyers. I. W. Lees

Isaiah was cheered to receive a prompt reply from Davies. He had telegraphed the Spanish authorities in New York and they had authorized the San Francisco consul to render Lees all necessary assistance in the matter. Furthermore, they would "cheerfully" pay the percentage which they had previously offered.

Isaiah must have cursed his bad luck, but this had been a very real danger from the start. One of the attorneys who loitered around City Hall had gotten wind of Pereda's problems. After a lengthy discussion with his new client, the attorney slapped Lees, Crowley, and Consul Martin with a suit for $30,000, an amount Pereda claimed had been taken from him, plus $100,000 for damages and costs of the action. The suit was commenced on September 28, 1871, and was followed a few days later by a separate suit against Martin for $50,000.

Isaiah began assembling his evidence. By the time the Martin trial had commenced in U.S. District Court on May 23, 1872, Lees had put together a good case. Pereda's statement that day was that he had been a sick man when the police officers and consul had bullied him into giving up his money. Questioned as to how he had obtained the questioned funds, he no longer claimed a boy had given it to him on the street. Now he insisted he had earned some $40,000 by loaning money to fellow soldiers. Prior to the trial Pereda had denied being a prisoner at the time

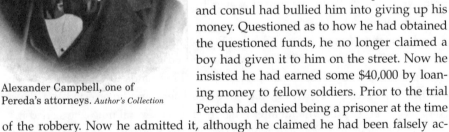

Alexander Campbell, one of Pereda's attorneys. *Author's Collection*

of the robbery. Now he admitted it, although he claimed he had been falsely accused. He also now admitted to being a deserter from the Spanish army.

On May 25 and 27, several witnesses gave testimony, but most of the time was taken up in hearing Consul Martin's relation of events. He fully sustained the police officers and reiterated that the money had been obtained without duress.

The trial was going badly for Pereda. W. H. Rhodes, his attorney, realized his whole case rested on the assumption that his client had been retained unlawfully and

made to sign over his funds to the police officers. When the document with Pereda's signature was offered in evidence, Alexander Campbell, Rhodes' partner, objected, saying that the chief of police should be ashamed to allow such an infamous document to bear the seal of his office. Rhodes then emphasized that the trial was for false imprisonment, and evidence in regard to previous character could not be offered. "Such a paper," he insisted, "would be hooted out of any court in the land!"

The next few days were spent trying to prove the plaintiff had been held in a locked room and threatened if he didn't sign the document. In the end, however, it was necessary to establish whether Pereda was suing for his own, or stolen, money.

On May 29, Lees produced his key witness. Ortega Garcia had been brought from Cuba, and he introduced himself as a captain of the guard in the Spanish army who had been on duty when the robbery occurred. Garcia described the theft and identified various drafts found in Pereda's possession as being signed by Antonio Lopez, cashier at the garrison. When Rhodes summed up on May 31, he must have known that his case was badly damaged. He tried desperately to overwhelm the defense effort with a spirited denunciation of the tactics of the police and the Spanish consul.

Captain Lees' good friend Reuben H. Lloyd represented the defense and summed up the prosecution's case with a review of all the damaging evidence against Pereda. Although Judge Ogden Hoffman cautioned the jury to disregard all testimony pertaining to the plaintiff's prior history, the damage to Pereda seemed irreparable when the jury began its deliberation on the evening of May 31.

Attorney Reuben Lloyd.
*Author's Collection*

Lees' methods in taking Pereda into custody and insistence that he give up funds in his possession had been criticised roundly in some quarters as the trial had progressed. After seeking counsel and the advice of the Spanish consul however, the detective had seen no other course of action to pursue. When the *Bulletin* censured his action, Isaiah prepared a statement and called on the editor, as reported on June 3, 1872:

> In our comments on the [Pereda] case in the *Bulletin* of Saturday, Officer Lees thinks we did him injustice in some important particulars....While we cannot change our opinion concerning the unlawfullness of a part of the proceedings, or the danger of such a precedent, we do not find any reason to suppose that Officer Lees had intended to make any improper use of the money taken from Pereda....Save one thousand dollars, which Pereda was allowed to retain, the whole sum went into the bank where it now remains. Officer Lees further claims that he never made any arrest, whatever. But that, as the agent of the Spanish Government, and knowing that Pereda had the money, he did his best to recover it without arrest and by

making as little fuss about it as possible....It is but justice to say that Officer Lees has an untarnished character for integrity....

The newspaper then printed a long summary of the case by Lees, in which he reviewed all the known facts of the robbery and its aftermath. "The money is claimed and owned by the Spanish Government," summed up the detective. "Will any honest man say that it should be given to the thief and not to the owner?"

This same day the jury announced it could not reach a verdict in the case. Seven jurymen held out for the defendants, while four agreed with Pereda's counsel. With the suit against Crowley and Lees scheduled in a few months in the Fourth District Court, attorneys Rhodes and Campbell didn't pursue a mistrial, but decided to concentrate on the upcoming litigation. Isaiah was relieved. He was still working hard on the case and hoped to have some surprises next time that would leave no room for doubt.

Prominent lawyer and judge Davis Louderback. *Author's Collection*

Isaiah's good friend Davis Louderback had taken office as police judge the previous January. A native of Philadelphia, where he had been born in 1840, Louderback had long been the assistant district attorney of the city and prosecutor in the police court. He had been criticized frequently by Mark Twain in 1864 for his inexperience and bad judgment, but the succeeding years had amply qualified him to tackle his new job.

Lawmen and citizens alike were cheered when Louderback read the riot act to the first hoodlum to appear before him."You belong to the criminal element of the city," stated the grim-faced judge, "and when one of your kind is brought before me and is proven guilty beyond a doubt of the commission of acts of violence or crime...he must expect nothing but exemplary punishment."

In August Chief Crowley's annual report announced a recent legislative act authorizing the augmenting of the one-hundred-man regular police force, subject to the board of supervisors' approval. Even more important, the act banned removal of police officers for political purposes. Crowley also alluded to the vicious gangs of juvenile offenders in the city and urged they be strongly prosecuted at every opportunity.

When the Pereda suit was taken up in the Fourth District Court on October 10, Isaiah was ready. Two important witnesses had been brought from Cuba and Pereda paled when he saw them. One was Captain Antonio Gomez Lopez, cashier of the army post that had been robbed. He had identified the stolen funds and would testify. The other witness was a young army drummer boy named Joaquin Barca, who was an accomplice in the robbery and had made a full confession.

At this point the plaintiff tried desperately to have the suit dismissed, but the judge refused. After statements of evidence by the opposing counsel, the jury quickly

Contemporary reward offer for the Brothertons in a city newspaper. *Author's Collection*

reached a verdict sustaining the defendants. "It is the purpose of the officers," reported the *Bulletin*, "to return the money to the Spanish government to which it belongs." The amount of the reward paid was not divulged. Isaiah must have felt a tremendous sense of relief...and vindication.

Late that same month the two Brotherton brothers came up for their third trial after a series of appeals. This latest hearing lasted eight days and meant long hours of testifying for Isaiah. The *Chronicle* of October 30, 1872 reported:

> Captain Lees was recalled and testified that he experimented upon checks written with the same kind of ink used by Seidentorff with the powder found in the baggage of the Brothertons, and took out the ink in ten minutes very nicely....

By now Lees had finally unearthed the Brothertons' criminal past. George had served a prison term for forgery under an assumed name in Philadelphia. Later he had been indicted for the same crime in Kentucky and Ohio. There was a smile of satisfaction playing about the whisker-shrouded mouth of the great detective as he heard the jury pronounce the brothers guilty on October 31. There was no doubt this time. The $5,000 reward was his.

At about eight o'clock on the evening of November 3, a lone deputy in the county jail thought he heard a noise. Earlier, a jail matron had reported becoming sick during supper and asked that one of the jailors come help her. Only R. P. Franklin was left on the premises. As he stood up to investigate the noise, Franklin was confronted by the two Brothertons and a trusty named Riley. George Brotherton had two pistols pointed at the deputy's head, while Lewis clutched a large knife. They quickly handcuffed Franklin and fled.

The escape caused great excitement in the city. Chief Crowley immediately sealed off the town, while police and sheriff's officers stumbled over each other trying to get a lead on the escaped prisoners. The brothers were scheduled to be taken over to San Quentin immediately, but had been held over because of the lateness of the day. This, and the suspicious actions of the

Despite their youthful appearance, the Brothertons were hardened and desperate criminals. Here George tries to spoil his mug shot. *Courtesy the Bancroft Library*

jailors, immediately raised the cry of foul play in the sheriff's office.

Isaiah and his men filtered through the Barbary Coast dives trying to pick up information, but the damp fog that swirled in from the bay seemed to have absorbed the fugitives completely.

Sheriff James Adams offered a $4,000 reward for the brothers and the city offered $1,000 more. Governor Booth was expected to contribute another $2,000 and private parties promised to swell the pot even more. The temptation was just too much for the fugitive's confederates. By November 8, Sheriff Adams, Crowley, and Lees were all in touch with parties wishing to turn the Brothertons into cold, hard cash.

Mary Ellen "Mammy" Pleasant, San Francisco's wealthy and influential black pioneer, was quite a shady lady, also.
*Author's Collection*

Crowley had finally arranged to intercept the fugitives one night as they moved to new lodgings. Taking Lees and Ellis, along with an equal number of men from the sheriff's office, the lawmen hid themselves along Howard and Twenty-first streets. Sheriff Adams, extremely touchy about the whole thing, refused to ride in the same hack with the city police officers.

At the appointed time of 6:45 P.M., the Brothertons and Riley were observed walking along the street with several others. They were easily taken into custody and found themselves in Crowley's office before the public was even aware of the capture.

One of their lawyers and several ex-convict friends were quickly implicated in the plot. The mysterious Mammy Pleasant had reportedly been engaged to find them a new hiding place. George Brotherton refused to admit there had been any confederates, but in the same breath castigated those who had sold them out: "....We were given away," he complained. "I knew that we should be and I was a damned fool for coming out to Twenty-first and Howard without knowing more than I did...."

Isaiah located a store basement on Washington Street where the fugitives had stayed. George O'Connor, a clerk in a neighboring shop, was one of those involved in the jail delivery, along with a man named Fern. Lees found various bits of evidence in the cellar which clearly indicated the Brothertons had stayed there.

This time the sheriff promptly rushed the brothers to their new home at San Quentin.

In November Isaiah was told Jake Chappell's body had been found in the bay. When his drinking problem had gotten out of hand some five years before, he had been dismissed from the force and his life had been all downhill since. He had recently left the inebriates' home, but it wasn't known whether the old detective had stumbled off a pier when drunk or had committed suicide in a fit of depression over an intemperance he found impossible to control.

## CHAPTER SIXTEEN / NOTES

The *Bulletin* announced the death of Police Captain James McElroy on January 7, 1871. His funeral and the large attendance of the department was noted in the same paper on January 9. Henry Ellis' appointment as captain was announced on January 13, 1871.

Lees engaged in much more activity than can be chronicled here. His trip to New York after the forger Van Eten is described in the *Bulletin* of March 4, 1871. Lees' and Bohen's capture of some New York forgers is reported in the same paper on April 7. The arrest of several burglars was covered in the *Bulletin* of May 6, while the breakup of yet another forgery operation was reported on May 25, 1871.

For an informative treatise on the gangs of young thugs that began plaguing the city in the late 1860s see Kevin Mullen, "Gangs of Old San Francisco," This World, magazine section, *San Francisco Chronicle,* October 29, 1989. The term "hoodlum" is reported to have originated in San Francisco in the late 1860s. One source of the term suggests these street gangs used the term "Huddle 'em" as a warning signal and gradually the term evolved into "hoodlum." Mullen states the name is a corruption of the Bavarian German word "holdalump," having the exact meaning as "hoodlum". The fact that San Francisco had a large southern German population in the 1870s adds credence to this theory. See John S. Farmer, *A Dictionary Of Slang,* Hertfordshire (England), Wordsworth Editions Ltd., 1987 (originally published in 1890) and the *Call* of June 6, 1886. Asbury's previously cited *The Barbary Coast* is also most informative.

Officer Cook's hoodlum scrap was reported in the *Bulletin* of June 8, 1871. Another officer's set-to was reported in the same paper on June 12. The murder of a Chinese merchant by hoodlums is detailed in the *Bulletin* of June 9 and 12, 1871.

Chief Crowley's annual report is quoted in the *Bulletin* of August 23, 1871, along with the noted editorial comments.

Captain Lees enjoyed a wide circle of friends and often attended social events of every kind. A few of his closest friends, aside from police officers, were John Nightingale, Anton Roman, Reuben Lloyd, W.H.L. Barnes, and Davis Louderback, all prominent local businessmen and attorneys. Isaiah would eventually make the prestigious *San Francisco Blue Book* and the many invitations to social events he saved over the years attest to his popularity and local prominence. His wife, on the other hand, did not enjoy social events and kept busy at her charities and home life. See the Lees Collection at the Bancroft Library for the many evidences of the captain's social activity. Obituaries of Mrs. Lees at the time of her death all comment on her charities, home life, and her small circle of friends. See the *Call* of January 16, 1897, and other local papers of the same date.

The Pereda case was given extensive covereage in the San Francisco press. This account is based primarily on articles in the *Bulletin* of September 29, October 3, 6, 1871, and May 23, 24, 25, 27, 28, 29, 31, June 3 and October 10, 1872. See also the *Chronicle* of March 15 and November 8, 1872.

There is some biographical data on Davis Louderback in Branch's previously cited *Clemens of The Call.* Judge Louderback's first few days on the police court bench are reported in the *Bulletin* of January 2 and 4, 1872.

Chief Crowley's annual report is summarized in the *Bulletin* of August 12, 1872.

The Brotherton case is reported in the *Bulletin* of October 22, 27, 28, 29, and 30, 1872. The *Chronicle* of October 30, reports on Captain Lees "as a chemical expert." The *Bulletin* of November 1 and 2, 1872, carried the story of the Brothertons' conviction and sentencing, with extensive converage being given their escape and recapture on November 4, 5, and 9, 1872. An investigation of the escape was reported in the *Bulletin* of November 15 and 16 and in the *Chronicle* of the same dates.

Jacob G. Chappelle's death is noted in the *Bulletin* of December 17, 1872, and the *Alta* the next day.

# Bull Run Battles and Newspaper Wars

BY EARLY 1873 HOODLUMS were a decided plague in the city. The papers were filled with their antics of harrassing merchants, street fights, crowding pedestrians from the sidewalks, and using loud and obscene language.

San Franciscans were cheered in late January when streetcar conductor John McCormick threw hoodlum John Coughlin from his car. Coughlin had been abusing both McCormick and his passengers and later threatened to "get" the conductor. When he again boarded the car with a drawn pistol, McCormick pulled his own and killed the bully. He was quickly exonerated. Even the police were not immune from these pests, as noted in the *Bulletin* later that year:

> ANOTHER OFFICER BEATEN. Policeman Forner attacked by a gang of hoodlums and severely beaten. Assaults on police officers are now of almost daily occurrence. During the last week four cases transpired, and in two instances the officers have been severely injured. Yesterday morning...Officer Forner...was struck in the back with a brick thrown by a hoodlum named Bill Harrington. The officer was not wholly disabled by the blow and succeeded in capturing the assailant who had fled into a Chinese wash house for protection. While passing along Dupont street a crowd of hoodlums known as the "Hill Boys" followed the officer, cursing and threatening him. On the corner of Jackson and Kearny streets the gang...surrounded the officer and his prisoner and prevented them from proceeding....Officer Carlisle responded to the cry for help....

During the ensuing melee the officers were separated. By the time Carlisle dragged his prisoner into police headquarters he found Harrington waiting there. He had given himself up and reported that Forner had again been struck down. Retracing his steps, Carlisle found Forner with a four-inch gash in his head and he helped the injured lawman back to headquarters. Other gang members in custody were arrogant as ever. "On the way to the City Prison," noted the *Bulletin*, "Dunn was very insolent and made threats against the officer's life, for which offense an additional charge was made."

Although horse-powered streetcars had been in use for some years, by 1873 the unique, new cable car system was being utilized. *Author's Collection*

San Francisco was steadily growing. The southern area was industrial and commercial, while to the west some one hundred and fourteen single-dwelling homes

had been built during 1873. The cost of a home and lot ranged from $2,500 to $4,000, with a few priced around $5,000. This Western Addition property was originally far outside the city limits, but now was rapidly being enclosed within the residential areas. Isaiah bought some lots on a speculative basis.

It was nearly ten o'clock at night on November 1, 1873, when Isaiah received word of a murder at the Bull Run Saloon on the Barbary Coast. Picking up detective Appleton Stone, Lees hurried over to Pacific Street. Ned Allen, the owner of the dive, had been stabbed in his doorway and when the detectives appeared, the Bull Run was quieter than Isaiah had ever seen it. Known as one of the worst deadfalls on the Coast, the Bull Run's basement and first floor were saloons and dance halls, while a second story served as cribs for the whores and waiter girls who worked below.

Looking down at the Allen's body, Lees must have mused at the bloody end of one of the most notorious characters of old San Francisco. Reportedly a veteran of the Civil War, Allen was a large man with a glowing nose to match. He frequently found it necessary to tone down his glowing and prominent proboscis with a dash of flour. "Anything goes here!" was his motto, and Isaiah well remembered the bloody brawl of Christmas morning in 1868 when one man was killed and three others horribly slashed. "The floor on which fallen women and depraved men had a few minutes before been dancing," noted the *Alta* at the time, "was splashed with blood in all directions...."

As many as forty women were often employed at the Bull Run as dancers and

waitresses. All were prostitutes as well, and when one passed out from the poisonous potions served in the barroom, she was often hauled upstairs and sold to all comers. For another quarter, it was said, a customer might watch his predecessor.

Allen had been stabbed behind a brightly wallpapered screen shielding the Bull Run's doorway. Some men had gathered about the entrance looking in and he had yelled not to block the entrance. When one man still lingered, the violent-tempered

Allen stormed from behind his bar with a club and a few minutes later walked unsteadily back inside and collapsed. An examination by one of the bartenders disclosed a chest wound which caused Allen's death. No one had actually seen the stabbing since the screen had hidden the two men from view from inside the saloon.

Isaiah quickly gathered statements from saloon patrons who described the man who had lingered in the doorway. Tom Field, one of Allen's fiddlers, had seen a man peek from behind the screen just before Allen had gone over to the doorway. Field, an ex-convict, thought he recognized a man named Freel whom he had known at San Quentin. It was a slim clue, but Lees was encouraged and he and Stone continued the search for witnesses.

Lees interviewed George Foster, an unemployed printer who roomed at a neighboring grocery store. Foster had been standing in the store doorway watching the scenes along Pacific Street when he heard the commotion at Allen's place. A man fitting Freel's general description left the saloon and walked up the street with several others. Freel had then abruptly returned to the Bull Run where Foster next heard someone say, "If you want to kill me, I will kill you." Detective Stone remained in the area to continue interrogating witnesses while Isaiah returned to headquarters and summoned Chief Crowley. Freel's name rang a bell. When Lees looked up his record, he found Bartlett J. Freel, alias Barney Flynn, had been sent up on a burglary charge and released from San Quentin in September.

Returning to Pacific Street, Lees found several other witnesses who identified a man fitting Freel's general description as being in front of the saloon at the time of the murder. The evidence was slim, but it was enough to now warrant picking up the suspect. The next few days were spent combing the Barbary Coast for some clue to his whereabouts, but the exhausted lawmen came up blank at every turn. Freel might well be out of the state by this time.

On November 3, a man named Jim Reynolds asked to see Captain Lees. Undoubtedly inspired by a reward offered by Allen's brother, Reynolds told the detectives he had been with Freel the night of the murder. This time he gave them the name of the suspect's boarding house, Lees and Stone were promptly on their way.

Freel's landlord told the detectives that Freel was gone, but had mentioned something about taking the Vallejo boat. The lawmen dashed off to the wharf where they thoroughly searched the waiting steamer. The suspect was not aboard, however. There was still some time before the boat left and they positioned themselves behind some cargo near the gangway. It was just after three in the morning and bitter cold and fog swirled around them.

At three-thirty a roughly dressed man answering Freel's description walked toward the gangplank. "It's him," muttered Lees. The suspect was quickly flanked and seized by the two officers. The startled man admitted his identity, but denied knowing anything of Allen's death.

At his boarding house Freel was stripped and examined for marks and bruises.

He insisted he had not been on Pacific Street the night of the murder and had retired early. As the suspect was being questioned later at police headquarters, an officer brought ten laborers and stationed them in the chief's office. Detective Stone had meanwhile brought in the five witnesses who had identified the suspect. When he was placed in the lineup of laborers, the witnesses all identified Freel as the man at the Bull Run entrance. Isaiah gave Pat Crowley a knowing glance.

The detectives were now certain they had the right man. Isaiah asked him again where he was the night of the murder and Freel insisted he had gone to bed about six o'clock. "That's rather early for a ranger like you to go to bed," remarked Lees. "Well," mumbled Freel, "maybe it was seven o'clock. It might have been seven thirty."

"Now, Barney," continued Lees, "where have you been hiding the past few days?" The suspect maintained that he had not been hiding—that he had been looking for work. When this was checked out, most of the names provided had not seen him. With Freel in custody, Isaiah continued the search for evidence. To date, all he had was circumstantial testimony of the worst kind—much of it from Barbary Coast Rangers and ex-convicts. It might be all he could find, but with enough of it perhaps the case could be worked up yet. The suspect had already been caught in some lies.

A preliminary examination was held in Judge Louderback's police court on November 4. The room was jammed to capacity, as noted in the *Chronicle*:

> Freel sat at the long table directly in front of Clerk McCarthy, and by the side of his counsel, Judge Tyler. Burke Phillips, flanked by Captain Lees and Stone, sat on the other side of the table and the intervening space was filled with lawyers, who were present, some from curiosity and others to study the legal phases of this mysterious case. Probably no case has ever occurred in San Francisco where the evidence has been so much of a circumstantial character as this of Freel's. No man saw the fatal blow struck, and whatever there is to fasten the crime upon the prisoner must be deduced from a web of circumstances which point to him as the guilty party.

The defendant's attorney was George Washington Tyler, the most colorful criminal attorney on the coast. Lees glanced at him warily. He was a good lawyer and would make the most of the character of the prosecution's witnesses. Tyler's first motion was to request removal of the witnesses to prevent them from hearing each other's testimony. The court assented.

The first witness was Allen's brother. He was a barber and recalled having shaved Freel two days after the murder. All witnesses agreed that the man

Forner Stockton judge George Tyler found criminal law much more lucrative than the bench. *Author's Collection*

they had seen had a ten day growth of whiskers. Next George Foster testified as to seeing Freel in front of the saloon at the time of the trouble. The defendant was holding that a knife he wiped on his coat sleeve as he left. The next witness was an army deserter who had served time on Alcatraz Island. He too had seen Freel wipe something on his sleeve at the time of the killing.

Tom Field, the fiddler, was next on the stand. He had recognized Freel as he stood in the doorway with several others. Dave Long, a bartender, had told the men to move on or come in, and while the others left, Freel had remained. Long had pushed him into the room, but Freel had staggered back into the doorway. It was then that Allen stormed from behind the bar and disappeared behind the screen. In a few moments he reappeared, mortally wounded. Charles Hunney also identified Freel as peeking from behind the screen.

Judge Tyler's eyes narrowed when he saw the next witness. Robert Montgomery was the cook on the schooner *Donald*, moored next to the Vallejo boat wharf. On a hunch Isaiah had questioned various people in the area and had struck paydirt with Montgomery, a large black man. A man fitting Freel's description had come into Montgomery's galley early in the morning and asked when the Vallejo boat would leave. After begging a cup of coffee and a biscuit from the cook, he had asked for some money. The man also asked Montgomery if he had heard of the Allen killing, but the black man shook his head. Taking out a knife he said, "This is what fixed the son of a bitch. Allen didn't have time to say his prayers." The cook was leaving for the market and the two men parted on the wharf.

Tyler knew, as everyone did, that Montgomery had recently married a white woman who was in San Quentin for killing a Negro lover named Sanchez. Here was a good chance to try to discredit this witness and cast aspersions on all the prosecution's testimony. Tyler began a series of bullying and repetitious questions, but he only managed to bring out the fact that Montgomery had seen what appeared to be blood on the man's cuff.

When Tyler continued to ask insulting questions calculated to show the black man was either ignorant or lying, the witness refused to respond to further grilling. Gently, Judge Louderback coaxed the witness into resuming his testimony. Although the audience was greatly amused at the show, the cook was furious, as was noted in the press account:

Robert: "I didn't come here to have my name befooled and have the papers give a big account of that damned old nigger on the stand...."

Tyler: "Who is the captain of the *Donald*?"

Robert: "I don't know his name. He's a German and I don't speak Dutch."

Tyler: "Now, don't you know that you're lying?"

Robert: "I don't lie! Now look here, you're down on me. I ain't going to answer questions three or four times. I came here to talk about that man there, and not

to tell you about the ocean and the names of Dutch captains. I told you once I didn't know his name...."

Again Judge Louderback tactfully persuaded the black man to resume his testimony. For nearly two hours the pair duelled verbally, everyone agreeing that the cook more than held his own with the noted barrister. His most telling blow was when Tyler was trying to catch him in a lie and asked if he had ever cooked for anyone else in the city. "Yes, a good many," responded Montgomery. "Name one," countered Tyler. When the cook named Mrs. Sackett who kept a house on Fourth Street, Tyler then asked what kind of house it was and the black man made his move.

"I don't know nuffin about what kind of a house she keeps. You ought to know, I've seen you there after eleven o'clock at night." Judge Tyler quickly changed his line of questioning.

Jim Reynolds testified next. He was Freel's companion who had reluctantly admitted the two were on Pacific Street the night of the murder. Following Reynolds, Lees and Stone described the suspect's capture and reported how all the witnesses had separately picked him out of the lineup. In the end the case had come together even better than Isaiah had hoped. Tyler commented:

> Your honor, I must confess that the circumstances of this case are very suspicious and I suppose you will not hesitate to hold this man. But I wish to say that the statements of that man Montgomery are false in every particular. I haven't entered any house on Fourth street for eighteen months....

This brought on some unrestrained chuckling in the courtroom and after gavelling for order, Judge Louderback announced the defendant would be held without bail on a charge of murder.

The coroner's inquest, held the same day, also charged Freel with the crime. At his trial in late April, Freel submitted a plea of self-defense and managed to get off with a manslaughter conviction despite all his previous lying. He was sentenced to eleven years at San Quentin.

Theodore Cockrill. *Author's Collection*

A new police chief took office in early 1874. Theodore Cockrill was a merchant and the first Democrat elected chief since vigilante days. Cockrill had run a reform campaign, but in his meeting with Isaiah and other executive officers, they were assured no major changes were contemplated other than some steps to correct various abuses.

In early February Isaiah became involved in a nasty little newspaper squabble he should have ignored. Through quick-witted, hard work, the de Young brothers had established a subscription list of some 40,000 for the *Chronicle* and made their fledgling paper one of the largest of the dailies. Both brothers were still in their twenties, but they were tough and expounded a wild and woolly brand of journalism that often got them into trouble. Isaiah admired the

boys and knew they carried pistols. From the tone of some of their editorials, he probably thought it a good idea.

It had all started on January 31 when the *Chronicle* responded to a subscriber's letter. The writer complained of being blackmailed by another local newspaper, a sleazy and disreputable sheet called *The Sun*. The de Youngs recommended the complainant turn the newspaper's proprietors in to the police if they made any more attempts at blackmail. In a brief editorial on the subject they offered a mild character analysis of the *Sun's* owners:

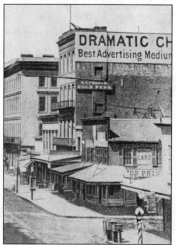

> ...Fitzgerald, the publisher of the sheet in question, is by his own confession a thief, a liar, a bigamist, and...a scoundrel. B. F. Napthaly, the nominal editor, is a graduate of the Industrial School, a professional blackmailer,...and...one of the most degraded specimens of hoodlumism....

The de Youngs knew both men well. Fitzgerald had indeed admitted to his character frailties in a court of law, while Napthaly had worked for the boys after being released from the Industrial School in 1870. He had been fired after various instances of drinking and petty thievery and had been in jail when approached to take an interest in *The Sun*.

The *Chronicle* building in the days when the de Young boys were building their newspaper empire. *Author's Collection*

That very afternoon *The Sun* retaliated with a verbal assault that libeled the de Youngs in very serious terms. The city loved a good fight and copies of the offending paper sold at a lively pace, issues being rented after the editions sold out. Fitzgerald was working at his printing press when Gustavus de Young, a younger brother of the editors, confronted him. He quickly punched the publisher to the floor and had beat him unconscious when several other *Sun* pressmen grabbed him. Gus beat a hasty retreat and joined his brothers in trying to run down Napthaly. They looked high and they looked low, but the *Sun's* editor appeared to have "set."

The de Youngs exploded in anger the following day when they heard another edition of the libelous issue was being prepared. They had obtained a libel warrant against *The Sun's* management, barring any legal issuing of the paper again.

Calling at police headquarters, Michael de Young explained the situation to Captain Lees and was probably rewarded with an amused smile. Isaiah tried to explain that there was no way of knowing if they really intended to issue the paper again. He couldn't arrest them for what they might do. But de Young was insistent. There was going to be trouble, possibly a shooting! He was going over there with his brother to find out what was going on, and Lees was asked along in case there was trouble. Reluctantly, the detective accompanied them to the newspaper office, taking along an officer in case there was indeed some difficulty.

At *The Sun* office the pressroom was found to be locked up. As Lees looked about for another entrance, Mike de Young kicked open the door. Inside, he pointed his pistol at several printers and told them not to move. Lees pushed him aside and asked if the offending article was indeed being republished. When he was convinced that it was, he put the printers into the custody of Sergeant Ward, and he and Charles de Young went off in search of a judge and a warrant.

Captain Lees had no sooner left than Michael began wrecking the shop and scattering all the type. When Isaiah returned an hour later with his warrants, the printers were escorted to headquarters.

That afternoon Napthaly heard what had happened and grabbed the first policeman in sight. Unfortunately, he was spotted being taken to headquarters. The *Bulletin:*

> ...The two were crossing Sansome street on California, when Gus De Young approached unawares from behind. When within a few yards of his quarry, Gus drew a revolver and commenced firing at Napthaly. The prisoner being unarmed, broke and ran from the officer, De Young continuing to fire some four or five shots. He was finally knocked down by a citizen....

Michael de Young, editor of the San Francisco *Chronicle. California State Library*

The officer lost one prisoner, but grabbed Gus and ushered him off to the city prison where he was met by his two brothers. The boys were discussing the day's events when Ben Napthaly, whose timing was something less than perfect, strolled in to again surrender himself. When Mike de Young pulled his pistol, Napthaly broke and ran. Mike was disarmed by an officer before he could fire and Charles was searched and arrested for carrying a concealed weapon. Gus and Mike were both charged with assault.

Ben Napthaly brought charges against Isaiah for his part in *The Sun* raid. The police commissioner's hearing was held on April 2 and, as usual, the veteran detective had prepared his case well. A parade of witnesses testified that Lees had not participated in breaking in the door or in scattering type, but had behaved as any officer would under the same circumstances. A typesetter admitted he was re-setting the libelous article and another witness testified that when he had asked for a copy of the article, he was told to come back in an hour. When Isaiah questioned Napthaly, the editor admitted the article was being re-set, but without his knowledge. After reading several passages from legal journals to support his actions, Lees was gratified when the board unanimously dismissed the complaint. The *Bulletin,* however, demurred:

> According to the unanimous decision of the Police Commissioners, Captain Lees was fully justified in the extraordinary course pursued by him in the *Sun-Chronicle* imbroglio....It is certainly at variance with the generally perceived opinion in relation to personal rights....

In February the police force had been increased by fifty-five additional officers. Lees' old friend Henry Johnson was one of the new policemen, and the two

must have reminisced about the old days. There were few old-timers from the '50s left. Most had either died, left the force, or been dismissed during political upheavals.

Isaiah had long lobbied for a records clerk to have custody of criminal records and the Rogues Gallery. When this new bureau was finally established in 1872, Officer Arnop "Tim" Bainbridge was put in charge. A native of England, Bainbridge had come to San Francisco from New York in 1865 and joined the department in January of 1869. The new clerk not only saved the officers valuable time looking up records and documents, but developed into a good sleuth himself and was eventually appointed a detective.

Arnop Bainbridge was put in charge of the department's criminal records, spending over thirty years on the force. *Author's Collection*

In February of 1871, Isaiah had gone to New Orleans and New York seeking the arrest of forgery suspect Louis Van Eten. The fugitive was captured by New York officers just prior to Lees' arrival. Isaiah remained for the trial and when Van Eten was convicted and sentenced to nine years in Sing Sing, Lees caught the next westbound overland train.

After learning Van Eten had secured a pardon in early July of 1874, Isaiah was again on a train heading east. Now in his mid-fifties, Van Eten had learned of an escape attempt and alerted the prison authorities. He was given a pardon for his action, but had no sooner left prison than he was picked up by New York officers accompanied by Captain Lees. The old forger still had a trump card to play, however, as was reported in the *New York Times* of August 3:

> Louis Maximilian Van Eten, the noted bond forger, who attempted to commit suicide by poisoning in the Hudson County [N.J.] Jail on Saturday, recovered conciousness yesterday, and hopes are now entertained for his ultimate recovery....He is to be conveyed to California as soon as he can undergo the journey. He was visited by Detective Lees yesterday, but he had very little to say....

After a brief rally, Van Eten died from the effects of the laudanum. As Lees prepared to return home, a message from San Francisco mayor James Otis caused the detective to alter his plans. He boarded a train for Canada on yet another investigation.

An 1870s San Francisco police mug book. *California State Library*

Earlier in the year Lees had become aware of certain suspicious incidents involving the county assessor's office. He had noticed several of the poll tax collectors making large bets at the race track. Curious, he checked on where one of

them lived and found the man in quarters which should have been far beyond his means. He noted the fellow wore diamond stickpins and dined at the city's finest restaurants and hotels, and the following was reported in a local paper:

> It was a delicate situation. Mayor William Alvord was just leaving office, but Isaiah sought a meeting and shared his suspicions. Alvord encouraged proceeding with his investigation and appraised the incoming new mayor, James Otis, of the circumstances.

Working alone, Isaiah now began a surveilance of four deputy assessors: Henry and Joseph Casey, Newton Morgan, and Alfred Eckstein. He spent several days watching them at work and became quite familiar with their tactics. "They very seldom gave receipts," Lees recalled later. "I never knew them to give more than a dozen or fifteen receipts to the Chinamen going on board the steamer. Sometimes one man would stand at the front of the gangplank and give receipts or stubs, and the other would stand at the head of the plank and take them away from the holders."

The detective captain watched them steadily and knew that the victims had to be given counterfeit receipts if the deputies were keeping the money. The assessor

The huge Palace Hotel dominated the San Francisco landscape for many years.
*California State Library*

had the genuine receipts in his safe and Isaiah wasn't sure of the difference between the phony and the genuine articles. He couldn't let the assessor himself in on the plan since he might very well be involved. "I did not dare to hunt up genuine receipts in the hands of citizens for purposes of comparison because I might by chance go to some friend of these deputies and thus spoil my plan," Lees remarked. Finally, he obtained a forged receipt from the previous year, along with some genuine items, while the assessors were off at the state fair. It was August before he acquired some

forged 1874 receipts and a comparison between them made the scheme quite obvious. Now he had to find where and how the bogus receipts were obtained.

After Van Eten's death, Isaiah received a wire from Mayor Otis advising him that Henry Casey had left for Montreal, Canada, to make some property arrangements. When he arrived at the Montreal depot, Casey was unaware that Lees was watching him from the shadows. He kept the deputy in almost constant sight for the next few days and finally followed him to an engraving plant where the counterfeit receipt plates were prepared. The detective managed to secure one of the plates, then stayed on Casey's trail to Chicago and Philadelphia. Lees was certain the printing was being done in one of these cities, but was unable to identify the source. Both Lees and Casey returned to San Francisco at about the same time.

On the ferry crossing the bay, Lees marvelled again at the magnificent Palace Hotel. It rose out of the city like one of the great bluffs on the plains of Nebraska and Wyoming. It was being built just west of his old home on Stephenson Street and when completed would be the larg-

San Francisco Mayor
James Otis. *Author's Collection*

est hotel in the West, and probably the country. Over 1,200 masons, carpenters, and laborers of all kinds were employed on the mammoth project. They were working on the seventh and last floor of the hotel at the time, and the huge structure dominated the growing city.

Back home again, Lees spent several days wrapping up his investigation, then presented his case to Mayor Otis. The evidence was obvious and plentiful.

During a police court hearing on October 3, Captain Lees was the principal witness. He displayed all the evidence and carefully explained the differences between the bogus and genuine tax receipts. After listing several hundred victims, the detective stated that he had many more that had not been catalogued yet. "Captain Lees," reported the *Bulletin*, "gave his evidence in a very straightforward, positive manner and the readiness and sharpness with which he replied to some of the questions of Mr. Campbell created some amusement in the courtroom."

It was estimated some $100,000 had been stolen by the deputies, but there was no indication of how long the scheme had been in operation. All deputies received richly-deserved terms in San Quentin.

## CHAPTER SEVENTEEN / NOTES

Conductor McCormick's hoodlum scrap is detailed in the *Bulletin* of January 20, 1873. The attack on Officer Forner is reported in the same paper on September 15, 1873. Western Addition home construction is reported in the *Bulletin* of November 1, 1873.

Ned Allen's murder is reported in the *Bulletin* of November 3 and the *Alta* of November 4, 1873. For the investigation and Freel's capture, see the *Chronicle* of November 4. Details of the police court examination are reported in both the *Chronicle* and the *Bulletin* the following day. Articles on the trial and sentencing appeared in the *Bulletin* of April 21, 23, 24, and 25, 1874. Freel was released from San Quentin for a new trial in December of 1874 and was convicted of manslaughter in late November of 1875. His sentence was for five years, but it was commuted on November 2, 1878. See *List of Convicts on Register of State Prison At San Quentin*, State Printing Office, Sacramento, 1889. Data on Ned Allen and his notorious deadfall can be found in Asbury's previously cited *The Barbary Coast*. The article on new Chief Cockrill was in the *Bulletin* on December 6, 1873.

The *Bulletin's* long account of the *Sun–Chronicle* imbroglio appeared on February 2, 1874. The editorial, "The Case of Captain Lees," was published in the same paper on April 3, 1874, with a long article on the hearing before the police commissioners in the same issue.

The article on the new police officers appeared in the *Bulletin* of February 3, 1874. Biographical information on Arnop "Tim" Bainbridge and his police career appeared in an unidentified obituary clipping in Volume 3 of the *Daggett Scrapbooks* in the California Section of the California State Library. Besides his connection with the criminal identification records of the department, Bainbridge was later appointed a detective and retired in 1907. He died in 1913. Establishment of the records department is reported in the *Bulletin* of March 18, 1874.

Lees' pursuit of forger Van Eten is detailed in the *Bulletin* of July 28, 1874. The *New York Times* of the same date gives further information. The *Times* of August 3 reports on Van Eten's attempted suicide and Lees' visit to his cell. The *Bulletin* of August 5, 1874, gives an account of Van Eten's career and death. A brief summary of Van Eten's New York bond escapade appears in Thomas Byrnes' *Professional Criminals of America*, New York, privately published, 1886

The investigation of the county assessor's office was detailed in a series of *Bulletin* articles beginning on September 29, 1874. Follow-up articles appeared on September 30 and on October 1, 2, and 3, 1874. Newt Morgan used his education and personality to obtain a position as clerk to one of the prison officials. By 1877 he was not even required to wear prison clothes, was known as the "Duke," and was the man other convicts sought out for favors. He had the run of the prison, frequently leaving the grounds to attend local parties and dances. He even managed to get a female convict pregnant. See the *Chronicle* for October 13, 23, and November 1, 1877. Details on the construction of the Palace Hotel were taken from a *Bulletin* article of September 29, 1874. See also Oscar Lewis and Carroll D. Hall, *Bonanza Inn, America's First Luxury Hotel*, New York, London, Alfred A. Knopf, 1939.

# Kidnappers and Rioters

ISAIAH LIKED NOTHING BETTER than to select a good book, light up a cigar, and relax in his favorite chair at home. He now possessed a large library. His crime books were kept at the office, but at home several bookcases were filled with his growing collection of finely bound volumes.

Despite his lack of formal education, Lees' literary tastes ran the gamut from poetry to religious works and war reminiscences. Western history particularly appealed to him. He was proud of the prominent California artists and writers—even that scamp Mark Twain. *Outcroppings,* the beautifully printed 1866 anthology of local poets, was always a joy to peruse. It had been published by his good friend Anton Roman and contained the haunting work of Edward Pollock.

San Francisco's own,
Toby Rosenthal.
*Author's Collection*

One evening in early March, Isaiah noticed a brief article on Toby Rosenthal in the *Bulletin*. Rosenthal, a twenty-seven-year-old San Francisco boy with a burgeoning art career, had been studying in Munich for years and had recently gained critical acclaim for an exhibition in Berlin. Although very representational, Rosenthal's work was often whimsical in character and quite popular. On a visit home in 1871, the artist had been commissioned to do a painting based on Tennyson's *Idylls of the King.* The finished work had been highly praised, as noted in the final paragraph of the *Bulletin* article:

> Rosenthal's last picture, "Elaine," created great interest and attracted sincere admiration at the last Berlin Exhibition of paintings. It represented the Elaine of Tennyson's ballad, Elaine the guardian of Lancelot's shield, whose flower-decked corpse, in accordance with her wish, is taken to the court of Queen Genevra.

When Rosenthal suggested increasing his price for "Elaine," he received no response from his patron, but he was able to sell the work to another local collector, Mrs. Robert C. Johnson. The painting was shipped back to the states and exhibited in Boston in early March. When "Elaine" arrived in San Francisco, it was displayed at the gallery of Snow and May on Kearny Street and exhibited as a charity fundraiser at twenty-five cents a head the following week.

All week long the local press devoted column after column to evaluations of Tennyson, Rosenthal's life, or minute details of the painting. The city was proud of its young artist and people flocked to view his work. By Thursday over 3,700 patrons had visited the gallery and "Elaine" had taken the city by storm!

On the morning of April 3, 1875, patrons filed into the gallery only to stare blankly at an empty frame. A frustrated attendant explained that the painting had

been stolen and the police were on their way to investigate. Soon hundreds of curious people were streaming through the gallery just to see the now-empty frame.

Lees pushed his way through the crowds to where the vacant frame was displayed. Any clues had probably been destroyed by all the curious visitors. He directed detectives Billy Jones and John Coffey to see what they could find while he toured the gallery with the owner. After studying the basement window where an entrance had been made, Lees returned to examine the empty frame. He noticed the canvas had been carefully cut from the stretcher bars. He could only speculate that it was to be held for ransom—a scheme not unfamiliar in the art world.

"Alas! Elaine," groaned the *Alta*. "Farewell Sweet Sister," wailed the *Chronicle*. Isaiah read all the papers hoping for a lead or idea, but he learned nothing new. He kept his men in the field talking to informants and nosing around the pawn shops while he attended to other matters.

The scar is readily apparent on the face of William Donahue.
*Author's Collection*

That afternoon Officer Wright interrupted him. There was someone to see him concerning the "Elaine" case. The visitor was quickly ushered into the detective captain's office and the door closed.

The caller didn't want his name involved in the matter, but he had seen several suspicious looking characters in front of the gallery the evening before "Elaine" was stolen. When one of the suspects was described as having a scar on his face, Isaiah's face lit up. He pulled a volume of his Rogues Gallery down from a shelf and turned to a page featuring a portrait of one William "Cut face" Donahue. "That's him," responded the witness. Lees barked orders at several of his men, then thanked his informant. This was an incredible piece of luck.

James Allen, another of the "Elaine" kidnappers.
*Author's Collection*

By evening detectives had located Donahue and his likely associates in the theft. The men were all followed, while their hangouts and rooming houses were being discovered. James Allen, one of the thieves, later recalled the events that night:

> ...We went around town until about a quarter to twelve when we went into Phil and Joe's saloon and was in there hut a few minutes when Jones, the detective, came in. He said nothing, but took a drink. As soon as he had his drink and went out, we all went out after him and met O'Neill and Murphy and Wallace walking up Stephenson street....We were wondering what the devil was bringing the police around here at that hour of the night and thought that something was wrong....

Allen should have acted on his suspicions. The detectives were "piping," or trailing, the suspects at the time and perfecting plans for their capture. Isaiah had already determined that a raid on the men in their rooms would be the best way to take them and shortly after two o'clock Sunday morning he and John Coffey entered a rooming house on Third Street. They knocked on every door in the place, prying open any that were locked. After handcuffing one suspect, the officers were leaving when they nearly bumped into Allen and Tom Wallace. "We just got in the front of the door," recalled Allen, "when Lees and Coffey jumped out and caught me and Wallace. Lees said, 'Allen, I want you,' so he ran us around into Stephenson Street and handcuffed us and Jones and Coffey took us down to the Station House."

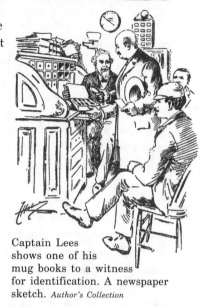

Captain Lees shows one of his mug books to a witness for identification. A newspaper sketch. *Author's Collection*

Meanwhile Donahue, John Curran, James O'Neill, and James Murphy had been picked up and Lees was confident they had the whole gang. Isolating Donahue from his pals, Isaiah convinced him the detectives knew everything. In a few minutes "Cut-face" was relating the whole story. Allen and Curran had been the actual thieves, hoping to hold the painting for ransom from either the owner, the artist, or the gallery. After listening to all the details, Isaiah jumped up and rushed downstairs, dragging Donahue along by the arm.

As Captain Lees hailed a hack, dawn was just beginning to break. In a short time they were on Langston Street, where Donahue singled out a shanty at the rear of a house. Inside, the prisoner pointed to

Cut marks along the edges are still visible in this image of the painting, "Elaine."
*Courtesy of the Art Institute of Chicago*

177

a bed in the corner. The detective sorted through some old clothes and blankets before seizing a roll of material labeled "Custom House Official Maps." Keeping an eye on "Cut-face," he unrolled the material and found "Elaine" spread out before him. It was safe and intact.

Back at headquarters, the painting was displayed on a table in Chief Cockrill's office. Word had quickly spread that "Elaine" had been found and crowds lined up at City Hall to see for themselves. "The scene," commented the *Bulletin*, "was suggestive of the remains of some illustrious departed lying in state." The crowd filed in one door and out another as Isaiah and Chief Cockrill stood to one side answering questions and shaking hands. Lees still couldn't believe his good luck. Just forty-eight hours had elapsed since the theft.

This is probably the portrait of Lees displayed next to "Elaine" in the art gallery.
*Courtesy of the Bancroft Library*

Prior to the display, the detective captain had informed Mrs. Johnson, Mr. Snow, and even Toby Rosenthal's father that the painting had been recovered. Snow, who had already cabled the artist to re-create the painting at his cost, was elated at the news.

Although receiving high praise in the local press for his work, Isaiah was even more flattered when "Elaine" was again displayed at the gallery. Now, however, in a large gilt frame next to the painting was a photograph of the famed captain of detectives. He must have taken Jane to the gallery to share his moment of glory.

Isaiah had previously considered running for the chief's office but had withdrawn when circumstances seemed unfavorable. This summer of 1875 he again tested the political waters but again dropped out, as noted in the San Francisco *News Letter & California Advertiser:*

> Captain Lees is an admirable candidate for Chief of Police, but he retires from the canvas. He finds that a nomination involved entanglements that would largely cripple him when he came to administer the department. His knowledge of what is required from the force teaches him that if he cannot be free to do the right as he knows it, he had better retire with honor, and he has done so....

It was disappointing, but there would be future opportunities.

Death claimed another old friend on July 30. Henry Johnson had been ill for some time, and as he sat quietly during the funeral, Isaiah must have thought fondly of the old days when he, Johnson, and Jake Chappell had been the three musketeers of the force. Now, both old friends were gone. Isaiah felt genuinely sad as he offered his condolences to Mrs. Johnson and the four children.

Another death struck even closer to home. In September of 1875, brother Joe died. He had been working on a steamer at Vallejo in January when Isaiah had

sent him some medicine. Now he was gone. Memories of the early Gold Rush days flooded over Isaiah as he recalled the two young brothers who had worked, sweated, and celebrated together so long ago. It was painful when he wrote out the particulars and gave them to a *Bulletin* reporter:

The new chief, Henry H. Ellis.
*Kevin Mullen Collection*

> Died—Wrigley—at Donahue, September 17, Joseph Wrigley, a native of England aged 61 years. Friends are respectfully invited to attend the funeral Sunday, September 19th at 1 o'clock P.M. from the residence of Captain I. W. Lees, 1022 Pine Street.

The fall municipal elections contest was between two of Isaiah's good friends, Captain Henry Ellis and former chief Pat Crowley. Both men were eminently qualified, though Crowley was labled a member of the "Ring," while Ellis was an Independent.

Undoubtedly, a prime reason for Lees' dropping out of the race for chief was his reluctance to run against two good friends. Such contests could become ugly, and already Crowley was being accused by the *Bulletin* of pressuring campaign funds from his men during his previous term. Although Crowley plausibly justified his actions, Ellis won the election. However, he had to work with Mayor Andrew J. Bryant, the "Ring" candidate, during his term.

In late January of 1876 Chief Ellis appointed nephew Edward Byram to the police force. A thirty-year-old local postman, Byram had left his Maine home in 1865 to follow his uncle to the West Coast. Lees liked the young man immediately and noticed that he kept daily journals of both his private and police work. The following month Byram was slashed by a Chinese burglar while walking his beat.

Though bleeding badly, he chased and captured his assailant. For years afterwards his scarred face was pointed out to rookie officers as an example of what could happen when you relax your vigilance with prisoners. However, the cool, new officer was widely admired for clubbing his attacker rather than shooting him.

In early March Billy Caldwell was being taken to municipal court for arraignment when he slipped off his handcuffs, dashed up an alley, and disappeared. Lees was furious. Caldwell belonged to a notorious burglary ring that had plundered the country's larger cities for years. After much work Lees' detectives had captured most of the gang, including Caldwell and his brother, Jim.

The men were wanted in various Eastern cities, including New York and Chicago. In Cleveland they had

The notorious burglar, Billy Caldwell. *Author's Collection* been interrupted during a large-scale burglary and had killed a police officer. Captured and jailed, the gang had escaped and fled to San Francisco where they planned to "work the town," as they put it. All were dangerous characters and invariably well armed. Maurice Duvall, one of the crowd, had shot and badly wounded a man whose home he was robbing.

Isaiah had only recently learned the records of these men and was determined that Caldwell, the reported killer of the Cleveland officer, should not escape. Taking Jones, Coffey, and John Meagher with him, Lees scoured

A Minna Street boarding house nestled next to a stable. Caldwell was captured in such a house, perhaps this very one. Note the police officer in the street. *California State Library*

the town for the next few nights. They combed the Barbary Coast and the sleazy lodging house sections, then sought out their stool pigeons. At intervals they met and compared notes.

After several nights they caught a glimpse of Caldwell in Minna Street, but he quickly disappeared. At four o'clock in the morning he was again spotted in a boarding house, dozing on a couch. He was using his coat for a pillow and had a cocked revolver in his hand. Getting as close as they could, the detectives suddenly swarmed over him and he was taken with only a minor struggle.

Of the gang that had arrived in town that year, Billy and Jim Caldwell were now in custody. Maurice Duvall, Henry Moore and James Kenny, alias McCarthy, were in San Quentin. Charley Perry had just recently been tried in municipal court and convicted

Handcuffs of the period. *Author's Collection*

on a burglary rap. Two other San Quentin inmates were thought to be members of the gang, also. The *Chronicle* concluded:

> ...To Captain Lees and his corps of excellent detectives, Coffey, Jones and Meagher, the highest praise is due for their untiring and vigilant efforts to house this gang. The Captain has received letters from all of the Superintendents East who were desirous of having the villains caged, congratulating him upon his success, and commenting in glowing terms of the efficiency of the detective force of this city.

John Meagher was one of Lees' best detectives. *Author's Collection*

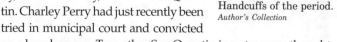

Isaiah had frequent conversations with the new chief about the city's increasing Chinese problem. Both men well remembered the 1867 South Beach riots and worried that the city was now heading for similar trouble. The oriental population had grown steadily, swelling the already bulging boundaries of Chinatown.

The Chinese Quarter now housed some 30,000 inhabitants, with thousands more arriving every year. The six-block area stretched from the fringes of the Barbary Coast to Stockton Street on the west, between Jackson and Sacramento streets. The anti-Chinese *Call* referred to the area as a "cancer that is slowly eating at the vitals of our city."

Just a few years earlier Washington Street had been a principal thoroughfare used for shopping access to Kearny and Montgomery streets. On Sundays it was utilized by residents attending the First Baptist Church between Dupont and Stockon. As the Chinese Quarter oozed out of its original boundaries, Washington Street was abandoned to the orientals who eventually even bought the church. Lately it had been converted into a shop for manufacturing, gambling, and worse. The old chapel had recently echoed to the shrieks of a Chinese being slashed to death within its walls.

No one in authority would deny the Asians their right to live in this country, to work or buy property. The Chinese customs, morals, and hatred of American ways, however, put them on a collision course with both society and the authorities. Their cus-

A street scene in San Francisco's Chinatown. The brick buildings lining the outlying avenues often hid appalling slums on back alleys and streets. *California State Library*

toms of tongs, gambling, and slavery made them a law unto themselves, and they seldom looked outside their own society for either help or protection. No respectable Chinese would even be buried in America, but invariably would have his bones shipped back to China.

In April of 1876, Mayor Bryant sent a letter to the Six Chinese Companies, warning that while they were entitled to full protection under United States laws, they must change their ways or trouble was inevitable. "I would also recommend you to

advise your countrymen in China of the present state of public opinion in this state," concluded the mayor, "and advise them to stay home."

There was also an increasing tide of juvenile crime in the city—assaults by the dreaded "hoodlums." They were a problem that wouldn't go away, committing assaults on the street and the interruption of picnics and other public gatherings by stealing and creating disturbances. The real horror of the hoodlum gangs was their seeming sheer joy in brutality.

As early as 1868 a gang of these young thugs dragged a Chinese crab-catcher under the wharves where they robbed him, then proceeded to beat and brand him with hot irons. Not content with this savagery, they slit his ears and tongue before running from the scene. Judge Louderback gave them maximum sentences whenever possible, but the hoodlum gangs were also suspected of many unsolved murders in the city.

Chief Ellis called the members of the regular police force together on the evening of August 19 for a stern lecture on the city's hoodlum problem. It was the fourth time he had done so, and he was both angry and frustrated:

> ...The residents of Hayes Valley are speaking of banding together as a vigilance committee for mutual protection. What a commentary on our inefficiency as guardians of the public safety! I am ashamed—and I hope you are—that the people should consider such action necessary for the safety of their persons and property....

The chief explained that hoodlums were frequently arrested, but witnesses refused to testify for fear of reprisals. After his talk the officers raised various complaints and Ellis promised to investigate.

In 1877 a general economic depression in the country was augmented by vicious labor strikes and conflicts in Baltimore and Pittsburgh. Unemployment and labor unrest were also serious problems in San Francisco. At large gatherings, leaders harrangued workers about the railroad strikes in the East and the burgeoning problems at home. Thousands of destitute and unemployed were given aid by various local organizations, while churches and other groups helped with the growing numbers of poor and unemployed.

The Chinese were convenient scapegoats. Having already alienated San Franciscans with their customs and exclusivity, the "Mongolians" could be hired at much lower wages than white workers and were monopolizing most low-paying jobs. In shoe and cigar manufacturing shops, they outnumbered whites four to one and had driven the wage down from twenty-five dollars a week in 1870 to some eight dollars in 1877. Both local and national efforts to resolve this problem were ineffective.

On July 21, 1877, a mass meeting of workers was scheduled for the evening of the 23rd. James F. D'Arcy, organizer of the United States Workingmen's Party, was to speak on the subject of solidarity with the Eastern strikers. Isaiah heard persistent rumors of trouble. In discussing the upcoming meeting with Chief Ellis, the two lawmen agreed that the city was a powder keg and it wouldn't take much to set it off.

In conferencing with his captains, Ellis concluded to prepare for the worst. The police force was divided into squads commanded by the captains with each to patrol a particular area. Fire was an overriding concern and in deploying his men around Chinatown, Ellis began to realize just how insufficient his force was. He contacted Mayor Bryant, and several national guard regiments were placed on alert and held in reserve at their respective armories.

Isaiah sent his detectives to hoodlum hangouts to see what could be learned. There were many rumors, and some anti-Chinese agitators reportedly were

Officer Michael Flannery saw duty during these troubled times. *Author's Collection*

going to take advantage of the meeting. After warning Jane that he would be out all night, the detective captain prepared for the fateful meeting. Perhaps all the rumors were just that and there would be no trouble after all.

Notices of the meeting appeared on the 23rd in all the morning papers. In

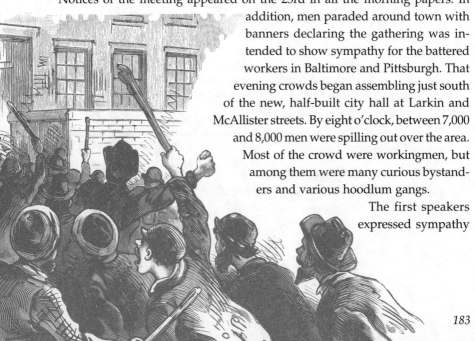

addition, men paraded around town with banners declaring the gathering was intended to show sympathy for the battered workers in Baltimore and Pittsburgh. That evening crowds began assembling just south of the new, half-built city hall at Larkin and McAllister streets. By eight o'clock, between 7,000 and 8,000 men were spilling out over the area. Most of the crowd were workingmen, but among them were many curious bystanders and various hoodlum gangs.

The first speakers expressed sympathy

for the victims of the Eastern troubles and spoke against violence and the destruction of property. The cheers seemed to assure a peaceful gathering.

By nine o'clock, as the crowd was beginning to thin out, the Anti-Coolie Club paraded into the meeting with a band and a group of followers. As several club members made inflamatory speeches, hoodlums began urging them on. Suddenly word spread that a Chinese was being attacked several blocks away. A portion of the crowd made a dash for the area, only to find two hoodlums in a brawl. Chief Ellis alerted his men that the hoodlums had run off shouting they were going to burn Chinatown. On Market street an officer was beaten and disarmed and his prisoner hidden in the crowd.

The situation was now out of control. A mob attacked a Chinese wash house on Tyler Street, breaking all the windows and doors and chasing the occupants down the street. Two policemen defended the shack briefly, but were pummeled into submission as the hoodlums sacked the place and then moved on to destroy another laundry. Breaking into a grocery store, the crowd passed out liquor before splitting into two groups. In a few minutes the sky was lit up as the wash house of Yee Wah on Geary and Leavenworth streets was torched. The screaming mob then rushed down Geary and began stoning another wash house and a fruitstand next door.

Police squads were now hurrying to their assigned locations. As firemen arrived at the conflagrations, they were stoned by the mob and fire hoses were cut. However, a crowd of hoodlums rushing towards Chinatown was suddenly confronted by a row of police stretched across Dupont Street. Captain Lees gripped a police club and cautioned his men to stand firm. The screaming mob stopped for just a minute, then surged forward. Lees later recalled that dangerous moment:

> ...We made a stand at Pine and Dupont streets. There were 2,500 or 3,000 men in the mob. There were young men, ranging from 25 to 30 years of age. I had sent one column of men over to the fire, but I ordered it back again. I divided the force into two columns, one resting on California Street and one on Pine. I ordered the crowd back, but it wouldn't go, when I ordered the Pine Street column to advance, and after a severe struggle it dispersed the crowd, part of it running up Pine, the other ran down Pine....Hoping to get in the rear of the police, but they there met the California Street column and were again driven back....I then dispatched Captain Stone with a force after them and he drove them clear to Meiggs Wharf....

The crack of clubs on hoodlum heads punctuated the curses and yelling as the police effectively dispersed the mob and closed the streets toward Chinatown. The *Chronicle* reported:

William T. Coleman once again took up the cause of law and order. *California State Library*

...The policemen behaved admirably. Their firmness and courage prevented a night of carnage and terror and the citizens of San Francisco owe them a debt of gratitude. Officers were stationed at all streets intersecting Dupont and no one was allowed to pass along that thoroughfare....

Some dozen Chinese wash houses were destroyed during the rioting, along with other buildings. The following day, a large number of merchants and property owners were called together by William T. Coleman, the vigilante leader of the 1850s. They were dubbed the "Committee of Safety" and were armed with heavy pick handles. Coleman placed his troops under municipal control and specified they were not to take any action except under direct police orders.

The following two nights were destructive and bloody. Catching what sleep they could during the day, the police were again out all night breaking up mobs and chasing down vandals and hoodlums. Several Chinese were murdered in their burning houses. The police fought with their pistols against a crowd of thugs who had taken possession of a building on Rincon Hill. When the lawmen and a squad of safety committee members charged up the hill, they succeeded in dislodging the hoodlums, killing and wounding several in the process.

Many officers were shot or bruised by stones, and a list of the killed and wounded of both sides filled half a column in the *Chronicle*. A huge fire resulted when warehouses at the Beale Street wharf were ignited. Thousands of gallons of burning whale oil also destroyed a nearby lumber yard.

And, suddenly, it was over. As though glutted on the mayhem and bloodshed, the unemployed, the union agitators, hoodlums, and thugs seemed to know the tumult was at an end.

A new political party was forged from the fires and rioting that had raged in the city. The Workingmen's Party met on sandlots, and Isaiah frequently attended their meetings. He watched with interest as a young teamster named Denis Kearney roused his listeners with talk of violence. From his constant monitoring of the pawn shops, Isaiah also knew the Chinese were arming. There would be more trouble.

A new police chief, a wine and liquor importer named John Kirkpatrick, took office on December 3, 1877. He was the last elected chief; from that time on they would be appointed by the police commissioners. At a reception held at Centennial Hall, Isaiah sipped champagne, puffed on his cigar, and wondered if he would ever be the guest of honor at such an affair.

## CHAPTER EIGHTEEN / NOTES

Captain Lees as a book collector is dealt with in the *Chronicle* of May 3, 1896. His extensive crime library is the subject of an article in the *Examiner* of July 14, 1889. Charles H. Shinn, writing in *The Overland Monthly* of October, 1888, remarks that "Captain Lees of the police force has a most admirable collection of about five hundred volumes of old Californian magazines and books." A complete list of the detective's excellent private book collection was compiled by his daughter, Ella Lees Leigh. It was published in Elisa D. Keith's "Report of Historical Landmarks Commission," The Native Daughters of the Golden West, 1902. After his death, Lees' fine collection was sold to bookseller Fred M. DeWitt, who lost it in the earthquake and fires of 1906. See the *California Historical Society Quarterly*, Vol. 23, March, 1944.

The Toby Rosenthal article appeared in the *Bulletin* of March 9, 1875. For biographical information on Rosenthal, see *California Art Research*, First Series, Vol. 3, WPA Project 2874 and William M. Kramer and Norton B. Stern, *San Franciosco's Artist, Toby E. Rosenthal*, Northridge, Santa Rosa Press, 1978. For a detailed story of the "Elaine" robbery, see Kramer and Stern, "The Great Elaine Robbery," *Journal of the West*, October, 1971. Excellent articles on the theft and recovery of the painting appeared in the *Call* of June 4 and the *Bulletin* of April 5, 1875. See also the *Chronicle* and *Alta* of April 3, 4, and 5, 1875.

Cut-face Donabue was sentenced to 5 years under the name Cloonan, while James Allen received a 7-year term according to the San Quentin Prison Register. Tommy Wallace, whose father had been implicated in the LaMeet murder with Cummings in 1863, turned states evidence on his pals and was discharged to go on to a lifetime of crime. See Edward Byram's Record No. 1 (one of three volumes in which Byram listed the names and records of both noted and obscure early criminals of the bay area—see later note in this chapter).

Isaiah's try for the chief's job is mentioned in the *Bulletin* of July 6. The quote is from the *News Letter & California Advertiser* of July 31.

Henry Johnson's obituary appeared in the *Alta* of August 1, 1875. His record as a Wells, Fargo detective was provided by Robert Chandler of the Wells Fargo Bank History Room, San Francisco. Joe Wrigley's death is reported in the *Bulletin* of September 17, 1875. A telegram informing Isaiah's brother that his medicine was on the way is in the private collection of Robert Chandler.

Political items regarding the contest for police chief appeared in the *Bulletin* of August 25 and 28, 1875.

When Edward Byram was appointed to the San Francisco Police Department in 1876, he began keeping detailed journals of his day to day activities as an officer. These large-format, bound volumes also contain pasted-in clippings, notes, letters, wanted posters, and mug shots of both famous and petty criminals. Byram's daughter Edith inherited the collection of journals and in turn passed them on to her son. This author is very grateful to the family for being allowed to utilize these diaries. Since Byram later became a detective under Lees, the diaries were an invaluable source of information. Besides his personal narrative of the encounter with the Chinese burglar, Byram had pasted several newspaper accounts and

follow-up articles in his journal; see the *Call* of February 20, 1876. The Byram journals are now in the collection of historian John Boessenecker.

Long articles in the *Call* and *Chronicle* of March 11, 1876, relate the story of the Caldwell gang.

The *Call* of March 27, 1876, contained much information on the Chinese, including "the number now in the city [and] what may be feared in the future." The *Call* had a tradition of catering to the anti Chinese crowd, as noted in the previously cited *Clemens Of The Call*. Further anti-Chinese rantings appeared in the same paper on April 10 and April 15, 1876. Nevertheless, the *Call* still contained much valid information taken from political investigative reports.

Judge Louderback's warning to hoodlums appeared in the *Call* of March 30, 1876. Typical hoodlum atrocities are noted in the same paper of August 13, 19, and 27, 1876. Chief Ellis' lecture to his men on the hoodlum menace was reported in a long column in the *Call* of August 20, 1876. See also his account in the previously cited *Kennebec To California*.

The labor problems and rioting during the summer of 1877 are well covered in Bancroft and other city histories. Richard Dillon tells the story well in his *The Hatchet Men* and a modern, more concise version appears in William Issel and Robert W. Cherney's, *San Francisco, 1865–1932*, Berkeley, University of California Press, 1986. For a real feeling of the horror of those tumultuous times, however, you can do no better than the contemporary press accounts such as the *Chronicle* of July 24–26, 1877. Lees' account of his confronting the mob appeared in the *Chronicle* of February 3, 1878.

The reception for the new police chief is reported in the *Chronicle* of December 2, 1877. On Christmas Eve, Chief Kirkpatrick's friends presented him with a handsomely engraved pistol and an ivory hilted dagger and carving set; see the *Chronicle* of December 25, 1877.

# The Great Duncan Hunt

ON OCTOBER 8, 1877, A NOTICE IN THE *CHRONICLE* announced the failure of the Pioneer Land and Loan Bank. The article was quick to assure its readers that this was an isolated instance brought on by faulty management. The other banking institutions in the city were perfectly sound. A crowd of howling depositors told many sad stories of lost savings and ruined lives, however. Isaiah had known Joseph C. Duncan, the bank secretary and general manager, for many years. Duncan had a shady reputation and his involvement in various lottery, gold bar, and land schemes had enabled him to acquire the funds to inaugurate his Pioneer Bank in September of 1873. He had acquired wealth and prominent friends and was involved in local church and social affairs. Because of his sleazy past Isaiah had recently looked into a rumor of the over-issuance of stock from another Duncan holding, the Safe Deposit Company. On the day the bank failure notice appeared, Captain Lees checked out the stock certificates and found they had been altered, rather than over-issued:

John Kirkpatrick, the new police chief. *Author's Collection*

...In one corner the figure "10" was written, then the word "ten" was written on the line in front of the word "shares," etc. In that condition the certificate was taken to Mr. Casserly for his signature. Upon being returned to the secretary, that official wrote after the figure "10" the figure "20," thereby raising the number of shares to 1020 and after the word "ten" he wrote "hundred and twenty shares." After having thus altered the certificate it was handed to Duncan who raised money on it....

The detective captain tracked down many of the certificates and found none dated prior to August 15. It seemed clear it was about that time Duncan realized his bank was insolvent. He decided to collect all he could from his faltering empire.

That same day, October 8, Captain Lees filed two charges of forgery against Duncan, but the wily banker could not be located. Benjamin Le Warne, Duncan's son-in-law and secretary of the Safe Deposit Company, was also missing. The detectives feared they had fled the city with some $800,000 in bank deposits alone. Thousands had also been raised on the stock certificates.

In the following months a careful watch was kept on all city exits, even

Wanted notice sent out for the fugitive Duncan. From Edward Byram's journal. *John Boessenecker Collection*

**ARREST** *son in law to Duncan.*
**BENJAMIN F. LE WARNE,** for the crimes of FORGERY AND FELONY, in RAISING and issuing fraudulent Stock of the "SAFE DEPOSIT COMPANY," of San Francisco, of which Company he was Secretary.
Englishman, Age 35 ; Height, 5 feet 8 inches ; Stout, well built, complexion dark ; Hair very dark--inclined to curl--very thin on top of head ; Whiskers very dark brown, curly, and parted under chin ; Short stubby nose--nostrils rather large ; Very dark heavy eyebrows ; Third finger left hand gone at second joint ; Conspicuous perpendicular scar (from sabre cut) on right temple ; Very little English accent ; Gentlemanly manners and appearance ; has been a LIEUTENANT in BRITISH NAVY.
**JOSEPH C. DUNCAN,** (the father-in-law of LE WARNE,) and late Secretary of, "PIONEER LAND AND LOAN BANK," for the same offence.  *Level how since 1849.*
Age about 60, Height about 5 feet 6 inches ; Hair iron gray--quite thin and worn rather long ; Eyes hazel gray ; gray chin whiskers ; slim built ; has a quick nervous way, and short elastic step ; very smooth and gentlemanly in his manner and conversation. Warrants are issued.
H. H. ELLIS,
SAN FRANCISCO, Oct. 9, 1877.  *Chief of Police.*

Joseph C. Duncan, fugitive banker, was the father of the famous dancer, Isadora Duncan. *John Boessenecker*

though the fugitives might already be in South America. Looking into Duncan's crumbled financial empire, Isaiah found him enmeshed in debt and mortagages that had crippled his business operations.

On a Monday morning, December 17, 1877, Chief Kirkpatrick informed Lees that Duncan and Le Warne had been discovered hiding at the home of Oscar White, a salesman for the Giant Powder Company. It was a terrible mess, confided the new chief. The previous Saturday he had been told the fugitives were suspected of hiding at the White home, but dismissed the matter as another false lead. The next day he had reluctantly put a watch on the house, but it was too late. Two men, identified as Duncan and Le Warne, were seen leaving the house on Saturday afternoon. To make matters worse, the White home was only three doors away from the chief's residence!

A grand jury investigation later revealed the two fugitives had been hiding at White's ever since their disappearance. Isaiah took pains to disassociate himself from the whole affair. When the *Bulletin* stated Lees had accompanied the chief when he finally searched the White home on Monday, Isaiah wrote the editor and explained he had not been asked to go along. Further, he had been required in court that day and couldn't have accompanied the chief in any case. The chief, the detective grumbled, was perfectly capable of making an arrest himself.

Since the Duncan disappearance Isaiah had never worked harder. A son, Willie Duncan, had been arrested, along with one William Du Vall, and accused of aiding the fugitives in their flight from the White residence. Little else had been accomplished, and Duncan was released on bail.

The city had been sealed off, but the fugitives could very well have left town over the weekend. Rumors were everywhere and although all had to be checked out, none were valid.

Isaiah established a pattern for searching the town and all likely places of concealment. Various friends of Duncan had to be watched and coupled with the constant searching it meant almost round-the-clock duty for the whole force. Every train, ship, wagon, coach, and ferry leaving the city must be examined. All the police worked long and tedious hours, although Ned Byram's journal indicates he had Christmas day off.

Duncan took Ben Le Warne, his son-in-law, and most of his family down with him. *Author's Collection*

Byram was assigned to "pipe" Willie Duncan and devotes many pages of his journal to following his quarry around town. The entry on January 8, 1878, reads: "Looks more discouraging than ever." Some idea of the desperate activity is reflected in several notes Isaiah sent to his daughter, who was ill at home:

My Dear Ella:        Feb. 15, 1878

Send me word by note how you are feeling. I am in great distress of mind about you. I would come home and see you, but am so deeply engaged in directing matters for the capture of Duncan that I cannot leave. Send me word how you feel Love, for I am full of anxiety about you. Send answer by note with return messenger.

         Your loving father, I.W. Lees

A ship seemed the obvious means of escape and the detectives made exhaustive efforts to discover the most likely vessel. A seventy-ton schooner named the *Ellen J. McKinnon* came under suspicion when it was cleared for a trip to Nicaragua.

The weather was stormy and miserable. While the *McKinnon* lay at the Harrison Street wharf, it was watched around the clock. The police contingency fund had long since been exhausted and Isaiah went to the Stevedores Association and was granted permission to use the steam yacht *Elaine*. The yacht was concealed at North Point and kept constantly under steam, to be ready at a moment's notice. Although the streets were torn up in the area, Isaiah ordered the fastest runner on the force, John McGreavy, to dash to the *Elaine* and report the moment the schooner left port.

At one o'clock on the morning of February 17, the *McKinnon* left the wharf and moved out into the bay. McGreavy made the run in just eight minutes. Byram was on board the *Elaine* and wrote:

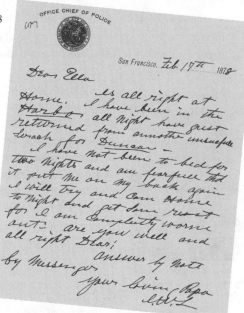

> This put new life into us and we were soon steaming down the bay, the wind was blowing quite fresh from the south. Off Alcatraz we hauled up on the lee side of the ship *Otago* and there waited to pounce on our prey....

The plan was to intercept the schooner before it got out through the heads, but if necessary, the *Elaine* could pursue it at sea. A strong gale and rough water made navigation difficult, but when the *McKinnon* hove into sight the *Elaine* was quickly alongside and the detectives scrambled aboard. Byram's journal detailed the drama:

> Making a hasty search, no Duncan could be found. Once more he had beat us, but all of his traps were on board...shirts, underwear, cuffs, a razor case marked "Joseph Moulder Duncan," two razors, pictures of the family...but the old boy himself was non est conectebus....We had dropped on the schooner too soon, the mate and some of the men admitted as much....

Lees quickly got his men back on board the *Elaine* and headed for shore looking for the *Joe Redmond*, previously seen alongside the schooner. One of the fastest tugs on the bay, the *Redmond* suddenly loomed up in the darkness, no running lights being in evidence.

When the tug suddenly pulled away under full steam, Isaiah knew they had been spotted. The two boats played hide-and-seek around Alcatraz Island before the chase culminated at the Mission dock, where the *Elaine* pulled up just four minutes behind her quarry. "A thorough search," wrote Byram, "was made of the *Redmond*, the wharf and all the vessels laying there, but no trace of Duncan could be found. A little late again." Men had been seen running from the area, but the fugitives had again made their escape. Lees was frustrated, exhausted, and drenched to the bone. His only consolation was giving an account of the incident to an *Alta* reporter, who closed with:

Officer Edward Byram. *John Boessenecker*

> The officers naturally feel chagrined at the unsuccessful issue of their enterprise...and claim that this is only one of a series of labors in this case which, when given to the public at the proper time, will entirely rebut the aspersions cast upon the department....An idea of the hardship endured in this affair can be found from the fact that many of the officers, among them Captain Lees, have had no sleep for sixty hours, being continuously on duty....

Isaiah and the rest of the force now stepped up the frantic search. They knew Duncan was in town now and desperately followed up every lead. Surveillance of all travel from the city was beefed up, and the officers and crew of the *Redmond* were subpoenaed. Duncan was obviously being aided by people in high places, and the desperate detective captain drove himself even harder to find the fugitives. An opportunity presented itself on the Friday following the *McKinnon* incident.

Ship in the bay just off shore from San Francisco, the scene of the fruitless, night sea chase after Duncan. Alcatraz Island is in the distance.
*California State Library*

Isaiah dropped into Oscar Lewis' Sutter Street saloon on the evening of February 22. Willie Duncan was there with Tom Van Ness and the detective talked with them for a time about the Duncan case. During the conversation Stewart Menzies, owner of the *Elaine*, came in and began talking with Lees. When the others wanted to go out for an oyster supper Isaiah begged off, saying he had some business to discuss with Menzies. Leaving Lewis' place, Duncan and Van Ness walked toward a Bush Street oyster saloon, while Lees and Menzies continued strolling down Sutter.

At Pine Street Captain Lees terminated his walk with Menzies, saying he was going home to rest. Rapidly retracing his steps, the detective took up a position where he could watch the door of the Bush Street oyster house. He pulled his hat down low and turned up his collar as he waited. The weather was cold and wet.

In a half hour Willie Duncan and his companion sauntered out and began walking up the street. When they split up, Lees followed one of them for over an hour. He never revealed which of the party he was "piping," only referring to him later as a "certain Individual." It was probably Willie Duncan. When his quarry met another man, Lees recognized him and knew where he was employed. The two went on home and Lees did the same. After napping for an hour and a half, he again headed back downtown.

The next day Lees cautiously told Kirkpatrick of his suspicions. He then began shadowing the man he had recognized the previous night. In the afternoon the fellow went to a three-story boarding house on Kearny Street. Following his quarry upstairs, the detective watched as he entered a room in an unusually careful manner. He waited for some minutes, but when the fellow didn't emerge, Isaiah returned to headquarters. There was no doubt in his mind. Every instinct he possessed told him Duncan had been found!

It was ten o'clock that night, February 24, 1878, when Ned Byram finished a surveillance and returned to headquarters. "There was something new in the wind," he wrote in his journal:

> Lees was there getting a crew together consisting of the Chief, Meagher, Jones, John Coffey, Dan Coffey. Cox and myself joined them in the upper office. Of the Patrol we had McDermott, McGreavy, Bee and Morehouse. Of the Substitute Force Kelly and Davis. [Lees] got us all together and said; I have reason to believe that Duncan is concealed in the building at 509 Kearny St. north of California on the west side, first brick building. I want you men to go in couples and in different directions and reach St. Marys street. There I will join you and tell you what to do then.

At the Kearny Street address Lees indicated the front, third-story windows and then detailed two men to the back of the building and two to remain in front. Others watched the roof. Lees then led the balance of the officers upstairs through two flights of darkened stairs. When one of them stumbled, Lees turned and hissed, "Who's that? If anyone makes any more noise, I'll kill him!"

# HUNTED DOWN.

---

### The Ex-Manager of the Pioneer Bank Captured at Last.

---

### His Arrest Last Night by Captain Lees in a Kearny-Street Lodging-House.

---

Joseph C. Duncan, the ex-Manager of the Pioneer Bank, was arrested at half-past 11 o'clock last night, by Captain Lees, at the lodging-house No. 509 Kearny street, west side, near California street. Since the failure of their water-front scheme, in which the McKinnon, the Redmond and the Elaine figured, the detectives had redoubled their efforts to discover the whereabouts of the great fugitive. The latest trail was struck by Captain Lees Friday night, and he followed it personally, until the labors of his department, extending through nearly five months, were crowned with success.

The story of this capture is, at present, a short one. Having satisfied himself that Duncan was quartered at 509 Kearny street, Capt. Lees, with Chief Kirkpatrick, took measures to proceed there and arrest him. The building was surrounded by a squad of officers, and all escapes cut off at front, rear, and roof. The following officers, besides Lees and the Chief, were in the detail: John Coffey, Meagher, Jones, D. Coffey, Cox, Gardenier, Mc-Greevey, McDermott, Morehouse, Byram, Bee, T. Kelly and Davis.

**THE ARREST.**

The building is a three-story house, and Duncan's room was on the top floor, a front room, opening on Kearny street. Capt. Lees went up with several

*Daily Alta California*, February 24, 1878. *Author's Collection*

On the top floor Lees halted before the front apartment door. At his knock the door was opened by a man who immediately recognized the captain of detectives. "You can't come in here," he blurted.

Lees recognized him too. Jamming his foot in the door he snarled, "By God, John, I will come in. Where's the old man?"

Duncan was in bed across the darkened room. He sat up when he recognized Lees. The fugitive was thin and haggard, with a full growth of beard, which he had darkened. The months of hiding had taken their toll. The detective captain had his pistol in his hand and was taking no chances.

"Don't move a peg or off goes the top of your head."

As the squad of officers flooded into the room, Duncan began dressing and was handcuffed. Several men were detailed to remain in the room while Lees led the parade back to headquarters. All the lawmen felt as though a great burden had been lifted from their shoulders. Detective Billy Jones voiced the sentiments of the whole force when he told a *Chronicle* reporter, "I would rather that a dozen McCoppin bills should pass reducing my salary than not to have captured Duncan tonight."

Exhausted by the months of searching, Isaiah could now relax at last. The police had taken a terrible drubbing in the press and now had been vindicated. The detective read with a grim smile a *Chronicle* editorial putting the arduous search in perspective:

> The force under Captain Lees have been actually worn out with their constant vigilance and hard service. Every road leading from the city has been guarded. Every vessel and every railway train has been searched. Hacks and all kinds of vehicles upon which he could have escaped have been watched. Hundreds of houses have been searched from roof to cellar. And this kind of work has been going on for four months and half without a moment of relaxation. Under these circumstances the officers, and especially Captain Lees, are deserving of the highest praise. They have won fresh laurels in their profession and are entitled to the thanks of the public. Captain Lees, whose persistence and skill finally triumphed over all difficulties, will add greatly to the credit of his office and to his reputation as a detective, which is already world-wide.

Despite indictments for forgery, perjury, and embezzlement, Duncan survived four trials and as many hung juries. Lees was disappointed, but he must have thought justice had been served after all when Duncan was reported lost at sea many years later.

Isaiah hadn't taken a vacation in years. He had long yearned to see Europe and now desperately needed a rest. Jane couldn't go. She was subject to asthma attacks and had to stay close to home. It was decided Ella would go instead, and Isaiah eagerly cleared his desk for the trip. He was provided some eighteen letters of introduction to European bankers and police officials to ensure as pleasant a trip as possible.

In late April of 1878, they were on their way and in early May were reported in Omaha on the first leg of their trip. Charles de Young and other prominent San Franciscans were along also, but Lees stopped for a few days in Cincinnati, telling his friends he would meet them in Paris. He couldn't ignore a loose end of the ordeal he was putting behind him.

A notorious forger named Carl Siscovitch had cashed some bogus checks during the Duncan hunt and Isaiah couldn't then spare the time to go after him. Receiving word Siscovitch had been picked up in Cincinnati recently, the detective stopped off in that city to verify the forger's identity. After pointing out Siscovitch in his cell, Lees demonstrated to local officials some of the forger's techniques for erasing figures on checks. Later he was wined and dined by the local lawmen, as reported in a dispatch to the *Chronicle*:

> ...Captain Lees was handsomely entertained by the police officials here. He has been escorted to all places of public interest and every possible courtesy has been shown him, he being well known here by reputation.

Isaiah was glad to see Siscovitch put away. He was an international thief who had escaped from a Turkish prison with Charley Becker and others in 1875, and was wanted in England on suspicion of murder. He was sentenced to a long prison term.

Charles Becker, an associate of Siscovitch in crimes both in the U.S. and abroad. Lees would later cross swords with Becker, also. *Author's Collection*

The trip to Europe was a fascinating experience. The detective visited London's Scotland Yard and the French Sureté in Paris. With Ella he toured the continent, being entertained by officials wherever they traveled. Soon it was time to return, and Jane was all smiles when they arrived home on October 14, 1878.

That evening a group of Isaiah's friends met at his home to welcome him back. Headed by a brass band, a large group of officers paraded down the street to his residence playing "Home Again," and "Auld Lang Syne." Colleagues and friends crowded into the house and Chief Kirkpatrick read a speech of welcome.

"Tonight," he began, "we are assembled in social union to welcome home our esteemed friend, apociato and companion, Captain I. W. Lees. His absence has been like a void in our midst. His return is like the birth of a new day, bringing with it sunshine, happiness and joy...." The Duncan chase was still fresh in everyone's mind

and the guests were reminded of how bitterly the police—and particularly Lees—had been treated by the press. It was recalled also how brilliantly he had vindicated himself and his associates after an incredibly difficult campaign. The speech was touching and testified to the deep affection and esteem in which Isaiah was held by his friends and fellow officers.

Remarking that "speech-making was not in his line," Lees gratefully thanked the crowd for this mark of their regard. Counselor Alfred Clark, Judge Ferral, and others also made speeches and the music and congratulations were kept up until a late hour.

In July of 1879, Chief Kirkpatrick filed his annual report. The force now consisted of the chief, five captains, a chief clerk, a property clerk, twelve detectives, twenty-five sergeants, twelve corporals, and 273 patrolmen. Over $142,000 worth of property had been reported stolen or lost, with $90,000 of it being recovered. There were now nine police sub-stations, two being connected to headquarters by telegraph. The riots had resulted in abolishing the Special Police and increasing the regular force accordingly.

The new city charter of 1879 provided for the appointment, rather than election, of the chief of police. In early December of 1879, Pat Crowley was unanimously appointed by the police commisioners to replace Kirkpatrick. Crowley had a long record of public service and the appointment was generally well received.

Rumors that some of the police captains would be replaced were quickly put to rest. Actually, the new chief didn't have the authority for such actions. Lees and Crowley were old friends dating back to the early 1850s and were well aware of each other's skills. As the powerful and famous captain of detectives, Isaiah's place was secure in any case.

Every inch the new chief, Patrick Crowley was an excellent lawman and powerful political figure as well. *Kevin Mullen collection*

## CHAPTER NINETEEN / NOTES

The *Chronicle* of October 8 and 9, 1877, reported on the growing excitement and speculation concerning the Pioneer Bank and Duncan's various financial problems. Duncan's early history is given in the same paper on October 11 along with an account of Lees' investigations. For more data on Duncan's life, see Adela Spindler Roatcap's, "Joseph Charles Duncan: Journalist, Art Dealer, Poet, Banker," *The Argonaut, Journal of the San Francisco Historical Society,* Summer, 1995. Chief Kirkpatrick's fiasco concerning the White family harboring Duncan is reported in the *Chronicle* of January 7, 8, and 10, 1878, which also explored the grand jury report on the incident. Lees' letter to the *Bulletin* appeared on January 12, 1878.

The *Alta* of January 12, 1878, reported the arrest of Willie Duncan and Du Vall. The letter from Captain Lees to his daughter is in the collections of the California Historical Society, San Francisco.

All of the Byram quotes are from his journal, volume 2, December 5, 1877–December 11, 1880.

Duncan's attempted flight by sea is described in much detail in the *Alta* of February 18, 1878. Lees story of events in police court was reported in the *Chronicle* of February 27, 1878. Duncan's capture caused tremendous excitement and was given extensive coverage in the local press. The *Call,* the *Alta,* the *Chronicle* and the *Bulletin* of February 24, 1878, gave every detail they could discover concerning the exciting events and Lees was the hero of the hour. The *Chronicle* editorial praising the work of Lees and his men appeared on February 25, 1878.

Duncan's various trials and eventual loss at sea are reported in Duke's *Celebrated Criminal Cases of America* and in the *Examiner,* November 13, 1898. For more on Duncan's history, see the previously cited Roatcap article, "Joseph Charles Duncan: Journalist, Art Dealer, Poet, Banker," and Allan Ross McDougall's *Isadora: A Revolutionary in Art and Love,* New York, Thomas Nelson & Sons, 1960. Duncan's daughter was the noted dancer, Isadora Duncan, born in the midst of all his troubles on May 27, 1878. Mrs. Duncan stood by her husband during his trials and the family was held up by defense attorneys as a model of probity. It was Lees' painful duty, however, to testify in open court that a woman was living with Duncan at the time of his capture. Duncan had brought her from New Orleans to San Francisco several years earlier, and when a baby was born he had abandoned her. She was living as a prostitute when Duncan again summoned her while in hiding. Mrs. Duncan quietly listened to the results of the detective's investigation and later filed for divorce. See the *Chronicle* of May 3, 1879. Joseph Duncan was reported lost at sea when his ship went down while on a trip to England in October of 1898. See Carol Pratl and Cynthia Splatt, *Life Into Art, Isadora Duncan and Her World,* New York-London, W.W. Norton & Company, 1993.

The many letters of introduction taken by Lees to Europe are in the Lees Collection in the Bancroft Library.

An account of the first leg of the Paris trip appeared in the *Chronicle* of May 1, 1878. Lees' stopover in Cincinnati is reported in the same paper on May 4. For Siscovitch's history, see Ben Macintyre, *The Napoleon of Crime, The Life and Times of Adam Worth, Master Thief,* New

York, Dell Publishing, 1997 and the previously cited Thomas Byrnes, *Professional Criminals of America.*

Lees' return from Europe and his welcome-home reception is reported on October 15, 1878, in the *Chronicle, Alta,* and other city papers. A copy of the speech welcoming Isaiah home is in the Lees Collection in the Bancroft Library.

A summary of Chief Kirkpatrick's annual report is given in the *Chronicle* of July 30, 1879.

For the political situation in San Francisco during this period, see Bancroft's *History of California, Vol. VII,* San Francisco, the History Company, Publishers, 1890. The *Chronicle's* fight for the new constitution is related in John P. Young's *Journalism In California*, San Francisco, The Chronicle Publishing Company, 1915.

Crowley's appointment as chief was reported in the *San Francisco Post* of December 1 and the *Chronicle* of December 2, 1879.

# A Stage Robbery and Other Mysteries

CHARLEY SEVERANCE LIVED AT THE LARGE Throckmorton Ranch in Marin County, across the bay. Employed as an agent and collector as well as a dairyman, he lived with his wife and Ah Lung, a Chinese cook and handyman. Severance made his regular rent collections the first of April, 1880, and was last seen at the Victor ranch on his way home. Mrs. Severance was out of town at the time.

On Sunday the Throckmorton cook was arrested at Sausalito while boarding the San Francisco boat. A neighbor, hearing the Throckmorton cows bellowing because they had not been milked Saturday night, investigated, and found no one home. Gathering others, the neighbors spread out over the countryside seeking their missing friend. Severance had returned home, insisted the cook, but was gone by the next morning when called for breakfast. Ah Lung made various conflicting statements, while Marin County sheriff George Mason looked about vainly for clues to the mysterious disappearance.

With mobs of Severance's friends threatening to take action if the law didn't do something, Sheriff Mason caught the Sunday afternoon ferry to San Francisco where he visited Chief Crowley. The chief and Captain Lees listened intently to the story of events as they had transpired to date. Realizing he was in over his head, the sheriff was frankly asking for help.

Isaiah agreed to take charge of the case. He wanted a free hand in the investigation as well as any rewards offered. The sheriff's only interest was in resolving the situation. Taking detectives John Coffey and John Avan along, Isaiah and Sheriff Mason were soon on the ferry heading for Sausalito.

At the Throckmorton Ranch Isaiah looked over the area, while Coffey and Avan began inserting rods into the ground at all likely spots where a body might be buried. Later Captain Lees went into San Rafael to interview the Chinese prisoner. Ah Lung crouched in his cell, the picture of despondency. He had accused a local Portuguese farmer named Jose Petars of being implicated in the disappearance, but no one really believed him.

Captain Lees was fifty years of age when he took on the Severance case. *Author's Collection*

When he became accustomed to the pidgin English spoken by Ah Lung, Isaiah talked quietly to him about his home and family in China. The detective listened attentively as he described a recent visit home and reunion with his many relatives. The officer sympathized with his present situation, urging him to always tell

the truth. It was a brief visit and soon Lees was riding back to the ranch to check on the progress of his men. Despite a great deal of probing and digging, nothing of significance had been discovered.

When several days had passed and no body had been produced, the locals began to think Severance might have merely left the area. But this didn't make sense. He was popular locally, had a happy marriage and children, and his parents lived nearby. The monthly rents he collected averaged about $1,500—hardly reason enough to abandon your family. As the whole area buzzed with excitement and speculation, Isaiah quietly probed and questioned the prisoner.

Another Chinese prisoner gave Lees an idea. Obtaining background on the man from Sheriff Mason, the detective interviewed him and proposed trading services. After the oriental was placed in Ah Lung's cell to see what could be learned, the ploy quickly bore fruit. Cut off from any ouside contact except the coaxing, prodding detective captain, Ah Lung eagerly received his countryman. The results of Lees' scheme was reported in the *Alta:*

> ...He gradually gained Lung's confidence, broached the Severance murder, and by constant and adroit tricks sought the coveted information. Lung knew his life was at stake upon his admission, and called every nerve to support him in his ordeal. He struggled hard to keep his secret, but his guilty knowledge and cruel inquisition conducted through his fellow murderer at last broke down his stolid reserve, and worried, tortured, and betrayed, he told of his crime....

Lees drank in every detail of the confession. Ah Lung had caught Severance at his milking and killed him from behind with an ax. Two Chinese accomplices had then shot him numerous times and dragged the corpse to a previously prepared

grave inside a woodshed. The cunning of the murderers was nowhere more evident than in digging the grave. Instead of a hurriedly excavated hole, the orientals had carefully removed each layer of sand, loam, and clay and deliberately kept them separate. When the body had been interred, each level of soil was replaced in sequence and tamped into place. Leftover dirt was scattered about the premises.

Back at the farm, Lees directed digging within the woodshed. A box containing a chicken's nest was removed and several feet down a man's arm was suddenly exposed.

A Chinese highbinder, or Tong warrior. *Author's Collection*

It was Severance and all the details began falling into place.

Mrs. Severance told Lees of a jacket she had helped Ah Lung make for himself. The apparel couldn't be found, but in checking a Chinese house in Sausalito where Ah Lung had slept the night of the murder, both the jacket and missing rent money were found. A pistol, with empty chambers, was also found there.

Several recognized San Francisco highbinders, or tong warriors, had called on the prisoner and were suspected of being his accomplices. Leaving Officer Avan to clean up any loose ends, Isaiah crossed the bay to take up other pressing business.

On the morning of April 18 large crowds gathered in San Rafael for the Severance funeral. Everywhere there was talk of lynching, but the crowds somehow remained restrained.

Returning from the funeral, Sheriff Mason and detective Avan looked in on Ah Lung. The corpse of the oriental was found hanging from the ceiling and turning ever so slowly. He had torn up an undershirt and fashioned enough of a rope to end his life. There would be no lynching that night.

Commenting on the case, the *Marin County Journal* of April 22 lauded the officer's work:

> ...And if it was a matchless piece of work by the murderer, the job of the detectives is no less so. It will give officer Lees rank with Vidocq and Mace. Sheriff Mason gives full credit to Lees. And he honors himself by it....The public are disappointed because the detectives do not give the secret history of their work. But they cannot. They rarely do. They may need to use the same methods again soon in some other place. It is probable that the culprit's suicide will cheat the officers of the State's reward....

Reverend Isaac Kalloch, dubbed the "Sorrel Stallion" because of his many affairs. *Kansas State Historical Society*

On April 23, 1880, San Franciscans were stunned by a not unexpected tragedy. The de Young boys had gotten into a squabble with a local mayoral candidate named Isaac Kalloch. In 1857, Kalloch, an itinerant minister and entrepreneur, had been caught with one of his church choir girls in a Boston hotel room and skipped out for the West after his adultery trial. He left a trail of bad debts through Kansas before showing up in San Francisco where he blustered his way into the ministry of the Baptist Metropolitan Temple. Kalloch was quite popular in the Bay City, but when he was nominated for mayor on the Workingmen's Party ticket, the de Young brothers were outraged. They published long and detailed exposés of Kalloch's sordid career, resulting in an ugly feud. When Kalloch began making reference to the old, scandalous *Sun* articles and threatening to reprint them in the summer of 1879, Charley de Young drove over and shot Kalloch down in front of his own church.

Although dangerously wounded, Kalloch recovered and managed to win election as mayor. His one term in office was undistinguished, however.

Charles de Young's shooting of Kalloch.
*Frank Leslie's Illustrated Newspaper*

Mayor Kalloch's son, Isaac M. Kalloch, was minister to a small congregation in the mining country. He had promised to see that Charles de Young was killed for attempting to assassinate his father, but when he had left town it was assumed the feud was over. De Young's trial had been postponed many times when young Kalloch appeared back in town in April of 1880. He was very morose and drank heavily. On a Friday evening he walked into the *Chronicle* office and shot down Charles de Young, who was standing at the counter talking to two men. De Young tried to draw his pistol, but died before he could get off a shot.

*Chronicle* publisher Charles de Young. *Author's Collection*

The funeral was large and well attended as befitted a leading newspaperman of the West. Isaiah noticed Amelia de Young wasn't present and later heard she had declined to look at her son's powder-burned face. The heartsick mother had preferred to remember him as he was and remained in her room during the proceedings.

Ella Lees had attended many social gatherings at Amelia de Young's home and was quite upset over the tragedy.

Claiming self-defense, young Kalloch managed to beat a murder rap and left town with his father when the latter failed to be renominated for mayor.

At the height of the late riots and labor troubles, Isaiah had no indication that one of his more noted exploits was being initiated. On September 1, 1879, a stagecoach rumbled down the mountain grades in the Gold Rush country east of the bay. Between Moore's Flat and Nevada City the coach was stopped by two highwaymen. One of the bandits held a shotgun on the passengers, who were lined up and searched alongside the coach. Banker William Cummings panicked when his valise was discovered. He tried to snatch it from the bandit and a violent tugging match commenced. The outlaw with the shotgun waited for an opening, then shot and killed the struggling banker. The coach was then ordered to drive off, leaving the body in the road. The bandits disappeared into the brush and trees with some $7,000 in loot, including a gold bar in Cummings' valise.

A posed stage holdup in the California foothills. Taken about 1890, the photo shows how Dorsey and Collins plied their trade. *Author's Collection*

The tragedy caused a sensation throughout the state but posses in the field could find little trace of the outlaws. Over $5,000 in rewards failed to create any immediate leads and weeks went by with little progress being made in the case.

The two robbers, Charles Dorsey and John C. Collins, were both ex-convicts from San Quentin. Promptly leaving the state following the robbery, the pair traveled to Arizona, New Orleans, and Louisville, Kentucky, then divided their loot and split up.

The murder was not forgotten, however. Jim Hume, Wells Fargo's chief detective, was first to isolate the suspects. Two masked men had been seen the night of the murder at Nigger Tent, a notorious resort just east of Downieville. The owner of the place, an old woman named Romargi, had sent some food and medicine to the men who were staying in an old mine tunnel. One had been wounded—probably by a shotgun pellet when Cummings had been killed.

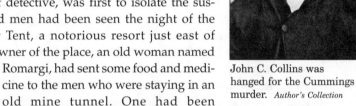

John C. Collins was hanged for the Cummings murder. *Author's Collection*

Obtaining descriptions of the highwaymen from his informant and the stage passengers, Hume then called on his friend Charles Aull who was at that time turnkey at San Quentin. The two men exchanged information and concluded the most likely candidates were Dorsey and Collins, the two ex-convicts.

The next break in the case came in December of 1879. A man named Sam Severs reported talking to Dorsey and Collins during a large Denis Kearny meeting in Nevada City several days prior to the holdup. The two told Severs they were camped a few miles out of town. With this information, Aull and Hume sent notices out to all the principal lawmen of the state, warning them to be on the lookout for the two fugitives. Lees received his notice and posted his men to keep a sharp watch for the outlaws, as the rewards were substantial.

Charles Dorsey, the murderous stage robber who lived to a ripe, old age. *Author's Collection*

In 1880, Aull went to work as a detective for Wells Fargo. When the Sonora to Milton stage was robbed in early November of 1881, Aull was instrumental in capturing the bandits. The notorious Bill Miner was the leader, but one of his partners, Jim Crumm, proved to be just as important to Aull. Crumm was another ex-convict and he promptly "fell down" in an attempt to save his own skin. Dorsey had lived with him for a time in Nevada County and had invited him to participate in the Moore's Flat stage robbery. Crumm declined at the time since he was making a good living stealing horses. The outlaw's testimony completed the chain of evidence leading Dorsey and Collins from San Quentin to Nevada County and the subsequent stage robbery and murder of Cummings.

Roger O'Meara. *California State Archives*

After splitting up with his partner, Collins had acquired a mistress and traveled about the country. He lived in high style until his cash ran out and his mistress left for greener pastures. Finding himself broke in Saint Louis, Collins was picked up on a burglary rap. He might have served a jail term and disappeared again except for a curious coincidence.

Roger O'Meara is reported to have had respectable California antecedents, but he spent much of his time trying to decide whether to lead an honest life, or one of crime. After serving three years in San Quentin, O'Meara was released in 1879 and took a job writing a history of Marin County. Later he worked in Arizona, then drifted to Denver and Chicago where he reported for a local newspaper. Involved in a Saint Louis burglary in the summer of 1882, he was soon once again behind bars.

While exercising in the jail yard, O'Meara felt a tap on his shoulder. Turning, he was surprised to meet an old San Quentin acquaintance, John Collins. The two exchanged news from the Coast and in the next few days became quite chummy. Collins mentioned the Nevada holdup and when O'Meara showed some interest he told him the whole story. He described Cummings' murder as well as the disposal of the loot in New Orleans and Louisville.

Later it occurred to O'Meara he had acquired information he could use. When he told his jailors Collins was wanted in California on a murder charge, a wire was sent to Wells Fargo. Hume was elated at the news and put Detective Aull on the case. O'Meara was assured by wire that his testimony would win him the sympathy of the court. Calling on his old friend Captain Lees, Aull proposed a joint venture.

Charles Aull, Wells Fargo detective and later warden a Folsom state prison. *Author's Collection*

Aull told Lees of Collins' appearance at Saint Louis. Photographs sent to Missouri had definitely established his identity, and Aull proposed Lees join him in picking up the fugitive and further investigation of the case. Isaiah readily agreed. A quantity of Dorsey mug shots were distributed to police around the country. The lawmen postponed their trip to Missouri hoping news of Dorsey would surface in the meantime. It was mid-September when the two detectives boarded the overland train and headed east to keep their appointment with Collins. It was a long journey and they arrived in Saint Louis on September 26, 1882. The *St. Louis Republican* reported their arrival:

PACIFIC PEELERS. They will take back to San Francisco an Alleged Stage Robber. Capt. I. W. Lees and Capt. Charles Aull of the San Francisco police arrived in this city yesterday and as soon as all arrangements are perfected will take away with them to the slope John C. Patterson, alias Collins, alias Kehoe, who is wanted in California on charges of murder and

robbery. Patterson is now confined to jail in this city on the charges of burglary and perjury. He has been tried on the first charge and the jury gave him three years in the penitentiary, but a motion for a new trial is pending....

The two lawmen hoped to obtain information on Dorsey from Collins, but that wily convict refused to even acknowledge them. When they showed him his Rogues Gallery photograph, he growled that he thought maybe he knew them after all.

In going through the prisoner's effects, Lees noticed depositions from a lawyer named Thorne in Union City, Indiana. The depositions alleged that Collins had been in Union City at the time of the burglary for which he was accused. There was the distinct odor of a rodent about the claims. In checking further, a letter from "lawyer" Thorne looked curiously familiar. It was Dorsey's handwriting! Hopping the next train to Indiana, the lawmen easily nabbed their quarry as noted in the *Union City Times* of October 7:

> Quite a furor was raised in our usually quiet city last Monday morning at the arrest of Chas. Thorne, partner of Moses Murphy, by two strangers....The arrest was made by Capt. Charles Aull, special officer of Wells, Fargo & Co's Express, assisted by Capt. I. W. Lees, Chief of the Detective Force of San Francisco. They found Charley eating his breakfast at Branham's restaurant and walking up to him the arrest was made without any resistance on his part. He was taken to St. Louis on the excursion train. During Thorne's (alias Law, alias Dorsey, alias half a dozen other names) residence in our city he has conducted himself in a straight forward business manner....At the time of his arrest he was engaged in the lumber business and was making a nice thing out of it....

Dorsey had surrendered without a struggle. Instead of resisting he played the mistaken identity ploy to anyone who would listen. The trio managed to leave town without incident, however.

Depositing Dorsey in Saint Louis, Lees and Aull concluded their investigation. They interviewed witnesses, collected depositions from Union City to New Orleans, and soon had the case wrapped up. Meanwhile, Isaiah was desperately working against time. Ella was to be married on October 26 and he had to be back home before that date.

Two tired and relieved detectives arrived in San Francisco with their prisoners on October 16. "Captain Lees," wrote a reporter, "remarked....that the trip from the East was tiresome and tedious in the extreme, and was rendered the more so by the ceaseless vigil kept over the prisoners night and day."

Isaiah received nearly $2,000 as his share of the reward money. The two outlaws were taken to Nevada City by Aull where their trial would be held.

The capture was celebrated throughout the West. The *Grass Valley Union* was particularly exuberant: "The manner in which the case has been worked up by Aull and Lees is one of the most creditable pieces of detective skill of the time."

Dorsey was tried first and sentenced to life imprisonment. One juror had held out against the death penalty because he and Dorsey were both ex-Confederate soldiers. Collins was also convicted and was hanged for the Cummings murder, even though Dorsey had fired the fatal shot. Isaiah attended the trials and brought along several San Quentin convicts to testify.

> Mr. & Mrs. J. W. Lees,
>
> Request the pleasure of your company at the marriage of their daughter Ella to Mr. Ernest A. Leigh, on Thursday Evening, October 26th, 1882, at 9 o'clock, at their residence, No. 1022 Pine Street.

The day of Ella's wedding finally arrived. Her fiance, Ernest Leigh, was the son of the city clerk, whom Isaiah had known for years. Two hundred invitations had been sent out, with some sixty people invited to dinner and dancing after the ceremony. Both events were held at the Lees residence on Pine Street. Among the guests were Mr. and Mrs. John Nightingale; Reuben Lloyd, the noted attorney; Mr. and Mrs. M. H. de Young; Raphael Weill, the wealthy merchant and superb chef; Chief Crowley, his wife and daughters; Dr. and Mrs. Martin Burke; Ben Bohen; Arnop Bainbridge; and others of the department. The home was beautifully decorated and the couple were married in the bay window under an elegant floral bell.

Afterwards dancing commenced until 10:30 when dinner was served. Dancing then continued until three o'clock in the morning. The couple honeymooned in the Napa Valley, and Isaiah was probably greatly relieved when it was over and his home returned to normal.

On the morning of August 16, 1883, three men were ushered into Isaiah's office. They introduced themselves as Sam Dixon, Donald McLea, and Mr. Fiood, all friends of a retired businessman named Nicholas Skerrett. A longtime resident of the city, Skerrett had sold a prosperous dry goods business and invested in real estate. Now he lived comfortably on rents and various speculations.

The men were concerned after not hearing from their friend for three days. Suddenly, each had received a mysterious telegram from Sacramento. The messages all conveyed the same story—that Skerrett had sold some property and was going to Colorado to settle the deal. All his local property was being turned over to a man named La Rue, who was referred to as "solid and reliable." None of the men believed the message was sent by Skerrett.

Wright LeRoy looked the part of the sinister lawyer he was. From a mug shot in Edward Byram's journal. *John Boessenecker Collection*

Sam Dixon lived in the same building as his friend and had seen the man La Rue on several occasions. Prior to

his disappearance, Skerrett had confided that he was indeed considering selling most of his real estate property to La Rue.

La Rue's description rang a bell with the detective captain. As soon as the men left he looked up the mug shot of one Wright LeRoy in the Rogues Gallery. LeRoy was a sleazy lawyer who had served time in San Quentin on a forgery charge. The description fit his mug shot and the similarity of names convinced Lees he was on the right track. He was sure whoever sent those telegrams would show up in person to help himself to Skerrett's belongings. When he contacted McLea to tell him of his suspicions, Lees was told that La Rue had already stopped by while he was at the police station and would return in a short time. Sending recently appointed detective Ned Byram ahead, Isaiah and Chief Crowley were later summoned to McLea's home where La Rue was being held.

Another mug shot of LeRoy from Byram's journal. *John Boessenecker Collection*

As they stepped into the house, Isaiah immediately recognized Wright LeRoy. A number of keys in the suspect's possession were found to open the door to the building and various doors and boxes throughout the house.

"Where did you get those keys?" demanded the detective captain.

"They are mine and I obtained them in a lawful way."

"Aren't these the keys to this house?" said Lees. But again LeRoy insisted they were his property.

"What am I charged with? Am I arrested?"

"You murdered Skerrett," stated the detective captain, "that is what you are arrested for. Where is he?"

"He is all right," countered LeRoy.

"If he is alright," said Crowley, "why don't you tell where he is? It will satisfy his friends if they know he is all right."

"No," growled Lees, "he is not all right. He is dead!"

Startled, the prisoner frantically denied anything had happened to the missing man. He insisted he had last seen him in Sacramento with two mining men. When asked if he had sent the telegrams to Skerrett's friends, LeRoy denied it.

"You did send those telegrams," said Lees. "The operator described you and will identify you."

At headquarters the suspect made a statement that Skerrett had gone to Denver with two mining men named Miller and Townsend, where they were to pay him off for all his property. The following day LeRoy called Lees to his cell and admitted his previous statements had been lies. Now he told a long story about

meeting two ex-convicts who had kidnapped Skerrett for money. LeRoy had agreed to help James Dollar and Thomas McDonald delude Skerrett's friends by posting notes on the doors of some of his property.

In questioning Dixon, Isaiah had learned Skerrett owned a vacant house on Ellis Street. Sending Detective Bob Hogan and a Skerrett employee named James Chichester to look over the property, Lees waited for a report. It soon arrived.

As they entered the house Hogan and Chichester were immediately confronted with a revolting stench. Hogan recognized the smell of death and they began a room by room search. Throwing open the door of a third-floor apartment, Hogan saw a closet which had to be the odor's source. The door was locked. When Lees arrived a few minutes after being called, Chichester opened the closet door.

Looking west down Post Street, from Montgomery. A view taken just after a rainstorm in 1880. *Author's Collection*

The fetid odor within the closet slammed into them like a wall and the putrified body was exposed. The corpse was half lying down, half sitting, with a hideous expression on the bloated and blackened face. Shielding his nose as best he could, Isaiah called Chichester over to look. Yes, it was Skerrett. He was difficult to recognize in this condition, but there was no doubt about the identity. In the summer heat the body had putrified to the extent that the blackened, jelly-like flesh was oozing through the clothes.

On August 27, 1883, an inquest was held in the Skerrett case. Lees testified at length, followed by a parade of other witnesses. The jury almost immediately returned a verdict that Skerrett had been murdered by Wright LeRoy.

"The Chief and Cap'n Lees," noted Byram in his journal, "visited the heads of all the papers and begged them not to publish anything as it would clog the wheels of justice greatly. They all promised not to, but the *Bulletin* and *Post* came out with it in their issue this evening."

Isaiah promptly put his investigating team together. John Meagher, Ned Byram, Bob Hogan, and John Coffey thoroughly covered the area where LeRoy lived, the Skerrett home, and the Ellis Street property where the body had been discovered. The

Sacramento telegraph operator was summoned and various friends and relatives who had identified the body were rounded up. Everyone who had seen Skerrett and LeRoy together was located and asked to be a witness. A negro chimney sweep had seen the two men enter the fatal Ellis Street house, and neighbors had seen LeRoy and two other men there. With his customary skill, Isaiah soon had a strangling net of circumstantial evidence woven around the accused killer. Meanwhile, a massive effort was made to locate James Dollar and Thomas McDonald, the two ex-convicts LeRoy had attempted to implicate.

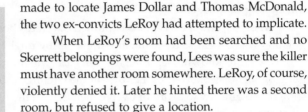

Robert Hogan was another of the astute detectives who helped make Lees famous from coast to coast. *author's Collection*

When LeRoy's room had been searched and no Skerrett belongings were found, Lees was sure the killer must have another room somewhere. LeRoy, of course, violently denied it. Later he hinted there was a second room, but refused to give a location.

Making six duplicates of a room key found in LeRoy's possession, Captain Lees directed a canvass of the area around the suspect's known room, but with no immediate results.

One night Isaiah and Bob Hogan went over to the Grand Hotel on business. As they were leaving Lees asked Hogan to wait for him on Market Street while he returned to the hotel for a moment. As he stood waiting, Hogan decided to try his duplicate key in the door of a rooming house at 620 Market Street. Amazingly, it worked! When Isaiah returned Hogan told him the good news and the two detectives returned to the address early the next morning.

Mrs. Ryder, the landlady, promptly identified LeRoy's photograph as that of one of her lodgers. In his room the lawmen found a grip sack and a large bundle of clothing later identified as Skerrett's. Other property of the murdered man was also recognized, as well as various personal items usually carried on his person.

The trial began in early October, with a packed courtroom. LeRoy's attorney, John D. Whaley, could do little more than fight a holding action, trying to discredit witnesses and accusing the police of threatening his client. When the black chimney sweep testified he had seen Skerrett and LeRoy enter the Ellis Street house, Whaley sneered, "Show me a nigger and

A note from Lees to several of his men who were working on a murder case in Marin County. He refers to his detectives as "My Dear Boys." The directive is in one of Ned Byram's journals. *John Boessenecker Collection*

209

I will show you a thief and a liar!" For this he was severely castigated by the Deputy District Attorney, Major Stonehill.

Isaiah spent much time on the stand. On October 5 he was testifying as to statements made by LeRoy when the defendant's counsel strenuously objected. Whaley insisted that anything his client said had been obtained by force and intimidation. "All of which," wrote Byram, "were a lot of lies. The Cap'n did not use any threatening language."

When a team of physicians exhumed Skerrett's body and testified that strangulation was the cause of death, any hope LeRoy might have had faded.

"So far as known," reported the *Chronicle*, "no human eye witnessed the strangling of Nicholas Skerrett by LeRoy, yet the circumstances of the latter's guilt were shown so plainfully to a jury of twelve men that on the first ballot, without an argument among themselves, they unanimously adjudged him guilty, and upon the first ballot as to the degree of guilt, placed it in the first degree."

Actually, it had taken only thirteen minutes to reach a verdict.

As counselor Whaley left the courtroom, he announced in a loud voice that "Guilty or not, it will be a long time before LeRoy hangs!" The crowd just laughed. "You bet!" someone shouted.

After the trial, the two elusive convict pals of LeRoy were finally located. Dollar's and McDonald's testimonies did little more than verify what had already been established, however, and there was nothing to link them to the murder. On January 16, 1885, Wright LeRoy was hanged for his terrible crime.

## CHAPTER TWENTY / NOTES

There is a long account of the Severance murder in the *History of Marin County, California and Biographical Sketches,* (no author given), San Francisco, Alley, Bowen & Company, 1880. The *Alta* announced the disappearance on April 5, 1880, followed by the *Marin County Journal* on April 8. Accounts of the investigation were published by the *Alta* on April 9, 16, 17, and 18, 1880. Ah Lung's suicide is reported in the *Alta* of April 19. On April 22, the *Journal* published its summation of the case, praising the work of Lees.

The *Chronicle's* exposé of Kalloch appeared on August 20, 1879, and took up much of a page. Kalloch's shooting was given wide coverage in the city press, the *Chronicle* account of August 24 being as restrained as might be expected under the circumstances. For a sometimes unreliable biography of Kalloch, see M.M. Marberry, *The Golden Voice, A Biography of Isaac Kalloch*, New York, Farrar, Straus and Company, 1947.

The shooting of Charles de Young was front-page news all over the country, and of course the San Francisco press of April 24, 1880, gave the incident much coverage. The *Chronicle* of April 26 reported the funeral and comments from other newspapers in the East. See also Bruce's *Gaudy Century* and Marberry's *The Golden Voice* for versions of the tragedy. Ella Lees' invitations to attend parties at Amelia de Young's home are among the Lees Papers in the Bancroft Library.

Accounts of the stage robbery and murder of banker Cummings appeared in the *Grass Valley Union* of September 2 and 3 and the *Nevada Transcript* of September 3, 1879. See also the account by Juanita Kennedy Browne, "The Murder of William Cummings in 1879," *Nevada County Historical Society Bulletin*, April, 1987. A detailed history of the investigation appeared in the *San Francisco Chronicle* of August 10, 1882, and November 30, 1883. The capture of Collins and Dorsey and the investigations in the Midwest are detailed in the *St. Louis Republican* of September 27 and October 10, 1882, the *Indianapolis News* of October 3, 1882, the *Union City Times* of October 2, and the *Winchester Journal* of October 4, 1882. See also the *St. Louis Democrat* of September 19 and the *Grass Valley Union* of October 4, 1882. Dorsey's conviction and sentencing are reported in the *Grass Valley Union* of March 2, 1883. After various prison escape attempts, one of which was successful, Dorsey was paroled in 1911 and lived an honest life, dying in 1935. Collins' hanging, following many appeals, was reported in the *Union* on January 2, 1884. There is a brief account of the whole affair in Duke's *Celebrated Criminal Cases of America*.

A collection of newspaper clippings and other memorabilia pertaining to her wedding was kept by Ella Lees Leigh and is preserved in the Lees Papers at the Bancroft Library.

Lees was involved in a great many other investigations between the Severance and Skerrett cases, including a trip to Mexico to retrieve an absconded official and various local forgery and fraud cases. The San Francisco newspapers gave excellent and detailed reports of the Skerrett investigation, but volume 4 of the Byram journals devotes many pages to the case—a fascinating, behind-the-scenes look at the work of the detectives by one of them. Besides two mug shots of LeRoy, Byram pasted into his journal many newspaper clippings describing the case as it evolved. The *Alta* began its coverage on August 19, 1883, and

reported on the coroner's inquest on August 28. There was good trial coverage in the same paper on October 5, 6, and 10. The *Chronicle* of October 10, 1883, announced LeRoy's conviction in superior court, while the *Alta* of November 1 and 2, 1883, gave the details of the minor involvement of LeRoy with McDonald and Dollar. The hanging of LeRoy at the county jail, along with a recital of the case, was reported in the *Examiner* of January 27, 1885. This case, too, is reported briefly in Duke's *Celebrated Criminal Cases of America*.

# A Fight for Life

THE SAN FRANCISCO POLICE FORCE had grown to number some 405 men by late 1885. City government had grudgingly increased the manpower of the department over the years, but as the city limits sprawled steadily westward into the sand hills, the department again lagged behind. Police patrol beats became ever more distant from main headquarters at City Hall, and sub-stations were established with holding cells where prisoners could be temporarily detained.

In 1850, the city had been divided into three police districts, from Rincon Point to the area north of Pacific Street. Now, in 1885, the city consisted of only two districts: north and south of Market Street. Captain William Y. Douglass commanded the Northern District, with Sergeant George W. Harmon as second in command. Their headquarters was in the basement of old City Hall where they supervised four sub-stations: North End Station at Jackson and Polk, Seawall Station, North Harbor Station, and South Harbor Station on Steuart

Captain William Y. Douglass. *Author's Collection*

Street. The North Harbor Station was commanded by Captain Andrew J. Dunlevy, who was in charge of the Harbor District.

Captain J ohn Short.
*Author's Collection*

The Southern District was commanded by Captain John Short, with Sergeant Thomas Kingsbury second in command. Headquarters was at the Southern Station on Folsom Street. Substations were the South Harbor Station, the South San Francisco Station and the Mission Station on Seventh Street, near Howard. All sub-stations were connected by telephone to the district headquarters, but most were terribly out-of-date and overcrowded. Rental of the stations ranged from ten dollars a month to eighty dollars, and Chief Crowley had long advocated the city owning its own stations, as it did with the fire department.

Peter Donahue passed away at his home on Rincon Hill late on the evening of November 26, 1885. Isaiah had seen his old friend occasionally at social gatherings, but both were quite busy. Besides his Union Iron Works, Donahue had constructed the city's first gas lighting system, built the first street railroad, and was one of the principals of the San Francisco and San Jose Railroad, which was later sold for over three million dollars. His later years were taken up with building the San Francisco & North Pacific Railroad in Sonoma County. A rush of memories must have flooded over Lees as he remembered the Gold Rush days in the old Happy Valley foundry. The city had changed so much since those pioneer times.

On the night of February 2, 1886, Richard Carroll's Van Ness Avenue home was burglarized. The theft of some $2,500 worth of diamonds was quickly reported, and Isaiah routinely ordered a list made up of the stolen property. As Lees was going over a printing proof of the notice, a clerk from the jewelry firm of Nathan Raphael & Company was shown into his office. A customer had brought in some jewelry to be appraised early that morning and the gems had been recognized as having been set for Richard Carroll some time before.

"What do they weigh?" asked the detective captain, who was acting chief at the time, as Crowley was ill. The response tallied exactly with the list Lees held in his hand. Isadore Cohen, a clerk in a Kearny Street pawn shop, had brought in the diamonds for appraisal. Lees grabbed his hat and headed for the Raphael store.

Burglar William Rees.
*California State Archives*

Isaiah knew Cohen and as he approached the Raphael shop he saw the jeweler and another man enter just ahead of him. The detective worked quickly. Asking Cohen to step into a curtained backroom, the officer followed the two men, then stood in front of the curtains, blocking the exit. By this time Cohen had called attention to his companion with several motions of his head.

Mistaking Lees for the owner, the stranger demanded he either be paid for his diamonds or have them returned.

"Who are you," responded the detective, "and where did you get those diamonds?" The stranger smelled a rat now. "My name is William Rees and the jewelry belonged to my family."

At this point Lees pulled aside the curtain and asked clerk Henry Myers to inform him when a Kearny streetcar came into view.

"Who are you?" asked Rees.

"My name is Lees and I'm a police captain. I arrest you for stealing those diamonds from Dick Carroll's home last night."

What happened next is best told by Lees himself:

> With that he caught hold of me and tried to fling me to one side that he might rush out, but I was as quick as he and catching him by the throat, backed him up to a table near a corner of the room and there I pushed him against the edge of the table to bend him over in order to get him off his feet, but that I could not succeed in doing. We struggled there for some time and he got one of his arms around my neck and tried to pull my face down to his. All this time he was grinding his teeth and I did not like that sound for I knew that meant bite if he was given the opportunity....

As they struggled, Rees once pulled the detective's face close enough to bite, causing blood to flow from a ragged wound in Lees' face. At that time Henry Meyers

came in and demanded Rees stop struggling or he would shoot him. The burglar managed to seize a cane on a table and dealt the clerk a fierce blow alongside the head. Suddenly Lees was startled and he reported the subsequent events:

> ...The next thing I know that fellow had a pistol up against my stomach and was trying to cock it, and as soon as I saw that I turned him around so as to get his face against the wall. He tried to get his hand behind him, but I worked on him til I got both my arms over his, above the elbows and then I held him as in a vise. But though I knew I had him secured, I could not disarm him.

Rees now made a desperate attempt to break loose, and the two men burst through the curtains and crashed into several display cases in the front showroom. Rees fired at Raphael, but missed due to Lees' implacable grip. A large crowd of people were now gathering in front of the shop wondering what was happening. Cohen and the clerks were terrified of the pistol-wielding burglar and afraid to aid the lawman. Lees' report continued:

> ...None seemed to have courage enough to render any assistance except a young plumber or gas-fitter, who came in at my request, took the revolver from the shooter and threw it on the floor behind us. Then the fellow became wilder and kicked. When he raised his foot I caught it with my leg in such a manner as to prevent him from getting it down again. At my request the gas-fitter...under my directions, hit the fellow alongside the head with a piece of gaspipe and then caught hold of his right hand, while another young man caught him by the left....

Nineteenth-century police nippers, when placed on a criminal's wrist, could be twisted and made quite painful. *Author's Collection*

At this time Officer Frank Merrifield suddenly pushed through the crowd and rushed to help the detective. He immediately clamped his "nippers" on Rees' wrist and twisted them enough to make the prisoner howl. The fight was over.

An 1887 view of Market Street. The streetcars provided an easy means of getting around the city now. *California State Library*

"The prisoner," noted an article in the *Call*, "was a powerful man about twenty-five years younger than the captain....Both were fagged out and each showed the strain of the struggle. The captain was bleeding from the wound on his cheek and one on the back of his right hand." "Lees," Rees told a *Bulletin* reporter, "was a tough old man."

In the confusion of the moment Isaiah didn't get the name of the fellow who had come to his aid. Later he located and personally thanked Thomas Ellis for possibly saving his life. When the young plumber expressed interest in joining the department, Isaiah was instrumental in securing his appointment. Rees was convicted and sentenced to a twenty-four year term at San Quentin.

Sweaty and worn out from his fight, Isaiah went out into the bitter cold and quickly took a chill. "The Cap'n," wrote Ned Byram in his journal, caught "a very severe cold from not taking proper care of himself after this tussle, and was confined to his house for several days."

Crime had become quite sophisticated by the 1880s. There was a new safe-cracking saw being manufactured that looked like an ordinary ribbon-bladed saw, but with no teeth on the blade. The blade was made of platinum and, when plugged into the electric light fixture that was common now in most large stores, cut through the iron of a safe twice as fast as an ordinary saw. Because this and other house-breaking or safe-opening devices were being used in various legitimate operations, they could be manufactured openly as tools for locksmiths, metal workers, and firemen. They were sold to the underworld through sleazy pawn shops and saloons and of course were exported throughout the world.

Contemporary newspaper drawing of
nineteenth-century burglar's
tools. *Author's Collection*

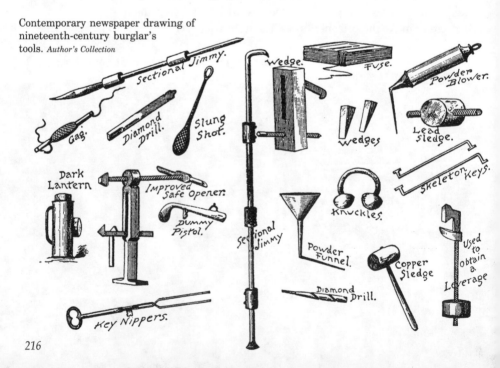

However, progress also worked against the criminal. The telephone was particularly useful in speeding up the gathering and conveying of criminal information. In September of 1886, Isaiah received a phone call from the village of Milton, in Calaveras County. The caller was F. J. Dake, a Wells Fargo agent in that town. He reported his safe had been broken into on the night of the 11th and some $1,400 taken. Also missing were a number of checks drawn by G. W. Grayson.

Sheriff Ben Thorn. *Calaveras County Historical Society*

The next day Sheriff Ben Thorn appeared at headquarters and gave Captain Lees details of the crime. Thorn was an old-time lawman whom Lees had known for many years. He was one of the most prominent officers in the state, having been appointed a deputy in 1855 and elected sheriff almost continuously since 1867. Lees respected him as both a tough, hard-riding thief-taker and as a detective as well. It was Thorn who had found the clues leading to the capture of Black Bart, the notorious stage robber, in November of 1883.

Thorn explained to Lees that two men had done the job and described in minute detail just how the safe had been blown.

"That's some of Schultz's work," remarked the detective captain. "Just the same kind of work he did before we arrested him back in '77."

Thorn then described two strangers who had been in the area just prior to the robbery. Lees again nodded his head. One of the suspects fit Henry Schultz's description, while the

other sounded very much like Charles M. Coleman, an East Saint Louis import whom the police had been watching recently. After some good surveillance work, several rousing chases, and a rough and tumble street fight, Lees and his men soon had the suspects in custody.

Both the prisoners were double-ironed when Ben Thorn and Wells Fargo detective John Thacker left with them for the return trip to San Andreas. As Isaiah shook hands with the sheriff, Schultz stepped up and commented with typical criminal logic: "Cap, this is pretty hard to have you push me the way you do. You know I haven't been bothering your city."

Burglar Henry Shultz had a long criminal record. *California State Archives*

Charles Coleman. *California State Archives*

A string of explosions had rocked the city recently. Isaiah and his detectives were convinced striking railroad carmen were behind the blasts, but no arrests had been made yet and the police were becoming more and more frustrated.

While uniformed officers patrolled the car lines, the bombers held back. When the patrols were halted, however, there were several more explosions. Byram devotes five pages of his journal to describing his riding on the cars and "piping" various suspicious conductors. He also writes of several battles with mobs of masked strikers who put obstructions on the tracks, then attacked the cars when they stopped.

Detectives were finally able to implicate several members of the striking Carmen's Assembly Union. The suspects were carefully watched on a twenty-four-hour basis.

Early on the morning of February 16. 1887, detectives observed John Stites leave his rooming house via a back alley door. It was after four in the morning and Stites' suspicious movements made the lawmen suspect something was in the wind. When he spotted the detectives following him, Stites panicked and began running. He was seen to throw something away, but kept running even after several warning shots had been fired.

Isaiah and Chief Crowley heard the shots while patrolling on nearby Larkin Street, but by the time they reached the scene Stites had been captured. A discarded dynamite cartridge was quickly found and a search of Stites' home turned up further damaging evidence. Another suspect named H. C. Dean was then arrested and his saloon yielded more bombing supplies. Byram wrote in his journal:

In April 1906, Charles Coleman was killed resisting arrest in Texas. *Author's Collection*

May 28, 1887. Stites was sentenced to States Prison at San Quentin for 2 years and 4 months. Dean got out of it. Nothing could be proved against him. The explosions ceased with their arrest.

It had been a long, hard investigation. "The Chief," noted the *Call*, "Captain Lees and officers engaged in working up the dynamite plots were very tired and sleepy last night, having lost a great deal of rest in working up these cases."

## CHAPTER TWENTY-ONE / NOTES

Data on organization and history of the San Francisco Police Department is taken from the previously-cited Luke Fay document and articles in the *Call* of September 15 and 22, 1885.

Peter Donahue's death was reported in the *Call* of November 27, 1885. For details on his financial holdings see the previously-cited pamphlet published by his wife, Dillon's *Iron Men*, and Issel and Cherny's *San Francisco, 1865-1935*. Donahue's forty-room mansion on Rincon Hill was surrounded by the homes of such dignitaries as Governor Milton Latham, William C. Ralston, John Parrot, Senator William Gwin, Hall McAllister, and William Tecumseh Sherman. Monuments to this pioneer industrialist are the town of Donahue, the terminus of his San Francisco and North Pacific Railroad in Sonoma County, and the memorial entitled "The Mechanics Monument," erected by his son at the intersection of Market, Battery, and Bush streets at the turn of the century. See Erwin G. Gudde's *California Place Names*, Berkeley, University of California Press, 1974, and Mildred Brooke Hoover, Hero Eugene Rensch, and Ethel Grace Rensch, *Historic Spots In Califoria*, Stanford, Stanford University Press, 1978.

Volume six of Byram's journals devotes six pages to the Dick Carroll burglary, including a brief account of Lees' fight with Rees. The *Call* of February 4, 1886, and the *Bulletin* of the same date give much more detailed accounts of the fight, each paper quoting Lees' own story of the desperate struggle. Rees was convicted of both the Carroll robbery and attempted murder in shooting at Nat Raphael, as reported in the *Call* of March 2 and 4, 1886.

Information on new burglary devices was reported in the *Fresno Weekly Expositor* of April 28, 1886.

The safe robberies in Calaveras County were announced in the *Examiner* of September 15, 1886. Lees' subsequent investigation and capture of Schultz and Coleman with Sheriff Thorn is the subject of a long article in the *Call* of September 18, 1886. Byram spends five and a half pages describing the incident.

Byram tells of the dynamite investigations in Volume 7 of his journals. Stites' capture is reported in the *Call* of February 17, 1887. His conviction and sentence are reported in the same paper on March 17 and 27, 1887.

# Jimmy Loses Hope

"OLD MAN" HOPE HAD BEEN RELEASED from San Quentin in November of 1886 and Isaiah had been watching his legal maneuvering ever since. Born in Philadelphia in 1836, James Hope had been trained as a skilled machinist at an early age. While employed by a safe manufacturer in the early 1860s, Hope decided it would be more profitable to put his skill to use opening them in the dead of night. Eventually he developed into the most skilled and daring bank robber in the country. Hope robbed the Philadelphia Navy Yard paymaster's safe in 1870 and a New York bank later that same year. Captured after the latter job, he was sentenced to New York's Auburn State Prison, but escaped with two others in January 1873.

Late that same year Hope, Big Frank McCoy, Jim Brady, and several others took the family of a Delaware bank cashier as hostages. Before they could loot the bank, however, a servant escaped and alerted the police who captured the whole gang without incident. All were sentenced to ten years and forty lashes for their attempted crime, but Hope again escaped a short time later.

Hope was credited with robbing the Wellsboro, Pennsylvania bank in both 1874 and 1875. In February of 1878, he was caught while attempting to rob another bank, but was tried and acquitted. Later that year he pulled off his most daring and lucrative job when he and several pals robbed the Manhattan Savings Bank on October 27, 1878. They took some $2,747,700, mostly in registered securities. Old Man Hope made his escape after this job, but his nineteen-year-old son, John, was picked up and sent to Sing Sing for the crime.

Feeling a change of climate might be in order, Hope headed west with Big Tom Bigelow and Little Dave Cummings. The movements of the gang are not known, but by June of 1881, they had surfaced in San Francisco. Lees learned of their presence from an informer and soon received indications they were in action.

A clerk at the Sather Bank reported finding plaster on his desk several mornings in a row and Chief Crowley and Captain Lees were soon prowling around the premises. On the floor above the clerk's desk the two lawmen found a section of floor had been removed inside a closet. Some checking disclosed the four-foot square opening was actually over the bank vault, behind the clerk's desk. Burglars had removed twelve

Little Dave Cummings.
*Author's Collection*

layers of brick and a like number of iron straps from atop the vault. They had labored nights the past week and the final protective covering of railroad iron was all that remained between them and their goal. Each morning they had replaced the floor boards and covered the area with supplies in the closet. The brick, mortar, and iron had been tossed into the wall cavity next to the vault.

Byram's journal noted that at 3:30 on the afternoon of June 27, 1881, he was called into Chief Crowley's office by Captain Lees. Detectives John Coffey, Billy Jones, Ben Bohen, and Ross Whittaker were also present and were briefed on the attempted burglary and the plan for the capture. Byram recorded the arrangements:

> Making all necessary preparations, getting tools, shotguns, keys, dark lanterns, provision satchel, stockings to wear over our boots, we separated to meet at the Chief's office at 5 o'clock.

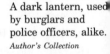

Byram, Coffey, and Whittaker took up their posts in lawyer E. B. Mastick's office directly over the bank, while Isaiah, Ben Bohen and Billy Jones waited in an alley across the street. When Hope's party entered the building, Lees was to signal his men to make the capture.

Hour after hour Coffey, Byram, and Whittaker waited patiently. They took turns watching the window for the signal, while one of them listened at the door for anyone entering the building. As the evening wore on, the third detective dozed on a leather divan in the office.

A dark lantern, used by burglars and police officers, alike. *Author's Collection*

Suddenly Captain Lees flashed a lantern signal. Hope and Little Dave Cummings had entered the building and proceeded to the closet. As Hope laid out their tools, Cummings went upstairs to another law office where he opened a window, creating an alternate escape route. When it was thought the second man had rejoined Hope, the detectives made their move. Byram recorded the subsequent actions:

Detective Ross Whittaker. *Author's Collection*

> Being all ready we sallied forth. I shouted to them to throw up their hands or they were dead men, the door leading to the water closets opened and closed and all was quiet. We made sure that both men were in there and I demanded it to be opened. I called a second time and a voice replied, "All right, I will." The door opened and one man showed himself.

Hope appeared and a moment after the capture, Lees and his men were bounding up the stairs. When told the other burglar was still at large and had disappeared, Isaiah rushed upstairs and jimmied open the door of Needle's law office. An open window indicated Cummings' escape route and Lees helped Byram through the window and onto the roof of Sorbier's restaurant. Cummings, however, had disappeared.

After all the intruder's tools had been gathered up, the prisoner was escorted to headquarters. He claimed his name was Thompson, but when he was stripped,

Byram wrote: "...he was found to be Jimmy Hope, the renowned Eastern bank burglar, having his name in india ink on his arm."

The rest of the night was spent trying to locate
Hope's room. At 6:30 in the morning Lees and his
men went out and had breakfast, then returned and
Isaiah again began grilling Hope. Finally he gave in.
Isaiah and John Coffey quickly drove out to 313 Geary
Street where Hope was rooming in a private residence,
a favorite ploy since it made him harder to locate.
They brought back his trunk and satchel. "In the
trunk," wrote Byram, "were 3 pair of nips, steel
wedges, gimlets, powder, dynamite, nitroglycerin and
a socket for a combination jimmy, which exactly
matched the jimmy found on top of the bank vault,
both made of the same piece of iron and sawed in
two. This will convict him."

Jimmy Hope was one of the most
famous, and "wanted," burglars in
the country. *Author's Collection*

When Isaiah escorted Hope to a photographer
for his Rogues Gallery portrait, the photographer told
a *Bulletin* reporter there were over 9,000 mug shots in
his collection now. Hope was furious at having his photograph made and tried
various gambits to frustrate the sitting. Finally, he gave up. "I shouldn't have to do
this," he grumbled, "when I haven't even been convicted yet."

While the detectives sought out the sources of the burglar's tools for evidence,
Mrs. Hope suddenly appeared in early August. She was kept under surveillance,
but appeared to be only interested in consoling her husband. Convicted in late October of 1881, Hope received a seven-and a-half year sentence to San Quentin.

Several Eastern lawmen were on hand when Hope was released in November
of 1886. Extradition papers from New York were signed by Governor Stoneman,
but were ruled invalid by a local court. Isaiah watched in disgust as lawyers and
judges squabbled for months over fine points of the law. It was late May of 1887
when Hope was finally found liable for re-arrest and extradition.

On the 24th, Captain Lees called in Ed Byram and told him he and Officer
Harry Hook were to accompany Hope and two New York officers as far as Chicago.
On May 27, 1887, the Hope party crossed the bay and entrained for the east. The trip
was uneventful, except for the crowds of people who gathered at the depots to see
the famous burglar. "He takes it in good part," wrote Byram, "he don't seek notoriety. Very good fellow traveler, kept him hand cuffed the first day and the two first
nights, then took them off and didn't put them on again. He said he was a gentleman and would go as a gentleman...."

Byram took advantage of his journey by visiting his hometown of Gardiner,
Maine, in early June. It was his first trip back home since leaving in 1865.

In October, Isaiah read that Sarah Althea Hill had won her celebrated divorce case against Senator William Sharon in the state superior court. The case was reversed in the federal circuit court, however, during the seemingly endless litigation. Lees had become involved in the case during its early stages, primarily to help his friend General W. H. L. Barnes. Barnes was Senator Sharon's chief legal counsel and Isaiah helped in the investigation of the Hill claims. When he and General Barnes were hoodwinked into buying some manufactured evidence, Lees quit in disgust. His hard won laurels as a master detective took a drubbing in the press.

Although there was a great deal of dismay when Sarah married one of her counsels, Judge David Terry, the couple seemed to be quite happy despite the difference in their ages.

The federal courtroom had been the scene of a terrible brawl the previous month when a "marriage contract" put forth by the Hill attorneys had been ruled a forgery. Ben Bohen was there and told Isaiah all about it. Sarah had blurted out an accusation that Judge Stephen J. Field had been bought, resulting in her being dragged screaming from the courtroom. Terry had pulled a knife during the melee and had to be disarmed by Dave Neagle and several other bystanders and officers. The couple served a jail term for their behavior and made numerous threats directed at Justice Field.

Judge Stephen J. Field.
*Author's Collection*

In her latest court appearance Mrs. Terry was again unruly. Her nervous attorney hurriedly plead her case "as if he feared a repetition of the famous courtroom scene."

Isaiah had known Terry since Gold Rush days and recalled the excitement caused by the Hopkins stabbing and Broderick duel. There had been other brawls as well. Terry had not mellowed with age and seemed to be a bomb destined to go off at any time.

Sarah, too, seemed unstable and apparently unable to accept her fate in the courts. Although the pair appeared contented enough on the surface, their destiny was not to be a happy one.

## CHAPTER TWENTY-TWO / NOTES

For a brief history of James Hope, see Byrnes, *Professional Criminals of America*. Much biographical information was also included in the press at the time of his death; see the *Call* and *Chronicle* of June 3, 1905. His wife's assertion that he "died of grief, broken-hearted because of the publicity which constantly kept his record alive" was greeted by yawns in both the East and West. His crimes had inspired the invention of time-lock safes, and it was more likely the resulting boredom from inactivity had caused his death at the age of 69.

Hope's capture was reported in the *Chronicle* of June 28, 1881, and in other city papers. A good first-hand account of the capture and investigation is in Volume 7 of Byram's journals. Hope's legal battles in seeking to avoid extradition are alluded to in the *Call* of February 27, 1887.

The news item on Sarah Althea Hill appeared in the *Call* of October 16, 1888. There are various references to the Sharon-Hill case in the Byram journals, notably when he was detailed with other officers to keep Sarah away from the funeral after Sharon's death on November 3, 1885. For the complete story of the Sharon-Hill case, see Robert H. Kroninger, *Sarah & The Senator*, Berkeley, Howell-North Books, 1964.

# Chapter 23

# A Detective's Library

ON FEBRUARY 1, 1889, ISAIAH RECEIVED WORD of Bill Rees' escape from San Quentin. The erstwhile burglar probably left the state, since he was never recaptured or heard from again in California.

Late the previous year Chief Crowley was made aware that his Chinatown police squad was heavily involved in taking bribes from the quarter's vice lords. There were always rumors that police were being paid off, particularly those assigned to Chinatown. Here was where the temptation was greatest, and to minimize any straying from duty, Crowley often rotated assignments to that area.

Sergeant George L. Gano was a ten-year veteran of the force when he took charge of the Chinatown squad in December of 1888. Four policemen were under his command, but Gano quickly asked that Officer McEvoy be replaced. Crowley complied with the request, although Gano's stated reason—that McEvoy was a "crank" and couldn't get along on his beat—seemed rather unusual.

The chief's clerk was discussing the McEvoy change with Officer Hugh Monahan one day when the patrolman intimated Gano was not doing his duty. "What do you mean?" inquired the clerk. "I mean he's taking money over there," responded Monahan.

The officer agreed to repeat his charge to Chief Crowley, who was visibly skeptical. Finally, he agreed to an investigation and Monahan spent the next week shadowing Gano to see what he could discover. He reported back to Crowley that Gano was indeed taking bribes from the Chinese Tan game gamblers and lottery merchants. He also reported that Sergeant Gano would be picking up his regular payoff the following Saturday night, at the corner of Jackson and Ross Alley, between ten o'clock and one in the morning.

When Gano didn't show up at that location for several Saturdays in a row, Crowley told Monahan to forget the whole thing. The officer was adamant,

Ross Alley stretched between Washington and Jackson streets, in the heart of Chinatown.
*California State Library*

however. He insisted he was right, and he reminded Crowley of how McEvoy had obviously refused to go along with Gano's schemes. Crowley now assigned Monahan to the Chinatown squad. During his first night out, a watchman told him the other officers were taking payoffs and he might as well get his share. When he agreed, a Chinese visitor paid him seventy dollars the very next night.

Monahan talked to the other members of the squad, including officers Chrystal, Robinson, and McCarthy. While making no accusations, they all intimated Gano was a "hog," that he wanted more than his share, and that they were being short-changed.

The honest officer now reported back to Crowley and turned over the seventy-dollar bribe. After a full report of the investigation, Crowley placed the case before the police commissioners. The grand jury brought indictments and caused the arrest of Sergeant Gano on February 19, 1889. He and his squad each faced a possible prison sentence of ten years if convicted.

Crowley was clearly upset over the incident and downplayed the affair to the press, remarking upon Gano's fine past record. But he was glad he had been able to clean up his own mess. A new squad was assigned to Chinatown, with freshly appointed Sergeant Monahan in Gano's place.

Bookplate of Isaiah Lees.
*Robert Chandler Collection*

An *Examiner* reporter cornered Captain Lees in mid-July of 1889. The detective's love of books was well-known, but the reporter sought to separate his history and literary interests from his notable collection of criminal volumes that burdened the shelves in his City Hall office. Isaiah was always delighted to discuss his more esoteric interests, even if with a reporter having an ulterior motive. The article proved to be quite interesting:

> If Captain Lees tomorrow were to collar the Whitechapel fiend, [Jack-the-Ripper] and be able to establish his identity by the clearest proofs, he would make no mention of the circumstance in the upper office, and treat it as an everyday occurence. When he runs down and scoops in a rare specimen of criminal literature the case is different. He glories in his success, brags of his achievement and will spend hours telling his friends how he was enabled to make the capture. He would not exactly give up the chase of a murderer in order to catch a coveted book on the wing, but if he could manage to drive his man down in the direction of the book and bring the book and the criminal back in the same car, his triumph would be complete.

The reporter was astonished at the scope of the detective's criminal library. Besides volumes dealing with murders dating back to the time of Socrates, there were works on gambling and criminal histories of New York, Chicago, London, and Paris. Isaiah pointed out shelves of work, in a locked case, on prostitution by Pierre Dufour, A. J. B. Parent, Du Challet, and W. W. Sanger. Charts and graphs showing fluctuations and effects of the "social evil" filled these works. A chart in Dufour indicated there were four times as many "unfortunates" in Paris in 1832 as there had been in 1817.

"Here," commented Lees, as he took a small volume from the shelf, "is a book which at first glance seems to have no connection with crime. It is a sort of agricultural report, and what I wish to call your attention to is a chart showing the fluctuations of the price of wheat for the period covered by Dufour."

The detective pointed out how the price and scarcity of wheat directly affected the increase or decrease of vice. The graphs made it quite clear that as the crops failed in a bad year, the daughters of the farmers went out on the streets to support their families. "The daughter's shame," as Isaiah put it, "was the last barrier against famine."

There was a series of bulky, leather-bound volumes of crime in Great Britain in which the detective took particular pride: the history of crime in England—*The Newgate Calendar, Haunted London* and many others.

"These two volumes," continued the lawman, "cost me considerable time and trouble to secure. I ran one (down) in London and the other in Philadelphia. I was on the trail of this one five years. It once belonged to a noted London detective, and I was anxious to get it on that account."

Chief Patrick Crowley.
*Author's Collection*

After displaying other treasures, such as an autograph of the great French detective Vidocq, various historical death warrants, and manuscript confessions of noted murderers, Isaiah ushered the scribe from his office so both of them might return to work.

In July the board of supervisors announced that $20,000 in tax levies had been set aside for signal and telephone boxes along every police beat in the city. This would enable officers to call in news and reports and greatly facilitate emergency response time. The system was already in use in Oakland and had been advocated by Chief Crowley for some time.

Along with the telephone boxes, it was again proposed that a patrol wagon be brought into service such as was used in other large cities. The wagon would be equipped with stretchers, handcuffs, first aid supplies, blankets, and other necessary equipment. A gong would ring as the wagon sped to its destination and it too would greatly facilitate the effectiveness of the department. Year after year Crowley had asked for new, more modern equipment, but his voice was seldom heard. There were always other places for the money to go. Maybe this time it would be different. Chief Crowley's annual report was delivered to the board of supervisors on July 19. The chief made his usual requests, also asking for the purchase of lots on which to erect modern police stations and for a mounted patrol for the outlying

districts. He also sought to increase lottery fines and to prohibit shooting galleries in Chinatown.

More than 23,000 arrests had been made, with just about half resulting in convictions; 388 lost children had been restored to their families; and of some $108,000 worth of stolen property reported, over $58,000 had been recovered. The number of licensed whiskey saloons was enumerated at 2,961.

Judge David S. Terry.
*California State Library*

On Wednesday morning, August 14, 1889, word of the tragedy at Lathrop reached the central police station. One of the detectives probably stuck his head in Isaiah's office to tell him that Judge David Terry had been killed while assaulting Justice Field. Trouble had long been expected.

The Terrys had continued to press appeals and countersuits in the courts after the Sharon business had been decided. When decisions were adverse to their interests, Sarah insisted on filing new litigation. Still bitter and vindictive over their stint in the Alameda jail, Terry and his wife made threats resulting in Captain Lees being summoned to the Palace Hotel on the evening of September 20. He was asked to provide an escort when Judge Field took the train to the Oregon border on his way east. Concerned that some of Terry's friends might be dangerous, several of Field's associates were willing to sustain the cost. Later Lees took Byram over to the Palace and made arrangements for him to accompany Field and his family north.

In October of 1888, Byram was retained again to escort federal judge Lorenzo Sawyer, who had also been threatened by the Terrys. When Judge Field returned to California the following year, Byram met the train at Truckee on June 19 and traveled with him to Oakland. Here they were greeted by United States marshal John C. Franks and deputy marshal David Neagle, who had been appointed bodyguard to Field during his stay in the state. Neagle and Byram then accompanied the judge's party to the Palace Hotel.

The restaurant at Lathrop where Dave Neagle shot down Judge Terry.
*Holt-Atherton Center for Western Studies, University of the Pacific*

In mid-August Judge Field was returning to San Francisco after attending court in Los Angeles. He was surprised to learn the Terrys had boarded the same train at Fresno. When a breakfast stop was made at Lathrop, a concerned Neagle suggested Field eat on the train. The jurist wanted to stretch his legs, however, and Neagle escorted his charge into the railroad restaurant.

Inside, Field was forking down his sausage and eggs when the giant figure of Terry loomed up behind him. Striking Field with a blow to the head, Terry was preparing to strike again when Neagle swiftly drew his pistol and jumped up. Even as he shouted "Stop!" Neagle fired twice at the snarling figure, and Terry fell sprawling in the aisle with a mortal wound. He lived only a few moments, as his screaming wife rushed in and

The beautiful Sarah Hill Terry was as much the cause of her husband's death as Dave Neagle. *Author's Collection*

threw herself on the body. Neagle pushed Field against the wall and shouted that he was a marshal protecting a United States judge. The two men quickly made their way back to the train.

The killing caused a sensation throughout the country. While Dave Neagle was briefly being held in the Stockton jail, Californians were wondering just who this diminutive gunman was. Isaiah knew most officials in the city and was acquainted with Neagle. Raised in San Francisco, Neagle had spent most of his adult life mining and drifting about the West. For the past few years he had been serving as a deputy sheriff and license collector, an appointee of Democratic party boss Chris Buckley. During several elections he had seen duty as a deputy U.S. marshal in particularly tough city precincts and had helped disarm Judge Terry during the courtroom melee that had eventually led to the Lathrop tragedy.

The papers were full of Neagle for the next few weeks. He had been orphaned when quite young and was mining in Western boom towns while still in his teens. After a shooting scrape at Pioche, Nevada, he had moved to Panamint, California, where he owned a saloon. In Arizona he was a mining contractor, a deputy sheriff, and chief of police at Tombstone. He killed a desperado in a personal encounter there before moving on to Butte, Montana, where he was involved in another shooting when a partner skipped out with some mutual funds. In 1884, Dave returned to San Francisco where his wife and child lived.

Deputy U. S. marshal David Neagle. *Author's Collection*

Neagle was a feisty character. Although only five feet, eight inches tall, he had a temper and would tackle anyone who got in his way. While a deputy sheriff of Cochise County in early 1882, he had ridden with a posse commanded by Wyatt Earp, arrested Sherman McMasters, and escorted him back to town. "He was hon-

est and courageous," Earp would later recall, "and did all [of Sheriff] Behan's work that needed a fighting man."

Judge Terry had made a fatal mistake. He was a son of the old South and lived according to all the traditions of that storied land. Honor was everything to him. In 1859, he had killed Senator Broderick during a political dispute. He was a respected attorney and jurist, but he badly misjudged Justice Field's bodyguard. Dave Neagle cared nothing for honor or the Southern traditions by which Terry lived. He was a tough, hardliving Westerner and gunman who took no chances. When you made a hostile move around such a man, you might very well die for it. Judge Terry didn't understand this, and as he lay on the floor of the restaurant staring at the ceiling with glazing eyes, it no longer mattered.

The San Francisco Federal Appraiser's Building where many of the Sharon-Hill divorce proceedings were aired, as well as Neagle's hearing on the Terry shooting. *National Archives*

Neagle was taken to San Francisco early on the morning of August 17, 1889. He was accompanied by San Joaquin County Sheriff Tom Cunningham and several others. The incident was rapidly becoming a legal free-for-all to establish whether the state or federal government had jurisdiction. Both Field, a politically powerful federal supreme court justice, and Neagle's boss, U.S. marshal Franks, maintained it was a federal case and not in the jurisdiction of the state. Also, Stockton, near Lathrop, was Terry's former hometown and there was concern for Neagle's safety when he was moved to the Bay City.

The hastily assembled charge against Judge Field, pressed by Sarah Terry, was easily thwarted and brushed aside and Neagle became the central figure of the case. In San Francisco, Isaiah and Chief Crowley took him into custody and placed him in the city jail. Accused wife-killer Dr. Milton Bowers had recently occupied cell 33, which contained a few pieces of furniture. Neagle was placed there until it was time for his court appearance.

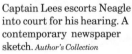

Captain Lees escorts Neagle into court for his hearing. A contemporary newspaper sketch. *Author's Collection*

Neagle's was an important case. When he made his appearance in the circuit court Captain Lees, Chief Crowley, Sheriff Cunningham, and Nick Harris, a federal secret service detective, all escorted him to the old Appraiser's Building at Sansome and Washington streets.

The hearing lasted several weeks. There seemed to be little doubt as to the outcome of the case, Field being present every day and spending all recesses with the two presiding federal judges. After extensive testimony of witnesses, Neagle was questioned at length about the encounter. The gunman readily admitted having shot to kill. After striking Field, Terry had been told to stop by the bodyguard who had already drawn his pistol. Neagle recalled that Terry had "...the most desperate expression I ever saw on a man's face...it meant life or death to him or me...."

With his pistol in his left hand and, steadying the barrel with his right, Neagle shot Terry through the body and fired again as the giant lawyer fell. The fact that no knife was found on the body was immaterial. Terry was known to always be armed. It was also speculated that Sarah, when she threw herself on her husband's body, might have taken his weapon. On September 16, 1889, a decision was rendered that Neagle had indeed acted to defend a federal official against a man known to be a desperate character with a violent past. He was discharged, but jurisdiction and the methods by which the case was handled were to be argued still further.

Crushed and distraught over her husband's death, Sarah Terry didn't even attend the Field and Neagle hearings. She was staying alone in a local hotel and refused to talk to reporters. When forced to attend court on another matter, she cried and held her head throughout the hearing. Neighbors reported she paced and cried in her room incessantly. Perhaps she realized at last the disastrous mischief she had fomented and carried through to its bitter conclusion.

Barely thirty years old when she had instigated the Sharon lawsuit, Sarah had, in her own way, killed off both the men in her life and she now found herself a disturbed, harried and haggard woman. A protracted quarrel with the Terry heirs contributed to her mental instability and in time she would be committed to the Stockton state insane asylum, where she died in 1937.

## CHAPTER TWENTY-THREE/ NOTES

News of Bill Rees' escape from San Quentin was reported in the *Bulletin* of February 1, 1889. Two other convicts escaped with him.

The Gano investigation is described in the *Bulletin* of February 20. The supervisors' allocations for updating the police department are referred to in the *Bulletin* of July 6, 1889.

The *Examiner* of July 14, 1889, contains a long and fascinating article captioned, "A Detective's Library." Other articles over the years made it clear that Lees had one of the finest libraries in the city, quite aside from his crime collection.

For Chief Crowley's annual report, see San Francisco *Municipal Reports*, Fiscal Year 1888–89, San Francisco, W.M. Hinton & Co., 1889.

The full legal story of the Sharon-Hill litigation and its aftermath is perhaps best told in the previously-cited *Sarah & The Senator*. The outrageous behavior of the Terrys in the U.S. circuit court was reported in the *Bulletin* of September 3, 1888, and the *Call* the following day. Judge Field's escort from the state and his later return are detailed by Byram in Volume 8 of his journals. Heretofore it has been assumed that Dave Neagle met the judge at the border and brought him into the state, but Byram makes it clear that he was hired for the job at the instigation of Captain Lees.

Under the heading, "THEY HAVE MET," the *Examiner* of August 15, 1889, devoted its whole front page to the killing at Lathrop. Other papers devoted similar amounts of space to the sensational event, notably the *Chronicle* of August 13. Neagle's arrival in San Francisco and Lees' involvement was noted in the *Bulletin* of August 17 and given four columns on the front page of the *Examiner* on the 18th. Many details of the shooting were revealed during Neagle's hearing in the U.S. circuit court and published in the *Chronicle* of September 7, 1889. Further information on the incident can be gleaned from the documents found in the General Records of the Department of Justice (Record Group 60) in the National Archives and Records Service, Washington, DC. Information on Neagle's background can be found in Stacy Osgood's "The Life and Times of David Neagle," *The Westerners' Brand Book*, Chicago, April, 1962, and in the author's personal collection of Neagle data. The gunman's Tombstone days are well chronicled in the many histories of that famous town, while Wyatt Earp's assessment of Neagle can be found in Stuart N. Lake's *Wyatt Earp, Frontier Marshal*, Boston and New York, Houghton Mifflin Company, 1931.

# Footpads, Cracksmen and Train Robbers

ISAIAH FELT A DEEP LOSS at the death of John Meagher on January 10, 1890. The fifty-three-year-old detective had been plagued with rheumatism for years and had been ill at home the past two months. Meagher had been on the force since 1864 and had quickly displayed his aptitude as a detective. Lees had always depended on "Old John" and had seldom been disappointed. But more than that, Meagher was a friend. A native of Ireland, the dead detective was an engineer by trade and Isaiah could talk with him in the technical terms of the trade they both knew so well. In a newspaper interview, the captain of detectives extolled the life and services of the dead lawman:

> John Meagher would have been a well man today, said Captain Lees, when asked about the dead detective, if it had not been for his devotion to duty. His health was broken by the Duncan case. Poor Meagher worked day and night on that case, and it broke him down. Before that he had never been sick a day, but the lack of sleep and overwork generally consequent of the case hurt him. He did not suffer alone, though. It killed a couple of my men and broke down a number more.
>
> ...Much of Meagher's success as a detective was due to his wonderful memory. If he saw a face once that face remained in his mind forever. If he was given the circumstances of a case, no matter how involved and minute, not the smallest detail could slip his mind. He had a bad spell of sickness once that I feared had affected his memory, so I determined to test him. I pretended to get into a dispute with John Coffey about the facts of a case that we had had ten years before. We were both wrong, and so Meagher promptly informed us. Then he went on and recited the facts without missing a single thing, though he had never had occasion before to recall the case....

The funeral was quite sad. Lizzie Meagher had spent the holidays nursing her ill husband. Now he was gone. "Old John's" two younger brothers would look out for her, and they escorted her to the requiem mass at Saint Francis Church and later to the Holy Cross Cemetery.

There had been a rash of shooting scrapes in town recently and when Chief Crowley railed in the press about the lack of punishment and lax laws, he was surprisingly contradicted by Ambrose Bierce, a columnist for the *Examiner*. Crowley maintained that stiffer penalties for carrying a pistol were needed. Not so, grumbled Bierce; the very fact that so many carried pistols was a deterrent to much greater slaughter.

As if to underscore the dispute, Samuel Jacobson was fatally shot early on the morning of August 17, 1890. He lived with his parents and sisters on California Street in the Western Addition. After an evening at the theater, Jacobson stepped off a streetcar about

Samuel M. Jacobson.
*Author's Collection*

one o'clock that Sunday morning near his home. A few minutes later he burst through the doors of his residence and collapsed, after telling his parents he had been accosted and shot by two footpads. A physician was hurriedly summoned, but Jacobson died.

California Street cable car. *Author's Collection*

The case was a particularly difficult one and occupied Lees and his men for the next few years. When Bob Hogan picked up a local burglar named Schmidt, detectives quickly isolated a twenty-seven-year-old drifter employed by the local Singer Sewing Machine Company. Sidney Bell and a fellow salesman named Campbell had grown weary of soliciting customers in the evening and branched out into holding up late-night pedestrians on the street. Schmidt had also participated in Bell's crimes.

Exhaustive detective work identified Bell as the suspected killer, but it wasn't going to be easy to prove. The case came to trial in April of 1891, with Bell's wealthy Ohio family prepared to spend any amount in defense of their venal offspring. As had happened so often before, finding it difficult to refute the evidence, the defense sought to confuse the jury by attacking the methods and integrity of the police, notably that of Captain Lees. This was particularly true after Bell's conviction, while he was trying for an appeal.

When the two accomplices were bought off and recanted their testimony, a new trial was granted and Lees decided it would be safer now to try him on robbery charges, which would be easier to sustain in court. Bell was again convicted and sentenced to sixty years in San Quentin, while Campbell fled to the East. Schmidt too was convicted, but committed suicide while on his way to prison.

Isaiah's malignment by the defense prompted Judge Murphy to set the record straight:

...The settled conviction in the mind of the judge is that in no manner, shape or form has Captain Lees done more or less than his duty called for, and had he done less he would have been derelict in the performance thereof....Instead of being condemned, in the judgement of the court Captain Lees is entitled to commendation, so far as this case is concerned.

Sidney Bell.
*Author's Collection*

*California State Archives*

In January of 1891, a series of safe burglaries kept Lees and his men scrambling for clues as to the perpetrators. It was obviously an out-of-town gang of "cracksmen" whose safe-cracking methods were repeated over and over again. After effecting an entrance through an adjoining building, the burglars would wrap the safe lock with rags to muffle the sound of a sledge hammer. When the lock knob had been broken off, it was a simple matter to punch out the levers holding the lock in place, and the safe was open.

Isaiah was well-acquainted with the methods of safecrackers, and he even admired some of the more skillful fellows. They were much like detectives. Patience and coolness were their trademark, as well as a thorough knowledge of the mechanics of their business. Expert safecrackers were usually intelligent enough to be a success in any legitimate business, but, like the detectives, they thrived on the danger and excitement of their chosen career.

After spending many hours talking to burglars and safecrackers, Isaiah felt he could open a safe with the best of them—and being an old ironworker, of course he could. When certain they were not being recorded in any way, cracksmen frequently discussed their methods with the detective captain. Men like Jimmy Hope and "Lightning" Davis stood at the head of their profession and didn't care to associate with riff-raff like prowlers and "porch-climbers." There was always hope for the petty thieves, however, as explained by Lightning Davis:

> ...A safe burglar stands at the head of all the profession. A young man who has been only a common house-breaker or "porchclimber" considers himself lucky to get a few years in state prison. There he has a chance to get a thorough education. He picks up points and ideas in regard to burglarizing which he would never hear of outside prison walls. Safe burglars, as a rule, will not associate with men below them unless circumstances bring it about. The state prison is the burglars university. It is there that he takes his final course in his education, and when he is set free he is ready for any enterprise from holding up a stage to breaking into a bank....

Breaking into a building could be accomplished in a multitude of ways, depending on circumstances. An old case knife inserted between the upper and lower sash would flip open a catch nine times out of ten. If this failed, molasses or a soft bar of soap was spread over the window glass. To this was applied a strong piece of paper. When the window was broken by a firm tap, the glass stayed adhered to the paper without noisily falling to the floor. This was called "spanking the glaze."

Other times skeleton keys might be used. A clever burglar made his own keys, since they couldn't be traced. All tools were either made or stolen for this reason, except for the more sophisticated items sold in the back

Contemporary newspaper drawings of nineteenth-century burglar's tools, including a dark lantern, chisles, drills, skeleton keys, a sledge, and wedges. *Author's Collection*

rooms of disreputable pawn shops and saloons. Lanterns of any kind were seldom used. A small piece of candle was much easier to carry, put out, or dispose of and did the job just as well once you got used to it. Top safe-crackers were skilled mechanics who made a constant study of safes and their locking methods. While doing time in San Quentin a "cracksman" once discoursed on his art:

> We make a study of safe locks and all the new improvements as they come out. How do I accomplish it? I go to a safe agent, say I am a saloon-keeper and want to buy a good safe. The agent, of course, is anxious to sell; he explains the intricacies of the lock, expatiates on the good points in the mechanism. Then I speak of rival locks. He shows me the weak points in them, also. Watching my chance, I take a match or a pencil and slyly measure the bolts, tumblers and portions of the combination, and get an idea of their proportions and make up. To get further facts I go to the rival agent. He shows me the weak points in the lock I have just seen, and in this way get posted on the different styles of the locks. We watch the displays of locks in show windows of the big safe houses always on the lookout for new improvements....

Upon arrival in town, cracksmen first broke into a local blacksmith shop to steal a sledge hammer, brace, and bit. The handle of the sledge was cut off to about six inches to make it simple to conceal. "It is easy," recalled a burglar, "to slip this short piece up the sleeve and conceal the hammer part in the hand and under the cuff. I have walked along a street with an eight pound sledge in my sleeve, passing policemen who never dreamed of what I was carrying."

Once the mechanics of a safe were known, breaking into it was just a matter of time. If the safe couldn't be opened with a sledge and drill bit, powder and fuse did the job. Even time-locks could be cancelled by dynamite on top of the safe, which usually ran down the clock machinery. However, certain kinds of safes were nearly burglar-proof and were avoided completely by safecrackers.

In November of 1891, the San Francisco Express out of Saint Louis, Missouri, was robbed and Isaiah became involved in the search for the bandits. The train had been stopped near the village of Glendale, Missouri. Four bandits had dynamited the express car and obtained over ten thousand dollars from the safe. As the car was being ransacked, several of the robbers had shot at the passenger coaches, then the gang jumped into a wagon and disappeared into some nearby woods.

Saint Louis police chief Lawrence Harrigan quickly isolated two suspects. Marion Hedgepeth and Adelbert Slye were ex-convicts suspected of several other train robberies. The two were also experienced burglars and dynamite users who had just recently left

Adelbert Slye. *Author's Collection*

town. Harrigan felt sure they were the leaders of the gang and promptly launched his investigation. He knew Hedgepeth had operated a restaurant in Los Angeles the past summer and that Slye had been reported there as well.

Robert Pinkerton was vacationing in San Francisco when Harrigan located him at the Palace Hotel. The Pinkerton Detective Agency was retained by the railroad and the agent was quickly in the field. Taking San Francisco police detective Roscoe J. Whittaker with him, Pinkerton was soon on his way to the angelic city.

Although Hedgepeth could not be located, Slye was found operating a saloon under the name of Denton. A watch stolen in the Glendale robbery was found on him and Pinkerton quickly had the outlaw on the next train to San Francisco.

Robert A. Pinkerton.
*Author's Collection*

Chief Harrigan had meanwhile learned of a trunk belonging to Hedgepeth that had been shipped to a "Florence Waterman, Oakland, California." Harrigan wired Chief Crowley and advised him of the trunk, then sent along mug shots of Hedgepeth and his wife, Maggie. The rest of the operation was turned over to Captain Lees.

It was late December when Isaiah took Ned Byram and three other detectives to watch the Oakland Wells Fargo express office. The vigil was interrupted when Lees and Byram caught a train and met Whittaker with Slye at Modesto. By the time they reached Sacramento, Lees had convinced Slye he might as well go straight back to Saint Louis and Byram and Whittaker soon were heading east with the suspected train robber.

Maggie Hedgepeth.
*Author's Collection*

Byram had been gone two days when an attractive young woman called for the trunk. Lees and his men followed her home in a driving rain and watched as she entered a room on Tenth Street in Oakland. As Maggie Hedgepeth was taking off her coat, the detectives rushed in and handcuffed her. After waiting several hours for Hedgepeth, Lees realized they had probably moved too fast, as they had missed catching her husband. The outlaw's lady was taken across the bay to headquarters and was soon on her way across the continent to join Slye in Saint Louis.

Following up other clues, the detectives learned Hedgepeth was staying at an Ellis Street hotel in San Francisco. When they missed their man, he was traced to a lodging house on O'Farrell Street, but he had again checked out a few hours earlier. Here the trail ended.

Isaiah put all the men he could spare to work checking rooming houses and hotels in the area. Just as he was beginning to suspect the outlaw had left the city, a

telegram arrived from Chief Harrigan. A Saint Louis lawyer had received a letter from Hedgepeth, asking that he look after his wife's interests. This was just the break the lawmen needed.

Lees knew Hedgepeth would now remain in the city until he had a response from the lawyer. Since he was constantly changing rooms, the letter must be sent general delivery in care of the outlaw's alias, "H. V. Swanson." Now it was just a waiting game.

For nearly two weeks Lees posted his detectives inconspicuously about the corridors of the post of-

Detective Ray Silvey.
*Author's Collection*

fice. Ned Byram stayed near the general delivery window and closely watched every patron. But mainly they waited. Patience was the most important attribute of any detective, then and now.

On the morning of February 10, 1892, detectives Byram, Cody, Silvey, and Officer Scotty Campbell drifted one at a time into the post office as soon as it opened. Lees was busy at City Hall. According to Byram's journal, it was 11:40 when a smooth-faced, well- dressed young man sauntered toward the general delivery window. Suddenly, the clerk hit a buzzer and the detectives smoothly moved into position. Byram recorded the events of the next few minutes:

Marion Hedgepeth. *John Boessenecker Collection*

...I stepped up to the left side of him between him and the street. Silvey and Cody got on the other side of him and behind him. Thought it was Hedgepeth, but he had his mustache shaved off. I looked at Silvey, he nodded. I rubbed against the man, and stuck my head in the window alongside of his, he had no pistol in his hip pocket, his right hand was in his overcoat pocket and he was handling his letters with his left hand. He drew back and looked at me, as he did so I grabbed his right arm with my left hand and my right hand on his left arm....We were face to face. He struggled violently to get his right hand to work, but I held to him, having broken his hold on his gun which he had in his right hand overcoat pocket. Silvey and Cody had him from behind, Silvey got his gun into his left ear and kept telling him, "you quit!" We kept him moving, smashed the glass in the door to the porters room as we went through. I got my handcuffs on to him and we had him sitting down in a chair in the porter's room before he knew where he was.

The capture in the post office. A contemporary newspaper sketch. *Author's Collection*

Two double-action Smith and Wesson revolvers were taken from the prisoner, and he was hustled off to City Hall in a hastily-summoned hack commanded by Captain Lees. At the city prison over a thousand dollars in currency, gold, and silver was found on the outlaw. He

240

also had a pair of burglar's nippers for turning keys in locks from the outside. While interviewing Hedgepeth later, Lees noticed a bulging trouser leg and, cutting the seam, drew out $120 in crisp, new bills. The owner of the Log Cabin Bakery in Oakland dropped by in the afternoon and positively identified Hedgepeth as the one who had held him up six months previously.

At four-thirty the following afternoon Hedgepeth left for Saint Louis in custody of detectives Byram and Whittaker. Isaiah cautioned his men to take no chances with the prisoner, who was weighted down with a ten-pound "Oregon Boot." The lawmen carried sawed-off shotguns and were instructed to deliver their prisoner in Missouri, dead or alive. During the trip Hedgepeth became ill in Colorado, but quickly recovered. "People are very curious at all the stations to see our prisoner," Byram wrote in his journal.

There was a great deal of excitement over the capture, and Lees and his men received high praise for their work. One telegram read as follows:

> New York, February 10, 1892
> Captain I. W. Lees, Chief of Detectives, San Francisco:
> Hurrah! It's a great victory and the greatest blow struck for train robbery in years. President Stanford, Vice President Lovejoy and Managers Weir and Damsel all join in sending Chief Crowley, yourself and officers engaged in the arrest, hearty congratulations. Hope you may get "Dink."
>
> Robert A. Pinkerton

The "Dink" referred to was Lucius "Dink" Wilson, another member of the gang. After killing a New York detective the following year, Wilson was captured, tried, and convicted and later executed at Sing Sing. A fourth member of the gang, James Francis, was killed while resisting arrest. Slye was sentenced to a twenty-year prison term in Missiouri. Although Maggie Hedgepeth was later released, her husband was sentenced to a twenty-five-year prison term. Pardoned after twelve years, upon release Hedgepeth soon resumed his life of crime. He was killed during a Chicago saloon holdup on December 31, 1909.

## CHAPTER TWENTY-FOUR / NOTES

John Meagher's death was recorded in the *Chronicle* of January 11 and 12, with a long article appearing in the *Examiner* on January 12, 1890. Articles on the shooting statistics of San Francisco for the past few years appeared in the *Examiner* of February 9 and 10, 1890, with Crowley's comments appearing in the latter article. Bierce's remarks were in his "Prattle" column in the *Examiner* of February 16, 1890.

The Jacobson shooting was reported in the *Chronicle* on August 18, 1890. Trial coverage began in the same paper on April 21 the following year, with articles appearing on April 23 and 30, 1891. "Bell on the Stand" was reported in the *Chronicle* of May 5, while further details were in the issue of May 7. Bell's first conviction was announced in the *Chronicle* on May 8, 1891. The conduct of the defense forces are dealt with at length in the *Chronicle* of July 7, 1892. Duke's *Celebrated Criminal Cases of America* gives data on various aspects of the case.

The exploits and comments of "Lightning" Davis are reported in a long article in the *Examiner* of May 3, 1891, while an extensive story on safe-cracking appeared in the same paper on May 10, 1891.

The Glendale, Missouri, train robbery and capture of Hedgepeth are dealt with at great length in the *Examiner* of February 11 and 12, 1892. Volume 10 of Byram's journals gives a good, firsthand account of the investigation, capture, and trip back to Missouri with the prisoner. More information on the careers of Hedgepeth, Slye, and Lucius "Dink" Wilson can be found in Roy O'Dell's "Marion Hedgepeth, The Derby Hat Outlaw," *True West*, August, 1993. See also O'Dell's much longer, two-part article, "Daring , Dashing, and Dangerous," Quarterly of the *National Association for Outlaw and Lawman History, Inc.*, January–March and April–June, 1996. There is some information in William A. Pinkerton's *Train Robberies, Train Robbers and the Holdup Men*, Chicago, New York, privately published by William A. and Robert A. Pinkerton, 1907. Hedgepeth's death during a robbery attempt is reported by Charles Fox, a descendant, in the Quarterly of the *National Association and Center for Outlaw and Lawman History*, Winter, 1988.

# Perfidious Policemen
# & Murderous Russians

CAPTAIN LEES CELEBRATED FORTY YEARS with the department in October of 1893. He was surprised by a large floral piece as he entered his office one morning, and was congratulated by a surrounding throng of friends and fellow officers. At the gathering he missed his long-time associate John Coffey, who had been ill for some time. Coffey had been on the force since the 1860s and Isaiah had always depended heavily on "Old John." Worn down by health problems and years of service, Coffey was considering retirement to his home in Redwood City.

In April of 1894, Chief Crowley became aware of more trouble in Chinatown. He found it hard to believe rumors that his men were taking payoffs, but when a prominent Chinese gambler offered *him* a bribe, he initiated an investigation. It turned out that not only were members of the Chinatown squad on the take, but Crowley's own clerk, Captain William E. Hall, was the instigator.

Hall was informing the Chinese gamblers of impending raids and getting rich in the process. By the end of the month the investigation had crested. Fourteen officers were dismissed from the force, including two of Lees' detectives. It was generally believed there would be no indictments, the principal reason being a lack of evidence strong enough to convict and the need to keep the methods of the investigation a secret to protect informants. Also, the investigation was to continue and further efforts would be hampered if a disclosure of methods and informants was made.

A by-product of the inquiries was a general recognition that new blood was needed in the department. The senior officers of the force—the men under whom the gambling scandals had taken place—were all of retirement age. It was a natural conclusion that these old men could not, or were not, paying close enough attention to the supervision of subordinates. Lees and Crowley realized they also were both in this category.

A look at these officers quickly emphasized the situation. Isaiah himself was sixty-four years old, while Crowley

A Chinese gambling game in 1890s San Francisco. A contemporary newspaper sketch.
*Author's Collection*

was several years older. Captain Appleton Stone, in charge of the prison, was over sixty. Captain John Short, commander of the southern division, was eighty-seven. Captain Andrew Dunlevy, of the Harbor Patrol, was over sixty also, while Captain William Douglass, of the northern division, was sixty-eight. A correlation between these old officers' ages and the scandals that had rocked the department seemed inescapable. Speculation now began on just who would be retiring and which sergeants would be promoted in whose place.

It was thought that more clout was needed in Chinatown, and as an initial reform move Captain Dunlevy was installed as head of the Chinatown squad on June 19. Gambling games were extremely hard to find in town after the April shakeup.

About ten o'clock on the morning of March 23, 1894, a call to police headquarters reported the Savings Union Bank at Market and Fell streets had just been robbed and a cashier shot and killed. The killer was quickly picked up and Isaiah set to work deciphering a journal the bandit had kept. It was written in some kind of code, but the detective soon discovered his prisoner was one of the most wanted men in the West.

William Fredericks was the man who smuggled the guns into Folsom prison for the George Contant break during the previous summer. After killing a Nevada County sheriff, Fredericks had fled the state and traveled throughout the West. He was promptly tried for the cashier's killing and hanged in July of 1895.

William Fredericks, whose right eye was injured during the attempted robbery.
*Author's Collection*

One of Captain Lees' strangest cases originated on a bright, crisp Sunday morning in Sacramento. It was a few days after Christmas 1894 when Luther Weber opened his father's store for business. For thirty years the elder Weber had been operating a grocery store across the street from the capitol. A German couple, the Webers were quite popular in town. They were noted for being prohibitionist in politics, their business being referred to as the "Temperance Store."

As young Weber stepped inside the store, he noticed a dark stain on the floor in a corner of the room. A chill came over him as he suddenly realized the stain looked like blood. Glancing about for the

A view of Sacramento taken from the dome of the state capitol building. The Weber shop and home was on one of the side streets as shown here.
*California State Library*

244

Francis H. L. Weber.
*Author's Collection*

source, he looked up and was startled to see the same red stain on the ceiling.

Luther's parents lived above their store and as he rushed for the stairs the young clerk must have been terrified at what he might find upstairs. When there was no response to several raps on the door, he rushed in to find Francis Weber sprawled on the kitchen floor, his head split open and his life blood staining the area around him. Horrified, young Weber ran through the apartment, only to find his mother dead in the bedroom. Dashing from the terrible scene, he quickly reported the double murder at police headquarters.

Mrs. Francis H. L. Weber.
*Author's Collection*

The Sacramento police were promptly on the scene. The Webers had apparently interrupted burglars late the previous night and been killed by the intruders. A bloody ax was found in the yard and some gore-blotched clothes indicated the murderers had put on some of Weber's clothing in a shed outside. Jewelry, clothes, and other items had been taken. There were apparently two burglars, one wearing heavy boots and the other barefoot. The officers found a complete dearth of clues, as noted in a dispatch to the San Francisco *Examiner* of January 1:

> Sacramento, December 31.—The robbers who murdered Mr. and Mrs. Francis H. L. Weber on Saturday night last may never be caught for the police and detectives have so far no clew to the criminals. The Coroner's inquest may possibly lead to some clew, but there is little hope even of that. Governor Markham has offered a reward of $1,000 for the apprehension and conviction of the murderers, and this will stimulate the search for them....

Otto "Billy" Heyneman, Lees' clerk, later recalled how his boss received a telegram from the Sacramento police chief asking San Francisco officers to look out for suspicious characters. Heyneman stated the Sacramento officer also asked for Lees' help to which Lees readily agreed.

Taking Heyneman and several detectives along, Isaiah traveled by riverboat to Sacramento. During the trip he re-read all the newspaper accounts of the tragedy, and by the time he reached the scene he knew as much as the local police. Lees and his men searched the premises relentlessly, but like the Sacramento officers, could turn up no clues whatsoever. "[Lees'] beautiful gray locks were black with soot," Heyneman recalled, "for even the chimneys were not overlooked. There was soot and dirt in his whiskers, and he presented an undignified appearance...."

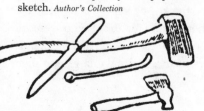

Murder weapons and burglar tools. A contemporary newspaper sketch. *Author's Collection*

When no further leads were turned up, Isaiah returned to the few clues that were available. Turning the bloody clothes of the killers over and over in his hands, he searched in vain for a label or scrap of paper in the pockets or lining. Suddenly his eyes lit up. He had been overlooking the obvious.

"It's the work of a couple of foreigners," Heyneman recalled him saying. "Do you note this cloth? That's foreign material. These are no common tramps or yeggmen."

In company of the Sacramento officers, Lees and his men now covered the foreign section of town where Russians, Poles, and Italians congregated. They talked to boardinghouse keepers and saloon owners, but still there were no leads. By now Isaiah was out of time and he returned with his men to San Francisco. The Weber murders might very well be one of those cases that would never be resolved.

On New Year's Day 1895, the previous night's drunks were herded from their cells for their appearance before the San Francisco police judge. While sweeping out the cells, a trusty found a small gold watch behind a water closet in the drunk tank. The timepiece was given to a guard, who rushed it up to Captain Lees' office. When told to examine the inscription, the old detective jumped to his feet. Inside the watch case lid was the lettering — "To M. Weber, from mother."

Isaiah stared hard at the watch as the terrible truth became clear. He probably had the Weber killers in his jail the previous night. A quick survey of the prison register and interviews with the officers who had picked up the drunks soon isolated several suspects. Some foreigners who had recently arrived from Sacramento had been spending freely on the Barbary Coast and had been thrown into the drunk tank when they became too obstreperous.

When Lees summoned Luther Weber from Sacramento, he immediately identified the watch as a gift his grandmother had given his mother. Isaiah must have gnashed his teeth in frustration. The rewards were now over two thousand dollars.

In the fall of 1894, Chief Crowley traveled to Honolulu for a much-needed vacation with his wife and daughters. The chief hadn't taken any time off in years, and age and the recent investigations had worn him out. He had returned to a continuing harangue in the newspapers launched by a crew of church reformers. Again Crowley began investigating his men, this time on charges they were in the pay of prostitutes. Once more the late hours began to tell on the old chief.

When the grippe again assaulted the city in late February of 1895, both Crowley and Lees were laid up. A nasty form of influenza, the grippe kept the city pharmacists compounding mixtures of quinine and phenacetine for those who were afflicted. "Thousands," commented the *Examiner*, "prefer whiskey, and half the people who drink straight whiskey over the many bars of the city make la grippe their excuse."

Ned Byram and Ross Whittaker were trying to locate a suspect in a Stanislaus County assault case at this time. In his journal Byram reported: "Ross went up to see Capt. Lees who is sick, at past 4. Chief Crowley is also sick."

Although bicycles had been around for many years, the two-wheeled vehicles took San Francisco by storm in the mid-1890s. Suddenly bicycles were everywhere. The U.S Army announced plans for a bicycle corps and the San Francisco police also briefly considered a bicycle unit.

A side effect of the cycling craze was the discovery that many of the busiest San Francisco streets were in bad need of repair. There was a brief flurry of concern also when several physicians announced the sport caused a dangerous curvature of the spine and other maladies. But this was of little concern to the thousands of cyclists who flooded the streets and country roads on weekends from spring well into fall. Sundays became a bicycle fashion parade as bloomer and shortskirted women wheeled through Golden Gate Park accompanied by boyfriends and husbands clad in tiny visored beanies and colorful, striped blazers.

In the mid 1890s, bicyclers were beginning to take the place of buggies and strollers in Golden Gate Park. *California State Library*

Isaiah was deeply involved in a mysterious murder case, in early June of 1895, when he was interrupted one day by Deputy Sheriff Martin Hughes and a man named Bennett. Bennett had confided to Hughes that a photographer named Stevens had told him he had some information on the Weber murders. Hughes had asked Bennett if he would accompany him to Sacramento to see if they would be eligible for the rewards. There were no details and Isaiah must have grunted when he heard the story. He had already run down dozens of phony leads—clues that led nowhere. Still, nothing could be overlooked.

The detective captain sent two of his men to check on the photographer's story. Stevens proved to know little, but he in turn acknowledged that he had originally heard of the crime from a

Russian carpenter named Zakrewski. The Russian was located and interviewed, then swiftly conveyed to City Hall, where he told what he knew to Captain Lees.

The story had begun in August of 1893, when some ten convicts had escaped from a Russian prison island in the far north. The men had suffered terribly after putting to sea in a small boat without food or water. They were nearly mad when picked up by the American barque *Charles W. Morgan*, bound for San Francisco. After reaching port in the Bay City on November 7, the convicts were treated with great kindness. They were permitted to stay after a court hearing established them as political prisoners and not criminals.

The rescued Russians as sketched by an *Examiner* artist aboard the *Charles W. Morgan*. *Author's Collection*

Zakrewski had met one of these Russian exiles in August of 1894 in a San Francisco saloon. He gave his name as John Durbroff and early the following year he was rooming at Zakrewski's house. Durbroff seemed to be troubled about something. During a drinking bout, he told his carpenter friend that he and another man had watched a house in Sacramento for three days. They broke into the place on the third night and when an old man accosted them, they killed him with a hatchet. The victim's wife was also chopped to death. After stealing some clothes and other property, the killers fled to San Francisco. The Weber murder case had received widespread publicity and the horrified Zakrewski knew exactly what his friend was describing.

Tscherbakov, one of the Weber murderers. *Author's Collection*

Zakrewski recalled that Durbroff and a friend named George Pettion had gotten drunk the previous New Year's Eve and been thrown in jail together. Isaiah was suddenly on his feet. He sent a detective off to find Pettion, while dispatching another to bring him the December jail register.

Pettion was soon in Lees' office. He said he had known Durbroff for some time and had been roused from bed on New Year's Eve to go out and get drunk with him. At that time he had noticed his friend was wearing a watch and chain—something he had never known him to do. Durbroff bragged of having plenty of money and they went out on the town to celebrate.

After visiting several saloons, Durbroff became more and more intoxicated. They stopped for a meal at a Kearny Street restaurant where Durbroff bought sev-

eral papers and insisted Pettion read the Sacramento dispatches. They continued drinking and later, while at breakfast, Durbroff again asked to be read accounts of the Weber murders. By noon both men were hilariously drunk and were picked up by the police for disturbing the peace in a saloon.

At the city prison, Pettion and Durbroff were registered and put into the crowded drunk tank. Both were released the following day and a short time later the watch was found by the trusty who was cleaning up. Pettion described the watch exactly, as Isaiah chewed his cigar a little more fiercely. At last, he must have mused, at last! When he saw both Pettion and Durbroff's names listed on the prison register, Lees grinned with satisfaction.

Zakrewski gave the detectives Durbroff's Howard Street address, and a moment later Lees and two of his men were on their way. Forcing the door, they found the Russian in bed and after a brief struggle quickly had him cuffed. After going through his possessions, the detectives packed up his meager belongings and the whole contingent headed back to headquarters in a patrol wagon.

When confronted with Zakrewski's statement, Durbroff denied everything. "I am a working man," he insisted while showing his hands. "I do not kill anybody." After accidentally admitting being in Sacramento the previous December, he claimed he had been picking cherries.

"Now Ivan," countered Lees, "how could you be picking cherries in December?" Durbroff could only stare at the floor.

At last there were tangible directions in which to reopen the investigation. Now began the patient and exhaustive detail work of gathering and assembling evidence of the crime. Isaiah had by now learned that Zakrewski, Durbroff (whose real name was Kovalev), and two others named Nikitin and Tscherbakov had traveled to San Jose after the Weber murder. The men quickly used up what little money they had and determined to again turn to crime. Zakrewski didn't like the idea and returned to San Francisco.

Lees learned that Tscherbakov had been fatally stabbed when he tried to rob a man named Dowdigan in San Jose. After the incident was reported, the dead Russian was found near where Dowdigan reported the attack took place. He had reportedly been stabbed in the side, but when found the body also had a knife wound in the heart. Two days later Kovalev was back in San Francisco wearing new clothes.

Ivan Kovalev, alias Durbroff, standing in the doorway of his jail cell. *Author's Collection*

When Isaiah put all this together, he immediately sent detective Charles Gibson to San Jose to exhume the body. He wanted to know if the corpse was wearing any of the stolen Weber clothes, or could otherwise furnish any

Detective Ed Gibson played an important part in the Weber murder investigation.
*California State Library*

clues. Meanwhile he had sifted through all of Kovalev's belongings and obtained other valuable bits of evidence. A pair of gold eyeglasses were tentatively identified as being the property of Mrs. Weber, while suspenders worn by Kovalev had belonged to her husband.

Enough preliminary evidence had been gathered for Lees to summon the Sacramento district attorney and the two Weber children to make some identifications. The glasses were recognized as belonging to the dead woman, while the daughter identified the suspenders as being a pair she had made for her father.

When Gibson returned from San Jose with Tscherbakov's clothes, Isaiah was disappointed. They did not match any of the stolen Weber property. Closer examination, however, revealed the clothes matched some of the discarded garments found after the murders. The case was coming together. Isaiah was sure that Kovalev had changed clothes with his comrade before burying him. He was just as sure he had stabbed him in the heart to make sure he didn't talk if he were taken into custody.

Under the heading "Clothes from a Grave," the *Examiner* noted the latest damning evidence on June 29:

> ...Captain Lees was very pleased when the identification and comparison was complete."I think this effectively puts an end to all doubt as to the guilt of Tscherbakov and Kovalev," he said. "The last link in the chain of evidence has been forged and I have not the slightest doubt but that we will be able to secure a conviction without any trouble. In all my experience I do not think I ever encountered such a gang of fiends....Mr. Levin told me that Kovalev had admitted changing clothes with his dead comrade....Believe me, he is a much cuter man than you would give him credit for at first glance...."

Ivan Kovalev paid a terrible price for the treachery he and his comrades had shown towar[d] their California hosts.
*Peter Palmquist*

For some reason, the two men must have exchanged clothes before Tscherbakov's death since there was no blood or cuts in the clothes now worn by Kovalev. The latter's oversize trousers were identified as being the former property of the dead Weber. The cold hand of death was on Kovalev and he seemed to know it.

Isaiah and his men were still busy rounding up witnesses when he had his preliminary hearing in Sacramento on July 2. The Russian finally confessed to being present at the murders, but insisted the actual killing was done by the dead Tscherbakov. Evidence to the contrary was overwhelming, however. He was convicted and later hanged on February 21, 1896.

In late January Isaiah traveled to Sacramento to push his claim for the Weber murder reward. At the hearing held in Governor Budd's office, attorneys for various claimants presented their respective cases. One of the claimants had given Lees information and complained of putting all his interests in the detective's hands. As attorney W. A. Anderson was questioning this claimant, Isaiah made several remarks, causing the lawyer to turn on him.

Governor James H. Budd.
*Author's Collection*

"You leave that man alone," he shouted at Lees. "Can't you see I'm talking to him? You have primed him enough."

"What's that you say?" demanded Lees, as his face flushed. "Don't you dare talk to me like that. I'll not have it."

"You heard what I said," returned Anderson. "You've primed this man and now I want a whack at him."

Isaiah was furious and rose from his chair, but Governor Budd quickly shouted for him to sit down. "You fellows stop this immediately," said the executive, "or I'll take a hand in it myself." Later, the lawyer and detective apologized and shook hands.

Lees' claim was finally rejected on the basis that he was a public official and was merely performing his sworn duty.

## CHAPTER TWENTY-FIVE / NOTES

Isaiah's forty years of service was recognized in the *Call* of October 29, 1893, and other local papers. John Coffey's illness and long years of service were recounted in the *Examiner* of February 14, 1892. Information on Mrs. Mary Coffey and her five sons is in the *Redwood City Democrat* of February 15, 1912, and the *Times Gazette* of November 13, 1931.

Crowley's investigations and the scandals in the police department can be found in a series of articles beginning in the *Chronicle* of April 17, 1894. Chinese gambler Big Jim's visit to Chief Crowley is reported in the *Chronicle* of April 18, while an article the following day details the chief's investigations of his men. Crowley's other comments on Chinatown are in the *Examiner* of April 22, 1894.

Retirement of the old captains was discussed in the same paper for April 30 and May 3, 1894.

George Contant's attempted breakout at Folsom was given extensive coverage in the press beginning on June 27, 1893. The *Examiner* of that date gave particularly extensive coverage, as did the *Chronicle* of June 29. The murder of Sheriff Pascoe is reported in the *Grass Valley Union* of July 1, 1893. The search for Fredericks is given much coverage in both the *Union* and the *Nevada Daily Transcript* of July 2, 3, 4, 5, 6, 1893. The *Chronicle* of March 23, 24, and 25, 1894, devotes much space to the attempted bank robbery and Lees' identification of the suspect as Fredericks. The trial and several escape attempts of Fredericks are reported in the *Examiner* of April 3, 6, and May 6, 1894. The murderer's execution was announced in the San Francisco press as well as the *Grass Valley Union* of July 27, 1895. The story of Fredericks is also briefly told in Duke's *Celebrated Criminal Cases of America*, as well as in Fanning's previously-cited *Great Crimes of the West*.

Detailed coverage of the Weber murder appeared in the *Examiner* of January 1, 1895. Local coverage was in the *Sacramento Bee* and the *Record-Union* of December 31, 1895. Otto Heyneman's recollections of the case appeared in the *Call* of January 8, 1911. The discovery of the Weber watch in the drunk tank was reported in the *Examiner* of January 10, 1895.

Crowley and Lees' illness is mentioned in the *Examiner* of March 1 and 6, 1895. The Byram reference is in volume 11 of his journals.

The discovery of Zakrewski and the arrest of Durbroff, or Kovalev, is detailed in a long article in the *Examiner* of June 27, 1895. The San Jose episode is reported in the same paper on June 29 and the strong evidence being gathered against the prisoner is listed in the *Examiner* of July 3 and 4, 1895. Kovalev's Sacramento trial is reported in the *Examiner* of November 12, 13, and 16, 1895, while the killer's hanging is reported in the *Chronicle* of February 22, 1896. The governor's office rumpus is detailed in the *Chronicle* of January 22, 1896, while Lees' further appeals are noted in Duke, which also gives a brief recounting of the crime.

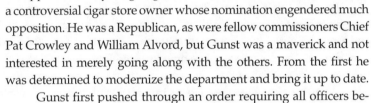

# The Beast in the Belfry

MOSES A. GUNST WAS APPOINTED a San Francisco police commissioner in early 1895. A last minute appointment by outgoing Governor Edwin Markham, Gunst was

ɔse Gunst and Lees
did not get along.
hor's Collection

a controversial cigar store owner whose nomination engendered much opposition. He was a Republican, as were fellow commissioners Chief Pat Crowley and William Alvord, but Gunst was a maverick and not interested in merely going along with the others. From the first he was determined to modernize the department and bring it up to date.

Gunst first pushed through an order requiring all officers below the rank of corporal to wear a helmet of the style worn by New York City officers. Corporals and above would wear visored caps. At this time policemen wore moderately wide brimmed, black hats. Many officers refused to wear the new helmets, which cost $3.50 each, but they soon came around. A grand review of the helmeted force was held in late May, but Gunst was just getting warmed up.

After a tour of the East, Commissioner Gunst returned and recommended belting of the police uniforms. By September the Bay City lawmen were wearing two-inch-wide leather belts stitched in red. The new accouterment cost $2.50 and was fastened in front with a gilt clasp on which the word "Police" was inscribed. Besides providing a carrying loop for the officer's club, the belts helped support the back during long duty hours in wet weather.

Gunst next targeted the aging police captains. All were aging and, despite a prodding to retire to make room for younger blood, the old fellows stayed on and on. Finally, Gunst got tough. Crowley and Lees were pretty much untouchable. They would have

The police commissioners: (from left) Moses Gunst, William Alvord, Chief Crowley and Robert J. Tobin. All were prominent San Franciscans. *Kevin Mullen Collection*

to make up their own minds, and they would obviously be difficult to replace. The new commissioner threw down the gauntlet in a statement published in June 1895:

All promotions in the Police Department will be made on merit alone. As the vacancies occur they will be filled by men who have shown their ability and fitness and this will be the

only thing considered in advancing men in the department. We have started in to retire the men whose usefulness has been impaired with age. From time to time others will be retired and in six months we will have a force that will be as efficient, active and up-to-date as can be made.

Police Commissioner Gunst.

In early July sergeants Bennett, Hanna, Helms, Esola, and George Wittman were appointed to the new rank of lieutenant. Late this same month Captains Stone and Short tendered their resignations to the commissioners. "My work as a policeman is done," commented eighty-nine-year old John Short. "Even a policeman cannot live forever. I realize the wisdom of putting younger men into the harness."

Appleton Stone likewise closed out a colorful, thirty-year career as an officer and detective. He was sixty-eight years old and, for the past few years, had been in charge of the city prison.

Captain Douglass was another matter. He flatly refused to resign and pulled every string he could to maintain his position. "I understand he will refuse to resign," commented one of the commissioners, "but...it will make no difference in the result. He must go...." Late in July, the old officer finally stepped down. It was a foregone conclusion the new captains would be selected from the recently appointed lieutenants.

On April 10, 1895, under the heading "Missing from Home," the *Chronicle* ran a brief article and portrait of a young girl named Blanche Lamont. A twenty-one-year-old student, Lamont had failed to return from school one afternoon and disappeared as though the streets had opened up and swallowed her. She had been missing for a week from the home of an aunt, where she lived.

Blanche Lamont, the missing young girl. *Author's Collection*

The girl's distraught aunt, Mrs. C. G. Noble, called on Captain Lees shortly after the disappearance. The old detective had soothed her as best he could. Most such cases, he explained, were the result of some natural occurrence that might be easily explained when the girl returned. Usually disappearances were the result of a romantic liaison of some kind. Mrs. Noble shook her head. She knew of no such interests of her niece at the moment. After describing the girl's clothes and jewelry and leaving a small portrait, the old woman returned home to wait for news.

Although he didn't let on to Mrs. Noble, Lees felt something was very wrong. A week was too long with no word. This might very well be serious. He called in Abe Anthony and discussed the matter. Anthony was a patrolman on temporary detective duty. Isaiah asked him to prowl around his old beat in the tenderloin and see if any new girls had turned up in the brothels. Lees didn't think this was the case, however, and he told him to see how far he could trace her from home and to school that fateful Wednesday afternoon. At some point she had disappeared and hopefully Anthony could find some clue as to what happened. Lees returned to other business.

Anthony checked at the girl's school and with her friends. After learning she was active in the Emanuel Baptist Church on Bartlett Street, he queried members of the young people's group to which she belonged. He came up with an assortment of information, but nothing that shed any light on her disappearance. A young medical student named Theodore Durrant had met her after school and rode with her on a streetcar. This seemed to be the most promising clue.

The detective found Durrant at his parents' home, where he lived. He readily admitted meeting Blanche after school and riding with her on the streetcar. After a brief ride, he had gotten off and that was the last he had seen of her. Durrant

The Emmanuel Baptist Church. Blanche's body was found where the two windows on the steeple are located. *Author's Collection*

offered to help in any way he could. Anthony reported back to Lees, who was preparing for a business trip to Los Angeles.

On Saturday morning, April 13, three women were busily decorating the Emanuel Baptist Church for the Easter Sunday services the following day. They strung vines and flowers about the pulpit and hung garlands of other greenery along the seats and walls.

When they had finished, a Mrs. Nolt looked about for a container in which to deposit loose leaves and other trash. She stepped into the pastor's study just off the lobby and, not finding anything there, opened the door to an adjoining small room. The sight that met her eyes made her gasp. She screamed in horror as she observed a young girl lying in a pool of gore, the blood-splashed walls and corpse turning the small chamber into a scene from hell. She ran screaming to her friends, and a policeman was quickly summoned.

Captain Lees was still in Los Angeles, but his clerk, Billy Heyneman, promptly telegraphed him about the murder. Isaiah couldn't get away immediately, but reported he would return as soon as possible. Heyneman accompanied Chief Crowley and a crew of detectives to the church and recalled the terrible scene some years later:

> It is an utter impossibility to give a vivid word picture of the repellent condition in which the remains of Minnie Williams were found. Her clothing had been literally torn from her body. She had been repeatedly stabbed, the knife blade still sticking in her chest. A portion of the unfortunate's clothing had been wrapped around

Minnie Williams, the other young murdered girl. *Author's Collection*

a broom handle and stuffed down her throat; even the muscular officers had difficulty in removing it. The recollection of that poor girl's corpse even now causes a shudder....

Theodore Durrant.
*Author's Collection*

Detectives quickly discovered the victim, Minnie Williams, had been a member of the same church and young people's group as the missing Lamont girl. Theodore Durrant belonged to the group, also. When Williams' parents were interviewed, it was discovered she had been quite friendly with Durrant...and with Blanche Lamont. There seemed to be an inescapable tie between these three young people. The detectives scattered and began interviewing neighbors, friends and classmates of Durrant and the murdered girl.

When several witnesses were found who had seen Durrant and Minnie Williams together the evening before her murder, it was enough to make an arrest. The suspect was out of town at the time—on maneuvers across the bay with his national guard unit.

Crowley agreed that Durrant was obviously a prime suspect and a warrant was given to Abe Anthony to serve. The national guard was reportedly in the vicinity of Mount Diablo, and Anthony caught the next ferry crossing the bay. Telegrams were sent to all neighboring peace officers alerting them in case Durrant attempted flight.

Meanwhile, police continued searching the huge, old church from top to bottom. It was a three-story structure with basement, attics, and a tall belfry. When the detectives discovered a locked door that led to the belfry, Crowley received a call asking what they should do. "Break the door down," the chief growled. "Destroy anything that stands in the way of a successful search."

Ten minutes later Crowley again answered the phone. "Don't touch anything," he bellowed, "we'll be right there!" Another girl's body had been found in the belfry.

Top landing of the church belfry where Blanche Lamont's body was discovered. *Author's Collection*

The police wagon was quickly summoned while Crowley rounded up several of the police commissioners. Soon the group of officers were on their way to the iniquitous church on Bartlett Street. News quickly fanned out across the city about the latest discovery. People filtered out of homes and businesses and were soon choking the streets, and the clanging wagon slowed until it was barely moving as officers cleared the way.

"Clubs were freely used," recalled Heyneman, "those feeling their weight cursing and swearing at the police. The chief and the members of the Police Commission...refused to fight the surging crush, but struggled for every inch of the way for fully half an hour before we finally reached the church door. We were in sorry plight, our clothing torn, our hats crushed, the perspiration dripping from us in streams, but we won the entrance."

Inside the church, Crowley's party was led up the narrow stairway to the belfry. Louvered windows surrounded the tower just below the tall spire, but it was

Detective John Seymour.
*Author's Collection*

a few moments before the lawmen's eyes could adjust to the dark and candles could be lit. The nude and ghastly white corpse of the murdered girl suddenly became apparent. She had a block of wood under her head and her hands were peacefully folded over her breast. She looked like marble. Instinctively, Crowley and the others removed their hats. When Heyneman had finished taking notes, one of the officers covered the body with his coat. There was no doubt the corpse was the missing Blanche Lamont.

As the body was being carried down the stairs to the first landing, an exposed arm and hand were suddenly seen to turn black. Crowley looked up at the belfry. Although the girl had been dead for some time, the cool ocean breezes wafting through the shuttered windows of the belfry had slowed decomposition of the body. Now the rapidly decaying remains were rushed to the city morgue, where a hasty autopsy was performed, but it could only establish that the girl had been strangled.

Detective Anthony had meanwhile located the national guard unit near Walnut Creek. He informed the commanding officer of his mission, but was met with a refusal to give up the suspect. The two men argued violently before it was finally agreed that Durrant would be released to the detective's custody when the command reached San Francisco. Ned Byram, John Seymour, and several other detectives met Anthony and his prisoner at Oakland. Byram noted in his journal that on the ferry Durrant had little to say:

> Someone said, "this is a pretty tough case against you." He answered, "Yes. It will break my mother's heart even if it should prove a mistake." Not a tremor in his voice or any show of feeling in speaking of his mother. As we neared the city, he took my left arm with Handley on the other side of him, and we got out on to the end of the boat, forward of the rope. The officers held the crowd back. Capt's Douglass and Dunleavy had more officers at the landing, and a hack for us....we rolled off the dock and up Mission st. with a howling mob after us. Great excitement.

In the interim Crowley had sent several of his men to the Durrant home on Fair Oaks Street. With permission, the detectives carefully searched the trunks, shelves, and dresser drawers of the suspect's room, with no immediate results. "Here!" barked one of the officers. He held up a woman's handbag taken from one of Durrant's coats in a closet. Also in the coat pockets were ferry tickets and other items identifying the purse as belonging to the murdered Minnie Williams. A photo album in the room was found to contain two portraits of the dead girl. The men looked at each other. They had all felt Durrant was a prime suspect from the start, but this was hard evidence.

Durrant still wore his uniform when he later confronted Crowley in the chief's crowded office. Byram described the tense meeting:

> Chief Crowley showed him Minnie Williams' purse saying, "I don't wish to convict you by your own testimony, I only want to ask you one question." He had all ready been asked about the purse by a newspaper reporter at Walnut Creek. He had his story all prepared for the chief, who said, "Where did you get this purse?" [Durrant replied:] "I found it on the corner of Bartlett and 22nd sts". He corrected himself and said he meant 23rd st. at 20 minutes to 12 o'clock on Friday night, April 12th, 1895. He was alone at the time, did not know who the purse belonged to. That was all that was said to him. I only wish that old Chief Ellis had a hold of him with Blanche Lamont's torn clothing which was in Captain Lees' office, to shake in his face. He would have got a confession out of him inside of 20 minutes.

General John H. Dickinson, one of Durrant's three defense counsels. *Author's Collection*

Durrant was fortunate that the local national guard commander was General John H. Dickinson, one of the most prominent criminal attorneys in the state. He promptly offered his services to the young student and member of his command. Eugene Deuprey, another top-flight criminal lawyer, was also engaged, along with W. A. Thompson. The double murder was being called "The Crime of the Century" and Durrant quickly became a pawn in a game of newspaper circulations, professional egos, and legal reputations. The Crime of the Century was to evolve into the fight of the century, with Durrant's life as the stake.

Harry Morse was a famous California detective and lawman. *John Boessenecker Collection*

Byram noted that "Capt. Lees handled the whole of it when he got back from Los Angeles." He returned about April 23 and was directing the exhumation of Williams' corpse on April 24 to try to establish the time of death from the contents of the stomach. William S. Barnes was district attorney and would prosecute the case. He was the son of Isaiah's old friend, General Barnes, whose career had suffered of late as a result of the Sharon case fiasco. Young Barnes must prove himself now—live up to the distinguished career of his father. Even Lees soon found his reputation on the line when the noted private detective Harry Morse joined the defense team.

On May 1, a coroner's jury indicted Durrant for the murder of Blanche Lamont. Lees had already initiated the search for evidence, as depositions began arriving from unexpected sources. Billy Heyneman later recalled:

> As soon as Durrant was jailed the chief of police was deluged with information from all sources proving that the man under arrest was a degenerate of the most perverted type. Young women called voluntarily at the office and recited conditions and circumstances barely

printable. Photographs were received from women of the half world (prostitutes) revealing the prisoner in all sorts of disgusting poses....The informants who came to the office day by day begged the old master (Lees) not to subpoena them as witnesses....

Officer Thomas Duke corroborated Heyneman. Duke wrote that he owned "...a photograph taken of Durrant at a picnic when he was only sixteen years of age, and the position in which he posed proves conclusively that he was a degenerate even as a child."

At the same time, Isaiah was collecting evidence of a more tangible sort. Several students identified Durrant as the man who had met Blanche as she left school and rode the trolley car with her on that fateful day. A prominent attorney had paused to watch some laborers on the street and had noticed Durrant and a young girl matching Lamont's description walking toward the church.

A Mrs. Leake who lived across the street from the church had been looking out her window that late afternoon of April 3. Her own daughter was overdue from a shopping trip and she was watching for her when she observed Durrant and a young girl enter the side door of the Emanuel Baptist Church. Again, the description matched that of Blanche Lamont.

George King, the church organist and a friend of Durrant, practiced in the church that evening. He had begun just after five o'clock when Durrant came down from the belfry. He was wild-eyed and disheveled, and claimed he had been repairing the gas jets and had almost been overcome.

A pawnshop owner positively identified Durrant as the man who had tried to pawn three of the murdered girl's rings sometime early in April. Little by little a strangling web of circumstantial evidence was being gathered.

Lees and Barnes decided to prosecute the Lamont case first. They would still have the option of trying the suspect for the Williams murder if he wasn't convicted at the first trial. The case was called on July 22, 1895, and merely selecting a jury turned out to be nearly impossible. Only when Judge Murphy became infuriated at the repeated rejection of prospective jurors was a jury finally impanelled. District Attorney Barnes made his opening statement on September 3, and the great contest was under way. The oppressive heat was stifling in the crowded courtroom.

In his careful marshaling of the evidence, Lees had ordered construction of a model of the church belfry to enable jurors to accurately envision what had taken place. But it was the witnesses who made the case. When Durrant claimed he had been at a school lecture the afternoon Lamont had disappeared, he could not prove it and no students would testify that he had been there. Still, it created a doubt that was exploited by the defense. This ploy was disposed of when Lees brought in Dr. Fred Graham, a friend of Durrant's. Graham testified that Durrant had asked to see his notes of the lecture so he could "compare" them with his own. Graham had refused, telling Durrant that he would get into trouble with such requests. Durrant,

of course, could not produce his own notes for the lecture even though known as a meticulous taker of notes.

Captain Lees produced another surprise witness in mid-September. Following up a series of leads, a woman named Mrs. Elisabeth Crosett was located. She had been on the car on April 3, and had watched Durrant and Lamont get off on the street that led to the Emanuel Church, just a few blocks away. Mrs. Crosett completed the chain of witnesses who had seen Durrant pick up the girl, get on the trolley, and walk down the street to enter the church. It was only with great reluctance that Mrs. Crosett agreed to talk, however.

"If I must be a witness," she told Captain Lees, "I will tell all I know. I will tell you the truth." Her testimony was extremely damaging to the already demolished defense.

Day after day the trial dragged on, with witnesses being questioned endlessly by the opposing counsels. The heat in the crowded courtroom soon began to tell on everyone. Lees and lawyer Deuprey almost came to blows one day in a spat over the handling of evidence. Isaiah held up well during the ordeal, but he was also sometimes at odds with District Attorney Barnes over the handling of the case. "Captain Lees," grumbled an article in the *Examiner*, "...is particularly averse to anything that may seem to him in the nature of an attempted interference with his plan. He receives suggestions somewhat testily and those who encounter him...are never allowed to doubt that Captain Lees is the directing genius."

As the trial wore on, there was much speculation in the press concerning the antagonism between the two great detectives, Lees and Morse. As a longtime sheriff of Alameda County, Morse had killed a number of badmen in personal encounters and brought numerous others to justice. In the late 1870s he founded the Morse

The prosecution (foreground from the left): Detective Ben Bohen, District Attorney Barnes and Captain Durrant is in the dark suit behind Barnes' shoulder. *Author's Collection*

Detective Agency and had gained further renown in private work. Eager to exploit the case for their own ends, newspapers pictured the two famous lawmen ready to start swinging as they stared fiercely at each other day after day. That wasn't the case, according to a newspaper interview with one of Morse's men:

> These stories about a feud between Captain Morse and Captain Lees are all rot and nonsense. They do not glare at each other, nor crouch down like lions ready to spring at each others necks.... Captain Morse was not inclined to touch the case at first. He spent a week looking into it. When he became convinced the young man was not guilty he went in as a matter of business and justice....

Early in the case the defendant had been told by his counsel that he should not talk to anyone about the case— "To open my mouth only to eat," as Durrant put it, "and to breathe through my nose." Yet, as the trial entered its

District Attorney William S. Barnes, who prosecuted the Durrant case. *Author's Collection*

final stages, it became increasingly clear that the situation was desperate. Finally, Dickinson reasoned that since Durrant had convinced him of his innocence, perhaps he could do the same with the jury. On the stand, however, he was impassive, smug, and completely self-controlled. He denied emphatically the stories of the many witnesses, yet could prove none of his alibis. When he finally stepped down he had done little more than fortify the prosecution, as noted by a correspondent of the *San Bernardino Sun* of October 16:

> From the first to last the strongest witness against Theodore Durrant has been himself. Though his testimony, if true, would convict of lying not less than a dozen people, not one of whom, apparently, had any conceivable motive for misrepresentation, yet that very testimony, on one point or another, corroborates nearly every one of them in respect to matters about which there might have been room for some sort of doubt....

During the trial both Deuprey and Barnes were struck down by exhaustion. Still ill, the attorneys struggled back to the courtroom and continued as best they could.

Following up the hundreds of leads and rumors concerning the case kept Isaiah and his detectives always on the move. A particular story that gained circulation concerned an anonymous young woman who accompanied Durrant to the church one evening. Once inside, Durrant excused himself and disappeared into another room. A few moments later, the girl was horrified when he returned completely nude! She ran screaming from the church; one version insisted Durrant had later returned her hat and gloves, threatening to kill her if she gave him away.

It was Lees' theory that since no particle of blood could be found on the suspect's clothes, he had committed the murders while stark naked. The persistent story of Durrant and the girl in the church dovetailed perfectly with this theory, and Lees was convinced it was true.

When the rumor first surfaced, Lees detailed Detective John Seymour to trace it to its source. The lawman tracked the tale from person to person, then followed it across the bay to Alameda County. After interviewing some fifty-two witnesses, Seymour traced the story to District Attorney Barnes. The two men met in the courthouse corridor, and Seymour queried Barnes about the incident.

"Did you relate that story, Mr. Barnes?" asked the detective.

"Of course I did," responded the D.A.

"Who told you the story?"

"Why, Captain Lees told me. He read a letter to me in which it was described."

The *Chronicle* gleefully printed the story:

> ...The scene that ensued in the inner office when Captain Lees discovered he had traced an important story back to himself can be imagined. The Captain still believed that the rumor has foundations in fact.

Building an airtight case against Durrant was one of the old detective's greatest achievements. *Author's Collection*

The final summing-up by the defense revolved around the lack of really hard evidence. "Where was the motive?" thundered General Dickinson. The prosecution had proved nothing. Certainly robbery was not the motive and the great mass of circumstantial evidence was just that—circumstantial. The defendant was innocent and the verdict must be "not guilty!"

District Attorney Barnes next addressed the jury. He carefully marshalled his facts before the packed courtroom. Accurately and thoroughly, the exhibits and evidence gathered by the detectives was dovetailed into the testimony of the many witnesses. The prosecution was complete, and devastating—the oratory, superb. "I have attended trials all over the United States," wrote Billy Heyneman, "listened to the most eloquent speakers before the public, but I have never heard its equal. It was a plain, magnificently delivered oration, pointing cleanly and cleverly beyond the peradventure of a doubt to the absolute guilt of the prisoner."

General Barnes rushed over and threw his arms around his son the moment he had finished speaking. The "Trial of the Century" was over.

Judge Murphy charged the jury late in the afternoon of November 1, 1895. When the jurors filed back into the courtroom twenty-five minutes later, Durrant and his parents assumed they were going to ask the judge for some legal clarification. When told a decision had been reached, Mrs. Durrant clutched her son, as the foreman read a verdict of murder in the first degree. Cheers burst out both in the courtroom and the mob-choked streets outside.

Deuprey had suffered a relapse and received the adverse news by telephone while on his sickbed. Durrant's defense team agreed that the jury had been a superb

one, but they were bitter at the loss. "They have not hanged him yet," growled General Dickinson.

"Well," opined Harry Morse, "I suppose we ought to be glad they haven't hanged us."

Isaiah received much good press for his work in the case—full-page articles relating highlights of his long career and praising his detective skills. But he was sixty-five years old and the investigation and trial had worn him out. Throughout the trial he had been working on other cases—particularly the Ingleside murder and robbery in March of 1895. Lees had located the rooms of two suspected train robbers and was convinced they were also the Ingleside killers. He was preparing to leave for Sacramento on this case when a *Call* reporter obtained a statement from him:

Theodore Durrant at San Quentin. It was just a matter of time, now. *California State Archives*

> It is for the people who witnessed the trial from the beginning to end to express their opinion as to how the guilty man has been ferreted out and proof obtained of his single participation in the crime....I have but done my duty and my associates have done admirably....I have had no doubt of the guilt of Durrant for a long time. His is a peculiar character.

Contemporary newspaper drawing of the Durrant hanging. *Author's Collection*

Durrant was sentenced to be hanged at San Quentin, and after a long series of appeals and delays he paid the price for his terrible crimes on January 7, 1898. The body was shipped to Los Angeles and disposed of when local mortuaries refused to accept it for cremation. Even today, the case is regarded as one of the most celebrated and bizarre incidents in American criminal history.

Later that month Lees watched as the old City Hall was being torn down. The department had only recently moved out, and memories still clustered thickly about the old building. He clearly remembered those faraway days of 1850, when the Jenny Lind Theater was built, then later bought and refurbished into the new City Hall.

The time had passed so quickly.

## CHAPTER TWENTY-SIX / NOTES

The appointment of Commissioner Gunst was announced in the *Examiner* on January 6, 1895, with further coverage on the 16th and 18th. The *Examiner* also provides information on changes in the police uniform on March 21, May 28, and September 10, 1895. Gunst's concern about bringing the department up-to-date is discussed in the not-always-accurate San Francisco *Police and Peace Officers' Journal* of December, 1929. The San Francisco 1895 *Municipal Reports* was also useful.

The retirement of the old police captains was apparently first discussed by the grand jury, according to the *Examiner* of June 10 and at a police commissioner's meeting of June 19, 1895. See also the *Examiner* of July 10 and August 1. The *Chronicle* of July 30 was likewise very informative. The appointment of the new police lieutenants was reported in the *Examiner* of July 2 and 8, 1895.

Appleton Stone's retirement is mentioned in the *Chronicle* of July 30, 1895.

The standard work on the Durrant case is by Assistant District Attorney Edgar D. Peixotto, *Report of the Trial of William Henry Theodore Durrant*, Detroit, the Collector Publishing Co., 1899. Duke was also utilized, as was Otto Heyneman's article on the subject in the San Francisco *Call* of January 22, 1911. The most useful sources, however, are the daily newspapers of the period, which gave minute coverage to the case, beginning with the *Chronicle's* issue of April 10 announcing the disappearance of Blanche Lamont. Several of the local newspapers not only printed day-by-day court testimony, but were responsible, in their zeal to outdo each other, for locating many witnesses.

Ned Byram's quotes are from Volume 11 of his journals. He devotes 13 pages to the Durrant case and pasted in several notes pertaining to the suspect. The detective was obviously disturbed at the way Crowley handled the first interrogation.

The Lees-Morse rivalry is discussed in the *Chronicle* of July 29, 1895. Lees and Morse were not friendly and had tromped on each other's toes in earlier investigations. For an insightful view of the Lees-Morse rivalry, see chapter 19 of John Boessenecker's excellent biography, *Lawman: The Life and Times of Harry Morse, 1835–1912*, Norman, University of Oklahoma Press, 1998. Harry Morse's comment about not being hanged was reported in the *Examiner* of November 2, 1895. Lees' quote on the trial was published in the *Call* of the same date. Typical of the laudatory newspaper articles published at the conclusion of the Durrant trial was "He Forged the Chain Around Durrant," which appeared in the *Call* of November 5, 1895. This long article also contained much biographical material on Lees and is frequently cited in this work.

For a unique perspective on the Durrant case, see Felix Cherniavsky, *The Salome Dancer; The Life and Times of Maud Allan*, Toronto, McClelland & Stewart, 1991. Maud Allan, a noted dancer of her day, was the sister of Theodore Durrant. She was studying in Europe at the time of her brother's trial and was forbidden by him to return home. *The Salome Dancer*, and another Cherniavsky manuscript on the Durrant trial, are both based on letters, diaries, and other family materials acquired from Maud Allan by Cherniavsky's parents. Based on these

intensely personal sources, Cherniavsky concludes that there is no doubt as to Durrant's guilt...that Durrant was a schizophrenic and intermittently insane. Felix Cherniavsky, via communication to the author, November 23, 1995 and March 11, 1996. Although quite speculative, a recent work is quite interesting: Virginia A. McConnell, *Sympathy for the Devil, The Emmanuel Baptist Murders of Old San Francisco,* Westport, Connecticut: Praeger Publishers, 2001. I am much indebted to Dr. Cherniavsky, Kevin Mullen, John Boessenecker, and the late Dr. Albert Shumate for sharing materials and interest in the Durrant case.

The murder and robbery at the Ingleside Inn was reported in the March 18, 1895, edition of the *Chronicle,* as well as subsequent issues. Lees was convinced that Jack Brady and his partner, who had been killed in an attempted train holdup, were the Ingleside robbers and he had located their rooms in San Francisco. For Brady's career, see the James B. Hume Scrapbooks at the Wells Fargo Bank History Room, San Francisco, and the prison record of Henry Williams, alias Jack Brady, at the California State Archives, Sacramento.

The *Examiner* of June 23, 1895, gives a good description of the demolition of the old City Hall.

# Chapter 27

# The Great Nevada Bank Forgery

IN EARLY JANUARY OF 1896, CAPTAIN LEES HAD A CALLER. It was a Saturday afternoon and John Kavanaugh, an officer of the local Nevada Bank, was ushered into the detective's office by Billy Heyneman. The banker came quickly to the point. A bank draft of $22,000 had been taken out at a Woodland bank on the Nevada Bank in San Francisco. In balancing their books at the end of the year, auditors discovered the original check had been made out for $12.00 but subsequently had been altered, or "raised," to the larger figure.

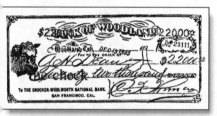

The "raised" check. *Author's Collection*

Kavanaugh showed Lees the check. The detective looked closely for telltale signs of the forgery, but there were none. Only when the check had passed through two clearing houses and been returned had the crime been discovered.

Calling in his clerk, the detective had him take down all the information Kavanaugh could relate. The man who had passed the bogus check was a handsome, bearded fellow named Arthur H. Dean. He had been doing business with the bank for several weeks and represented himself to be a general merchandise broker with an office in the Chronicle Building. As Kavanaugh described the man's friendly demeanor, his small talk with the tellers, and his regular cashing and depositing of small checks, Isaiah smiled. It was the standard operation of the confidence man and forger.

As soon as Kavanaugh left, Lees detailed one of his detectives to leave immediately for Woodland, a small town above Sacramento. Here he was to gather descriptions and other information on the man Dean. Another detective was sent to interview any local bank employees who had dealt with Dean. The check had been cashed on December 18, the gold being delivered in sacks containing $5,000 each. A balance of $2,000 was left in the account. There was no chance the thieves were still in town.

Taking Billy Heyneman along, Isaiah called on the superintendent of the Chronicle Building. Another detailed description of Dean was obtained, along with other information. In Dean's office, Captain Lees found several pieces of cheap furniture and a supply of stationery, billheads, and business cards. All were labeled "Arthur H. Dean, general merchandise broker, room 56, Chronicle

The Chronicle Building where Dean's office was located.
*Author's Collection*

Building." A rented typewriter was traced to its source and another description obtained.

The detectives located a boy named Wiley Lytle who had accompanied Dean to the bank and helped carry the gold to a rented buggy. The stable where the team was rented was also thoroughly checked out. Robert Pinkerton was promptly apprised of the crime, since the Pinkertons represented the American Bankers Association. "We'll need them on the eastern side of this thing," Lees noted to Heyneman. When his detective returned from Woodland, Lees gathered and compared his descriptions, most of which differed in details. Heyneman later recalled:

> ...He got up and locked his door, issuing preemptory orders that no one was to disturb him....I shall never forget as long as I live the two hours he spent over those puzzling, varying descriptions, each one vitally different from the next one, and after a long, tedious research, he made one composite description which was a marvel in its absolute correctness of every feature of Dean as I later knew him....

Dean, the tight-lipped con man, eventually talked.
*Author's Collection*

Dean's description was sent out to the Pinkerton agents and every major bank in the larger cities of the country. Although Dean had used various disguises in his San Francisco dealings, Isaiah's description had sifted Dean's true features from the phony. The description was as accurate as Heyneman later recalled. On February 29, an alert Saint Paul, Minnesota, bank clerk recognized Dean during a transaction and notified the Pinkertons.

Although he claimed his name was G. W. Woods, Dean was detained and definitely identified. Also picked up was a companion named Joe McCluskey, another notorious con man. They were soon back in San Francisco, where a *Chronicle* cartoon caricatured Captain Lees holding the two suspects with the caption, "Got 'em!"

Isaiah was well satisfied with the work, but he knew the most important facet of the case was yet unresolved. He wanted the penman who had actually forged the note. There was still no clue to his identity, but there were few men with such a flawless talent. The detective thought he might know who the forger was, but he had to verify the information through Dean to be sure.

Otto Heyneman recalled that Dean was aloof and cocky when first confronted by Captain Lees. By now his mug shot had been found in various police Rogues Galleries and his prison record in Maryland had surfaced. While being questioned, Dean laughed and cautioned the old detective.

"Oh no, Cap," he said, "no third degree for yours truly. I'll rot here before you'll get anything out of me. You've got nothing on me, even though I should—which I won't—be identified as your man Dean. I'll stand pat. Go as far as you like. My past record is against me, I know, but it's up to you to convict me."

Isaiah returned the smile. "That's all right. One of these days, soon too, you and I are going to have a matinee just by our two selves—one of those regular Ella Wheeler Wilcox heart to heart talks, you understand? Then we'll come to some real, definite conclusion. I'm not worrying, old boy."

Before he left, Lees asked the prisoner if there was anything he could do for him. "I'm going to treat you fine," grinned the detective. Dean asked for a "cold bottle and a hot bird," and later was surprised when it was served. He was also surprised at the comfort of his cell. He quickly discovered the price of his quarters, however. Every day Lees wheedled, coaxed, and questioned him concerning the forgery. Heyneman recalled:

> For three days the old master and Dean kept up their duel of wits. Dean spent hours in the chief's office. I was always secreted during these interviews, and had my instructions that the instant any matter pertaining to the case at issue was discussed I must be sure and get the report verbatim. Lees and the prisoner would swap stories like two old pals. Dean would brazenly tell of his experiences in the different European prisons in which he had been incarcerated, and he and his listener would burst into laughter many times.

Finally Lees saw the telltale sign he was looking for. Repeatedly reminding the prisoner he had been abandoned by his partners, the detective was steadily wearing him down with tougher queries. In the end, Dean was answering questions almost without knowing it. Eventually, Lees had his confession.

At his trial in early April of 1896, Dean's friend McCluskey was found not guilty. Although the man had a long record of criminal activity, there was little to connect him to the forgery case. Dean's confession had also kept his friend in the clear. Isaiah hated seeing McCluskey walk away, yet his plan was working well, even though few understood what was taking place. The *Chronicle* grumbled:

Creegan as he appeared for Captain Lees' mug shot. *Author's Collection*

> McCluskey and Dean occupied one of the best cells in the city prison. They were accorded every privilege and allowed to see visitors at any hour. Every day they have been permitted to leave the prison in company with Detectives Whittaker and Seymour and visit various places of amusement. Sunday they took a trip to the Cliff House and...were met by two well dressed rather handsome young women. Just why Dean and McCluskey were given such privileges is a source of worriment....While denying that the men were granted undue liberties, Captain Lees admitted that they were allowed to leave the prison, but were always closely guarded by two detectives.

On May 8, Dean gave his confession before the grand jury, resulting in a secret indictment of Charles Becker and James Creegan, the two other principals in the Nevada Bank forgery. Becker and Creegan had already been detained in Philadelphia, but had been released for lack of evidence. The Pinkertons kept the two men under surveillance and were aware they had already purchased tickets for South America. Both were picked up by the Newark, New Jersey police on May 14, 1896. Under the headline "Check Raisers Caught," the *New York Times* gave a detailed account of the capture:

> ...Patrolman Loftus, whose detail is the corner of Broad and Market streets...was on duty today a little after noon. He was accosted by a man who showed his credentials as a (Pinkerton) detective, and pointed out to Loftus two well-dressed, business-like appearing men. He said they were noted criminals and were fugitives from justice. Loftus at once arrested Creegan, while Detectives Fallon, Muenster and Laddel took charge of Becker. Becker appeared surprised, but said nothing. Creegan protested against arrest, and threatened trouble, but Loftus informed him he would use his club if there was anything but calm consent...and Creegan wilted....

Isaiah was jubilant at the news. The case was complete. And, if Otto Heyneman tended to overstate the old detective's abilities at times, it didn't seem so in all the laudatory telegrams and press accounts from around the country. The *New York Times* reported that "George D. Bangs, General Superintendent of Pinkerton's agency in this city, said yesterday that the principal credit for the arrest of the gang of check raisers and forgers belonged to Capt. I.W. Lees, Chief of Detectives in San Francisco." Isaiah had wanted Becker badly and now he had him. Byram penned in his journal:

Becker as he appeared upon his return to San Francisco to face Captain Lees. *Author's Collection*

> Wednesday, May 13th 1896. They were arrested in Newark, New Jersey. Creegan gave [name] of Joe Howard, and Becker as Charles Baker. They had tickets for Guatemala, by steamer. They were skipping out of the country, leaving Dean in the lurch. The "Fall Fund" provided by them all, was not forthcoming for Dean's defense. McCluskey was in there trying to raise it, but they said Na! Na! Dean and McCluskey then turned on them, and agreed to testify.

Charley Becker, "The Scratch," as he was called in the trade, was one of the most notorious forgers in the world. Born in Württemburg, Germany, in 1848, Becker came to America when just a child and learned the engraver's trade. At an early age he became involved with such master forgers and criminals as George Wilkes and George Engles. After robbing a Maryland bank in 1872, he fled to Europe where he, Joe Chapman, Carlo Siscovitch, and others flooded the continent with forged drafts of large denominations. They escaped from a Turkish prison and made their way to England, then back home to the states. Numerous other crimes followed, some with

his father-in-law, the lithographer Clement Hearing. Becker lived with his wife in their Brooklyn rooming house when he wasn't off on one of his forging expeditions.

Creegan was the middleman in the operation. He provided money and was the contact between Dean and Becker, who had altered the check in Sacramento. McCluskey had kept his eye on the bankers, as well as his partners.

The trial of Becker and Creegan began on July 1, 1896. The courtroom was packed with bankers who considered these men to be the most dangerous forgers in the world. Lees detailed Ned Byram and John Seymour to remain with the prisoners throughout the trial.

Isaiah had his usual airtight case. Besides his local witnesses, he had summoned porters, trainmen, and hotel clerks who placed the defendants in San Francisco and Sacramento at the time of the forgery. Becker's previous court testimony that he was a master forger was used against him, as was his prison record and criminal career. Mrs. Alice Becker was in court also and watched the proceedings closely. Dean's and McCluskey's testimonies were, of course, the final touch.

When first picked up in Philadelphia, both Becker and Creegan had been carrying new double eagles with San Francisco mint marks. Becker also had in his possession a forger's kit, consisting of water colors, fine brushes, goose-quill pens, and a collection of different types of banknote paper. He had thrown the outfit into the river when capture was imminent, but it had been recovered and used by Lees to show how the forgery had been accomplished.

During the trial, Byram was disturbed when a frustrated defense took its usual course and attacked the prosecution:

> Thursday, July 9th, 1896... Dunn commenced his argument, 4:20. He closed and court adjourned. Dunn is a very brilliant talker, would have liked him better if he hadn't roasted Lees. The most of McPike's argument was roasting Lees. Dunn went to Lees after he got through and apologized for McPike, but in his argument he clinched McPike's slurs and abuse.

The trial lasted ten days. After deliberating an hour and a half the jury found them guilty on July 11, 1896. Becker and his wife were shaken by the verdict, but were even more upset when both defendants were given life terms in San Quentin.

Becker in court, center foreground. Creegan sits next to him in the dark suit. *Author's Collection*

Upon appeal they were granted new trials on a technicality, and Becker wound up with a mere seven-year term. Creegan's appeals stretched out for several more years, and in March of 1899 he was finally sentenced to two years at Folsom after making a complete confession.

Isaiah was greatly relieved. "Captain Lees," noted the *Chronicle*, "looked ten years younger after the verdict was announced." Telegrams from lawmen and bankers came in from around the country. Robert Pinkerton's message was typical:

Becker in San Quentin.
*Author's Collection*

> Accept my sincere congratulations on the conviction of the greatest forger of the age. The banks of the world owe you and the Police Department and District Attorney a debt they can never pay. It is a great victory.

Dean, whose real name was apparently Frank Seivers, wound up being held in the city jail for nearly four years as the case was being appealed.

"I don't suppose," he commented as he left the jail in March of 1899, "that I will ever be a good man, but I will never be so cussed bad as I have been."

Isaiah had no time to rest on his laurels. Although he was increasingly concerned with Jane's asthma attacks, the pressures of his office still left little leisure for home life. In the midst of the Becker-Creegan case, the old detective was wrestling with an equally frustrating local case.

Early on the morning of February 14, 1895, there was a disturbance at the California Street residence of wealthy Julius L. Franklin. Sam Solomon, a son-in-law living there at the time, heard a pistol shot about three A.M. and roused himself to investigate. In the basement he found a side door open and the family butler lying on the floor, groaning in pain. Frank Miller, the butler, gasped that he had surprised a burglar and during a struggle had been kicked in the stomach and knocked down. He had fired a shot at the fleeing robber just moments before Solomon found him.

Miller was the hero of the hour. Touched by his nineteen-year-old employee's bravery, Franklin presented him with a new watch and a $200 check.

The Franklin home at 2930 California Street.
*Author's Collection*

A year later, almost to the day, the young butler had an encounter with another intruder. Miller had gotten up as usual at five A.M. on the morning of February 14, 1896. After retrieving the paper, he was investigating a noise in the basement when he confronted three men in the hallway. One of the intruders held a pistol on him, while the other two disappeared. Noticing his captor was shaking with excitement, Miller grabbed him and a desperate struggle followed. Several shots were fired, and the servant received minor wounds in the neck and hand, but he managed to draw his own pistol and shoot the intruder in the head.

Waking from a sound sleep, Sam Solomon rushed to a window and blew his police whistle. Officers Green, O'Connor, Alvares, and Herlihy were promptly on the scene and found the wounded servant lying next to the dying burglar. Physicians were summoned and the officers took the statement of everyone in the house. It was still quite early when Captain Lees, Billy Heyneman, and several other officers arrived in a hack at the Franklin home.

Frank Miller, whose heroics quickly came under suspicion. *Author's Collection*

Isaiah had known Julius Franklin for many years and the merchant quickly took him to where the dead burglar lay in a pool of blood. Lees carefully looked over the body. "Instinctively," Heyneman later wrote, "I shuddered as the chief ordered me to take down in my book minutely and carefully the details of every wound, every abrasion, the color of the eyes, hair, complexion and position of the bullet wound. This done, he gave immediate orders to have the body removed to the morgue."

As Heyneman made his notes, the old detective prowled about the scene of the crime. He was shown the jimmied door where the intruder had gained entry and where the burglar alarm wires had been cut. The gas and telephone lines had both been tampered with in out-of-the-way places. Lees was carefully scrutinizing the entry doors when Heyneman caught up with him.

The dead "burglar." All Miller case illustrations from February, 1895 issues of the *Chronicle. Author's Collection*

"Inside job, Billy. Whoever cut those wires was very familiar with this house. And look at that door. It was unlocked from the inside, not the outside."

As they stepped into Miller's room, Lees was quite probably thinking of the butler's previous run-in with a burglar. This was all too much of a coincidence. Still, he had to keep an open mind.

Throwing back the sheets on Miller's bed, Lees pointed out vermin in the bed. Calling in one of his men, the detective captain told him to get down to the morgue and see if the burglar's body had vermin also. Lees next went through a stack of newspapers found on a shelf above the bed. After carefully searching through each issue he picked out one paper and initialed it, telling Heyneman to mark it "Exhibit A." As they left the room the secretary glanced through the paper, but could only discern that four pages were missing. "Guess the old man has gone dippy," he mused.

The detective captain next wanted to interview the wounded hero, but was stopped at the door of the room in which Miller was being treated. Franklin insisted the doctor didn't want him disturbed. Isaiah promptly telephoned the attending physician, who finally agreed Miller could be briefly questioned. Taking only Heyneman with him, Lees entered the room and stood next to the bed where the apparently unconscious hero lay.

Heyneman later recalled that Lees spoke roughly to the patient, throwing back the covers to look at his wounded thumb and otherwise treating Miller as something other than a hero. He was probably trying to get a rise out of his suspect. After removing the bandage from Miller's neck, the old detective called Heyneman to the bedside.

"Come close. Take a description of this horrible wound. You needn't be a doctor to see that it is the merest superficial scratch."

As he lay in bed, Miller was closely examined by Lees, whose suspicions had already been aroused.
*Author's Collection*

After detailing an officer to guard Miller night and day, Lees returned to headquarters.

Isaiah knew that identification of the dead intruder's body was the key to the case. If he was indeed a known burglar, it was possible Miller's story was true. All the evidence seemed to point otherwise, however. A *Chronicle* reporter caught the old captain in a talking mood some time later:

> I am satisfied that he is not one of the burglar class. I have searched every available record and have written and sent his description to various prison officials, but all to no avail. The burglars who would conceive the details of such a daring crime are not of the class of men of the deceased. They do not allow themselves to get into the filthy condition this man was. That leads me to believe that he was a tramp picked up for the occasion.

Although Julius Franklin was outraged at the police suspicions, there was little evidence that would tend to support Miller's story. Franklin again rewarded his employee and vowed to spend his entire fortune to see that he was cleared in the case. The detectives maintained that two fleeing burglars would most certainly have been seen by the many milkmen, newsboys, and bakers on the streets at that hour of the morning. Yet, only one neighbor had "thought" he had heard someone running on the street.

Finally, there was a break. A hobo named Welsh contacted the police and told a curious story. He had a friend named Franklin Hayes, known among the tramp fraternity as "Dakota Slim." Slim had told Welsh that a man who looked like Miller had given him some eating money on the night of February 11, near the Plaza. It was shortly before midnight and Slim had been asked if he would like to make

some more money and get a new suit of clothes. When he showed interest, the tramp was told to meet Miller at a house on California Street. Friends convinced him not to keep the rendezvous and after the story broke in the newspapers, Slim recognized Miller's picture. "That fellow wanted to shoot me," he told his friends.

Slim also had the Franklin address scribbled on a piece of paper bag. He said Miller had given it to him that night. Isaiah showed him a group of over a dozen photographs and asked the hobo to point out the man he had met. Two portraits of Miller were identified immediately. When Slim saw Miller on the street one day, the butler also gave an inadvertent sign of recognition.

On February 27, the inquest was held. It was a two-day affair and Lees confidently presented all the evidence collected to date. There was still no identification of the dead "burglar," but he was later identified as Billy Murray, an indigent from Butte City, Montana. Miller still stuck to his story with his employer's support. "I will defend him with my life," stated Franklin. "It is an outrage to charge him with such a crime."

Although several occupants of the Franklin home insisted Miller had not been out of the house on any night prior to the killing, a former cook contradicted this alibi.

When Isaiah took the stand, he presented the evidence which suggested the incident was an inside job. The testimony of Dakota Slim and several other tramps strongly implied that Miller had sought out an indigent in a cold-blooded plan to make himself a hero again and collect another liberal reward from his employer.

To Lees the story was clear. The dead tramp was enticed to the Franklin home and told he could sleep in Miller's bed that night. When he put on his clean clothes and discarded his filthy underwear, Miller wrapped the old garments in a newspaper and discarded the package in the street, where it was later found by detectives. Isaiah showed where the paper had been obtained displaying "Exhibit A." Early that morning, Miller had roused his guest and was showing him to the door when he suddenly shot him in the head. Quickly, he then scratched his neck with thumb and forefinger, intending to give himself a flesh wound. Unable to see what he was doing, he also wounded himself in the thumb—powdermarks lending credence to this theory.

When Miller took the stand, Lees made him give a history of his life There were periods of time for which he made no accounting and the detective knowingly nodded his shaggy head. "I am satisfied," he commented, "that if that man's record could be discovered we would find that he probably did not want to remember that period."

At one point Lees asked Miller to demonstrate his fatal, early morning fight with the supposed burglar. Billy Heyneman played the burglar's

part and as the two men grappled, the butler's strength became readily apparent. Heyneman choked and grew red in the face as Miller got him into a headlock and forced him down.

"It is not the first time he has held a man up," said Lees. "He gave my man the 'strong arm' in the most approved fashion."

On February 28, the coroner's jury brought in their verdict. The killing was pronounced to have been done in self-defense. Isaiah shook his head as Miller thanked the jury, then walked up to him. "Thank you, Captain, thank you."

"I don't know what kind of a jury that was," commented the detective later. "The verdict was totally unwarranted by the evidence. I do not know what to make of this man Miller. He is a mass of contradictions."

Lees continued the investigation, hoping the grand jury would come up with an indictment. Arresting Miller again, he knew, would be fruitless. Franklin would not press charges and would free him in a matter of minutes.

Carefully backtracking from what Miller had told of his past, Lees traced his earlier life to Plymouth, Connecticut, where he struck paydirt. His real name turned out to be Hoefler, and although Miller had stated his father was dead, Isaiah found Kaspar Hoefler alive and well. Other lies were discovered and it seemed clear the suspect was trying to shield a shady past.

Ed Wren and Tom Gibson were kept on the case, and they succeeded in finding several other tramps who had been approached by Miller. When the butler's attorney became convinced his client was guilty and dropped him, Franklin was forced to reassess his position. In mid-April the *Chronicle* reported a new development:

> "I am thoroughly satisfied," said Mr. Franklin yesterday, "that Captain Lees is correct in his theories about Miller. I have become so disgusted with him that I don't want to see him anymore. I kept him as long as I could in order to give Captain Lees an opportunity to arrest him, but there is nothing we can do now. We went to see District Attorney Barnes also, but he is doubtful about securing a conviction with the testimony that could be gathered.
>
> I discharged him today and he went to the bank, got his money and left town...."

Lees was disturbed that he had not been able to hold the suspect. He had to be content with the unsettling news in mid-August that Miller was being held in Santa Barbara for an attempted abduction of a young girl. He was convicted and sentenced to San Quentin for five years. At least he would do some prison time, but it was a small price to pay for a cold-blooded murder.

## CHAPTER TWENTY-SEVEN / NOTES

For Otto Heyneman's recollections of the Becker forgery case, see the *Call* of January 1, 1911. The forgery was announced in the *Chronicle* of January 6, 1896, and followed up during succeeding days. Lees' description of Dean is noted in the *Chronicle* of March 2, 1896, with an account of Dean's and McCluskey's Minnesota arrest. Dean's confession and McCluskey's release were reported in the *Chronicle* on April 14. See also the *Call* of May 13 and 24, 1896.

Ella Wheeler Wilcox was a prominent lecturer and poet of the day who had frequently visited San Francisco. See Oscar Lewis and Carroll D. Hall, *Bonanza Inn, America's First Luxury Hotel*, New York, London: Alfred A. Knopf, 1939.

Edward Byram's comments are from Volume 12 of his journals, covering the period from September 2, 1895 to May 28, 1897.

The indictment of Becker and Creegan and Dean's turning of state's evidence was announced in the *Chronicle* of May 13, 1896. The capture of Becker and Creegan was described in the *New York Times* of May 14 and 15, 1896, and in the *Call* of the same date. Becker's trial was covered in the *Chronicle* from July 1 to his conviction on July 12 and sentencing on August 29, 1896. Articles on Dean's life in the San Francisco city jail and other sidelights of the case appeared in the *Examiner* of March 21, 1898, and March 26, 1899, and the *Call* of the latter date. Duke's *Celebrated Criminal Cases of America* contains an account of the case, as does an article by Frank Smith in *Police and Peace Officers' Journal*, San Francisco, April, 1932. See also Fanning's *Great Crimes of the West*. Information on Charley Becker's career can be found in the previously cited Byrnes *Professional Criminals of America* and Robert A. and William A. Pinkerton's, *Adam Worth, Alias "Little Adam;" Theft and Recovery of Gainsborough's "Duchess of Devonshire,"* New York, Pinkerton National Detective Agency, 1904. See also Ben Macintyre, *The Napoleon of Crime, The Life and Times of Adam Worth, Master Thief*, New York, Dell Publishing, 1997. Other details of Becker's life can be found in the *New York Times* of May 14 and 15, 1896. Heyenman recalled in his January 1, 1911 *Call* article that after his release from prison, Becker was employed as an engraver for a large New York banking firm. He was paid a good salary and the authorities could keep an eye on one of the most dangerous forgers in the world.

The *Chronicle* of February 15, 1896, devoted the complete front page to the dramatic story of Miller and his alleged fight with the burglar. Coverage continued on February 16, 17, and 18, 1896. Lees' comments on the dead man being a tramp and not a burglar were reported in the *Chronicle* on February 19. Details of the coroner's inquest were given on February 29, while Franklin's discharge of his erstwhile butler was related on April 11, 1896, in the *Chronicle*. Miller's attempted abduction in Santa Barbara was reported in the *Call* and the *Chronicle* on August 16, 1896. Heyneman's account of the Miller affair was featured in the *Call* of November 27, 1910. Lees' initial questioning of Miller, as reported by his secretary, was utilized by the author, although it may have taken place later than noted in his story. Duke also relates this case.

# Chapter 28

# A Just Tribute to Captain Lees

ON MAY 16, 1896, NED BYRAM made a fateful entry in his journal:

> 9:30 A.M. At the Hall. A telephone came in that there was a murder at 1225 Geary St. Harry Reynolds and I went up there. Coroners men there. They had telephones to our office. Mrs. Philopena Langfeldt, a divorced woman, lay dead on the floor in a back upper room with her throat cut....

Mrs. Langfeldt, the murdered woman. *Author's Collection*

Lees and his men went quickly to work on what turned out to be a particularly frustrating case. It was difficult locating the rooms of a man who had recently been calling on the middle-aged victim. The suspect was one Joseph E. Blanther, a young man of German or Austrian heritage, who had boasted of his European family connections. Mrs. Langfeldt enjoyed the company of younger men and evidence seemed to suggest she was looking for a means of support when her divorce money ran out. Although Blanther had claimed he was making good money as a writer, when his room was located and friends interviewed, it became plain he was so penniless as to be on the verge of starvation. He had recently told a friend he was contemplating suicide, yet was reported to be in good spirits the day after the murder. Isaiah must have seen the whole sordid story coming together.

The detectives quickly sorted out the details. Blanther had been seen washing bloody hands in the sink at his room and had sold Mrs. Langfeldt's jewelry through a friend. Further questioning of witnesses made it clear that both Mrs. Langfeldt and Blanther had misrepresented their circumstances to each other and each had hoped to obtain security through the other. Undoubtedly, when the woman had refused a loan to Blanther, he had stepped behind her, slit her throat, stripped the rings from her fingers, and fled.

Time spent in locating the suspect's room had allowed him to successfully flee the city, although Isaiah had covered all the trains, roads, and ports as soon as a description had been obtained. The detective captain was furious when he learned that a wire sent to Los Angeles had gone astray and the detectives there had just missed their man. Blanther had disappeared.

One of the reward notices sent around the country in the hunt for Joseph Blanther, the murderous Austrian fortune-hunter.
*Courtesy John Gilcrease*

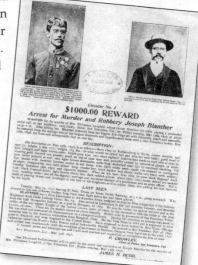

Joseph Blanther. *Author's Collection*

Lees never gave up, and he now covered the country with circulars describing the killer. He had learned in the meantime that Blanther was a deserter from the Hungarian army and was suspected of several other murders. "First let me catch my hare," he told a reporter, "then watch me skin him."

The circulars finally paid off. In March of 1897, Lees received word Blanther had been seen in Texas, teaching school under an assumed name. He had attempted to draw a pistol when being arrested, but was jailed to await arrival of one of Lees' men.

Isaiah sent Ed Gibson and a friend of Blanther's to Texas, but they arrrived too late. On the morning they were to leave for the Coast Blanther was found dead in his cell. Although Lees had specified the suspect be thoroughly searched, he had hidden cyanide in his hat band. There was no doubt as to his identity and Gibson had photographs taken of the body to wrap up the case. Blanther's long trail of treason, deception, and murder had come to an end.

Mrs. Isaiah W. Lees; 1829–1897
*Courtesy The Bancroft Library*

Jane's asthma had become steadily worse. The summer of 1896 was excessively warm, and Isaiah rented a cottage for her in San Rafael. He had hoped getting away from the humid city would somehow help, but while visiting one weekend he realized there was no improvement. After two months, she was brought home more ill than when she left.

By early January of 1897, Jane was confined to her bed, and it became apparent she was slipping away. Pulmonary problems had undoubtedly put a strain on her heart, and her gasping attacks must have been extremely difficult for the family to witness.

Deeply involved in several investigations, Isaiah was probably grateful to be busy. He could do nothing, and it was more than he could bear to sit idly by and watch her suffer. We can only imagine that he held her hand in the evenings, read to her, and talked of the days when the city, and they, were young.

It must have come home to him now just how fragmentary their life together had been. He had always been there when she needed him, but mostly he was at work—days, nights, weekends. Always at work. She knew the strain of his job and never begrudged him those evenings at the Palace Hotel bar when he did have some free time. Now, when it was too late, the realization of his neglect of this good woman must have startled him. The separate lives they had lived suddenly became painfully obvious.

The *Call* published a notice of the end on January 16, 1897:

> After a last short illness Mrs. Jane Amelia Lees passed away yesterday morning. She was surrounded by the members of her family and death came peacefully after the years of pain she has suffered. The sturdy old captain, hardened in the contemplation of the sorrows of life, as evidenced in his daily routine of business during the past quarter of a century, melted away yesterday afternoon in hot and burning tears as he gazed upon the features of his lifelong companion.... Mrs. Jane Amelia Lees was a most charitable woman. She was essentially a homebody, seldom being seen in the society circles to which her attainments entitled her. She had a little coterie of friends who gathered about her and through whom she did many acts of benevolence....

John Nightingale had come to California with Lees and remained the detective's lifelong friend. *California State Library*

The funeral was large and impressive. A throng of mourners flooded into the Lees home on the afternoon of January 18, spilling onto the stairs and sidewalk outside. In the parlor, huge flower displays nearly hid the casket and scented the air throughout the house. Large bouquets sent by prominent citizens and city officials filled the home, and Robert and William Pinkerton telegraphed two magnificent floral pieces from Chicago.

After the services, Fred and Ella followed their father and Reverend Stebbins out the door after the casket.

The honorary pallbearers were Chief of Police Crowley, W.H.L. Barnes, Reuben Lloyd, Thomas W. Walkington, Dr. John Nightingale, A. C. Widber, Davis Louderback, Joseph Bee, John T. Harmes, and Anton Roman. A detail of officers carried the casket. Two platoons of policemen commanded by Captain Wittman took the lead in the long procession of carriages.

At Laurel Hill Cemetery, a brief prayer was offered before Isaiah and his friends followed the casket into the impressive family vault.

San Francisco in the 1890s was a beautiful, modern city, but crime never seemed to let up. *Author's Collection*

That evening the crowds finally dwindled away at the house until only Fred, Ella, and close friends remained. Then he was alone. Isaiah had never realized how important it was to know someone was home waiting for him. She had always been there, night after night. Now she was gone.

Anton Roman, the prominent publisher, was a longtime Lees friend and helped him find many rare books.
*California State Library*

The memories flooded over him as he looked around the empty house. He had always shielded his family from his job, never talking shop at home. This had never made much sense to Jane, since the newspapers constantly ran articles about him and his work. He had once told a *Call* reporter: "I don't allow a volume of crime to get into my home. I try to forget that phase of my life when I go home. It's really not a pleasant business, anxious as so many amateur detectives are to get into the profession...."

It was so true. To laymen the business seemed romantic and exciting, but when on a case there was no stopping to go home for dinner or rest. You had to work on and on. Time was always your great enemy. Time allowed the criminal to escape. Time obliterated clues and destroyed evidence. Often he had worked around the clock and slept only when he dozed from exhaustion at his desk. Jane had understood this, but it had carved great chunks out of their lives together. Now he had to finish their story alone.

In late February of 1896, Pat Crowley tendered his resignation as chief of police. He had been deeply affected at the recent death of his son, and although in good physical condition the long years of responsibility had made him yearn for a rest. He had never forgotten his Honolulu vacation. Far from the reach of telephones and emergency situations, he had relaxed in a world of which he was totally unaware. It was the only vacation he had ever had, and now in the twilight of his life he longed to spend his remaining years in the carefree company of his wife and daughters.

Crowley had told the police commissioners, Lees, and others of his plans and determined to leave office on March 10. The old chief was interviewed extensively in the city's press and left no doubts as to whom he would like to see take his place. The *Examiner* of March 1, 1896 reported:

> I would like to see Lees succeed me. He has been in the department a great many years and, like myself, has given his whole life to the service of the people. It has been his ambition to become Chief of Police, and I think that if he were appointed to that office he would be content to hold it a few years and then retire. Of course, I do not know what action the Commissioners will take in the matter, but I think it would be only a just tribute to Captain Lees and a proper recognition of his long service to appoint him my successor....I do not

know any man who could take charge of the department with as firm a hand and with the knowledge of its requirements as he can. I do not think that I could have torn myself away if it had not been that I knew Lees was there to take my place.

Although several others were mentioned as candidates for the position, Lees was the obvious and logical successor.

"I do not hesitate to say," Isaiah told a reporter, "that I would like to be Chief of Police. It is a matter, however, which I cannot discuss." He was thrilled to know his long-sought ambition might be fulfilled, but it was not immediately to be.

Informed that a proposed pension law amendment might result in higher retirement pay, Crowley postponed his resignation. It was just over a year later that the legislature passed the amended bill, and Crowley submitted his final resignation on the evening of April 7, 1897. The commissioners immediately appointed Isaiah the new chief. Both Crowley and Lees favored Ben Bohen as the new captain of detectives and this appointment was also made.

The new chief was sworn in that morning, as reported in the *Evening Post*:

> Everybody was on hand in the upper office early today. The ex-chief came down and waited in his private office while his successor filed his bond and took the oath of office before Judge Slack, with Mayor Phelan, Dr. John Nightingale and Martin J. Burke as sureties for $10,000....

It had long been Isaiah's wish to become chief, and few men were ever better qualified for the position. *Author's Collection*

When Lees came into Crowley's office, the two old friends met, shook hands, and with lumps in their throats and tears in their eyes each saluted the other as "chief."

"I wish you all the success in the world, old man," tremulously remarked Pat Crowley.

"I know you do," replied the new chief executive.

"If you ever need me during a riot," remarked Crowley, "call on me."

"I will," responded Lees. "You'll remember I did once before when you were out of office and I was acting chief while Kirkpatrick was absent."

The Palace Hotel bar was San Francisco's elite watering hole in Isaiah Lees' time. *California State Library*

"Yes, I don't forget that occasion. I had 200 men under me then."

The *Chronicle* reported, "the leave-taking between Chief Crowley and the commissioners was most affecting. The meeting was held with closed doors, and at its conclusion there was not a dry eye in the room."

The following week was a succession of dinners, congratulatory telegrams and well wishes for the new chief. John Nightingale had rushed to be the first to put up the bond for his old friend. Isaiah was stopped on the street, in the Palace Hotel bar, and interrupted in restaurants by friends and acquaintances in every walk of life who wished him well in his new position. But he always had to go home at night. If only Jane could have shared his triumph.

The new municipal city hall had been under construction since 1871 and was at last in the final stages of completion. The Hall of Justice portion of the building would house the courts and main police headquarters. This would be the second headquarters Isaiah would occupy, and he spent much time helping to plan the police chambers of the facility.

Criminal photography had been shown to be a vital aspect of detective work over the years. The Blanther case had again proven its worth, and most large police departments in the world utilized the Rogues Gallery system.

The new city hall complex was finally completed. Over twenty-five years under construction, due to graft and labor union shenanigans, it would be destroyed in a few years by the great earthquake and fires of 1906. *California State Library*

Private photographers had been used by the police until the mid-1880s when Isaiah was finally able to set up his own camera. The only room he could obtain was in the basement of headquarters, and the poor light made for long exposures. Still, it was more practical to be able to control the process. Lees learned to operate the camera himself and did so when necessary. The French police had been taking both profile and full face views in the 1880s, sometimes simplifying the process by having the subject stand next to a mirror. Other Rogues Galleries had utilized this mirror process also, but Lees still took a full face and side view of all prisoners.

The new police headquarters would have the most modern photographic facilities available and this time Chief Lees could plan it himself, as he stated to a *Chronicle* reporter on April 18:

Two or three rooms in the new buildings," said Chief Lees yesterday, "will be devoted to the new gallery. I am determined to make it one of the finest in the country. As the work of the new building progresses I will tell Architect Shea where I believe will be the best location for the gallery, which will be on the same floor as the prison, the light being the principal consideration in its location.

The annual Memorial Day parade was scheduled for May 30 and this would be the first time Isaiah would ride at the head of the department as chief. He had seldom worn a uniform in the past, but now he would be a focal point of the parade and he had his new cap and coat carefully prepared. It was a proud moment for the old detective as he rode in front of the two companies of officers headed by Captain Wittman. "For nearly forty-four years," commented the *Chronicle*, "Lees has been connected with the department, but the memory of the oldest inhabitant does not run to the time when the veteran wore the blue clothes and brass buttons of an officer."

In early August of 1897, Chief Lees filed his first annual report with the board of supervisors. After listing the number of arrests and the amount of fines paid into the city treasury, Isaiah continued the policy of his predecessor in seeking city ownership of the police sub-stations throughout the city:

> The history of the police departments in other cities and particularly in the large and more progressive eastern cities, fully justifies the position which I am assuming in this matter. In these cities the police stations are city property and are fitted up in a substantial and adequate manner to accommodate all officers in the district in which the station is located, thus giving the force a place of rendezvous where they can be concentrated in cases of riot or popular outbreaks. It is my duty to remind you that ultimately it is the tax-payers who are

Chief Lees leads his first parade. *Courtesy of the Bancroft Library*

obliged to make good losses resulting from the conduct of riotous mobs, and I urge seriously upon your most careful attention the proposition that the reasonable precautionary measures here suggested for the adequate equipment of this department would be a very cheap insurance against the heavy losses which may be incurred by neglecting to take that care of the public interest....

Other equipment needs were stressed, along with a beefing-up of the mounted patrol. The old lawman closed his report with a warm tribute to his predecessor.

On the morning of October 26, 1897, Chief Lees was pleasantly surprised as he walked into his office. A large floral wreath composed of chrysanthemums, roses, and carnations in the form of a seven-pointed policeman's star was placed on an easel flanked by Ben Bohen, Tim Bainbridge, and other department associates. At the top of the wreath was inscribed "44 Years," with his name beneath. A broad grin creased the old man's handsome face as he shook hands all around. The veteran lawman confessed to a *Chronicle* reporter that he had "an uncomfortable lump in his throat as he surveyed the good-will token of his fellow officers."

The celebrated Botkin case occupied much of the following year. When the spoiled and frivolous Cordelia Botkin poisoned her paramour's wife through the mail, Chief Lees was involved in an investigation carried on between the West Coast and Delaware, where the victim lived. It was an ugly case involving poisoned candy and two spouses who behaved with no thought as to how their illicit actions affected others. John Dunning had to live with the fact that his lover had murdered the mother of his children.

Lees and his men did their usual masterful job of assembling a mass of evidence assuring Mrs. Botkin's conviction. An appeal gained her a second trial, but she was again convicted and died in San Quentin in 1910.

There had been a state and municipal election recently. Under date of November 9, 1898, Byram noted, "Republican Victory except Mayor Phelan and some others." Isaiah was pleased with the results, but there would be trouble the following year from the new mayor.

Mrs. Cordelia Botkin murdered her paramour's wife by sending poisoned candy across the country. *Author's Collection*

## CHAPTER TWENTY-EIGHT / NOTES

The Byram quote pertaining to the Langfeldt murder is from Volume 12 of his journals. The *Chronicle* and *Call* of May 17, 1896, announced the crime, with both papers following the actions of Lees and his men in succeeding issues. On May 23, the *Chronicle* announced a one thousand dollar reward offer and gave details of Lees' frantic attempts to intercept the fugitive as he fled south. Blanther's capture and death in Texas was confirmed on April 7, 1897, when the *Chronicle* published sketches made from photographs of the body. Otto Heyneman's recollections of the case appeared in the *Call* of December 11, 1910, while Duke also recounts the tragedy.

Jane Lees' pulmonary problems are reported in the *Chronicle* of January 15, 1897. She passed away this same day after what was termed years of suffering. On January 16, the *Call, Evening Post, Chronicle,* and the *Examiner* all paid high tributes to "the beloved wife of the veteran Captain of Detectives." On January 19, the press gave extensive coverage to the funeral, the *Chronicle* producing a large, three-column sketch of the scene outside the vault at Laurel Hill Cemetery. "To know her was to esteem her," stated a large headline in the *Call.*

Lees' comment on detective work was culled from the *Call* of November 5, 1895.

Pat Crowley announced his retirement to the police commissioners on February 29, 1896, with the story appearing in the *Examiner* and other city newspapers on March 1. The following day the *Call* published a long article in which Crowley, Captain Wittman, and others boosted Lees as the man most qualified to head the police department. Lees' appointment as chief was heralded a year later in the *Chronicle* of April 8, 1897.

The cornerstone for a new city hall was laid in 1871, at the corner of Larkin and McAllister streets. The city government at this time was still in the old Jenny Lind Theater building. By 1878 the municipal headquarters was still only partially built, but some local government was able to move in, the police department remaining at its old quarters until a Hall of Justice could be completed. All through the 1880s construction lagged, until in the early 1890s the still uncompleted structure was referred to as "the new City Hall ruin." Portions of the municipal headquarters were still uncompleted in late 1899 and, of course, it was only in use for a few years when it was destroyed by the great earthquake and fires in 1906. See Issel and Cherny, *San Francisco 1865–1932.* For contemporary information, see the *Chronicle,* August 20 and October 29, 1899.

Lees reminisced about the first mug shots he had taken in a previously cited article by Theodore Kytka, "The First Rogues Gallery in the World." Kytka was a famous handwriting expert and criminologist who had worked with Lees on many cases. He wrote that the San Francisco Rogues Gallery was the first in the world, which it was not. Other police photographic history, and the quote of Lees and his new gallery, are reported in the *Chronicle* of April 19, 1897. Information on French criminal mug shots and identification is reported in the *San Francisco Post* of September 27, 1890.

The Memorial Day issue of the *Chronicle* appeared on June 1, 1897, with a full page devoted to various celebrations and some history of the yearly event. For Chief Lees' report, see the *Call* of August 4, 1897, or the *San Francisco Municipal Reports* for 1896–97.

"Chief Lees Counts His Official Milestones" was the heading of a long article in the *Chronicle* on October 27, 1897, which described the occasion and briefly outlined his life and career.

The Botkin case is dealt with in both Duke and the Heyneman series in the *Call*, although Heyneman doesn't always agree with the contemporary press. All the local papers covered the bizarre case, of course; see the *Chronicle* of August 24, 1898, and the *Examiner* of August 21, 23, 28, and 31. The *Chronicle* of October 5, 11, and 12 dealt with the squabbling over extradition and the arrival in San Francisco of the witnesses. The *Chronicle* covered the trial beginning on December 9, and on January 1, 1899 announced the verdict. Duke, an officer at the time, gives details on Mrs. Botkin's behavior in jail and her death in San Quentin.

# *"A Newspaper Is a Powerful Thing"*

THE ANNUAL POLICE PARADE was scheduled for the day of Washington's birthday. Parades were important. Isaiah recalled how the armed legions of Chief Burke, drilling in the streets, had done much to curb violence during Civil War days. But more than that, citizens felt more secure knowing they had the protection of these four hundred blue-clad officers, marching in formation with their white gloves and belts and glittering badges and rifles. The noted police drum corps and band added to the impressive display as cheering crowds lined Montgomery Street to California and along Kearny to Market.

Isaiah had gradually become aware of the enmity of Andrew Lawrence, managing editor of Hearst's *Examiner*. He had watched the newspaper's rise to power through the use of sensational news stories, together with bullying antics in acquiring advertising. "The Monarch of the Dailies," as the paper termed itself, liked to think it could bring powerful politicians and captains of industry to their knees, and occasionally it actually did initiate needed municipal reforms.

Little boys frequently ran alongside Chief Lees' horse during parades. *Courtesy of the Bancroft Library*

Anyone familiar with editor Lawrence's record, however, knew there were ulterior motives for most of his social campaigns. Described as a "dapper, unscrupulous man who always maneuvered for political connections," Lawrence had a checkered background. He had served a brief term as a Democratic member of the California state legislature and managed to cozy up to U.S. senator George Hearst. The old senator had owned the *Examiner* before giving it to his playboy son, William, who surprised everyone by working hard and eventually making his toy a profitable enterprise.

Young Hearst had once fired Lawrence for being involved in a blackmailing scheme, but later re-hired him—some said because Lawrence had something on Hearst himself. The "Monarch" was a Democratic political organ and editor Lawrence slavered for power. With Hearst in the East or Europe much of the time, Lawrence had things pretty much his own way as long as he stayed in the black. He cast greedy eyes at the police department, long a Republican political bastion. For many years the chief and the balance of commissioners had been Republicans. Isaiah was also a staunch Republican. There was power in the police department and editor Lawrence determined to have it. Chief Lees thought at first the attacks on him

Lieutenant William Price was a pawn in the *Examiner's* political shenanigans. *Kevin Mullen Collection*

were simply a matter of politics, but he soon learned the stakes were even higher.

In late February 1899, the *Examiner* devoted most of a page of its Sunday magazine section to police lieutenant William Price's article, "My Ten Years' Struggle with the Hatchetmen." It was a rousing tale of the police efforts to control the Chinese tongs and gamblers, and Isaiah was glad to see one of his officers get some good press from the "Monarch." Price described the highbinders as "a pack of deep-dyed devils—every one of them blood-thirsty...." His tale was one of danger and excitement.

Chief Lees was surprised a few weeks later to see a prominent article in the same paper describing Lieutenant Frederick Esola's attacks on various Chinese gambling halls a few years before. But now it was a changed scenario:

> Up to that time numerous police officials backed by large squads made feeble efforts to stop the wide-open gambling in the Chinese Quarter. It was frequently noticed that those officers and the members of their squads grew wealthy enough in a few months to be retired from the Police Department. Gambling became so prevalent that the police decided to put a stop to it and Lieutenant Esola was chosen to lead the squad. Axes and sledge hammers were his weapons of reform....

Lieutenant Frederick Esola *Author's Collection*

The chief was puzzled at first. What was Lawrence up to? Suddenly, it all came together. The Price article was meant to establish the danger of Chinatown duty. A few weeks later Price is no longer the hero, however. Now it is Lieutenant Esola who bravely tackles the highbinders and chops his way into the evil Chinese gambling dens. Esola! Now things were beginning to make sense.

Isaiah and everyone in the upper office were aware of Frederick L. Esola. He had worked in Andy Lawrence's legislative campaign in 1886 and had afterwards been rewarded with a job in the Democratic caucus in Sacramento. He also did work for Senator Hearst. Later, Lawrence secured his appointment as a guard at San Quentin. When he resigned that post, Lawrence obtained a commitment from one of the San Francisco police commissioners to name Esola to the force at the earliest opportunity.

Appointed a patrolman in 1892, Esola was not an outstanding patrol officer, yet was promoted to sergeant within two years and was soon a lieutenant. On duty he was frequently seen in the company of Lawrence and the two took

A Chinese highbinder of the 1890s. *Author's Collection*

vacation trips together. The young officer made it clear by his demeanor that he had powerful friends and strong political connections.

When corrected or given an order, Esola was sometimes haughty and distant—"He got up on his high horse," as Lees once expressed it. His superiors complained that he avoided drills and duties he considered unnecessary. He was also often away from his California Street station and difficult to locate.

Isaiah had always been friendly with Esola but, like others, was alert to his connections with Lawrence. When Lees complained that the lieutenant was not pressing as hard as he should as head of the Chinatown squad, Esola blurted out— "Oh well, I have a right to aspire to Chief of Police if I want to." Isaiah was startled, but agreed with him. At the time he didn't understand why the officer had suddenly made that statement. Later, when Lawrence unsuccessfully tried to obtain for Esola the Democratic nomination for sheriff, the objectives of the two men became quite clear.

Meanwhile, Chief Lees had his hands full in the Quarter. The Chinatown squad composed of Price and four men was still active, but the area was under the control of Captain Wittman of the California Street station. Occasionally Wittman would send Esola and several men out to break up a game, but the Quarter was thought to be rea-

Chinatown was a festering problem that would not go away. An open-air meat market, as shown above, might very well have warning buzzers under the counter to alert gambling room operators in the back of the shop. *California State Library*

sonably quiet so far as gambling was concerned.

In late March the *Examiner* was conducting an investigation in Chinatown for its own purposes and found lottery and fan tan games in operation. Lees had also been appraised of clandestine gambling and ordered Captain Wittman to break up all the games he could find. The *Examiner* commenced a series of large, three-column illustrated articles playing up the gambling and wickedness in Chinatown. An "immense corruption fund" was raised weekly in the Quarter, according to the "Monarch," a fund used to bribe the police. Esola had broken up the games a few years earlier and his methods should be used again, wailed the newspaper.

Isaiah must have smiled. The truth was that Esola had previously been pulled out of Chinatown because he was constantly accompanied by Lawrence, and it was

causing unfavorable talk. When his protege lost his high-profile position in the Quarter, Lawrence was furious and commenced his attacks on the department.

As for the so-called "corruption fund," the chief was always open to any proof of such a situation. Nevertheless, between February and April, some $19,520 had been paid by Chinese in bail and fines. This was certainly the major part of any "fund," as reported by the *Examiner*.

Numerous privately chartered Chinese clubs had recently been used as a cover for gambling, and on the evening of March 31, Lieutenant Esola was directed to take a squad of men and break into several of these clubs. Some thirty-two prisoners were taken, along with $4,000 from a safe. The *Examiner* was jubilant. "This is what an honest, active squad of healthy policemen can do," Lawrence glibly announced.

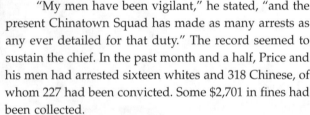

Day after day the *Examiner* articles hammered away at Price and his men, constantly suggesting they were the recipients of the mysterious "fund." Chief Lees refused to believe his officers were corrupt and doggedly defended them at every opportunity.

"My men have been vigilant," he stated, "and the present Chinatown Squad has made as many arrests as any ever detailed for that duty." The record seemed to sustain the chief. In the past month and a half, Price and his men had arrested sixteen whites and 318 Chinese, of whom 227 had been convicted. Some $2,701 in fines had been collected.

Two contemporary *Examiner* views of Chinese gambling. *Author's Collection*

The rumors of Chinatown graft finally surfaced at the police commissioners' meeting on the night of April 5, 1899. Lees had been investigating the situation for some time and read a report that wasn't released to the press. Although no charges had been made against Price, Commissioner Tobin commented later that there was circumstantial evidence to suggest that something was wrong in the Quarter. It was Lees' firm belief that the Chinese gamblers wanted to get rid of Price because he was too vigorous in his gambling raids. He also knew that the *Examiner* was stirring up things for its own reasons. Throughout the meeting the commissioners declined to inform Lees of what evidence they had, insisting their sources must be protected.

The meeting lasted some three hours, with Chief Lees doing much of the talking. He defended Price and his men and produced a list of over two hundred Chinese clubs and societies, most of which were actually gambling joints. Evidence was ex-

tremely difficult to obtain against these organizations, and when damage was incurred during raids and no evidence found, lawsuits were the result. Esola's last raid was already involved in a lawsuit. It all seemed black-and-white in the newspapers, but it was a difficult business.

The chief was appalled when the other commissioners finally voted to remove Price and his men from Chinatown. Lees cast the sole "no" vote. The removal might be postponed until replacements could be appointed, however. No charges had been filed and no evidence produced. Isaiah was frustrated, but steadily maintained his men had done a good job in Chinatown.

Chief Lees grew used to cartoons such as the above as the *Examiner* kept up its campaign to make Esola chief. *Author's Collection*

During a police commission meeting on April 12, Lees had recalled Esola had been removed from Chinatown in 1894 because of unfavorable talk resulting from his constant association with Andrew Lawrence. The chief further showed that, far from stopping gambling in the Quarter as the "Monarch" claimed, Esola had made only sixteen arrests and had collected only some $600 in fines during the month he was on duty there. At the time there were a reported 133 fan tan games running and some ten large lotteries.

The *Examiner's* editor was furious. For the next few weeks he vilified Lees outrageously in the paper, using large headlines to proclaim him a liar and cartoons that suggested he was somehow involved in Chinatown graft. "He is simply a human rattlesnake," wailed Lawrence.

The chief had personally appointed Price's squad and couldn't believe they were corrupt. The *Examiner* innuendos against Price, he discovered, had mostly been culled from ex-convict Tom Droulet, who had recently been seriously injured after being thrown from a window by a prostitute named "The Galloping Cow."

Price himself had no doubt about the source of his troubles:

> This is a diabolical scheme to get rid of me. Esola, anxious to run Chinatown to suit himself, has conceived the bold plan of accusing me of accepting money from the gamblers in order to carry out his purpose....He poses as an officer far above the rank and file of the department. There is one thing he lacks, however...and that is brains.

Price went on to accuse Esola of taking along his own "evidence" when he had made his recent, highly-publicized $4,000 raid.

The better part of two police commission meetings was taken up by Lees reading and discussing a large collection of records assembled to bolster his claim that the department was not tainted by Chinatown. The commissioners, however, in-

sisted Lees' records did not refute the secret witness's testimony concerning Price and his men.

Chief Lees closed his report to the commissioners on the evening of April 17, 1899. In attendance were editor Lawrence, *Examiner* attorney Garrett McEnerney, and a stenographer. McEnerney stated he was present to defend his client because of remarks the chief had made to the press. The commissioners quickly dismissed the trio. Quarrels between Lees and his enemies, commented President Tobin, had no place on the agenda. Isaiah stated he had never accused Esola of dishonesty as reported in the "Monarch," but he would stand by anything he had said about Lawrence.

The chief and his fellow commissioners must have been thoroughly weary of the whole thing by now, as reported in the *Chronicle:*

> More than once during the discussion Chief Lees impressed it on the Commissioners that he was determined to defend his department and its trusted officers to the last, but it was unfair to expect him to make any headway if no charge was brought against Price. Chief Lees said he couldn't fight shadows and that if the accusers would come out in the light he could deal with them. In the meantime all he could do was to put the Commissioners in possession of the facts in relation to Chinatown and to show that Price had a better record than any other officer who had ever been in the district.

The chief was feeling the pressure of the *Examiner's* attacks, although he consoled himself with the hope that few San Franciscans took the paper's wild charges seriously. Still, it hurt to see his years of public service reduced to nasty cartoons in a newspaper more concerned with power than good government. Noting the bitterness and anger in the old chief's face, toward the end of the meeting Commissioner Tobin sought to put the record straight:

> You know that when we first brought this matter to your attention we told you the Commissioners were a unit in their absolute belief in your personal honesty, integrity and ability. We are all of the same opinion still. You are not on trial here, no matter what any newspaper may say.

Always eager to go on record against the bullying tactics of the *Examiner*, other city newspapers rallied to the chief's support. The *City Argus* growled on April 22:

> Long Green Lawrence, the bunco manager of Hearst's *Examiner*, has been directing the dirty mud-flinging machines of that sheet against Chief Lees. As he cannot attack his reputation for honesty, by his orders Lees is ridiculed simply because the vigilant chief is a man that dares to do his duty and will permit no sheet to tell him what to do in its bogus reform crusade to gull the people....Chief Lees...knows that the managing editor of the *Examiner* wants to dictate who the next mayor of this city shall appoint as Police Commissioners so he can name a successor to Chief Lees.

The *Bulletin, Call,* and *Chronicle* were also well aware of what was going on. Under the heading "Esola out for Chief of Police," the *Bulletin* commented:

> Members of the Police Department declare that Esola is no more fitted for Chief of

Police than a Chinaman; that he lacks experience and all of the qualities that ought to go with the guardian of the "Cops." But that is to count for nothing. The *Examiner* is already being used to advance this young stripling. He is being featured as making Chinatown raids and performing all kinds of valorous deeds, all for the purpose of keeping the name of the youth before the public in the hope that when the proper time comes to announce his candidacy he will not be laughed out of town.

Sergeant James Donovan.
*Author's Collection*

Isaiah was disappointed on the evening of April 19, when the commissioners formally voted to withdraw the Chinatown squad and reduce Price to the rank of sergeant for alleged inefficiency. The old detective had fought hard for his men—often working around the clock, checking records and documents—but now it was over.

The *Examiner* whooped with glee: "Lees is no longer the bully that he was. He has been shorn of his power." This was typical "Monarch" nonsense, of course, but there was no doubt that "Long Green" Lawrence had won a round.

The next day, Lees appointed Sergeant James T. Donovan to head up the new Chinatown squad. The chief sternly lectured the officer on the responsibilities and temptations of the Quarter, then directed Sergeant Price to show him around. The old chief must have known nothing would really change. The Chinese would gamble. It might be possible to hold down the Quarter, but it would never be controlled. He had studied Chinese history and been familiar with the Quarter since its beginnings, yet the mysterious world of Chinatown and its denizens would remain a dark and inscrutable enigma.

Price was quite bitter over his demotion and threatened to resign, but was dissuaded by his attorney, Davis Louderback. "This is pretty hard," grumbled the big officer, "after 21 years of service and nothing wrong ever charged against me. Inefficient! I thought it was corruption I was accused of....If I had been given a chance to defend myself, I wouldn't mind it so much...but they wouldn't let me do that." Later he did resign.

When a solitary automobile appeared in the city's annual Fourth of July pa-

Sergeant Donovan's Chinatown squad. Chinese interpreter is third man from left. *Kevin Mullen Collection*

rade, it evoked a great deal of interest. These so-called "horseless carriages" were not yet common in the West. Many cities had initially banned them from the streets because they frightened horses, but the marvelous machines seemed to be an obvious and inevitable means of future transportation.

With his mechanical training, Isaiah had quickly envisioned the adaptation of the automobile to police work. In his July annual report to the board of supervisors, he recommended changing the existing horse-drawn patrol wagons to the new engine mode of power. He also recommended acquiring a steam launch for the harbor patrol, a bicycle squad for various beats, and the adoption of the Bertillon System of criminal identification. The number of arrests for the year to date was 27,769.

The *Examiner* couldn't resist publishing a cartoon showing Lees on a motorcycle-type "infernal machine," which would allow him to make the run "from city hall to the Palace Hotel bar in one minute and 49 seconds."

In late August 1899, the First Regiment of California Volunteers returned from the war in the Philippines. The city prepared lavish welcoming celebrations through a number of benefits and committees in charge of raising funds. Chief Lees and Commissioner Tobin were in charge of the police contributions to the committee, which was chaired by Isaiah's friend Michael de Young.

Late in the year, Isaiah and his friends lobbied in every way possible for his re-appointment as chief when his term came up on December 4. "Notwithstanding the newspaper attacks which the old chief has withstood," commented the *Bulletin*, "he is very strongly backed by some of the best men in the city." He desperately wanted to round out a full fifty-year career, hoping it might be possible since no outstanding

Chief Lees (far right) delivered the $2,000 contribution of the police to the welcoming committee for the returning soldiers. *Author's Collection*

candidates had come forward. Captain Bohen was too old and had been ill lately. Captain Wittman showed promise, but had only briefly held his present rank.

The only other likely applicant was Lieutenant Esola, and Isaiah would not stand for that. It was incomprehensible that he had worked all these years to turn the department over to the incompetent pawn of a power-hungry newspaper. He discoursed on the subject with *Bulletin* reporter Miriam Michelson:

> Look here, if a newspaper gets control of the Police Department, you know as well as I what a gold mine it will have in the way of "scoops." ...It's a fact that Chinatown might be exploited by an unscrupulous newspaper man, working through a chief of police whose appointment he had procured. That would be a richer mine than "scoops." ...But there's this: A newspaper, no matter how bad, is a powerful thing. There is no more powerful instrument for good—and bad—than the press....

In November the department began moving some of its offices to the new Hall of Justice building. Isaiah was nervous at the next police commission meeting but the worst didn't happen, as Byram noted in his journal:

> Wednesday, Dec. 6th, 1899. Meeting of the Police Commissioners. No Chief of Police was appointed. Chief Lees will hold office until his successor is appointed by the incoming Commissioners.

The commissioners declined to reappoint the veteran chief, preferring to let their successors name their own choice. Isaiah could understand their position. The old detective had suffered a number of setbacks recently, but was pleased when he read the year-end report of the grand jury:

> Whatever may be said of other departments in our municipal government, our city can congratulate itself upon its Police Department as being equal to that of any city in the world, and if it were backed up by the police courts and heed given to its demands as outlined by the Chief of Police in his annual reports, we could well feel that the suppression of crime and the protection of life and property is as secure here in this city as anywhere in the world. No greater argument in proof of this can be used than the small percentage of crime as shown by the records of the Police Department of this city.

On December 23 Isaiah must have been delighted with a series of *Bulletin* articles detailing Andy Lawrence's shady past and his plans for Lieutenant Esola. "Lawrence's Plan to Loot the City" was the large front-page headline of the first article. Follow-up stories gave particulars of an erstwhile Lawrence blackmail plot, featuring testimony of the victim. It was a rich dose of "The Monarch's" own medicine.

## CHAPTER TWENTY-NINE / NOTES

The Washington's birthday parade was well covered by the press, my account being taken from the *Call* and *Examiner* of February 23, 1899.

For information on William Randolph Hearst, the *Examiner* and Andrew M. Lawrence, see W.A. Swanberg's *Citizen Hearst*, New York, Charles Scribner's Sons, 1961. See also the *Examiner* of January 20, 1900. Lawrence and his brother Frederick worked for the *Chronicle* at one time before Andrew became a political writer on the *Examiner*, then later editor. Eventually he was appointed publisher of Hearst's *Chicago American*. For Lawrence's later money-grubbing schemes in Chicago, see Ferdinand Lundberg's *Imperial Hearst*, New York, Equinox Cooperative Press, 1939. Material on Lawrence's extortionist past appeared in the *Bulletin* of December 23, 25 and 28, 1899.

The article by Lieutenant Price appeared in the *Examiner* of February 26, 1899. The feature story on Lieutenant Frederick Esola, including a lively illustration, appeared in the same paper on March 10. Esola's early life was covered in the *Examiner* of January 14, 15, and 20, 1900, during the police commission investigation. Quotes of Lees and Esola are taken from testimony during these same hearings. Ned Byram mentions Esola from time to time in his journals and seems to have gotten along with him well enough. Byram was a detective, however, the elite of the force, and Esola would necessarily want to cultivate such people. Byram does write about dropping into the California Street station to visit Esola, only to find him gone most of the time—see Volume 13, pages 257, 258, and 259. Lawrence's attempt to obtain for Esola the Democratic nomination for sheriff is noted in the *Bulletin* of April 6 and December 23, 1899.

The *Examiner* began to publicize its Chinatown investigation on March 31, 1899, and continued into the following month. Lees' comments on Esola's unsatisfactory stint of duty in Chinatown was reported in the *Call* and *Bulletin* of April 13. Lees' "corruption fund" remarks are noted in the *Bulletin* of April 16, 1899. Esola's $4,000 raid is given most of a full page in the *Examiner* of April 1, 1899.

Lees' steady defense of Price's Chinatown squad is reported in the *Call* of April 6, the *Chronicle* of April 13, and the *Bulletin* of April 16, 1899. The statistics quoted are from an article in the *Bulletin* of April 1, 1899.

The police commission meeting on the evening of April 5 was reported the following day in most of the city press. The fact that the *Examiner* devoted nearly half of its front page to the meeting, while the other newspapers gave it only an inside column, is an indication the "Monarch" was using the situation for its own purposes. Again, on April 7, the *Examiner* followed up the story with another two full columns on the front page and three more columns, with a large illustration on the inside.

Chief Lees' comments on Chinese gambler fines levied in police court were quoted in the *Examiner* of April 4 and 6, 1899. The order to remove Price from Chinatown was made at the April 6 meeting, as reported in the same paper. Under the heading "Esola and his Wild Raids," the *Bulletin* didn't even mention the dismissal, the article being concerned with Esola and the *Examiner's* part in the developing Chinatown situation.

On April 13, both the *Bulletin* and the *Call* published Lees' devastating comments about Lawrence accompanying Esola during the course of his Chinatown duties. The *Chronicle* quoted from Lees' report directly, in which he stated at the time "there was talk...of a soft bed for Esola to lie on, of money, corruption funds and lots of other things...." Lees also displayed his scrapbook, showing *Examiner* articles highly critical of the department published at the time. On April 14, 15, 16, and 18 editor Lawrence retaliated by vilifying Lees unmercifully with long, name-calling articles and large caricatures indicating the chief was a thief in league with the Chinese.

Lees' investigation concerning convict Droulet is reported in the *Call* of April 13. Price's remarks are taken from the same paper of April 6, 1899.

The commissioners' meeting of April 17 was reported fully in the *Chronicle* and *Examiner* the following day. As usual, the articles were so different in tone they seemed to be reporting different events. Under a large front-page headline stating, "Lees admits that he lied," the *Examiner* again devotes most of its space to vilifying Lees, while the *Chronicle* devotes one interior column to the story under the headline, "Lees Closes his Report." Judge Tobin's quote is taken from the *Chronicle* article.

The *Bulletin* article, "Esola out for Chief of Police," appeared on April 6, 1899. All of the major papers in the city covered the meeting where Price had been demoted. Again, the *Examiner* devoted three front-page full columns to the meeting, concentrating on embarrassing Lees. The other papers devoted interior pages and much less space to the meeting. Sergeant Donovan's appointment is reported in the *Call* of April 21. Price's comments are taken from the *Bulletin* of April 20, 1899.

In an illustrated Sunday feature published on July 9, the *Examiner* discusses the introduction of the "automobile" and its impact on the world. See also the *Bulletin* of December 24, 1899. Chief Lees' annual report is in *San Francisco Municipal Reports* for the years 1898–99. The cartoon of the chief riding his "infernal machine" appeared in the *Examiner* of July 28, 1899.

The return of the California soldiers from the Philippines was heralded in the *Examiner* of August 24, 1899. A large photograph of Lees handing over the policemen's donations to the soldier's fund appeared in an article in the *Chronicle* on August 12, 1899, and is reproduced in this chapter. Byram mentions the decorations and large crowds as the soldiers paraded through the city.

The *Bulletin* article noting the efforts of Lees to retain his position appeared on December 28, 1899. Billy Heyneman commented in several of his articles on Lees' ambition to serve out a full fifty-year term. Captain Bohen's illness is mentioned in Volume 13 of Byram's journals, as is the move into the new Hall of Justice.

Lees' interview with Miriam Michelson appeared in a Sunday morning feature of the *Bulletin* on April 16, 1899. His prophetic description of the power of unscrupulous newspapers was borne out in 1912, when the mighty William Randolph Hearst was able to defy a congressional investigation looking into some stolen letters he had allegedly purchased for political purposes. Lees' concerns were further confirmed during this same case, when Andy Lawrence kidnapped an investigator named Stewart who was trying to secure some

information. Released, Stewart promptly preferred charges with the Chicago police, only to be ushered into the chief's office where Lawrence sat grinning at him. It was well known that Hearst owned the chief. For the full story of these incidents, see the previously-cited Hearst biographies by Lundberg and Swanberg.

The dashing of Lees' reappointment hopes was covered by the *Examiner* in its issue of December 7. The grand jury Report is taken from the *Bulletin* of December 23, 1899, while the series on Andy Lawrence ran in the same paper on December 23, 25, and 28.

# The Parting Hour

JAMES D. PHELAN HAD BEEN ELECTED MAYOR IN 1896 as a reform Democrat. A new city charter had bitterly divided merchants, labor, and other factions and failed to pass, but the new mayor immediately worked out a revised version. When Phelan was re-elected in 1898 a renovated charter was part of the package. An important provision allowed the mayor to appoint his own police commissioners—something the Democrats had been salivating over for years. It seems clear now that even more than politics had been involved, however.

During a series of meetings in the *Examiner* office, Mayor Phelan pledged, in exchange for the newspaper's support, to appoint new police commissioners who would "rid the city of the autocrats of the upper office" in the police department. Phelan admitted later that Police Lieutenant Esola had been present during several of these meetings, and that Esola's friends "expected for him some recognition in the line of promotion in case I was elected to office." The mayor's comment later turned out to be something of an understatement.

Mayor James D. Phelan learned too late that he had made a pact with the devil. *California State Library*

Hoping he could somehow salvage another term as chief, Isaiah was more active than usual in local Republican politics during late 1899. He had lobbied, called in favors, and asked friends to intercede, but by the time his term was up on December 4, he realized there was little chance of his being reappointed. Although his term of service was already one of the longest in United States police history, it had still been his determined ambition to serve a full fifty years.

At the police commission meeting on the evening of December 6, he was publicly informed that the commissioners felt morally obligated not to appoint a chief who might be objectionable to the new commissioners. Mose Gunst had never gotten along with Lees, but Tobin and Alvord were good friends and disliked the situation in which they found themselves. Despite the chief's private warnings about Esola, the commissioners' integrity overruled politics and Lees hoped for the best.

"The Finish of Lees as Chief" trumpeted large headlines in the *Examiner*, but Isaiah was to remain in office until a successor was appointed by the new commissioners in January. Maintaining a petty partisanship to the end, the "Monarch" began referring to Lees as the "acting chief" whenever he was mentioned in print.

Judge Robert Tobin,
one of the retiring
police commissioners.
*Author's Collection*

When Mayor Phelan announced the appointment of the new police commissioners on December 31, Isaiah knew it was over. He was a fighter, stubborn and set in his ways, but in the past few weeks he had come to terms with the realities of his situation. He wasn't going to be reappointed, but perhaps it wasn't the end of the world after all. He was old. Maybe it was best that changes be made at the beginning of a new century. Police work had been his life, but now it was time to step aside.

On the afternoon of January 2, 1900, Ned Byram was standing in front of the Bank of California talking to Officer Tom Walsh when Commissioner Alvord passed by. As he walked into the bank he said, "You boys have no Chief of Police. We have just retired him."

Byram looked at Walsh. "This was astounding news," he wrote in his journal. "Heard later that his clerk, the Property Clerk, three sergeants and nine patrolmen were also retired at their own request....Great excitement on the street at Lees' retirement."

Chief Lees had met with the police commission that morning and asked to be retired. The request was granted. It was a historic moment, Judge Tobin being visibly affected. All of those present realized it was the end of an era. Later, the old detective admitted he was still a candidate for chief when the new commissioners were seated, but as of now his police career was over:

> I had a special reason for retiring at this time. For twenty-two years I have been connected with the present Board of Police Commissioners and I felt that when the men with whom I had so long been associated were not reappointed I, in all manliness, should go down with the ship. The Commission about to retire has made a splendid record....

On January 1, the *Call* had predicted Esola would be Lees' successor, insisting the new police commissioners were pledged to do the mayor's bidding by appointing the young lieutenant. Although sometimes critical of the old chief and the department in the past, the *Call* was beginning to feel faint stirrings of the mayor's perfidy. "Phelan's First Deal Has Been Completed" blared the *Call's* headline on January 3. "Chief of Police Lees Retires to Make Way for Esola." In a long article the paper reiterated its charges, but paid the outgoing chief a stirring tribute:

Chief Lees had a career that few others could match, but now it was over. His name and legend would inspire future generations. *Courtesy of the Bancroft Library*

> In retiring, Chief Lees closes almost half a century of active consecutive work in the Police Department of San Francisco. The department as it is today, in its efficiency, is the

result more of his work than of any other man. It is due to him that modern methods of police work are in vogue. His ideas have not only prevailed in the local police department, but have been introduced into other metropolitan systems. Through his efforts very largely the department has grown until now it is the rival of any of the great departments of the world....

Captain George Wittman, the acting police chief. Later he would make chief on his own. *Author's Collection*

When Isaiah stepped down Judge Tobin was appointed acting police chief, and he in turn placed Captain George Wittman in temporary command of the department. Isaiah kept busy the following week settling business and gathering up his belongings. A false rumor, initiated by the *Call*, reported Lees was removing the Rogues Gallery and other records from headquarters, but inquiries disclosed he was only taking his personal collection of early photographs and memorabilia. "All our records from 1860 to the present day are here," reported detective Tim Bainbridge.

The ex-chief was present at the first meeting of the four new police commissioners on January 8, 1900. He formally turned over all police property to the board, as well as any funds of the department. He also presented a long catalog of all the record books and albums in the Rogues Gallery, which he said was complete from 1853 to date. Much of this material had been gathered at his own expense. At this time new commissioner William J. Biggy was appointed chief until a new head of the department was selected.

The new commissioners had announced that candidates for chief would be accepted up to noon of January 10, but rumors were circulating and the public was becoming concerned. Besides Esola, Bob Hogan—one of Lees' old detectives—and several others had announced themselves for the office. Editor Lawrence should have been getting nervous by this time, but if Ned Byram's journal is any indication, he was busy enlarging his schemes:

> Friday Jan. 5th. Morning at the Hall. Heard that Jules Callundan, Superintendant of Harry Morse's Patrol System, had been appointed on the force as a patrolman. A fine job is put up by Andy Lawrence and the *Examiner* to make Esola Chief of Police, Callundan Captain of Detectives. Throw out all the old detectives, then Harry Morse would control the Force, and what a squeezing the town would get from the *Examiner* gang. Esola couldn't stop them. Later Callundan came into the Bank of California and I had a talk with him. He gave me a yarn about better pay and a chance at promotion with the other men. He told it nice.

Just what kind of bargain Callundan and Harry Morse had made with Lawrence is not clear, but the other city newspapers now fully realized the threat posed by the *Examiner*

Jules Callundan, Harry Morse's right-hand man. *Author's Collection*

303

should it control the police force. In mid-January the *Call* published accusations that Callundan was at one time a defaulter and fugitive from justice. When Morse protested, in a letter to the police commission, that Callundan had been employed by him for the past eighteen years and had been an honest and faithful employee, the *Call* announced it was Morse himself whom Callundan had robbed!

On January 13, 1900, editor Fremont Older of the *Bulletin* filed formal charges with the police commissioners, specifying nine serious allegations against Lieutenant Esola. The charges were primarily based on the deposition of one Al Meador, a hoodlum friend of the lieutenant, and ranged from a petty robbery committed during Esola's youth to associating with degraded characters, having used an alias, and being dismissed from his job as guard at San Quentin. An investigation was promptly scheduled.

Robert A. Crothers, owner of the *Bulletin*. He was not about to let another newspap control the police departmen
*Author's Collection*

Just how involved Lees was in all this is not known, but he was certainly determined to do what he could to thwart Lawrence's plan. The *Bulletin*, and its owner Robert Crothers, was concerned that the "Monarch" would control the police force for its own ends. Also, Crothers was a Republican and fought the Democratic *Examiner* on general principles. It would have been quite natural for Lees, Crothers, and Older to pool their efforts to prevent Esola's appointment as chief.

The *Examiner*, of course, was furious at this unexpected turn of events. Lawrence accused Lees, his friend private detective John Curtin, and *Bulletin* editor Older of engaging in a vicious conspiracy against Esola. The virulent old ex-chief was jealous, raged Lawrence, and determined that if he couldn't be chief, neither could Esola. Curtin immediately wrote the *Examiner* and the *Bulletin*, denying any involvement in the affair and calling the "Monarch's" informant a "liar and cur." The *Bulletin* printed the letter, while the *Examiner* did not.

Day after day the *Examiner* devoted its front page and several inside pages to a defense of Esola, while Harry Morse and his men kept busy digging up character witnesses to refute as many of the derogatory charges as possible. Interviews with public figures were always carefully slanted or edited to only reflect well on Esola. It was overkill on a grand scale and a desperate, last-ditch attempt by Lawrence to salvage his scheme to control the police department.

The commissioners' investigation began on January 18, with a parade of witnesses relating the charges against Esola. The hearing was very damaging, despite the fact that several of the witnesses called by the *Bulletin* suddenly re-

canted their previous testimony. "Harry Morse and his *Examiner*-paid detectives were in the corridors," complained the *Bulletin*, "buttonholing witnesses and whispering in their ears alternate threats and promises." Al Meador, the main witness and a former hoodlum pal of Esola's, had disappeared after recanting some of his *Bulletin* testimony.

Even ignoring testimony that Esola had formerly associated with hoodlums, engaged in robberies, and used an alias, it became increasingly clear after several days that he was a mediocre officer with little executive ability who had received promotions and favored treatment through the influence of Lawrence and his newspaper. When called to testify, Esola mortally damaged his own case by claiming he couldn't remember ever meeting with the commissioners prior to his hearing, even though Lawrence testified later of several such meetings the past month. Mayor Phelan had earlier admitted Esola had attended several conferences with him and the new commissioners. When the *Bulletin's* attorney, Frank McGowan, proceeded with a series of minor questions dealing with the law, Esola's lawyer protested that his client was not required to know all legal matters involved in the chief's office.

"A Chief of Police," responded McGowan, "is necessarily a good criminal lawyer. I am engaging in no flattery when I say that ex-chief Lees is one of the best criminal lawyers in the state."

When Isaiah took the stand he maintained he had been the best friend Esola had while they were on the force, but he left no doubt as to his qualifications for the position of chief.

Isaiah's testimony before the new police commissioners left little room for doubt that Lieutenant Esola was in no way compentent to be chief. It must have been difficult for the old detective to be in the same room with editor Lawrence, who sits at extreme right. *Author's Collection*

"If you were a Commissioner, would you pick him from the department and make him chief?"

"I would not!" replied Lees, "for I do not think he is capable."

After running through a litany of the various department complaints against the candidate, Lees was asked why Esola was kept on the force—especially since he had once submitted his resignation.

"For peace and quiet. I knew that Andrew Lawrence was behind him and that there would be a row."

Esola's candidacy had been badly damaged during the hearings, but on January 26 the *Examiner* filled up its front page with photos and headlines declaring the lieutenant had been "completely vindicated" in the course of the hearing. The commissioners had indeed unanimously voted to clear the lieutenant of Older's charges, but it was only a temporary victory. The following day, commissioners Biggy and Newhall angrily stated they had only voted to dismiss the charges when it was agreed that Esola would be dropped as a candidate for chief. The commissioners were split now and although the two loyal Esola commissioners kept the lieutenant in the running, it was announced that a new chief had still not been selected. Callundan saw the *Examiner* schemes collapsing and quit the force without having served a day as a patrolman.

When Commissioner (and acting chief) Biggy was removed from the board by Mayor Phelan, all hell broke loose. Biggy decided he wanted to stay on as chief, and Commissioner Thomas resigned in protest of the constant turmoil on the board. Two more commissioners were appointed and at their February 13 meeting it was announced that a new chief of police would finally be selected. In his journal entry of that date, Byram noted a surprise event during the meeting:

Commissioner William Biggy helped throw cold water on the *Examiner*'s plans for the department. In 1907 Biggy would become chief again. *California State Library*

> ...At this time Esola appeared and handed in a letter withdrawing from his candidacy. The letter was read. He did not wish to remain the occasion of contention which might weaken the efficiency of the Police Department. Mr. Newhall thanked him and said he had made the way easier and smoother for them and we shall not forget your kindness.

It was the only thing he could do. Furious at the treatment he had received, ex-Commissioner Biggy finally blew the whistle on the whole sordid scenario:

> The truth is, and the public ought to know it, that it was Lawrence and not Phelan who selected all four of the Commissioners. Mr. Phelan totally abdicated his functions in that respect in favor of Mr. Lawrence....

So there it was. What many had suspected for some time was verified now by one of the principals in the scheme. How sweet it was to see the "Monarch" toppled.

Isaiah had triumphed over Lawrence but, more than that, he had helped assure the department would not become the pawn of men who would use it for their own ends. It had meant more vicious, personal attacks in the *Examiner*, but it had been worth it.

Mayor Phelan now saw the web he had been drawn into by the *Examiner* and quickly distanced himself from that journal. "They then turned loose the vials of their wrath upon him for ever after," wrote Ned Byram. "The Department had a very close call." Phelan decided against running for re-election the following year.

Isaiah was undoubtedly disturbed when the board appointed William P. Sullivan, Phelan's private secretary, to the post of chief. But he could do no more. At least the *Examiner* was out of the picture. The department had survived political appointments in the past, and the captains could run things until the new chief got his feet on the ground.

Fred Lees in 1893, when he was San Francisco's chief license collector. *Author's Collection*

Isaiah Lees had given much to his adopted city. He had devoted most of his life to the department—to protecting San Francisco from the criminals who had flocked to this metropolis of the West. Time and again he had risked his life and worked around the clock for his city. But he had always done much more. He had paid for the early Rogues Gallery daguerreotypes out of his own pocket in the days when the city had no funds for such frills. Many thousands of dollars of his own funds had been spent on record keeping, traveling, and other expenses incurred in his work. He had personally made the locks on the prison cells in the old city hall, and his was the first name on the list of Exempt Firemen, that select group of unpaid volunteers who had risked their lives so many times in the early days. He had been an inspiration of integrity and devotion to duty to several generations of fledgling police officers.

In the end, one of his more important contributions was helping to deliver his beloved department from the grasp of Lawrence and his "Monarch."

Most of the city newspapers devoted generous space to the retiring chief and his long service to the city. "Best Man in the Police Department Goes Out with the Old Commission" headlined the *Chronicle* over an article covering most of a page and featuring a large portrait of the old detective.

His police colleagues insisted on taking up the usual collection for a retiring officer. Two hundred and ninety-eight dollars was gathered to purchase a suitable gift, the largest contribution of twenty dollars being made by Captain Seymour.

On the evening of March 3, 1900, a testimonial was held at Isaiah's home. It was a large gathering, the policemen nearly overflowing the house. At the appropriate moment, the old detective was ushered into the back parlor where the cover was removed from a large and elaborately decorated pen portrait of the ex-chief. Former prosecuting attorney Joseph Dunn made the presentation speech:

> It seems that the forty-seven years of your service is more of a testimonial than any that the cunning hand of the engraver can put on parchment. It is to your credit too, that not withstanding your duties you have found time to make of yourself a friend of the department. The intrinsic value of this testimonial accounts for nothing; it is only as a testimonial of the personal opinion of those who have been associated with you so long that it is worth anything.

Isaiah responded briefly, relating some of his experiences of the early days. He praised the department and urged those who honored him to support his successor. Ex-Chief Crowley then toasted his old comrade and told of their long association. The nostalgic gathering lasted until after midnight.

It was hard to break old routines, and Byram often mentions Lees visiting Captain Seymour and others at headquarters. Alhough there were rumors that he was going into the private detective business, he never formally did so. When asked, he frequently did consulting work or aided in various investigations. The great mind could not lie idle, and he worked for years on litigation involving the James G. Fair estate.

In October 1902, Lees' health began to fail. An ear abcess was complicated by diabetes and he was bedridden for a time. When he rallied enough in mid-December for an outing with Ella it was thought he was recovering, but his mighty stamina and fighting spirit was giving out at last.

An old newspaper print shows the casket of the legendary lawman being carried by a squad of police officers.
*Author's Collection*

On Saturday evening, December 20, Fred and Ella were called to the house by Dr. John Gallwey. It was obvious the end was near. At three o'clock Sunday morning he seemed to be slipping into a coma and was asked if he could recognize his two children. He couldn't speak, but nodded his assent. Oxygen was applied to make him more comfortable, but at five minutes past seven o'clock that morning the great heart quivered and stopped. "A smile was on his lips," reported the *Examiner*, "and he looked as if he was sleeping when the heart ceased to beat."

The tough old warrior had fought his last battle.

Isaiah had wanted a simple Masonic ceremony, but his friends and family were unable to let such a man pass from this life without a public tribute to his long civic service. A large number of police officers and friends flooded into the Lees home for a private service just before a contingent of police bore the body to the Masonic Temple for the public funeral. Crowds lined the streets for many blocks to view the casket—people from every walk of life, from pioneer friends to curious young people. The temple's largest hall was crowded to overflowing, with the casket being nearly hidden by large floral displays. Dr. Jacob Voorsanger delivered the eulogy.

Dr. Jacob Voorsanger.
*Author's Collection*

The honorary pallbearers included former chiefs Pat Crowley, Henry Ellis, and John Kirkpatrick, Judge Davis Louderback, attorney Garrett McEnerney, Reuben H. Lloyd, and the pioneer publisher, Anton Roman. Police officers were the actual pallbearers who escorted the body to the cemetery. Soon, he was with his beloved wife in the Laurel Hill vault.

A long list of public officials paid high praise in the press to one of the most prominent California pioneers of his age. When he adjourned his department of the superior court in tribute to Lees, Judge William P. Lawlor voiced a moving tribute to the departed lawman:

> The State of California and, it may be said in some measure, the entire Nation owes a debt of magnitude to the deceased. Isaiah W. Lees, above all men who have ever been connected with the administration of justice in California has done much to vindicate the law and discourage crime. This is a fact so well recognized that it would seem as if a court devoted to

Judge William P. Lawlor.
*Author's Collection*

the administration of criminal justice were wanting in proper consideration if it allowed this occasion to pass without saying that much in his memory. He was a man born for the prosecution of criminals and, while this may be said of him, it is not to be forgotten that his sense of justice was ever fair and that no innocent person was ever made by him to suffer unjust punishment....It may be said of him that no member of the bar or even the bench had a better understanding of what was required in a case depending upon circumstantial proof for the establishment of the commission of a public offense than he. And it must be gratifying to those bound to him by ties of love, as well as to the citizenship of California, that his fame has not been confined to the state in which he lived so long and served so well.

During his last hours, perhaps the old detective's mind had focused briefly on the blurred pageant of his fascinating life. Cunning criminals, famed peace officers, and close friends were by his side once again. And dear Jane. In those final moments he might well have remembered Edward Pollock, his poet friend of so long ago. He had always enjoyed Pollock's work, and the haunting stanzas of "The Parting Hour" now summed up a life that was quietly fading into history:

> There's something in the parting hour,
> Will chill the warmest heart,
> Yet kindred, comrades, lovers, friends,
> Are fated all to part.
>
> But this I've seen—and many a pang
> Has pressed it on my mind—
> The one that goes is happier
> Than those he leaves behind.

The End

# CHAPTER THIRTY / NOTES

For brief overviews of Phelan's mayoral career, see William A. Bullough's *The Blind Boss And His City*, Los Angeles, London, University of California Press, 1979, and the previously-cited *San Francisco 1865–1932*. Phelan admitted to a series of meetings with *Examiner* personnel and Lieutenant Esola in an extended article published in that newspaper on January 17, 1900. The *Call* had earlier charged the mayor with these meetings, and on January 17 and 19 the *Chronicle* commented on the mayor's actions and the various discrepancies in his story.

Lees' political activism is indicated by his reported arrangment of a meeting between Martin Kelly, the Republican political boss, Horace Davis, the Republican mayoral candidate, and several other party figures. See the *Examiner* of October 29 and 30, 1899.

The *Examiner* of December 7, 1899, gives an account of the police commissioners' meeting of the previous evening, as does the *Chronicle* of the same date. Mayor Phelan's new police commissioners were announced on January 1, 1900, in all the city newspapers.

The charges against Lieutenant Esola were substantiated to a great degree, but the new commissioners had vowed to appoint him and apparently two of them would do so no matter what the investigation revealed. If they did nothing else, the charges forced Esola before the commissioners for a critical examination—an examination which he failed, by any fair judgement. Lees must have been certain if this happened Esola would discredit himself, and he was right.

The charges against Esola were announced in the *Call*, *Chronicle*, and the *Examiner* on January 14, 1900. The *Chronicle* gave the story two columns, while the "Monarch" and the *Call* devoted their entire front page to the story. The *Examiner* gave the resulting investigation much more space than any of the other city newspapers, for rather obvious reasons. Testimony of witnesses is reported in the city press beginning on January 20, the *Examiner*, *Call*, *Bulletin*, and *Chronicle* reporting much of the testimony. The *Chronicle* and the other papers called attention to Lieutenant Esola's loss of memory pertaining to Phelan's meeting with the *Examiner* staff, while the "Monarch" skips over it. Lees testified at great length on January 19, knocking Esola "with his largest hammer," reported the "Monarch." The dismissal of the charges against Esola were announced by the commissioners on January 26, 1900, as reported in the city's press.

John Curtain's letter was published in the *Bulletin* of January 15, 1900. The *Examiner's* frantic campaign to refute the charges against Esola by getting witnesses to alter or recant their original stories, and digging up new and satisfactory character witnesses, began on January 14. An example of the "Monarch's" editing of testimony is a favorable quote from ex-Commissioner William Alvord. As published in the *Bulletin*, however, Alvord's comments included the remark that he would never have selected Esola for chief of police.

In the opinion of the author, any fair-minded observer of the Esola hearing could have reached only one conclusion: The lieutenant was in no way qualified to be chief of police. Even discounting Lees' devastating comments, Esola's association with hoodlums, his use of an alias on Al Meador's marriage license to which he was a witness (the license had

"disappeared" by the time it was called for at the hearing, as had Meador), and his loss of memory pertaining to his prior meetings with the mayor and commissioners—all were more than enough to disqualify his candidacy. High officials at San Quentin testified that Esola was kept as a guard only because it was feared Lawrence would unleash another attack on the prison in his newspaper. Biggy's long statement of the behind-the-scenes impropriety, as published in the *Bulletin* of February 14, 1900, was in itself proof enough of Lawrence's schemes.

McGowan's remarks on Chief Lees' legal abilities were reported in the *Chronicle* of January 21, 1900. Lees' comments on Esola were published at length in both the *Bulletin* and *Examiner*. Biggy's and Newhall's rebellion at being hoodwinked into exonerating Esola was covered in great detail in the *Bulletin* of January 27.

Fred Esola made captain in 1902, but soon left the department to work for William J. Burns, head of the newly-established National Bureau of Investigation, precursor to the F.B.I. In 1924 he was appointed U.S. marshal for Northern California, serving for nine years. He died in San Francisco on January 26, 1949, as reported in the *Chronicle* the following day. An exaggerated account of his life appeared in the San Francisco *News Letter* and *Wasp* of March 14, 1936.

The resulting troubles among the members of the new police commission were reported in the *Chronicle* on January 24 and 27. The various Byram quotes are from Volume 13 of his journals.

Lees' many personal contributions to the efficiency of the department are cited in various biographical articles, previously noted, and also in the *Chronicle* at the time of his retirement. Even the *Examiner* grudgingly notes these public services in several articles.

The "Monarch" made the statement that Lees was "one of the wealthiest men in the city," but this was an exaggeration, and although well-off he was not a millionaire as the *Examiner* implied. His will, made only two days before his death, listed his personal property at $11,492—this figure apparently including his Pine Street home. His personal library was valued at $3,000. Also part of the estate were forty-two city lots valued at some $300,000. See the *Chronicle* of December 30, 1902. Deeds for various mining properties dating from the 1860s and 1870s are held in a small Lees Collection at the California State Library, Sacramento.

A list of contributions to a gift for the retiring chief from his men is among the papers in the Lees Collection at the Bancroft Library. The *Chronicle* of March 4, 1900, has a lively article on the testimonial gathering held for Lees at his home. Byram notes he was sick and couldn't attend.

Lees' remarks on establishing a private detective agency appeared in the *Chronicle* of January 5, 1900. There are many references to the old detective's work on the Fair case; see the *Examiner* of January 29, 1897, and February 18, 1900. Several letters and papers in the Lees Collection at the Bancroft pertain to consulting work he had done.

Lees' Sunday morning death was reported in the city press on December 22, 1902. Even his old enemy, the *Examiner*, published a large photograph of the chief at his desk to illustrate

an extensive and laudatory summary of his life. On December 24 the *Call, Chronicle,* and *Examiner* all published long, highly-illustrated articles on the funeral, which was heralded as one of the largest in city history. Judge Lawlor's comments were in the *Call* of the above date. Some details of the detective's death were obtained from a brief biography his daughter Ella gave to the California Historical Society.

Ned Byram made a terse reference to his old commander's funeral in his personal diary. "Fred Lees fainted away," he noted. This would seem to be a symptom of the heart disease that would result in his death a short time later. Byram retired from the department in 1908 and died in September of 1918.

Lees' admiration for Edward Pollock's verse is noted in one of the old detective's obituaties. The *Examiner* of December 22, 1902, relates how Lees bought all the copies of Pollock's published verse he could find and gave them away to friends whom he thought would be appreciative.

There were many formal resolutions presented to the family by various organizations at the time of Lees' death. A copy of a Society of California Pioneers Memorial was given to the writer by the late Dr. Albert Shumate, while a presentation from the Union League Club of San Francisco is in the Lees Collection at the California State Library. A resolution from the Veteran Police Association is in the Bancroft Lees Collection. Fred Lees died at his father's old home on February 22, 1903. His sister, Ella Lees Leigh, passed away in San Francisco on May 5, 1927.

# Index

**B**orn in Fresno, California, in March of 1930, William B. Secrest grew up in the great San Joaquin Valley. After high school he joined the Marine Corps where he served in a guard detachment and in a rifle company in the early years of the Korean War. Returning to college, he obtained a BA in education, but for many years he served as an art director for a Fresno advertising firm.

Secrest has been interested in history since his youth and early began comparing Western films to what really happened in the West. A hobby at first, this avocation quickly developed into correspondence with noted writers and more serious research. Not satisfied in a collaboration with friend and Western writer Ray Thorp, Secrest began researching and writing his own articles in the early 1960s.

Although at first he wrote on many general Western subjects, some years ago Secrest realized how his home state has consistently been neglected in the Western genre and concentrated almost exclusively on early California subjects. He has produced hundreds of articles for such publications as *Westways, Montana, True West*, and the *American West*, while publishing seven monographs on early California themes. His book *I Buried Hickok* (Early West Publishing Co.) appeared in 1980, followed by *Lawmen & Desperadoes* (The Arthur H. Clark Co.) *Dangerous Trails* (Barbed Wire Press), *California Desperadoes* (Word Dancer Press), *Perilous Trails* (Word Dancer Press) and *When the Great Spirit Died* (Word Dancer Press)